Opening the Scriptures

Psalms II

Opening the Scriptures

Psalms II

Frans van Deursen

Translated by
Nelson D. Kloosterman

General Editors
Jordan J. Ballor and Stephen J. Grabill

Grand Rapids · Michigan

© 2015 Christian's Library Press
An imprint of the Acton Institute for the Study of Religion & Liberty

98 East Fulton Phone: 616.454.3080
Grand Rapids, Michigan 49503 Fax: 616.454.9454
www.clpress.com

Originally published in Dutch as *De Voorzeide Leer*. Deel I K. *De Heilige Schrift. Inleiding op de Geschriften. Psalmen (II)*. Door F. van Deursen. 3rd ed. (Barendrecht: Liebeek & Hooijmeijer BV, 1986).

All rights reserved. No part of this publication may be reproduced, stored in a retrieval system, or transmitted in any form or by any means, including electronic, mechanical, photocopying, recording, or otherwise without the prior permission of the publisher.

ISBN: 978-1-942503-12-5

Scripture quotations not referenced by chapter and verse are translated from the author's Dutch translation or paraphrase.

Unless otherwise indicated, Scripture quotations referenced by chapter and verse are from the ESV® Bible (The Holy Bible, English Standard Version®) copyright © 2001 by Crossway, a publishing ministry of Good News Publishers. Used by permission. All rights reserved.

Scripture quotations marked NRSV are from the New Revised Standard Version Bible: Catholic Edition, copyright 1989, 1993, Division of Christian Education of the National Council of the Churches of Christ in the United States of America. Used by permission. All rights reserved.

The Message is copyrighted © 1993, 1994, 1995, 1996, 2000, 2001, 2002. Used by permission of NavPress Publishing Group.

Cover image: Map of Jericho (14th-century Farhi Bible by Elisha ben Avraham Crestas), public domain.

Cover design: Peter Ho

Printed in the United States of America

20 19 18 17 16 15   1 2 3 4 5 6

Contents

	Abbreviations	ix
	The Uniqueness of Opening the Scriptures	xi
1.	Psalm 59: A Psalm of David for Vengeance, When Saul Almost Murdered Him	1
2.	Psalm 56: David Arrested by the Philistines	43
3.	Psalm 57: When David Sat in the Cave	65
4.	Psalm 34: Praise and Wisdom from the Cave of the Oppressed	81
5.	Psalm 52: After the Mass Murder in the Priestly City of Nob	115
6.	Psalm 74: Weeping for God's Church	131
7.	Psalm 79:8: Do Not Remember against Us the Iniquities of Former Generations	175
8.	Psalm 88: In the Last Stage of a Fatal Illness	211
9.	Psalm 90: Not a Psalm for New Year's Eve	229
10.	Psalm 104: How Numerous are Your Works, O Yahweh. You Have Done Them All with Wisdom	253
11.	Psalm 111: I Will Give Thanks to Yahweh!	303
12.	Psalm 119: The Prayer of a Solitary Persecuted Person in a Church World Full of Contempt for God and His Word	313
13.	Psalm 139: O Yahweh, You Have Searched Me and Known Me!	331
14.	Psalms 145–150: The Book of Psalms Ends with Pure Praise	341
	Name and Subject Index	359
	Scripture Index	381

This series in English translation is provided by
John and Jenny Hultink
as their legacy to their children and grandchildren,
for generations to come.

*"I have no greater joy than to hear that my children
are walking in the truth." (3 John 4)*

Abbreviations

Old Testament

Gen.	Genesis	Song	Song of Songs
Exod.	Exodus	Isa.	Isaiah
Lev.	Leviticus	Jer.	Jeremiah
Num.	Numbers	Lam.	Lamentations
Deut.	Deuteronomy	Ezek.	Ezekiel
Josh.	Joshua	Dan.	Daniel
Judg.	Judges	Hos.	Hosea
Ruth	Ruth	Joel	Joel
1–2 Sam.	1–2 Samuel	Amos	Amos
1–2 Kgs.	1–2 Kings	Obad.	Obadiah
1–2 Chr.	1–2 Chronicles	Jonah	Jonah
Ezra	Ezra	Mic.	Micah
Neh.	Nehemiah	Nah.	Nahum
Esth.	Esther	Hab.	Habakkuk
Job	Job	Zeph.	Zephaniah
Ps(s).	Psalm(s)	Hag.	Haggai
Prov.	Proverbs	Zech.	Zechariah
Eccl.	Ecclesiastes	Mal.	Malachi

New Testament

Matt.	Matthew	Rom.	Romans
Mark	Mark	1–2 Cor.	1–2 Corinthians
Luke	Luke	Gal.	Galatians
John	John	Eph.	Ephesians
Acts	Acts	Phil.	Philippians
Col.	Colossians	Jas.	James
1–2 Thess.	1–2 Thessalonians	1–2 Pet.	1–2 Peter
1–2 Tim.	1–2 Timothy	1–3 John	1–3 John
Titus	Titus	Jude	Jude
Phlm.	Philemon	Rev.	Revelation
Heb.	Hebrews		

Old Testament Apocrypha

Add. Dan.	Additions to Daniel	Pr. Man.	Prayer of Manasseh
Add. Esth.	Additions to Esther	Ps. 151	Psalm 151
Bar.	Baruch	Sir. (Ecclus.)	Sirach (Ecclesiasticus)
Bel	Bel and the Dragon		
1–2 Esd.	1–2 Esdras	Sg. Three	Song of the Three Jews
Jdt.	Judith		
Let. Jer.	Letter of Jeremiah	Sus.	Susanna
1–4 Macc.	1–4 Maccabees	Tob.	Tobit
Pr. Azar.	Prayer of Azariah	Wis.	Wisdom of Solomon

General

art.	article
ASV	American Standard Version
ch.	chapter
ESV	English Standard Version
Heb.	Hebrew
KJV	King James Version
mg.	marginal reading
NRSV	New Revised Standard Version
OtS	Opening the Scriptures
v(v).	verse(s)

The Uniqueness of Opening the Scriptures

Opening the Scriptures is not a new series of technical commentaries that explain the Bible word for word, although this series of volumes does rest upon careful exegesis. Nor is it a collection of sermons, although now and then the authors shine the light of Scripture on our modern world. Actually, there is no familiar category of Bible studies that serves as a suitable classification for Opening the Scriptures. This series has a unique character. It offers devout church members a series of popularly accessible primers, with no display of scholarly expertise, so that the average churchgoer can easily grasp them.[1]

As far as their approach is concerned, these volumes begin by telling you about the structure of the biblical book that you want to study. This is because an overview of the whole enhances insight into the parts. After all, Scripture is not a loose-leaf assortment of essays or a collection of isolated

---

1. [*Translator's note:* In keeping with this purpose and where the flow of argument does not suffer, footnotes appearing in the original as well as some more technical references in the text have been omitted from this translation, since they refer primarily to Dutch and German literature, which for most readers of this series will be inaccessible.]

texts. Therefore the ABC of the authors of this series is this: pay attention to the text, the context, and the canonical place of the biblical book (or the other way around). What is the scope of a particular book, and how is it organized? What is its place in the totality of Scripture? For example, what ties Joshua, Judges, Samuel, and Kings together? What does Lamentations have to say to us today? In short, Opening the Scriptures resembles a museum guidebook that opens your eyes to the beauty and meaning of the treasures, large and small, being exhibited.

The organization of this series follows the four main sectional divisions of Holy Scripture (Luke 24:44). For the Holy Spirit has joined together all the books of the Bible into an imposing edifice. The Torah, or the five books of Moses, is the foundation upon which the entire Scripture rests. Therefore this section of the Bible is discussed most extensively in Opening the Scriptures. The many prophetic books form the walls. The Psalms and Wisdom books are the windows. Over all of this the Holy Spirit has laid the golden dome roof of the New Testament. The authors of Opening the Scriptures would like to guide you through this immense building. They will ask, "Have you seen this, and did you notice that?" And when you respond, "Surely the Bible is a wonderful book, and I would like to know more about it!" then they will have achieved their purpose.

Genesis, the book beginning the series, constitutes the introduction to the Torah. After telling us about the perfect creation and beautiful garden, human rebellion and divine graciousness, the flood and the Table of Nations, Genesis speaks extensively about Abraham's salvation and God's covenant with him and the other patriarchs. This covenant is not just one among a number of topics that the Bible talks about. Nor is it an isolated subject in theological dogmatics. God's covenant with Abraham exists still today. It consists of God's *solidarity* with us in the Lord Jesus Christ, and thereby it forms the basis beneath all our living, and it is the air that we breathe. We walk, we sit, we eat, we drink, we sleep, we work, we live, and we die *within and in terms of* that regulation-saturated and sanction-filled treaty relationship with Almighty God. The authors of Opening the Scriptures are constantly showing that Holy Scripture is from A to Z the Book of God's covenant with his people.

In his faithfulness to this covenant, the Lord delivered Israel out of Egypt, and in addition to the first covenant he established a second covenant. He even came to dwell among these people. Therefore, the Torah of Moses, which deals with this, is hardly a dry collection of antiquated laws. It teaches us to know Yahweh the Lord as the God who despises sin and death, and heartily loves life, especially the life of us human beings. He loves life so much that he sent his Son into the world to restore it. The entire Torah sparkles with that divine love of life. The tabernacle with its worship and all of God's life-enhancing statutes and ordinances bespeak that love.

The prophetic books (Joshua–Malachi) show what Israel did with God's covenant and his Torah. They show how Israel received the promised land of inheritance, but also how Israel forfeited and lost the land. God honored the covenant, however, by means of Israel's return from the Babylonian captivity, so that the Messiah could be born one day from this nation and in that land.

God reveals himself as the God of life even more clearly and powerfully in the New Testament than in the Torah, the Prophets, and the Psalms. For he proclaims that he so loved human life that, in order to save it, he sent his Son Jesus Christ to earth to be born as a son of Abraham. God did so in order that through faith in Jesus Christ he might grant eternal life not only to Jews, as in the old covenant, but now in the new covenant, to believers from every nation. And this is precisely as he had promised earlier under oath to Abraham, as we learn in Genesis.

Tracing the unfolding of this plan, then, is the design of Opening the Scriptures.

Frans van Deursen

Note to the reader: In this volume the author explains how to understand the Psalms in general. Therefore, he does not discuss every psalm but treats a selection of covenant songs whose themes lie at the heart of the Psalter and reappear often throughout the Psalter.

Chapter 1

Psalm 59: A Psalm of David for Vengeance, When Saul Almost Murdered Him

Night has fallen in Gibeah. A patrol of soldiers from King Saul is sneaking around David's house. They were commissioned to prevent the king's son-in-law from leaving his home at all cost. David was to be arrested. His death sentence had already been signed, so to speak. And it seemed that his last day in the land of the living had now dawned. Inside the house, however, the guards were on alert. High tension and alarm! David and Michal were keenly aware that they didn't need to have any illusion about Saul's intentions: David had to be cleared out of the way.

This tension-filled night forms the background of Psalm 59.

Naturally, we need not assume that David sat down to compose this poem while Saul's gang was sneaking around his home and Michal was preparing his escape. Only later would he write down how scared he had been during that dreadful night and what he had prayed to Yahweh that night.

He had prayed for help and rescue, understandably so, but also for the death and defeat of his enemies. In his distress David had cried out that night, "O God, kill them; exterminate them in your wrath." But many a Bible reader would have a hard time justifying these petitions. Granted, David was just a man, and he was probably deathly afraid, but is a child of God allowed to pray for the death of his opponents? When reading such imprecatory requests, many Christians wear a grimace on their faces, whether they read such thoughts in Psalm 59 or in Psalms 5, 35, 58, 69, 109, or 137.

But are we right to condemn such petitions?

Superscription and Background

That agonizing night formed the background of Psalm 59, as we just observed, at least if we are properly understanding the superscription above the psalm: "To the choirmaster: according to Do Not Destroy. A Miktam of David, when Saul sent men to watch his house in order to kill him." Many commentators ascribe no historical value to this superscription. But what do they offer in its place? Unfounded assumptions and timeless explanations. We are rather sympathetic to what Spurgeon observes in connection with this superscription: the heading "does not seem unsuitable to any verse, and in some the words are very appropriate to the specified occasion." Therefore we will be reading Psalm 59 against the background of 1 Samuel 18–19, where the events being referred to in the heading are narrated.

The prediction of this agonizing night

Let us take care that we do not unwittingly turn David into a kind of demigod, for he was an ordinary young man just in his twenties who loved his wife and could also become afraid, even though he had killed Goliath. David and Michal must have endured very distressing hours "when Saul sent

1. Psalm 59: A Psalm of David for Vengeance

men to watch David's house in order to kill him," all the more so because earlier they had endured so much danger.

It began immediately after David had slain Goliath, and the Israelite women and girls had celebrated the victors with a poem: "Saul has struck down his thousands, and David his ten thousands" (1 Sam. 18:7). "And Saul was very angry, and this saying displeased him. He said, 'They have ascribed to David ten thousands, and to me they have ascribed thousands, and what more can he have but the kingdom?' And Saul eyed David from that day on" (1 Sam. 18:8–9). On the very next morning, Saul tried twice to pin David to the wall with his spear. When this did not succeed, he appointed David as a commander of troops in the hope that his rival would perish in a military action. When this trick didn't work, Saul promised him his daughter Michal as wife on the condition that he pay as dowry the foreskins of one hundred Philistines. Perhaps he would perish in that endeavor. After all of these sly plans failed, Saul came clean with his palace personnel: he wanted David dead. Jonathan was initially able to restrain his father by having him declare under oath that he would not kill David, but shortly thereafter Saul broke his oath. On the day preceding the night of Psalm 59, Saul threw his spear at David for the third time.

Having barely recovered from the shock of Saul's further attempt to kill David, David and Michal heard soldiers walking around during the night. Michal did not underestimate for one moment the seriousness of the situation: "If you do not escape with your life tonight, tomorrow you will be killed" (1 Sam. 19:11). People have assumed that David's house was similar to Rahab's (Josh. 2), built on the city wall. So it was understandable that Michal rescued her husband by helping him escape through the window and down the city wall. Afterward she was able to give him enough time to flee by misleading the arresting troops by placing the teraphim in David's bed (1 Sam. 19:11–17).

This is what David had experienced when he composed

Psalm 59—several real attempts on his life. He was locked up in his own house like a bird in a cage, with the accomplices of his mortal enemy at the door. This is enough to give a person a heart attack!

These threats did not leave David unaffected, as we will see when we get to Psalm 56. The response of his stressed-out nervous system would not be long in coming.

Our plan is to discuss Psalm 59 first, and then Psalms 56, 57, 34, and 52. We will read these psalms in this sequence because the events they sing about occurred during David's persecution by Saul: Psalm 59, when Saul had almost killed him; Psalm 56, when the Philistines had arrested him in Gath; Psalm 57, when David fled from Saul in the cave; Psalm 34, praise and wisdom from the cave of the oppressed; and Psalm 52, after the mass murder in the priestly city of Nob.

"Do not destroy"

We discussed the word *miktam* in connection with the superscription to Psalm 16. The translation "Do Not Destroy" (Hebrew: *'al tashkhet*) is a bit puzzling. Our English Bibles insert "according to": the translators assume that "Do Not Destroy" were the first words of a well-known song, according to whose melody Psalm 59 was to be sung or played.

However, the Peshitta (an ancient Syrian translation of the OT, dating probably from the second century AD) provides an explanation of *'al tashkhet* that is worth considering. Johannes Cocceius adopted it in the seventeenth century, and it was still defended in the nineteenth century. During his years of distress, David supposedly took on his lips the words "Do Not Destroy" as a kind of quick prayer.

Could we not understand *'al tashkhet*, however, as a short proverbial description of David's *attitude* during his persecution under Saul? On one occasion, Saul lay sleeping at David's feet. Abishai whispered, "Shall I kill him?" But David forbade him, using the very same Hebrew words that we find above Psalms 57, 58, 59, and 75: "*Do not destroy* him, for who can put out his hand against the LORD's anointed and be guiltless?" (1 Sam. 26:8–9).

Was not the phrase "Do Not Destroy" the code that governed David's attitude during the years of his persecution? "Do not destroy! Do not avenge yourself! Make room for the wrath of God! Do not give free rein to personal partisanship, but take your appeal higher to Yahweh." This is how David showed himself to be "the man after God's heart." It didn't matter that Saul had treated him unrighteously; David's attitude remained one of "Do Not Destroy." Do Saul no evil, even though with one thrust of his spear David could have put an end to all his misery (1 Sam. 24; 26).

We find this explanation of *'al tashkhet* even more attractive because these words stand above a psalm that calls for being avenged! Maybe they are a key phrase of some sort? David himself did not destroy Saul and his gang. He prayed for God to do that.

Verses 1–10: Deliver Me from Bloodthirsty Men!

The language of Psalm 59 points clearly to a poet who was also a soldier. He uses expressions like "protect," "people who rise up against me," "God of hosts," "our Shield," and similar military terms. But the content of this psalm is characteristic of those who are genuinely humble, who are averse to every worldly method of fighting for the kingdom of God. That will come out as we read now what David prayed and what he did and did not do during and after that agonizing night.

Verse 1:
Deliver me from my enemies, O my God;
   protect me from those who rise up against me.

This is how David prayed, the one who conquered Goliath

and the one beloved among all Israel and Judah (1 Sam. 18:16). The women and girls sang songs about him. Soldiers would pass through the fire for him. And still more significant was that Samuel had anointed him in the name of Yahweh as Israel's future king. So what did this popular David do? He prayed and fled! After escaping, he fled to Samuel (1 Sam. 19:18).

This course of action proceeds from a spirit that is entirely different from the spirit with which many Christians today live and think. They could easily imagine that David would have uttered this appeal: "By its attempts to murder the faithful officer David, the government of Saul has become guilty of intolerable violations of justice and can no longer be recognized as the lawful Israelite government. Israelites, arm yourselves! Rise up against Saul the dictator; fight for David, whom God has identified as Saul's lawful successor!"

What a temptation it must have been for David to travel that revolutionary path. The history of the later ten tribes shows how the military leaders like Baasha, Zimri, Omri, Shallum, Menahem, Pekah, and Hoshea abused their military power to dethrone the king. But David fled and brought his appeal in prayer to the Judge of heaven and earth. In fact, who else could have obtained justice for him, now that Saul, the highest judge, was persecuting him? "Deliver me from my enemies, O my God," David prayed, and for the rest, he "did" nothing.

In this way, David showed increasingly that he was "the man after God's heart": by his respect for Saul as "the anointed of Yahweh," by placing his case in God's hands and waiting for years for God's intervention, and by constantly reminding himself: "*'Al tashkhet!* David, do not destroy him!" This is how David lived from the same Spirit as our Lord Jesus Christ, who also, "when he was reviled, . . . did not revile in return; when he suffered, he did not threaten, but continued entrusting himself to him who judges justly" (1 Pet. 2:23). Waiting on God is far more difficult than surrendering to an

1. Psalm 59: A Psalm of David for Vengeance

unbelieving impulse to act, even though it can be performed under the banner of faith!

Verse 2:
**Deliver me from those who work evil,
and save me from bloodthirsty men.**

It is wonderful that we know the historical situation of this psalm so accurately, for now we can read it concretely and not as a generic religious poem. But that also creates other challenges. Precisely because we know the historical situation so well, David's manner of praying impresses us all the more.

The phrases that David uses are in flagrant conflict with the view that generic Christian religion harbors nowadays about brotherly love. Who today would dare call fellow Christians what David calls his fellow Israelites? In this verse he calls them "bloodthirsty men" and "those who work evil"! Was this being very brotherly on David's part, condemning Saul and his followers with such harsh words? People can agree that what they did was wrong, but shouldn't David have done his best to continue loving them? After all, all Israelites, including Saul as well as David, were together God's people and thus brothers of one another, weren't they?

This way of talking is everywhere today.

Guido de Bres not only authored our Belgic Confession, but sealed it with his blood, leaving behind his wife with a large family. You can read about this in his moving farewell letters. But a generic Christian religion is growing in our generation that prefers as much as possible to blur the lines of separation between obedience and disobedience toward God's Word and to relativize that separation. This includes lines of separation in church history, like those which Guido de Bres spent his life defending.

Viewed superficially, this kind of religion, which blurs everything, appears to be speaking genuinely out of Christian love, and David looks like a hateful man with the way he talks in Psalm 59. Here is someone who ventured to call brothers his "enemies" and "workers of iniquity and bloodthirsty men"!

Nevertheless, you will find this line of talk throughout all of Scripture.

David is definitely not speaking here as a "typical Old Testament person," for our Savior himself said to his disciples, "Behold, I am sending you out as sheep in the midst of *wolves*" (Matt. 10:16). He was referring here to Israelites who were hostile to the Word, for in Matthew 10:5 he gave the emphatic command "Go nowhere among the Gentiles and enter no town of the Samaritans" (the mandate to preach to the Gentiles didn't come until Matt. 28:19). According to our Savior, his disciples would therefore encounter "wolves who were brothers" *among Israel.* And thus David was not crossing any boundaries when, after Saul's numerous attempts to kill him, he called the king and his followers "workers of iniquity" and "bloodthirsty men."

We saw in our previous commentary on the Psalms (vol. 1) that Holy Scripture does not usually call all the members of God's people *sinners*, even though there is no one who does not commit sin. Here we see that Scripture also does not say, "All people intend what is good." God's Word speaks with greater nuance than often is the case in generic Christian language. Scripture distinguishes more sharply, for example, between oppressors and the oppressed, those who cause distress and those who suffer distress *among God's people.* During the St. Bartholomew's Day massacre in Paris, there was a difference among the brothers, wasn't there? In the sixteenth century many *Christians* were "bloodthirsty men" toward their own brothers, weren't they, even though such occurrences need not involve the flowing of real blood? In connection with this psalm, Calvin talks about those "who persecuted the saints under the guise of brethren, and overthrew those laws which were of divine appointment" (commentary on Ps. 59:4). Calvin could join this conversation: he lived not only in an age of phenomena such as the Inquisition and the St. Bartholomew's Day massacre, but also in a time of wrestling against the Anabaptists.

In this psalm David mentions no names. That renders his prayer suitable as a model prayer for brothers and sisters who would become distressed on account of "bloodthirsty men" and "workers of iniquity." The spirit of the age may well condemn such a prayer, but God's Spirit supplies it!

Verse 3a–b:
For behold, they lie in wait for my life;
   fierce men stir up strife against me.

Indeed, lying in wait and stirring up strife! What had Saul and his men done if not these, stalking around someone's house in the darkness of night and scheming against David in his own backyard! Still, David did not think of himself as someone successful, despite his popularity after his victory over Goliath. "I am a poor man and have no reputation," he once said to one of Saul's servants (1 Sam. 18:23). Even now he looked up to his persecutors. He calls them "fierce men." For months they had been lying in wait for him, until they came to surround his house. "O Yahweh, *behold* . . . !"

Centuries later Jeremiah encountered something similar: "I was like a gentle lamb led to the slaughter." But his fellow villagers were concocting plans for getting rid of the prophet (Jer. 11:19). How many others have traveled down this same pathway of suffering as David and Jeremiah?

Could our Savior have been referring to Psalm 59 when, after his resurrection, he recalled "everything written *about me* in the Law of Moses and the Prophets and the Psalms must be fulfilled" (Luke 24:44)? From the Gospel of Matthew (cf. Matt. 12:14; 16:1; 22:15; 26:3–5; 26:14–16, 47–48) we know that the church leaders of his day certainly lay in wait for him like bloodthirsty men!

Verses 3c–4a
For no transgression or sin of mine, O Lord,
    for no fault of mine, they run and make ready.

After all, David was no rebellious officer who had carried out a revolution, such that Saul had to arrest him in order to prevent something worse. David had rendered invaluable service and brought significant benefit to the king. Later he demonstrated his unfeigned loyalty once more when he spared the life of Saul as he slept: "For by the fact that I cut off the corner of your robe and did not kill you, you may know and see that there is no wrong or treason in my hands. I have not sinned against you, though you hunt my life to take it" (1 Sam. 24:11).

That was indeed what it looks like to love your enemies as yourself!

On the other hand, here we are not listening to this same David arguing very "nicely" that "we all have guilt" in this dismal situation because "we are all miserable sinners"—David as well as Saul. On the contrary, David does not hesitate to declare in God's ears that in this matter involving Saul he was innocent. With complete loyalty he had to endure attempts to kill him and the ambush of his home (he is using military language about people executing orders and taking up positions). We mentioned in connection with Psalm 26 that the manner in which David confesses his innocence here has been lost among us Christians today. The tastes of many in our day would require David to say, "Brothers, we are all to blame for the current differences!" Jeremiah should have said something similar as well to the men of Anathoth who wanted to get rid of him. People could even accuse the Lord Jesus of not trying harder to "get along" with the brothers of the Sanhedrin.

But as we said, here in Psalm 59 David is not using such "nice" talk. Don't forget, he was innocent after all, despite being persecuted! Surely God's Word does not require that one

1. Psalm 59: A Psalm of David for Vengeance

declare his guilt in such a situation, does it? For such declarations of innocence we may refer the reader to our discussion of Psalm 26 in volume 1 of our commentary.

> Verses 4b–5:
> Awake, come to meet me, and see!
>   You, Lord God of hosts, are God of Israel.
> Rouse yourself to punish all the nations;
>   spare none of those who treacherously plot evil.

Isn't this pretty impertinent talk, telling God, "Wake up!"? But God's Spirit invites us to pray with such confidence. That is how David was permitted to pray amid mortal danger. It is remarkable that in doing so, he calls Yahweh "Lord God of *hosts*." Saul had mobilized his soldiers, but David, the popular commander, looked away from the throne of military power entirely and called upon the God of the heavenly armies. In David's day it was not so long ago that Yahweh had enlisted the stars of his heavens to join in the battle to deliver his people (see the commentary on Josh. 10).

"Treacherous plotters" he calls his enemies in verse 5. What else could they be called? "The king is fond of you; he'd like you as his son-in-law," said Saul's servants, but the dowry would likely cost David his life (1 Sam. 18:20–21; cf. 1 Sam. 19:1).

All of this was, after all, worldly prattle, wasn't it? Paganized manners? It's easy to understand why David asks God "to visit all the *heathen*" (KJV), isn't it? To explain this phrase, some have assumed that the poet was talking amid a mixed population, part Israelite, part pagan. This is one of the reasons some people doubt the historical value of the superscription. People took the word *heathen* literally and saw a conflict with 1 Samuel 19, which mentions only Israelites. The difficulty disappears, however, when we hear David characterizing Saul and his compatriots as *heathen* (cf. Ps. 9:15). That is what Israelites were "who say that they are Jews and are not, but lie" (Rev. 3:9). Isn't this being expressed in a pretty strange way? How often did our Savior refer to the Jewish church leaders and their coterie with the word *world* (cf. Jn. 16:20, 33; 18:20)? How was Saul's thirst for murder and traitorous conduct any different from what pagans were doing? In fact, we ourselves also speak of "surrendering to the pagans," and perhaps we too have Christians in view on occasion. *Barbarian* is nothing but another word for "pagan," isn't it? So in verse 5b we are certainly not reading a prayer for punishment upon all pagan nations. What would such a reference be doing here suddenly in a prayer that has arisen because of persecution by brothers? No, David's brothers were behaving like real pagans!

But was he therefore permitted to pray that God would show them no grace? Is a child of God allowed to pray for something like that? Or did God's church only outgrow that with the New Testament? We will discuss these questions in connection with verses 11–13.

Verse 6:
Each evening they come back,
   howling like dogs
   and prowling about the city.

In Israel, dogs were not faithful house pets; they were stray dogs, repulsive animals, skinny and famished. During the day they lay sleeping in the sun so that at night they could roam the streets howling and barking as they scrounged for something to eat. Even today, the safety of Near Eastern villages is threatened by such packs of wild dogs.

David must have been thinking of them when he saw Saul's henchmen that night. "Just like prowling dogs looking for prey!" Walking the streets at night to attack a righteous man like David! Such behavior resembles that of a mean Near Eastern street dog.

1. Psalm 59: A Psalm of David for Vengeance

Verse 7:
There they are, bellowing with their mouths
　with swords in their lips—
　for "Who," they think, "will hear us?"

Saul wanted to provide his campaign against the popular David with an apparent judicial basis, by unleashing a rumor campaign that portrayed David so darkly that well-intentioned people would accept it as true. That's how it often goes with especially pious lies.

And he was doing all of that as though Yahweh weren't listening!

But this was consistently one of the characteristics of the wicked among God's people: despite an outward appearance of piety, in the practicalities of life they acted as though Yahweh saw nothing, observed nothing, and heard nothing. That is why Scripture calls them fools. And that is how Saul behaved, too: continually taking the name of Yahweh on his lips but ignoring the fact that God was listening to his harsh lies about David.

Although he looked like a wise, believing man who had Israel's well-being in view, Saul and his accomplices walked around "with swords in their lips." For "who will hear us?"

Verses 8–10:
But you, O LORD, laugh at them;
　you hold all the nations in derision.
O my Strength, I will watch for you,
　for you, O God, are my fortress.
My God in his steadfast love will meet me;
　God will let me look in triumph on my enemies.

Here as well a soldier-poet is speaking, but one who, in spite of using military terms, completely renounces military might for acquiring the kingship in Israel. David abandons himself entirely to Yahweh's promise in that regard, even though murderers are breathing down his neck. "Soon I will look in triumph on my enemies!" That is how firmly David counted on Yahweh's intervention. In this ancient psalm David is the man par excellence who gave God the opportunity to show that he was God.

Verses 11–13: "Kill them . . . !"

> Verses 11–13:
> Kill them [ESV "Kill them not"], lest my people stumble;
>   make them totter by your power and bring them
>   down,
>   O Lord, our shield!
> For the sin of their mouths, the words of their lips,
>   let them be trapped in their pride.
> For the cursing and lies that they utter,
>   consume them in wrath;
> consume them till they are no more,
>   that they may know that God rules over Jacob
> to the ends of the earth.

First a word about the translation of these verses.

The ESV, together with most other translations, reads in verse 11, "Kill them *not*. . . ." David would then be praying for Yahweh to exterminate the enemies, but only gradually, "lest my people forget." But why would the people have forgotten a sudden destruction? It is far better to read and to translate this as follows: "O God, kill them—so that my people would not forget." It is our view that this translation fits better in the context of verses 11–13. In view of the other petitions in these verses, David was praying that God *would indeed* want to exterminate his enemies. "Make them totter . . . bring them down [to the realm of the dead] . . . consume them . . . destroy them." All of these are petitions asking for the destruction of David's enemies. "Kill them" fits better with these than "kill them *not*."

1. Psalm 59: A Psalm of David for Vengeance

Now we turn to the content of these verses.

Was it okay for David to pray this way?

"Kill them . . . consume them!" What do you think about such terrifying requests on the lips of a child of God? Didn't our Savior teach, "But I say to you, Love your enemies and pray for those who persecute you, so that you may be sons of your Father who is in heaven. For he makes his sun rise on the evil and on the good, and sends rain on the just and on the unjust" (Matt. 5:44–45)? "Do good to those who hate you, bless those who curse you" (Luke 6:27–28). On the cross the Lord prayed for his enemies: "Father, forgive them, for they know not what they do" (Luke 23:34). And Stephen imitated his Master by doing the same (Acts 7:60). Didn't the apostles hold before us to "bless those who persecute you; bless and do not curse them" (Rom. 12:14)? "See that no one repays anyone evil for evil, but always seek to do good to one another and to everyone" (1 Thess. 5:15; cf. Rom. 12:19; 1 Pet. 4:19).

How can David's prayer ever be harmonized with these passages? We cannot say that David could not have known this instruction, for loving one's enemies was taught already in the Old Testament (see Exod. 23:4–5; Lev. 19:18; Prov. 20:22; 24:17; 25:21–22; Job 31:29–30).

On the basis of these and similar Scripture passages, people have often condemned the imprecatory psalms (Pss. 5; 35; 58; 59; 69; 109; 137). Under the influence of humanism with its idol of the noble man who does no one harm, people declared these psalms to be in conflict with the rest of Scripture, especially with the love command given by the Lord Jesus and his apostles. In fact, the imprecatory psalms are supposedly unchristian. Others let themselves be guided by their feelings and on that basis consider it impermissible to pray down God's curse upon their enemy.

Admittedly, people moderate that condemnation by appealing to the mitigating circumstances of the poets, such as "they lived in a completely different time. The mentality back then was completely different. They were still living under the Old Covenant. They did not yet know the teaching of the Lord Jesus. They were passionate Easterners. The passionate language of these psalms fits with such temperaments. In Babylonia such curse formulae were employed as well." In these ways, people wanted to avoid the full impact of ascribing the imprecatory prayers to the psalmists but believed that a Christian cannot possibly take such prayers upon his lips any longer.

We need little argument to recognize that anyone seeking either to accuse or excuse particular psalmists is actually trying to accuse or excuse God, the Holy Spirit, the Author of Holy Scripture. Human understanding and sentiment function here as autonomous authorities sitting on the judge's bench in sovereign judgment over God's holy Word. We already mentioned the influence of humanism with its sovereign noble man. In this expression of so-called Scripture criticism we taste once again the evolutionism that we identified in connection with Psalm 16. According to this dogma, throughout the course of the centuries, not only this world but also the knowledge of God supposedly evolved to a nobler and higher level. In this way of thinking, the imprecatory psalms could be compared to stages of growth in the knowledge of God, which we fortunately have progressed beyond.

When it comes to explaining God's Word, however, we may allow neither our understanding nor our sentiment nor any evolutionary hypothesis to function as authorities, but only this Word itself. These imprecatory psalms are part of this Word. In response to this fact, it is far more suitable for us to adopt a posture of humble submission.

But David did not avenge himself!

True enough, the apostle wrote, "Beloved, never avenge yourselves, but leave it to the wrath of God, for it is written, 'Vengeance is mine, I will repay, says the Lord'" (Rom. 12:19;

cf. Deut. 32:35). And that is precisely what David practiced with full integrity! David did not avenge himself against his enemies in the least. This entire psalm, with its petitions for the destruction of his enemies, provides the proof that he did so with hearty faith: "Leave it to the wrath of God." David gave God plenty of opportunity to take up his cause. He initiated no campaign against Saul, the ruling king. David *fled* and in prayer called upon Yahweh for help. In this he was acting entirely in the Spirit of our Lord Jesus Christ, who also, "when he was reviled, . . . did not revile in return; when he suffered, he did not threaten, but continued entrusting himself to him who judges justly" (1 Pet. 2:23).

There are Christians who strongly condemn the kind of requests we are now discussing as being harsh and unloving. But just wait until their own rights must be maintained and defended! Then they will have no objection against reaching for various worldly means of power and even force, even though the route of normal jurisprudence lies wide open to them. One wonders where such Christians get the right to condemn someone like David. A wicked government tramples upon his rights and there is no judge willing to listen to his complaint. Saul, the highest judge, was chasing him. In this situation the popular military leader David renounced all military force and did nothing other than ask God for intervention, but he raised not a finger against his king!

Rather than be dominated by the choice between loving or being avenged, our discussion of the imprecatory psalms could better be guided by the contrast between maintaining your rights *by yourself* with every possible means, or handing it over (presuming the path to justice is blocked) *to God*. This latter choice is what righteous people like David did, together with the composers of other imprecatory psalms, even under the government of the wicked Saul or under the Babylonian world power that had trampled upon Israel's rights (cf. Ps. 137). In this respect, their attitude differs widely from the

Maccabean mentality underlying an activist and revolutionary Christianity.

And David did love his enemies!

Lecturing David because he should have loved his enemy rather than praying for such terrible things to befall him, gains no traction, simply because he *did* love his enemy!

Twice Saul had almost pinned him to the wall with his spear. Don't close your eyes to that! Would you have gone to sit next to Saul after those attempts, in order to calm and soothe him? Well, that's what David did (1 Sam. 18:11; 19:10). Did he love his enemy, or not? In addition to this, the book of Samuel shows in two lengthy chapters that David allowed two very opportune situations for killing his archenemy to pass, even though he himself would not have needed to strike the mortal blow (1 Sam. 24; 26). Saul acknowledged as much himself: "You have dealt well with me, though I did you evil" (cf. 1 Sam. 24:18). Do you want to find a more unimpeachable witness of David's love for his enemy than that enemy himself? Read once the moving "In Memoriam" that David composed not only when his friend Jonathan died but also in honor of his enemy, Saul, and then you will see how much the composer of the imprecatory 59th psalm loved his enemy (2 Sam. 1:17–27).

MOREOVER, DAVID CLOTHED THESE PETITIONS WITH ARGUMENTS

But if David was not praying for the destruction of his enemies out of personal hatred or vengeance, why did he do it? We will need to find the explanation in David's extraordinary love for Yahweh. David was standing in the flames for the sake of Yahweh's honor, Yahweh's cause, and Yahweh's people. This love for Yahweh was the motivating impulse as much for stepping up to Goliath as for composing this psalm. That becomes evident when we study the reasons David used to clothe his "problematic" petitions. He brought his request to Yahweh

1. Psalm 59: A Psalm of David for Vengeance

on the basis of the following four grounds: (1) the well-being of God's people, (2) the arrogance of God's enemies, (3) the justice of God's wrath, and (4) the acknowledgment of God's lordship. All of these are issues that involve the righteousness of God far more than the personal interests of David.

On behalf of the well-being of God's people

As we mentioned earlier, we prefer this translation of verse 11: "O God, *kill them*, so that my people do not *stumble*"—in contrast to the ESV: "Kill them *not*, lest my people *forget*." As we explained, a request for God to kill them seems to us more compatible with the petitions for their destruction than a request not to kill them. And "not stumble" or "not be moved, not totter" seems to us to fit better than "not forget." For what was the wider historical context?

Right after the time of the judges

In David's younger years the period of the judges had barely passed. The last judge, Samuel, was still alive. After his successful escape, David went to Samuel in Ramah (1 Sam. 19:18). After the abominable Canaanizing of Israel had occurred, many in Israel joyfully greeted the promising effort to return to Yahweh and his covenant that had arisen in Israel through Samuel's teaching of the Word of God (1 Sam. 4:1).

To be sure, the spirit that had led Israel to ask for a king signified a relapse into pagan worship of human power and idolization of a great man ("our king . . . [will] go out before us and fight our battles," 1 Sam. 8:20), but the beginning of Saul's rule looked quite promising. The Spirit of Yahweh took hold of him and was with him (1 Sam. 10:6–7, 10–11). "He shall save my people from the hand of the Philistines," Yahweh had said to Samuel (1 Sam. 9:16). Nothing came of this, however. When Saul died, the Philistines were the superior power throughout Canaan. For although Saul did deliver Jabesh in Gilead thanks to the Spirit of God, he subsequently showed himself more and more to be a man who threatened to destroy Samuel's reforming work entirely. Rather than relying as a humble king in complete trust on Israel's Master King, Saul increasingly took refuge in worldly instruments of power, such as a mighty army. Saul saw no chance of deliverance for the kingdom of God—which is what Israel was!—without military power (1 Sam. 13:11). In this way he undermined Samuel's teaching that had continued to echo the ancient sound of Moses, Joshua, Caleb, and Gideon, namely, that Yahweh was asking only one thing of Israel: trust in God, for then he would take care of the rest. Instead, with Saul there arose in Israel that equally ancient, unbelieving, and worldly calculating impulse. In the wilderness it had come to expression from the ten spies, and later it repeatedly drew Israel away from Yahweh.

There lay the precise cause of Philistine domination. With the light of the Torah (Lev. 16 and Deut. 28), Saul was supposed to have seen that in the return of the Philistines, the wrath of Yahweh was falling upon Israel, because Israel had dishonored Yahweh as its Master King (1 Sam. 8:7). Unfortunately, Saul did nothing but arouse the wrath of God even more. Jonathan sensed the issue very well: "My father has troubled the land" (1 Sam. 14:29).

For this reason David's victory over Goliath signified far more than neutralizing an irritating giant. Under Saul, Israel had become just like the nations (1 Sam. 8:20). But when David came on the scene, Israel knew once again that she had one God and "that the Lord saves not with sword and spear" (1 Sam. 17:47). David pointed that discouraged army, and later that joyful people, to Israel's "living God" (1 Sam. 17:26, 36) and called upon them to believe in the name (i.e., the reputation and the powerful deeds) of Yahweh (1 Sam. 17:26, 45). That was reformational language in the line of Joshua, Hannah, and Samuel. Just as David's victory over Goliath was a reformational event of the first order, comparable with Elijah's victory on Carmel and, in subsequent church history, with the Reformation begun on October 31, 1517: each of them a return to God and his Word.

1. Psalm 59: A Psalm of David for Vengeance

Now Saul's soldiers were walking around the house of this David! This was no ordinary rivalry, but represented the hatred that Cain had harbored against Abel—religious hatred. Here we have before us a fragment of the quarrel that God's people in every age have with their "pious" enemies.

In this historical context Psalm 59:11–13 was composed.

We must read this imprecatory psalm within the framework of the fierce confrontation between the arrogant and the humble groups within Israel. Or between the reformational and the deformational groups within the Israelite church. The young leader of the movement for return to Yahweh is being threatened with death. The requests for destruction in Psalm 59 are not an expression of personal feelings of revenge; they are requests coming from Israel's new deliverer, who had already been anointed as Israel's new king, the messiah David, the national deliverer who was to succeed Samuel.

This was the source and character of David's petitions to Yahweh.

How David must have suffered, filled as he was with his deep love and zeal for Yahweh and his cause, watching the dismantling of Samuel's life work. In that work Yahweh had begun to take pity on Israel by allowing Israel to continue living in Canaan and by allowing Israel to keep that inheritance, which had come to be despised and endangered despite the depth of Israel's sin in the period of the judges.

Of course David loved his neighbor, King Saul, even when he became his enemy. He sought his good. He calmed him with music. He spared his life. He respected his authority. But Saul's revolution, whereby he was destroying God's work and was leading God's people into worldliness, was something David could no longer stand by and watch. So from that love for God's cause and sorrow for God's people, David prayed: "O God, kill them, so that my people do not stumble! Make them totter by your power and bring them down!" (v. 12).

A TERRIBLE REQUEST?

Indeed it is a terrible request, but that is because it was a terrible situation!

Or wasn't it terrible that the entire deliverance of the people of Israel was on the verge of being smothered in its infancy? Wasn't it terrible that God's people were in danger of sinking away into Canaanitism and thereby in danger of calling down God's curse upon themselves (Lev. 26; Deut. 28) and of losing their inheritance, the land of Canaan? At this point we may properly weigh competing interests and remember that a human life does not have the highest value on this earth. As A. Janse has observed, such a notion belongs to a kind of universal human love that resembles the "love" of some parents who would rather let their child die than have that child undergo a painful operation. On this earth, full of strife, anyone who wishes to spare every human life will watch humanity be destroyed as his wish is being fulfilled. Such thinking places the human person above God, above the most sacred good belonging to the human race. Together with this most sacred good, in connection with our psalm (in fact, with all of the so-called imprecatory psalms), we can include matters like a church reformation, the well-being of God's people, averting God's wrath, and preserving the inheritance promised by God. These are far and away more significant interests than the length of King Saul's life. We speak intentionally of the length of his life, because when we consider David's request, "O God, kill them," we must not read into it, "O God, send them to their eternal destruction." After all, Scripture knows of other people whose lives were shortened because of punishment, including the life of Moses. Was Moses therefore lost eternally? We must distinguish at this point between a person's temporal fate and his eternal destiny.

It was that deep interest in Israel's continuing return to God and his covenant that David had in view when he prayed to Yahweh as one called to be a deliverer or when he prayed

1. Psalm 59: A Psalm of David for Vengeance

for the death of the leaders in Israel who were leading the people back into the carnal worship of human strength that is an abomination to God (Luke 16:15), thereby unleashing even more severe judgments upon Israel. Rather than sentimentalizing about David's "harsh" petitions, his critics would do better to take into account God's harsh judgments, as they were being executed by means of the Philistine terror that fell upon Israel. Saul's actions led to those judgments. David was seeking to avert them. So when he prays for the removal of the causes of Israel's misery, why should he be rapped on the knuckles for harshness and lovelessness?

THE LORD IS OUR SHIELD (V. 11)

In the situation of desperate need in which David composed Psalm 59, he confessed, "*Our* Shield is the LORD!" Here again David was not praying personally but continued praying both as the appointed deliverer of Israel and as the king who had already been anointed. In this critical time he was the "Immanuel figure" through whom Yahweh was going to deliver his people. In the near future Israel's salvation would be tied to David. So David was praying his petitions for the destruction of his enemies as an intercessor: he is talking about "my people"!

In addition, with his confession of God as "*our* Shield," we must see him as the spokesman of the meek in Israel, who had learned from Hannah and Samuel: "Not by might shall a man prevail" (1 Sam. 2:9). In this connection we could think of the godly who were being trampled upon, who would later be gathered with David in the cave of Adullam (1 Sam. 22:1–2), who were victims of Saul's despising of the Torah. On behalf of all these poor or righteous or meek, David confessed, "*Our* Shield is the LORD!"

Naturally one can understand the word *shield* to refer to the familiar military protection. But here the word can also mean "Suzerain, Great King," as it does in other passages. (The word *suzerain* refers to an ancient feudal lord who granted people protection in exchange for their loyalty.) Such rulers were identified in the ancient Near East with the term *shield*. No matter which meaning is preferred, it is clear that David is expressing here a genuine confession. He is standing up for the truth precisely at the point where it is being challenged in his day and where such confession is inevitably coupled with suffering. Saul's soldiers had surrounded David's house, but he and his sympathizers did not meet strength with strength; instead, they fled and confessed, "Our Shield is the Lord!"

That kind of language is characteristic of the meek.

On account of the arrogance of David's enemies

The second reason that David adduced for the defeat of his enemies was their arrogance and the campaign of lies with which they attempted to supply their persecution with an appearance of legitimacy. At that point David prayed, "For the sin of their mouths, the words of their lips, let them be trapped in their pride" (v. 12).

Here as well the question arises, was David allowed to pray that?

This question can be answered only if we view David in the historical context of Psalm 59 in its entirety. When did David utter these petitions? At which point of time in the struggle between the meek and the arrogant groups within Israel did this happen? Had God issued a pronouncement about Saul by this point?

God had already rejected Saul

Saul's failure as king wasn't a fate that hung over his head from the outset. As far as God was concerned, he could have been allowed to deliver Israel from the Philistines (1 Sam. 9:16). Yahweh had given him his Spirit and had allowed him to liberate Jabesh (1 Sam. 9:16; 1 Sam. 10–11). But Saul became disobedient, and though he was warned severely, he went from bad to worse, to the point that Samuel had to bring him the message "You have rejected the word of the Lord, and the LORD has rejected you from being king over Israel" (1 Sam. 15:26). Wouldn't Samuel have told David, once he had anointed him as Saul's successor, that Yahweh had already rejected Saul as king? In any case, David could easily have seen from Saul's outbursts of fury that the Spirit of Yahweh had left Saul (1 Sam. 16:14). In fact, wasn't this evident from Saul's fear of that blasphemer Goliath as well? And recently Saul had brushed off the serious warnings of Samuel and Jonathan and made yet one more attempt to get rid of David. David fled to Samuel in Ramah (1 Sam. 19:18), and had the prophet not mentioned it earlier, he surely would have told David at that point that Yahweh had rejected Saul as king—indeed, that Yahweh had indicated that he would rather not see Samuel grieving any longer for Saul (1 Sam. 16:1).

This sequence of events can help us understand David's prayer for Saul's defeat. God himself first made known, as David most likely knew, that Saul had already been rejected as king by God. Only after that did David come to God with Psalm 59. He was praying, so to speak, in the light of Samuel's prophecy, and only after Saul's impenitence was thoroughly obvious.

Regarding the requests of verse 12, we will return later to the fall of Saul as one who was arrogant. "For the sin of their mouths, the words of their lips, let them be trapped in their pride," David asked. After Saul's public fiasco at Naioth in particular (1 Sam. 19:19–24), the controversy between Saul and David emerged from behind the scenes of palace life into the public. The perception of Saul as a liar traveled all the way to the far corners of the land. The wise woman Abigail, a farmer's wife from Maon, saw through the excuses of Saul's courtiers, and the time was coming when all Israel would see clearly the difference between Saul and David (2 Sam. 5:2).

That was the divine response to Psalm 59:12.

On behalf of God's justified wrath

The third reason that David adduced for his disputed

petitions was "Consume them *in wrath;* consume them till they are no more" (v. 13a).

We must read these as dated, time-specific words. Then it becomes evident that David did not lift up this petition from personal revenge, nor was he thinking exclusively of God's wrath over Saul's campaign to surround David's house and arrest him. No, David understood his time as a period when Yahweh had a quarrel with his vineyard.

David learned that from Samuel.

And Samuel heard that from his mother.

DAVID WAS PRAYING AS A STUDENT OF HANNAH

We have already observed that Psalm 59 was written in the historical context of the close of the period of the judges. That was a period when Yahweh was often and severely angry with Israel. Some of the faithful Israelites saw God's hand pressing down upon his inheritance, like the judges and like the man of God who had come announcing judgment on Eli's house (1 Sam. 2:27–36). But from no member of the remnant in that period do we have such a penetrating analysis of this time and such a prophetic overview of the contemporary situation and future as from Hannah, the mother of Samuel. This woman was richly endowed with the gift of discernment! In her psalm, as she was led by God's Spirit, she was given to speak about the events that were about to occur in the next fifty years in the Hebrew church. Indeed, she was allowed to "see" even further into the future, for the composer of Psalm 113 and Mary in her Magnificat (Luke 1:46–55) cited Hannah's psalm extensively.

Hannah, who in her own barrenness physically experienced Yahweh's covenant curse on Israel (Deut. 28:18; cf. 7:14), had her eyes open to Yahweh's quarrel with the Israel of her day. But Yahweh exalted the despised Hannah by giving her a son, and with her knowledge of Yahweh she saw in that gift the fact that "the Lord awoke as from sleep" (Ps. 78:65–66) and a prelude of what he would do with all his arrogant enemies and his humble covenant partners in Israel: "The adversaries of the LORD shall be broken to pieces; against them he will thunder in heaven" (1 Sam. 2:10).

At that time, those arrogant ones were people like the priest's sons, Hophni and Phinehas, who had degraded God's holy dwelling to the level of a Canaanite idol temple, complete with accompanying sexual immorality (1 Sam. 2:22). While God's wrath was rolling over Israel in terms of the Philistine domination, those arrogant ones would at one point reach in "faith" for the ark. Hannah called them and their kind "the enemies" who "talk proudly," the "mighty ones with a bow." They "fight against Yahweh," and thus these church people through their wickedness bring down upon Israel Yahweh's covenant curse.

In addition to these wicked ones, however, Hannah saw an entirely different Israelite. "Feeble," she calls them. "The poor," "the hungry," "those with little," those who had sunk down to the realm of the dead, the powerless. And what did Hannah prophesy at that point? That Yahweh was ready to turn the entire order (or disorder) in Israel upside down. Samuel's birth was the start. She characterized the events now underway with the words "The adversaries of the LORD shall be broken in pieces; against them he will thunder in heaven" (1 Sam. 2:10). The wicked in Israel, who at that time were playing first chair in the orchestra, would be punished and oppressed just as surely as they and their cohorts now enjoyed the places of honor. Through the storm clouds of God's wrath, as they had gathered above Israel in the period of the judges, Hannah saw the rays of sunshine of divine compassion breaking out over his people.

This prophecy of Hannah in 1 Samuel 2:1–10 certainly became the "compendium" of all the teaching that she gave her son Samuel. In turn, he taught Israel in the same spirit. David learned from Samuel to understand his time in the light of Hannah's prophecy about Yahweh's divine rejection of all human pride and bragging about human strength and about his certain and sure imminent judgment upon all the arrogant in the church.

Didn't David see that prophecy being fulfilled in some sense? Hadn't Yahweh "thundered" over the arrogant priests Hophni and Phinehas (1 Sam. 4)? Weren't the Israelites defeated by the hundreds in the battles at Aphek (1 Sam. 4)? Hadn't Yahweh handed over his own dwelling to the Philistines, along with the ark (1 Sam. 5)? Hadn't Yahweh removed the entire house of Eli from the priestly service? Hadn't Yahweh chosen David from the tribe of Judah to be king and thus passed over the self-sufficient tribe of Ephraim (Ps. 78:67)? In the time of Psalm 59, weren't the land and the people once again under the wrath of God, so that their possession of the inheritance of Canaan was once again endangered? Hadn't Yahweh already begun to humiliate the arrogant Saul?

We will have far less difficulty with Psalm 59 if we read it as a dated, time-specific composition, in the light of Hannah's prophecy. The shocking things for which David prays in his psalm had already been prophesied by Hannah in her psalm! Through Samuel, David had learned from Hannah to see that Yahweh was angry with his people, and not just since yesterday or the day before. Yahweh had awoken like someone who had been asleep, Psalm 78 says, in reference to this same time. He awoke to take up the quarrel of his poor remnant, for that was God's own cause.

Many Christians are too obsessed with their own rights. In Psalm 59 David places himself wholly on God's side. He is here speaking out of the full acknowledgment of God's covenantal justice that makes his wrath on Israel entirely legitimate and his covenant curse entirely justified. David came at that point with his "curse petitions" asking Yahweh for help (cf. Judg. 5:23). As someone has put it, not the injured human being but the holy God and his righteousness constitute the central point in these OT psalms.

They allow us to hear the echo of prophecy.

On behalf of the acknowledgment of God's lordship

The fourth reason that David adduces for his requests was this: "That they may know that God rules over Jacob to the ends of the earth" (v. 13b). This reason, too, was not rooted first of all in David's personal interest.

David loved Yahweh's honor and Yahweh's cause very deeply. He walked away from Goliath with words similar to the ones we've just read (cf. 1 Sam. 17:26). He gave a preview of his defeat of the giant with these words:

> You come to me with a sword and with a spear and with a javelin, but I come to you in the name of the LORD of hosts, the God of the armies of Israel, whom you have defied. This day the LORD will deliver you into my hand . . . *that all the earth may know that there is a God in Israel*, and that all this assembly may know that the LORD saves not with sword and spear. For the battle is the LORD's, and he will give you into our hand. (1 Sam. 17:45–47)

Here in Psalm 59 David shows the same concern about the acknowledgment of God's dominion. In this connection we may recall that in Scripture this dominion comes down to being king—ruling, performing justice, defending the oppressed, punishing the evildoers.

So then, who was the real king in Israel? Saul? Or Yahweh? Who was really the suzerain ("Shield," v. 11) of the vassal nation of Israel? Would people be allowed to defy God's authority with impunity? Would Yahweh do nothing in response? With an eye on Yahweh's honor as the suzerain, David prays here for the defeat of his enemies so that every spectator could see that Yahweh rules in righteousness: faithful to his covenant, defending the oppressed, and opposing the oppressors.

In Psalm 58, which could be dated from the same period as Psalm 59, David prays with fiery expressions for the defeat of his opponents: "Let them be like the snail that dissolves into slime" (v. 8). And we must think of Psalm 59:13b when we read the end of this psalm:

> Mankind will say, "Surely there is a reward for the
>   righteous;
>   surely there is a God who judges on earth."
>
> (Ps. 58:11)

Imprecatory prayers are not characteristic of the Old Testament only

But aren't imprecatory prayers like the ones David prayed characteristic of the old dispensation? Now that Christ has given his teaching, haven't these psalms been conquered by "the spirit of love"? This widely heard claim can be refuted in no better way than by referring to the New Testament itself.

For a start, the apostles also cited these psalms in their writings, showing that they too consider the imprecatory psalms as belonging to the authoritative divine Scripture. With apparent agreement they cite not only other parts of these psalms but also the imprecatory prayers themselves (compare Acts 1:20a with Ps. 69:25; Acts 1:20b with Ps. 109:8; and Rom. 11:9 with Ps. 69:22–23).

Furthermore, in the NT we read from Paul's hand, "If anyone has no love for the Lord, let him be accursed. Our Lord, come!" (1 Cor. 16:22). And this: "If anyone is preaching to you a gospel contrary to the one you received, let him be accursed" (Gal. 1:9). Concerning Alexander the coppersmith we read, "The Lord will repay him according to his deeds" (2 Tim. 4:14). In this respect we hear in the last book of the Bible some remarkable prayers. While on the island of Patmos John saw in a vision those "who had been slain for the word of God and the witness they had borne." Wholly in line with Psalm 59, they were praying for God's wrath to fall upon their enemies: "O Sovereign Lord, holy and true, how long before you will judge and avenge our blood on those who dwell on the earth?" (Rev. 6:9–10). We see in Revelation 18 the response to this prayer in the fall of the great Babylon. We hear in Revelation 19 the subsequent reactions to this execution of divine wrath. John heard a multitude in heaven (the heavenly council) raise up a mighty "Hallelujah!" and a mighty voice sounded forth from the throne to the people on earth: "Praise our God, all you his servants, you who fear him, small and great" (Rev. 19:5).

So all the way to the very last book of the Bible, we read imprecatory prayers, and we encounter joy because of the execution of divine wrath. Thus, the imprecatory psalms do not at all contradict the tone of Scripture, nor the tone of the New Testament.

But then mustn't we pray for the conversion of our enemies?

Of course it is proper that we exercise great care with the kind of prayers like the one David composed in Psalm 59. God and our Lord Jesus Christ are not about to come to the defense of every possible inappropriate endeavor of Christians (1 Pet. 4:15). That is why we will need to be careful about singing psalms like this one if we are consumed with religious fanaticism or partisanship. Thomas Müntzer and John of Leiden identified their revolutionary Anabaptist "heavenly kingdom" with God's cause and sent up imprecatory psalms as part of their effort. When, during the peasant rebellion in Germany, Thomas Müntzer spotted a rainbow in the sky shortly before the battle, he thanked God for this sign of his faithfulness. But in his blindness the man failed to see that in their revolutionary disturbance his followers had abandoned God's covenant. Their army was completely defeated.

The imprecatory psalms are also covenant songs, included in God's Word, the Book of his covenants, to be taken upon the lips of those only who keep God's covenant. So great care is fitting here.

But shouldn't God's children pray for the conversion of

their enemies instead of for their defeat? The fact that God's Spirit has given psalms like Psalm 59 to instruct us in the school of prayer can teach us that we should not answer this question in the affirmative in all circumstances. We need to discern the times.

Samuel must have loved Saul very much, for after Saul was rejected as king, we read, "Samuel grieved over Saul" (1 Sam. 15:35). The old judge certainly prayed much for Saul's conversion.

Such prayers, however, are not always welcomed by the Lord!

In 1 Samuel 16 Yahweh asks Samuel, "How long will you grieve over Saul, since I have rejected him from being king over Israel?" (v. 1). Meanwhile, at God's command, Samuel had already anointed David as Saul's successor. Is it appropriate, then, to demand that David, who had already been anointed, still pray for the conversion of Saul, the one who had already been rejected as king?

The elderly Eli also understood that there were times when it was simply inappropriate to pray for conversion. He said to his wicked sons Hophni and Phinehas, "If someone sins against a man, God will mediate for him, but if someone sins against the LORD, who can intercede for him?" (1 Sam. 2:25).

"Do not pray for the welfare of this people," Yahweh commanded his servant Jeremiah: "Though they fast, I will not hear their cry" (Jer. 14:11–12). "Though Moses and Samuel stood before me, yet my heart would not turn toward this people. . . . I am weary of relenting" (Jer. 15:1, 6).

THE MARTYRS DARED TO DO SO

The persecuted "sacrificial lambs of Christ" living in the sixteenth century had less difficulty with this psalm than many modern Christians. We can see that in our sixteenth-century Reformed confessions. This was a generation that taught its children to recite Heidelberg Catechism, Lord's Day 19, question 52:

1. Psalm 59: A Psalm of David for Vengeance

> **Q.** What *comfort* is it to you that Christ will come to judge the living and the dead?
> **A.** In all my sorrow and persecution I lift up my head and eagerly await as judge from heaven the very same person who before has submitted himself to the judgment of God for my sake, and has removed all the curse from me. He will cast *all his and my enemies* into everlasting condemnation, but he will take me and all his chosen ones to himself into heavenly joy and glory.

They made this confession on the basis of, among other passages, 2 Thessalonians 1, where they read, "Since indeed God considers it just to repay with affliction those who afflict you, and to grant relief to you who are afflicted as well as to us, when the Lord Jesus is revealed from heaven with his mighty angels in flaming fire, inflicting vengeance on those who do not know God and on those who do not obey the gospel of our Lord Jesus" (vv. 6–8).

Anyone who has ever read a book about Christian martyrs will know a bit about the sea of misery that swept over faithful confessors of Jesus Christ in the sixteenth century. One of those martyrs was Guido de Bres, the author of the Belgic Confession. His confession constitutes "a devotional church book with a double golden clasp" (C. Vonk, *De Nederlandse Geloofsbelijdenis*, 2:549) for it concludes with a twofold appeal: an appeal to the earthly government (art. 36) and an appeal to the heavenly government (art. 37). But then these appeals went forth "in the hearing of enemies, persecutors, cowardly hypocrites like the Libertines, and especially governments who violate consciences by condemning their subjects to death, against their better knowledge, for the sake of the gospel" (Vonk, *De Nederlandse Geloofsbelijdenis*, 2:699). The Belgic Confession concludes with a dreadful wail arising from the oppressed spirit of a martyr church on account of the bitter injustice rendered by judges. These poor Christians had more important things to do than criticize Psalm 59 as harsh and unloving. In the hearing of friend and foe, they confessed that the thought of this judgment

> is horrible and dreadful to the wicked and evildoers, but it is a great joy and comfort to the righteous and elect. For then their full redemption will be completed and they will receive the fruits of their labor and of the trouble they have suffered. Their innocence will be known to all and they will see the terrible vengeance God will bring upon the wicked who persecuted, oppressed, and tormented them in this world. . . . and their cause—at present condemned as heretical and evil by many judges and civil authorities—will be recognized as the cause of the Son of God. (Belgic Confession, art. 37)

Verses 14–17: The Response to These Petitions

We need not say very much about verses 14–15. Verse 14 is a repetition of verse 6. In verse 15 David is developing a bit further the comparison of his pursuers with ravaging dogs: they must find their prey.

> Verses 14–15:
> **Each evening they come back,**
> **howling like dogs**
> **and prowling about the city.**
> **They wander about for food**
> **and growl if they do not get their fill.**

What a contrast with David, who burns with zeal for the cause and the name of Yahweh! They hound an innocent brother and simply refuse to factor God into the picture.

The binoculars of faith

Faith is a bit like a pair of binoculars: it brings the horizon of God's promises close to the viewer. That happens because God speaks so cordially in his promises—sometimes so cordially and divinely self-assured that he speaks about things that he will yet provide as though he has already provided them. This firm promissory speaking of God brings about in his people a firm believing response, so that not only the divine Promise Maker but also the human promise believer can talk about matters still to be given and received as though they were already given and received. We can see this manner of speaking with David in Psalm 59.

> Verses 16–17:
> But I will sing of your strength;
> > I will sing aloud of your steadfast love in the morning.
> For you have been to me a fortress
> > and a refuge in the day of my distress.
> O my Strength, I will sing praises to you,
> > for you, O God, are my fortress,
> > the God who shows me steadfast love.

David certainly did not compose this psalm immediately after he had slipped out of his house through the window and down the city wall. Perhaps he had escaped earlier that night from his murderers, and we should read these verses as thanksgiving for that deliverance. But we know how much danger and suffering still lay around the corner, and we recall that dreadful night when David's kingship over Israel seemed more like an illusion than a divine promise. Nevertheless, after that night David trusted so firmly in Yahweh's promise that he never lifted his hand against Saul, and was satisfied to live from the position of his future deliverance: "For you have been to me a fortress and a refuge in the day of my distress."

David did not end up ashamed in this faith.

Yahweh answered his prayer completely!

All the petitions granted

Of course, David had to wait a few years before his requests were answered, but then Yahweh did indeed answer every petition of Psalm 59.

"Deliver me from my enemies, O my God," David had pleaded (v. 1). Yahweh did so. "Awake, come to meet me, and see!" David went on to plead. "You, Lord God of hosts, are God of Israel. Rouse yourself to punish all the nations!" So, Yahweh rose up for David. David himself did not need to lift a finger. His posture was, in fact, to do nothing and to refrain from any kind of action, since Yahweh obviously took so much pleasure in his servant that Yahweh himself put his armies in service to David. He mocked David's enemies, as David had requested in Psalm 59:8. And he became a fortress for David (Ps. 59:9). This included the most agonizing and tense moments, for where did the miraculous deliverance of 1 Samuel 23:26–29 come from but from God? Yahweh granted even David's petition for the death of his enemies. They fell, among other places, in the hill country of Gilboa (1 Sam. 31).

With this last fact—the death of Saul and his compatriots—don't all the objections against this psalm of David evaporate? People can argue about this psalm as they wish; they can criticize David for some of these requests as they wish. But Yahweh, the God and Father of our Lord Jesus Christ, to whom David directed his controversial requests, answered every one of them!

Reading Other Imprecatory Psalms in the Light of Prophecy

We have read Psalm 59 in the light of its own contemporary prophecy, especially that of Hannah in her psalm. Given our approach, we will have less difficulty with similar imprecatory psalms if we read them in the light of the prophecy of their time. This also applies to perhaps the most offensive passage in this genre of psalms, namely, Psalm 137:7–9:

> Remember, O Lord, against the Edomites
>   the day of Jerusalem,
> how they said, "Lay it bare, lay it bare,
>   down to its foundations!"
> O daughter of Babylon, doomed to be destroyed,
>   blessed shall he be who repays you
>   with what you have done to us!
> Blessed shall he be who takes your little ones
>   and dashes them against the rock!

Here God's wrath is prayed for against two enemies of God's people: Edom and Babylon. Babylon, because it destroyed Jerusalem, and Edom, because it assisted in that destruction and took so much pleasure in Jerusalem's distress. The Lamentations weep intensely because of the misery that the Babylonians wreaked against Jerusalem's children and infants in particular (cf. Lam. 2:11–12, 19; 4:4). We must understand the severe punishment being prayed for in Psalm 137 in the light that God himself had shone on these events beforehand through his prophets. For through the ministry of Isaiah, Yahweh had announced concerning Edom that he would be holding "a day of vengeance, a year of recompense for the cause of Zion" (Isa. 34:1–17; cf. Jer. 49:7–22; Ezek. 25:12–14; Amos 1:11; Obadiah). All of these prophets had announced before Psalm 137 what a terrible vengeance Yahweh would be executing against Edom. So as far as Edom was concerned, the psalmist was praying altogether "along with Yahweh." Consequently, any criticism of his psalm leads inevitably to criticism of the God of Holy Scripture, who has a quarrel with his enemies and is pursuing his justice in terms thereof. As far as Babylon is concerned, Isaiah had already issued an extensive divine speech about the abominable Babylon, the scourge of the world of that time, who had starved and killed so many children and infants in Jerusalem (Isa. 13–14). That cruel Babylon stood at the threshold of Yahweh's "burning wrath" with which he would come to visit merciless Babylon with mercilessness. In that context Isaiah had already declared,

> Their infants will be dashed in pieces
>   before their eyes;
> their houses will be plundered
>   and their wives ravished.   (Isa. 13:16)

The other prophecies against Babylon are similar (cf. Isa. 47; Jer. 50–51). Babylon would be destroyed after terrible battles. In that connection the dashing of infants was a customary military tactic. This is how Yahweh himself had spoken about Edom and Babylon through his own prophets.

Only afterward were the prophecies of Psalm 137 composed.

Read in the light of prophecy that was both contemporary and earlier, Psalm 137, like Psalm 59, is not surprising; it is consistent with the tone of the rest of Scripture and isn't an incidental unburdening of a vengeful Israelite. In both psalms is embedded the language of faith granted by God's Spirit, faith that is most closely born out of God's already revealed prophetic Word. Here as well, just as in so many psalms, we hear the echo of the Prophets reverberating.

By David's time, God had seen to it that his plans for Israel's immediate future had already been prophesied by Hannah. Yahweh would turn the entire "order" upside down. David was affirming that in Psalm 59. What Hannah had prophesied in her psalm, David was now praying in his psalm. Similarly, more than a century before Psalm 137 was composed, God had made known through Isaiah and other prophets what he thought about cruel nations like Babylon and Edom and what he intended to do to them. So Psalm 137 was speaking not out of its own impulse, but with the help of divine speeches like Isaiah 13:16 and other prophecies: Blessed is the one who will be the instrument in God's hand for doing justice in Zion's just cause! Doesn't criticism of this psalm betray the wish to have a different God than the one proclaimed to us by Isaiah and the other prophets?

Imprecatory Psalms, Yes; Imprecatory Hymns, No

Although we harbor serious objections to many Christian hymns and songs, because such singing easily leads believers away from God's covenant, we don't want simply to reject singing hymns in general. Scripture itself does not furnish an absolute prohibition against singing hymns, and there is no Scriptural objection against singing good Christian hymns (cf. Eph. 5:19; Col. 3:16).

Having said that, we want to conclude our discussion of Psalm 59 by mentioning one particular objection against many hymnbooks: Where are the "imprecatory hymns"? Where are the Christian songs that cry out to the God and Father of our Lord Jesus Christ to perform justice on behalf of his oppressed people and to deliver his people from the hand of various wicked and bad people—songs that stand up just as fervently for God's honor, God's kingship, God's righteousness, as David does in Psalm 59? Where are the songs that sound forth prophecy just as clearly as the much maligned imprecatory psalms?

Christians who stumble over the imprecatory psalms, who have formed an image of a God who detests such psalms, will not be annoyed by the usual hymnbooks in this respect. In many of these pious songs, everything is focused on the lovely Jesus who loves everybody.

Is that really the case? Does Jesus love the unrighteous who do not repent or the wicked who trample over God's people?

The story is told that during the inquisition in Seville, the first *auto-da-fé* was celebrated in the city in 1559, when Don Juan Ponce de León and others were burned alive in the city plaza. Juan Gonzalez was burned alive for preaching Protestant doctrines. He was accompanied by his two sisters, who had also been condemned to die at the stake, and when the gag had been removed from his mouth, Gonzalez sang the 109th psalm: "Be not silent, O God of my praise! For wicked and deceitful mouths are opened against me, speaking against me with lying tongues" (be sure to read the rest of Psalm 109, yet another imprecatory psalm). The sisters were strangled, and he was burned alive. Do such brothers and sisters live today? Are they groaning in prisons and possibly being tortured in ways more refined than in the sixteenth century?

Shouldn't the church of Christ in our day be singing more often with that suffering fraternity, rather than being preoccupied in particularly beloved hymns with themselves, with their personal needs, their own doubts? Shouldn't the church be singing songs in the style of Zechariah—"That we should be saved from our enemies and from the hand of all who hate us" (Luke 1:71)? What modern hymn says that?

With these facts in mind, the constant yearning for newer hymns can have deeper unspiritual roots than many might assume. Let the Psalter remain the prayer book and songbook par excellence for the church of this new dispensation. The more estranged God's people become from the Psalter, the greater injury they will suffer and the less stable they will stand in the face of various winds of doctrine that misunderstand God's covenant, neglect God's historical acts of redemption in our generation as well as in our families, and close their hearts to the quarrel between the godly and their wicked oppressors.

This kind of Christianity can wallow in loveliness and sentimentality, but will it be aflame for the honor of the living God? Will it pant for the acknowledgment of God's lordship? Will it pray for justice on behalf of God's oppressed people? And even more importantly, will it suffer in the face of the trampling of God's justice? A saccharine humanism that views itself as being beyond this hatred of the imprecatory psalms, one that is brash enough to call itself Christian, is ignorant of such convictions.

May the remnant of Christians who still fear God and tremble before his Word pray fervently in the Spirit of Psalm 59 for the coming of Jesus Christ on the clouds, who will return to judge the living and the dead. What can offer the suffering Zion of our day any richer comfort?

CHAPTER 2

Psalm 56: David Arrested by the Philistines

This is the psalm of a man who is trapped: the poignant lament of a thoroughly miserable, lonely, endangered, and persecuted righteous person, one whose tears have almost filled a water bottle and whose nervous system had finally collapsed at a particular moment, so that those nearby thought they were looking at someone who was mentally deranged.

This is a person destroyed by his enemies.

That is how far gone David was when he composed Psalm 56.

Let's first look a bit more closely at this historical background.

Was David Merely Pretending in Gath, or Was There Really Something Wrong with Him?

In the superscription to this psalm, we read this: "To the choirmaster: according to The Dove on Far-off Terebinths. A Miktam of David, when the Philistines seized him in Gath." This history is narrated in 1 Samuel 21:10–15. From Nob, where the priest Ahimelech had given him the showbread and put the sword of Goliath in his hand, David fled about thirty miles farther to the Philistine town of Gath. There, however, he was arrested.

We see no reason to question the accuracy of this superscription. On the contrary, it appears to us to provide the key to the correct—which means, first of all, the historically situated—understanding of this psalm.

No affectation

We should not suspect too quickly that David was pretending before the people of Gath. According to 1 Samuel 21:10 David "went to" (i.e., paid a visit to) Achish, the king of Gath, surely in order to take counsel with this opponent of Saul. At that moment David saw no other option. But that Philistine king let himself be influenced by those around him (and later again, 1 Sam. 29:6–7). His servants approached him with the question (i.e., with the certain claim) "Is not this David the king of the land? Did they not sing to one another of him in dances, 'Saul has struck down his thousands, and David his ten thousands'?" (1 Sam. 21:11). David was overtaken by a dreadful panic, for "David took these words to heart and was much afraid of Achish the king of Gath" (v. 12). We get the impression that Achish had the city gates shut immediately, followed then by what we are told in 1 Samuel 21:13, that David "pretended to be insane in their hands and made marks [pounded?] on the doors of the gate and let his spittle run down his beard."

What was David doing? Was he pretending something at that moment when he was facing mortal danger? Was David performing a clever military ploy, or was there really something wrong with him? In this context this is an important question!

The common view proceeds from the premise that David was indeed pretending to be insane in Gath. In those days people who were mentally deranged were viewed as

2. Psalm 56: David Arrested by the Philistines

untouchable and were not killed. David supposedly tried to save his life this way. But if this were so, then Psalms 56 and 34 would come to stand in a strange light, for in the former, David confesses his sure reliance in faith upon Yahweh, and in the latter, he brings all gratitude for his rescue from Gath to Yahweh! If the common interpretation were correct, then David would first have saved himself by means of a trick leading to his escape and thereafter praised Yahweh as his deliverer.

We think, however, that this contradiction between the narrative of 1 Samuel 21 and the content of Psalms 34 and 56 does not exist. David was not pretending to be insane in Gath, but was genuinely confused.

We base this on the following considerations.

A crisis of nerves

Does the text of 1 Samuel 21:13 require us to believe that David pretended to be insane in Gath? This question is of decisive significance for the issue at hand.

The English translations of the Bible proceed with this common opinion by translating the verse, "So he changed his behavior before them and pretended to be insane" (ESV). The Hebrew text of 1 Samuel 21:13 does not require us to see this as a reference to feigned insanity. The Hebrew word translated as "pretend" (*halal*) can also be understood in terms of genuine mental bewilderment.

We would retain the translation referring to *change*. But we would interpret this in an intransitive sense: *David* changed. The Hebrew word for *behavior* or *understanding* can be taken as an accusative of respect, such that David's change occurred with respect to his behavior or mental capacities. The phrase "before them" can be rendered more literally as "in their eyes," and we have already indicated that the phrase "made marks on" can be understood as drumming on, banging on, or beating on. Taking all of this together, we would render 1 Samuel 21:12–13 this way: "And David took these words in his heart and was very afraid before the face of Achish, the king of

Gath. And he changed, namely, with respect to his mental capacities, at least in their eyes. And he conducted himself in their hands as one insane. He banged on the doors of the gate and let his saliva run down his beard."

For these reasons we are of the opinion that the text of 1 Samuel 21 does not require us to see David acting here as a clever pretender who was intentionally deceiving those around him. Something else was going on here, something that gave Achish and his servants the impression of insanity. But was that impression of Achish and his servants correct? Was David suddenly genuinely insane?

This need not be inferred from the text. For recall the trauma that David had just endured! We discussed this extensively in connection with Psalm 59. Whether he fled immediately from Nob to Gath, he had endured a long period of mortal danger. Think of Saul's attempts at murder, the ambush of his home, his narrow escape, his bidding farewell to his bosom friend Jonathan. For the emotional David, each of these events was nerve-racking. Presumably, he was already exhausted when he arrived in Gath. And there, to top it off, he was arrested! In 1 Samuel 21:13 we read literally that he behaved like a madman "in their hands." David was forcibly seized. We read earlier that these events had made David very afraid (1 Sam. 21:12). And then this dreadful panic was the last straw that made David's nervous system collapse. David changed, at least with respect to his understanding, his grasp of proper relationships, his capacity for evaluating things with discernment. At a given moment he lost his self-control completely. The Hebrew verb used in 1 Samuel 21:13 to refer to David behaving like an insane person is used in Jeremiah 25:16 and 51:7 in connection with drunkenness. David's manner resembled someone who had had too much to drink. In such a situation, a person is not being guided by his full mental capacity.

Rather than understand this as genuine insanity, we would prefer to think of David suffering powerless rage and irrational

2. Psalm 56: David Arrested by the Philistines

fear, causing him even to try to force the city gates open. Even now, having to read this about our beloved brother can be a moving experience. This same powerless rage can also explain why David allowed his saliva to run down his beard. No, not as a calculated part of a refined trick, but as a sign of complete loss of self-control. After all, it is not without reason that our own colloquial language has the expression "foaming with rage."

Achish makes an error in judgment

An entirely different question, naturally, is what Achish and his servants saw in the irrational fear and powerless rage of David. From 1 Samuel 21:13 we learn that "in their eyes" David was insane. The narrative continues to say after this, "Then Achish said to his servants, 'Behold, you see the man is mad. Why then have you brought him to me? Do I lack madmen, that you have brought this fellow to behave as a madman in my presence? Shall this fellow come into my house?'" (vv. 14–15). In Achish's opinion, David was genuinely insane.

But Yahweh used this error in judgment on the part of Achish as an instrument for rescuing his faithful servant David, and for that reason David could later praise and thank Yahweh with a clear conscience as his deliverer (Pss. 34 and 56). This subsequent response hardly comports with the traditional understanding of the events in Gath.

The superscriptions to Psalms 34 and 56 are fitting

Now that we have seen that the story of David's experiences in Gath recorded in 1 Samuel 21 does not require us to see David as a pretender, another argument that is often advanced against the accuracy of the superscription above Psalms 34 and 56 falls away. Both psalms can be explained very well against the historical background of this shocking episode in David's life, when he snapped psychologically and became totally confused due to his distress. At least that was the impression made on the superficial spectator.

We would like to read Psalm 56 in terms of this background.

The Day That I Am Afraid, I Put My Trust in You

From our youth, many of us have known the stories of David's flight from Saul, but that only increases the danger of our romanticizing them without realizing it.

Has anyone attempted to murder you? Have you ducked from a spear thrown your way, barely avoiding it by jumping out of the way? Has your home been surrounded during the night by soldiers who came to grab you for execution? David experienced all of these.

Fine enough, David could flee, but what he said later at his farewell to Jonathan characterized David's entire position: "Truly, as the Lord lives and as your soul lives, there is but a step between me and death" (1 Sam. 20:3).

As we read David's psalms composed during this period, we must picture him in the rocky wilderness of Judah. A man who lost everything in one fell swoop: his wife, his friend, his home, his work, his safety, his honor, his food and drink. A wretched outcast for whom life was no longer certain.

As you read Psalm 56, you must see him walking cautiously through the Judean hill country. Climbing every bluff carefully, setting up guards for the night, and lying down to sleep in a cave. You must see him getting up during the middle of the night to pray or to listen tensely to suspicious sounds. Slumbering. Being startled awake. Listening. Standing up. Filled with tension day and night. You must see him anxiously surveying his supply of bread and water, and remember that every hour of the day he had to face possible ambush.

And recall that this was the conqueror of Goliath, celebrated as a national hero, the king's son-in-law, a decorated military leader, and more than all these: a man whose heart was filled with the Holy Spirit, fervent on behalf of Samuel's

2. Psalm 56: David Arrested by the Philistines

efforts for return to Yahweh and his Word! And then to be hounded in the wilderness!

Surely you understand why David was lamenting to God at that point.

> Verses 1–2:
> **Be gracious to me, O God, for man tramples on me;**
> **all day long an attacker oppresses me;**
> **my enemies trample on me all day long,**
> **for many attack me proudly.**

This is what you're seeing: an outcast is lifting up to the ears of God a lament about his need. A man who is safe nowhere, one who faces danger on every side, who has lost everything, who has no other person to help him—not even prince Jonathan and the elderly prophet Samuel.

All of this was true not just for a moment but "all day long," every day. Each new morning brought with it a day full of uncertainty and mortal danger coming not simply from one person but from "many." Add to all of this his homesickness for the sanctuary, for his wife, and for his friend Jonathan. Add to this suffering his sorrow over the breakdown of Samuel's reformation efforts by the radical conduct of Saul, and then you have a bit of a sense about who is speaking in Psalm 56.

> Verses 3–4:
> **When I am afraid,**
> **I put my trust in you.**
> **In God, whose word I praise,**
> **in God I trust; I shall not be afraid.**
> **What can flesh do to me?**

This fits precisely with what we read in 1 Samuel 21: that David was severely distressed in Gath. Of course, he had lived for a long period in mortal danger and consequent fear and trembling, but the events in Gath were the icing on the cake. We have already seen that David was very afraid before Achish, the king of Gath, indeed, that the wretched outcast finally snapped. At a given moment, he was so bewildered that he was beating on the locked city gates of Gath as one foaming at the mouth from impotent rage, irrational with fear and completely shaken.

God's servants are not "personalities"

But could a man like David be so afraid? After all, he had just slain Goliath in faith, hadn't he? How can such a believing man now suddenly be overcome with fear? Indeed, some Bible readers might find it a bit off-putting to see this godly man David, the psalm writer, the man after God's heart, irrational with fear and crazy with distress. For some Christians perhaps it might be too hard to swallow: a David whose nerves are frazzled and shot? That hardly fits with the portraits of "strong personalities" and "imposing figures" that many Christians have always cherished! People like that aren't allowed to be afraid in public. And that's precisely what David was, with his slobbering and dripping beard in front of the gates of Gath! The complete opposite image from someone whom you can idolize with pride.

But here again we see the humanistic trace in our Christian thinking, whereby we participate in a hero worship that is somewhat Christianized but no less purely worldly. Christians fall for what might be called geniuses, strong personalities, born leaders. People usually look on these people as authoritative fellows who are able to match their opponents tit for tat. People who are like Nimrod, so to speak, hardy hunters before the face of the Lord. Leaders whom people admire even for the way they hold their pipe in their mouth, leaders to whom people devote scads of time and money.

That lineup of "personalities" has no place for a man who goes around like a maniac, scraping his fingernails on the city gates and letting his saliva run down his beard. Naturally

2. Psalm 56: David Arrested by the Philistines

David was nothing to look at, with his filthy beard and dirty face. But aside from that, what kind of impression did he make beyond Gath? A penniless man, with glistening eyes and trembling lips. He admitted as much in Psalm 56:8: "Put my tears in your bottle!" If only he had initiated a guerilla campaign against Saul! But what had David done? He had fled! And strummed psalms on a harp. That was pretty pious, but "strong" Christian "leaders" will surely observe that there are times when you need to "stand up" and do something—but where can you begin with such a pious psalm writer? No, in our day a Christianity that has become so worldly would have little to boast of in someone like David.

Yet Yahweh saved Israel by this man! That has always been God's way of acting, hasn't it? This is entirely consistent with the style of the kingdom of God (1 Cor. 1:28–29). Yahweh saved Israel from the morass of the period of the judges not by means of a heroic bruiser but through a man like David, who could suffer a nervous breakdown, to the extent that bystanders got the impression they were dealing with an insane person. Someone who stood beating against the city gates with a beard full of saliva. A man who could arouse the world's contempt. It still hurts to read the mocking words of the Philistine king about our brother David: "Do I lack madmen?"

The same thing happened later with other deliverers.

Elijah once suffered a deep nervous depression as well, leading to his collapse. How deeply depressed he must have been when he prayed, "It is enough now, O LORD, take away my life, . . ." (1 Kgs. 19:4). He was an exhausted man, tired of being a prophet. Jeremiah groaned: "I have become a laughingstock all the day; everyone mocks me" (Jer. 20:7–8). Indeed, Jeremiah shed a lot of tears. He was a man who at times was so distressed that he called out for his mother (Jer. 15:10). Daniel was exhausted by everything he had seen (Dan. 8:27).

Concerning all these righteous men (David, Elijah, Jeremiah, Daniel, etc.), Isaiah prophesied:

> He had no form or majesty that we should look at
> him,
> and no beauty that we should desire him.
> He was despised and rejected by men;
> a man of sorrows, and acquainted with grief;
> and as one from whom men hide their faces
> he was despised, and we esteemed him not.
>
> (Isa. 53:2b–3)

Think of this in connection with the way that Achish and his people treated David, acting with carnal pride, mocking and despising David.

But who was the supreme example in this line? The mocked, dressed-up, spit upon, stripped, and crucified Jesus of Nazareth, who during the night before he died was crawling on the ground at Gethsemane out of fear! "My soul is very sorrowful, even to death" (Matt. 26:38). "And his sweat became like great drops of blood falling down to the ground" (Luke 22:44). In fact, when Jesus's family came to get him, didn't people say about our Savior something similar to what people in Gath said about David: "For they were saying, 'He's out of his mind'" (Mark 3:21)?

Often that is how God's most faithful servants were and are treated.

> Verses 5–6:
> **All day long they injure my cause;**
> **all their thoughts are against me for evil.**
> **They stir up strife, they lurk;**
> **they watch my steps,**
> **as they have waited for my life.**

Here, of course, David is describing not only his experiences in Gath but the entire sphere in which he had been living in that time. Traitors, connivers, and bootlickers had seized the chance to earn a few points with Saul. Government officials like Saul inevitably attracted such folk, even among God's people. You can be sure that slander about David had been circulating throughout Israel and that the most baseless lies had obtained credence among some brothers.

In these verses you need to hear how all of that had wounded David!

How bitter it must have been for this hunted hero and believing composer of psalms to have to lead such a life: living every hour of the day looking out for his persecutor, having to leave all those lies unanswered, sneaking through valleys, spying from the hilltops, fleeing in caves, and constantly running the risk of someone betraying him—with no idea how long this all would last. For as Bible readers we know how Saul met his final end, but David did not know that when at that point he was wandering throughout the wilderness of Judea.

Church history is chock full of this kind of suffering. Isn't this how the wicked within the church have always oppressed the righteous and persecuted the prophets? Isn't this how they oppressed Elijah, Jeremiah, the Lord Jesus, and the apostle Paul—with intrigues, by twisting their words, with spying, and by watching their conduct with suspicion like religious voyeurs? That alone would make a person nervous, and what did David experience even beyond that!

Verse 7:
Free us from their malevolence [ESV "For their crime will they escape?"],
  In wrath cast down the Gentiles [ESV "peoples"],
    O God!

The first line of this verse is difficult to translate, though the main idea is clear. David did not take the law into his own hands, but appealed to a higher authority, Yahweh himself. This explains why people have seen the words in the superscription, "According to the Dove on Far-off Terebinths," as a reference to David's posture in the face of this injustice, namely, that of a hunted dove, mourning yet unable to make a sound. David expected his deliverance from God. To God he turned with the prayer to cast down "the Gentiles" (or the pagans). Just as in Psalm 59:5, he was referring with these words to his hostile Israelite brothers, who were persecuting him, with Saul at the head of the line. Those men were acting toward him like pagan Gentiles. In Israelite ears, "Gentile" had the same ring to it as "worldly" has in our ears. After all, in Saul and his compatriots, hadn't the Israelite church become paganized or worldly?

But did David have the right to pray for such terrible things to befall his enemies? Or is he standing here as an Old Testament believer below the standard of the New Testament, in which Jesus taught (Matt. 5:44), "But I tell you: Love your enemies"? We have discussed these and similar questions that arise in connection with such prayers, and did so in terms of Psalm 59, where David even prayed, "O God, kill them." See that discussion for our responses to objections that people raise against such prayers.

God's wrath, about which David is speaking here, is the same as that to which he was referring in Psalm 59. There was not a long period between the time underlying Psalm 56 and the time underlying Psalm 59. Perhaps a matter of weeks or months. So then, just as we did with Psalm 59, so too we need to read the words in this psalm about God's wrath in terms of the date or the situation of David's experience. Hovering above the Israelite church of his day—during the transition years as it moved from the period of the Judges to the period of the kings—was the cloud of divine wrath about which Hannah had already prophesied (1 Sam. 2).

The ESV has rendered the first line of verse 7 in a way consistent with Scripture, one that fits well with the next line: "For their crime will they escape? In wrath cast down the peoples, O God!" But the translation we have chosen also has some attractive features: "Free *us* from their malevolence." For

2. Psalm 56: David Arrested by the Philistines

then we hear David, just as in Psalm 59, not praying an individualistic prayer for deliverance from personal distress, but turning to Yahweh as appointed deliverer, as anointed king, as intercessor on behalf of the entire remnant among Israel that still feared Yahweh. In this connection one can think of the prophets in Naioth, the elderly Samuel, the believing Jonathan, the wise Abigail, all of them powerless under Saul's reign of terror and persecuting efforts mounted against David (Ps. 11:2).

On their behalf David was praying, "Deliver *us* . . ."

Verses 8–9:
You have kept count of my tossings;
    put my tears in your bottle.
    Are they not in your book?
Then my enemies will turn back
    in the day when I call.
This I know, that God is for me.

Here we must see the outcast before us in his cave. Arrested in Gath, having escaped alive through God's leading, he faces the question once again: Where now? He has lost his home. A person who returns to his home each day after work can hardly imagine this kind of aimless wandering.

David doesn't keep still: "I have cried aloud."

Nor does he piously beat around the bush, concealing the fact that he has enemies among his brothers (cf. Ps. 59:2). But here the sorrowful refugee is comforted with the soothing knowledge that God knows everything about his situation. He even writes it down. God knew exactly how many nights David had spent in caverns and caves, how many days he had wandered aimlessly. Even David's tears were preserved. The second line of verse 8 has also been translated, "You *have put* my tears in your bottle." We must not separate these words from the preceding verse: "In wrath cast down the Gentiles, O God!" With that divine day of reckoning in mind, David knew that his suffering had been recorded and his tears preserved. "This I know, that God is for me."

These definitely are the words not of a hardened, cursing psalm writer but of a meek man who could surrender his cause into God's hand and not seek vengeance himself, of one who loved his enemies and handed vengeance over to him who one day will judge righteously.

And that is what Yahweh did, at Gilboa, among other places. In his own time, Yahweh arose to answer these prayers of David and to recompense his tears against his cruel oppressors. That is true enough. But how many tears of how many others who have been oppressed are still waiting to be avenged, recorded in God's notebooks of the tears and suffering of his people? The tears of Jeremiah: "Oh that my head were waters, and my eyes a fountain of tears" (Jer. 9:1); those of Paul, whose pen at times was dipped in tears, as it were (Phil. 3:18); and those of numerous unknown lambs slain for the sake of Christ in subsequent centuries.

Luther commented in connection with this psalm, "What then? Does God have nothing else to do than to keep count of David's tears and wanderings? Is he not far more occupied with ruling the world and listening to the praise of the angelic choirs, which is unending? And yet it is true: God's care includes this: that he keeps count of the tears and wanderings of David" (*Luthers Psalmen-Auslegung*, ed. Erwin Mühlhaupt, vol. 2 [Göttingen, 1962], 244). He does this in order to wipe them away from their eyes once and for all with his own hands (Rev. 7:17; 21:4).

> Verses 10–11:
> In God, whose word I praise,
> > in the LORD, whose word I praise,
> in God I trust; I shall not be afraid.
> > What can man do to me?

Once again we hear the quintessential David. Such

2. Psalm 56: David Arrested by the Philistines

language is characteristic of David, and with this humble posture of faith, he was showing himself to be "the man after God's heart." David let God be God.

At this point, we wish to provide paraphrases of the Rev. J. C. Sikkel (1855–1920), who penned some important thoughts about David's experience and his psalm.

> How different the life of grace is from the worldly human life, even though it be led by those who boast in their knowledge of God and of his service!
>
> How small David must be in the eyes of all those polemicists among Christian leaders in our day, even though they boast about being representatives of the Christian faith!
>
> How these Christian men would have wielded the sword when Saul, David's great opponent, oppressor, and pursuer, twice lay at David's feet vulnerable and exposed, and the Lord, as David's men supposed, had given David's enemy into his hand.
>
> How these Christian men would have wanted David, during his wanderings and flights, to be ceaselessly busy with all kinds of outward means to increase his strength and resistance—rather than as David decided to do once—when he had considerable strength yet—to let Nabal go and not touch him.
>
> But the psalms on the harp, and prayer, his fleeing to God with pleading, for himself and for his people—indeed, that was the godly David, a fine man, but in the way of a simple soul. A strong man isn't like that, and a great man doesn't live like that. Christians must learn how to strike a blow. Weeping? Real men, partisans, don't weep. Practical women with a cause don't weep either. Christians in the world, world-Christians, they go along, they need to be made of granite.
>
> See to it that you overcome the other person. That is being a real man. Especially if you can do that for

someone else with a great name and power in the world; someone for whom you can devote your life.

David was a weakling, for he was a runaway. A wilderness hobo. Someone surrounded by destitute wretches. He sat there on a rock in the desert, strumming his harp. Lifting up his eyes to heaven. His tearful eyes. With trembling lips. Then he wept. He fell in solitude to his knees. He stuttered his soul's distress. He sobbed. He let go of the harp, and with trembling hands and fingers, reached upward, praying, pleading.

Only the Lord could deliver.

But that deliverance was in direct opposition to all the worldly nonsense in Saul's make-believe world, where according to accepted doctrine, souls and lives existed only to pave the way for strides of the great ones, who had to walk over that path as those bearing fame and honor, who trampled over others as they wished.

Blessed is the one who flees that world illusion, also in terms of religious weapons!

Blessed is the one who knows the distress of being kidnapped and enslaved by the power of the devil, the world, and sin! The one who hopes and trusts in the Lord alone, and waits upon the Lord alone! Together with all Israel! Looking for salvation and exaltation through the good pleasure of the Lord alone! Such a person prays. Such a person always prays.

That person will continue bearing the image of the wilderness man and the wilderness woman. With tearful eyes. With trembling lips. With bent knees. With shaking but uplifted hands. But also with the harp, with the psalms playing on the harp. The psalms of Israel. The psalms of the Holy Spirit.

And on that one's head a crown will one day glisten! (*De vreeze des Heeren en de verborgenheid des Heeren* [Haarlem, 1928])

To these thoughts of J. C. Sikkel we would add that David sang of this confidence after severe nervous exhaustion. In the confession of faith in Psalm 56 we may there see at the same time a confirmation of the explanation of the events in Gath. David's strange behavior there was a matter not of weak faith but of weak nerves, not a case of rescuing himself through a military trick but a divine deliverance by means of an error of judgment on the part of Achish. How else could David have so heartily praised Yahweh and his Word!?

Was David thinking of Hannah and Samuel?

Was David referring to a special portion of God's Word? David undoubtedly loved all of God's Word very much, the priceless Torah of Moses, dealing with Yahweh's covenant establishment with Abraham (Genesis), with Israel at Horeb (Exodus, Leviticus, Numbers), and in the fields of Moab (Deuteronomy). A man like Samuel would have taught his pupils in Naioth from that Scripture. After his escape from his house, surrounded by Saul's men, David fled immediately to Samuel! It must have been a great encouragement to him as he spent some time there.

But here in Psalm 56, wasn't David thinking specifically of the Word that God had spoken, for example, through the service of Hannah (1 Sam. 2), primarily with that particular time in mind? For Hannah had shed prophetic light on the period of Samuel and David. She had already "seen" and declared that Yahweh was ready to turn the entire order in the Israelite church upside down. Powerful wicked people, like Hophni and Phinehas and Saul, would be thrown down from their perches, and God would give poor righteous people like Hannah, Samuel, and David the seats of honor in his kingdom. No doubt this prophecy was known to David through Samuel's preaching.

Is it not obvious, however, that here David was boasting in the word of God that Samuel had brought him in the meantime, when David was but a shepherd boy working for his father, Jesse—namely, the divine word that Yahweh had chosen David to be the shepherd of Israel? This was the word that, after his anointing, David could have smelled in his clothing.

In that word, David would have boasted in a special way—not with military tricks and increasing military power, but in this promise of Yahweh, who cannot lie and who David firmly believed to be sufficient to fulfill his promises in his own time. David did not have to lift a finger for that fulfillment. That was Yahweh's cause. In that matter David did not want to move ahead of Yahweh with unbelieving nervous activism.

In this praising of Yahweh's word or promise lies the secret of David's attitude during his period of fleeing, when he didn't raise so much as a stick against Saul and when he had given over the kingship one hundred percent into the hands of him who had promised it to David.

God's Word teaches us to see power relationships

With the light of this word David was able to evaluate properly the dimensions and relationships involved in his struggle. In verse 1 he says, "Man [singular] tramples on me," where he uses the word *'enosh*, referring to man in all his weakness and fragility. Regarding verse 2, instead of "for many attack me proudly," the translation "How many attack me, *O Most Exalted One*" has been suggested. This too is proof of how believing David viewed the relationships in this situation. Saul was indeed exalted, but David had the *Most* Exalted One on his side. In verse 4 David wondered, "What can *flesh* do to me?" Saul's strength was only carnal, human strength. Here in verse 11 we read, "What can *man* do to me?"

God's Word teaches a person to view these power relationships properly. In comparison to God's most exalted majesty, all our enemies and oppressors are merely human, merely flesh and blood. The Philistines were but flesh and blood. Saul and his gang were but flesh and blood. What could they do to David apart from God's will (cf. Prov. 29:25)? Our Savior spoke

2. Psalm 56: David Arrested by the Philistines

from the same faith: "I tell you, my friends, do not fear those who kill the body, and after that have nothing more that they can do. But I will warn you whom to fear: fear him who, after he has killed, has authority to cast into hell. Yes, I tell you, fear him!" (Luke 12:4–5).

> Verses 12–13:
> I must perform my vows to you, O God;
> > I will render thank offerings to you.
> For you have delivered my soul from death,
> > yes, my feet from falling,
> that I may walk before God
> > in the light of life.

During those tense hours in Gath, when he was recognized as the one who had defeated Goliath and when he was arrested by the servants of Achish, out of his deep misery David surely made vows to Yahweh. These vows were part of the peace offerings discussed extensively in our commentary on Leviticus 3. A praise offering was the particular peace offering that an Israelite often brought when he wanted to testify of his gratitude to Yahweh for blessings enjoyed (cf. Ps. 116:13–14). One need not have promised this kind of sacrifice to Yahweh. But if one had made a vow after receiving a blessing of some sort, then he would bring what was called a votive offering. David must have made such a vow amid his fearful panic and nervous crisis that he experienced in Gath.

But now it was time for him to honor those vows.

So now he is saying that he needs to pay his vows (Num. 30:3; Deut. 23:21–23; Ps. 50:14; Eccl. 5:4–5): "For you have saved my life from death. King Achish had almost commanded my execution, but through your intervention he came to believe that he was dealing with an insane person, and my life was spared." Perhaps David was and remained an outcast for a time afterward, so that the wilderness was his home, but the acute mortal danger had subsided and he saw the sweet sunlight that is so intimately bound up with life (Eccl. 11:7).

So we can explain verses 12–13 as the language of experience. But we can also explain these verses as the language of faith. It was David who often expressed his firm confidence in the future fulfillment of God's promises by speaking as though God had already fulfilled them. "For you have delivered my soul from death" (v. 13). Seen in this way, verse 13 is expressing the language of faith. Here David was seeing himself in the future entirely rescued from the constantly threatening mortal danger coming from Saul and his men, and he saw himself already entering the sanctuary to pay his vows to Yahweh. And this despite the fact that when he composed the psalm he was still facing intense mortal danger. Imagine talking that way as an outcast!

That is trusting in God's promises!

And that melody makes this psalm so lovely.

Not a Lament about Human Suffering in General, But a Song Born of Persecution

Not all suffering is suffering for the sake of righteousness. We need to remember that in connection with Psalm 56. There are millions who suffer poverty. There are innumerable sick people. There are numerous starving people. But not all poverty is poverty for the sake of righteousness. Not all sickness or hunger is suffering on account of righteousness or on account of fidelity to God and his Word, or for the sake of Christ. Hunger, poverty, sickness, surgeries, and unfulfilled longings are experiences often shared by Christians and non-Christians alike. "It is the same for all, since the same event happens to the righteous and the wicked, to the good and the evil, to the clean and the unclean, to him who sacrifices and him who does not sacrifice. As the good one is, so is the sinner, and he who swears is as he who shuns an oath" (Eccl. 9:2). In many respects this is true. In the world there

2. Psalm 56: David Arrested by the Philistines

is much generically human suffering that is the consequence of sin in general.

As a result of the custom of singing psalm stanzas rather than the entire psalm, many will be tempted to think of human suffering in general in connection with Psalm 56. This psalm, however, is not a lament about human suffering in general, a share of which comes to believers and unbelievers alike; rather, Psalm 56 is the song of someone being persecuted. It is not the song of a person who, for example, has lost his house or family because of an earthquake, or who faces mortal danger because of a traffic accident, but of someone suffering on account of his faithfulness to Yahweh and his commandments! The former is suffering common to all humans; the latter comes only to believers. Psalm 56 was born out of being persecuted for one's faith. That is what the Lord Jesus had in mind when he spoke centuries later about "taking up one's cross." The Savior was not referring to such generic human suffering as sickness, poverty, natural catastrophes, and similar experiences as being our "cross," as we often do when we say that everyone has a cross to bear. It would be hard to speak of "taking" on oneself this generic human suffering, something the Lord was in fact requiring of his followers. The kind of suffering he was describing is laid upon a person. Suffering on account of righteousness or suffering for Jesus's sake is what our Lord meant by "our cross," and in light of Matthew 16:24, that suffering is indeed something we ourselves can take up—or leave lying on the ground! Psalm 56 was composed precisely for such a cross bearer!

Singing psalms with the church of all ages

Not all members of God's people receive in equal measure that kind of suffering for righteousness' sake. It is an honor to suffer for bearing Christ's name, and not everyone is judged worthy of that honor (Acts 5:41). Then again, what Paul wrote is also true: "Indeed, all who desire to live a godly life in Christ Jesus will be persecuted" (2 Tim. 3:12).

Therefore it is necessary, when we read all of God's Word and all the psalms, and certainly such psalms as Psalm 56, that we know ourselves to be bound in faith with God's one people of all times and all places. At a particular moment our own suffering for righteousness' sake may be rather minimal, but nonetheless we sing Psalm 56 heartily with our brothers and sisters. For then we will have learned once and for all to stop talking or singing or hearing about ourselves! Then we will know how closely we are bound with all those known and unknown brothers and sisters, today and yesterday, living and dead, who had to bear all kinds of suffering for the sake of the name of our Savior and faithfulness to God's Word—suffering that was avoided by those who denied the Lord and his Word.

As we sing Psalm 56, we are busy first of all with David. He was our brother, after all, whom they sought to destroy in Israel and in Gath. But as we read and pray this psalm, we think at the same time of that entire incomprehensible line of righteous saints who were trampled upon, distressed, exhausted, about whom Scripture and history have so much to tell. We have already mentioned Isaiah, Jeremiah, and Elijah. But this psalm was fulfilled—that is, it reached its climax, its zenith, or nadir—in the suffering of our Savior, who was abused like no one before or after him. People twisted his words, and he was surrounded by spies throughout his entire ministry. But he also turned everything over into the hands of him who will one day judge righteously. Amid his suffering and humiliation he could, just like David, give expression to all of those courageous declarations of faith. So we sing Psalm 56 about, and with, our Lord Jesus Christ, and with those who complete his sufferings (Col. 1:24).

Chapter 3

Psalm 57: When David Sat in the Cave

Have you ever been in a cave? Then you can imagine the decor of Psalm 57 somewhat, for it was sung for the first time in a cave. You could call it the prayer of a cave dweller.

Except for the fact that he was in his cave for an entirely different reason than you were in yours. For you, visiting a cave was probably a nice tourist stop. Perhaps you walked down in a romantic, dimly lit area with modern spotlights illuminating the spooky rock formations and the underground rivulets. You were there for enjoyment, and after a bit of time you left the cave unhindered to enjoy the warm and welcome sunshine again.

But not so with David, the composer of Psalm 57.

David was in his cave not as a modern tourist visiting for the purpose of enjoyment; he had fled in mortal fear to hide out in his cave. David was sitting there as a hunted, destitute outcast, probably still suffering the effects of the frightening events in Gath, where the Philistines had recognized him and seized him, where he had suffered nervous exhaustion from all the tensions of the recent days, and practically speaking, suffered a time of being crazy with worry. We discussed this extensively in the preceding chapter, in connection with Psalm 56, which arose in that situation. A person doesn't simply get over that kind of psychological crisis. And now David was sitting in a cave. The king's son-in-law, Goliath's conqueror, Yahweh's anointed, sitting in a cave! That was his home. There he slept, and into its depths he fled whenever danger threatened.

But in that cave, once again it became clearly evident that the light of God's salvation radiates most brightly for his children when they traverse along dark pathways. At that point God's Word can be such a fountain of comfort, and exactly at that point you realize that God is a Rock for his people. For David the poor outcast composed in that dark, cold cave this most wonderful Psalm 57. A song in which the worship, jubilation of faith, and praise for Yahweh arose so gloriously.

Psalm 57 is aimed not first of all at God's people, but at God himself. It is directed to the heavenly address of Yahweh, the God and Father of our Lord Jesus Christ. But this psalm was apparently so pleasing to God that he had it preserved in the Psalter, to serve God's people from then on as a precious practical example in the school of prayer.

The Superscription

Let's discuss the superscription to this psalm first.

It reads thus: "To the choirmaster: according to Do Not Destroy. A Miktam of David, when he fled from Saul, in the cave." We discussed the term *miktam* in connection with Psalm 16, and the phrase "Do Not Destroy" in connection with Psalm 59. What remains to be considered, then, is the historical situation being referred to here.

Adullam

Which cave is the superscription referring to? During his

3. Psalm 57: When David Sat in the Cave

flight from Saul, David often spent time in caverns and caves (cf. 1 Sam. 23:14; 24:3). By itself, it is possible that Psalm 57 originated in one of those unknown mountain hideouts. Nevertheless, in terms of the decor of this psalm, given the placement of Psalm 57 after Psalm 56, we prefer to think of the cave of Adullam.

The latter psalm places us near the events in Gath, where David experienced a collapse. The narrative of David's experiences in this Philistine city ends in 1 Samuel 22:1, with the observation that "David departed from there [viz., Gath] and escaped to the cave of Adullam." Since Psalm 57 is placed immediately after Psalm 56, may we not then infer that the historical sequence was being taken into consideration, so that here the cave in view is the one to which David fled from Gath, according to 1 Samuel 22:1?

We will stick with the cave of Adullam.

We should not imagine that this was a large alcove in a cave, but rather a number of underground, excavated rooms. Some of them could easily hide hundreds of people without anyone discovering them.

David gains a following

God granted brothers there to this solitary outcast, in both senses of that word: brothers who were sympathizers and brothers who were related by blood. For in 1 Samuel 22:1 we also read this: "And when his brothers and all his father's house heard it, they went down there to him." They had heard that David was sitting in the cave of Adullam, about twenty miles from Bethlehem (cf. 2 Sam. 23:13–17).

Every word here is worth looking at carefully.

"His brothers." Do you recall how Eliab greeted David among the soldiers? "Why have you come down? And with whom have you left those few sheep in the wilderness? I know your presumption and the evil of your heart, for you have come down to see the battle" (1 Sam. 17:28). And this when they knew that Samuel had anointed their brother in the name of Yahweh to be king! Now those brothers are coming to David. Converted, perhaps?

In addition, David's father and mother came there.

What a tragic scene: the elderly Jesse has fled from Bethlehem because Saul's soldiers were looking for David, that son concerning whom Jesse's family had learned such a wonderful secret from God. The elderly man and his sons are no longer sure about their own lives. Saul could arrest them as hostages to force David out of his hiding place. So Jesse and his other sons became homeless as well.

But David got even more of a following. In 1 Samuel 22:2 we read this: "And everyone who was in distress, and everyone who was in debt, and everyone who was bitter in soul, gathered to him." The word *distress* could also be rendered as *oppressed* (cf. Ps. 119:143; Deut. 28:53, 55, 57; Jer. 19:9).

That we are dealing here in the cave of Adullam with *oppressed* people becomes more evident from what we read further in 1 Samuel 22:2, namely, about those in debt. The kind of oppression involved here was social oppression and social oppressors. The refugees who joined up with David were perhaps running the same risk as the poor prophet's widow in the time of Elisha (2 Kgs. 4:1–7), whose creditor had threatened to sell her children as slaves if she did not pay her bill!

And this was going on despite the fact that in Leviticus 25, for example, Yahweh stipulated how creditors among his people were to treat debtors. This was precisely the opposite of what the Canaanites did. Yahweh's people were not to oppress such a poor fellow and sell him into slavery or inflict high interest, but help and support him. Literally, Yahweh had told Israelite creditors, "You shall not rule over him ruthlessly but shall fear your God" (Lev. 25:43; cf. Deut. 15).

King Saul was supposed to have ensured that!

But from this single sentence about the poor refugees in 1 Samuel 22, we can see the entire picture, in all its harshness, of Israel's covenant abandonment and apostasy in the time of Saul. In direct opposition to God's evangelical Torah, in the

Israel of Saul's day the poor were chased and oppressed by their creditors.

For those who still knew Yahweh, this was enough to make them cry!

Did David's coterie consist of a bunch of troublemakers and nuisances?

Did the group that gathered to David in the cave of Adullam consist of troublemakers and nuisances, quarrelsome folk who were always and forever at odds with everyone else? One might infer that from 1 Samuel 22, which refers to "everyone who was bitter in soul." But we must not read this to say that these people were simply bitter people, but people who lived in bitter distress, a distress that penetrated their souls. For the godly in Israel, under the rule of Saul there was every reason for being bitterly distressed. Like a fanatic opposing reformation, Saul threatened to ruin the wonderful reforming work of Samuel. Godly deliverers of the people like David were persecuted, and harsh creditors were allowed to do as they pleased. The priests at Nob were slaughtered and an Edomite like Doeg enjoyed Saul's favor. Wasn't this enough to make the godly remnant is Israel weep? Wouldn't Samuel and Jonathan and a wise woman like Abigail have been in bitter distress? To say nothing of David's father, Jesse, and all the unknown "quiet ones in the land" who had observed with holy joy the endeavors of David.

Such people joined David in the cave.

These were not troublemakers and embittered fellows, but poor, oppressed righteous ones who were distressed in their souls because of the destruction of the foundations of the Torah in Israel (Ps. 11). And as that psalm says, "If the foundations are destroyed, what can the righteous do?" (v. 3).

To those poor righteous ones, David said, "Stay with me; do not be afraid!" (cf. 1 Sam. 22:23). Saul chased them away, but David pastured them like a good shepherd, entirely in the Spirit of the Lord Jesus, who later said to the exhausted children of God in the church of his day, those oppressed by the "Sauls" of Jesus's day, with their harsh fanaticism: "Come to me, all who labor and are heavy laden, and I will give you rest.... For *my* yoke is easy, and *my* burden is light" (Matt. 11:28–30).

Now we can proceed to read Psalm 57, for we now know at least who was sitting around David when he first composed and sang this psalm. A cave full of "lost sheep of the house of Israel." Moreover, we now see clearly that Psalm 57, just like Psalm 56, is hardly a strictly personal prayer regarding David's personal need; he stands before us here as Israel's future king. And one who in that respect pleased God. A shepherd-king with a heart for his sheep, especially for the ones who had become weak and lost. He functions in Psalm 57 as their spokesman appearing before the face of Yahweh and as the intercessor on behalf of these bitterly distressed, oppressed poor ones.

Once again, as in Psalm 56, he is praying not for deliverance from various generically human needs shared by church and world alike, but from that unique suffering known only by God's children: suffering for the sake of righteousness.

Psalm 57 cries out amid the oppression of the faith of God's children.

The prayer of a cave dweller

Verse 1a:
Be merciful to me, O God, be merciful to me.

You may feel free to adopt this reading as well: "Take pity on me, O God, take pity." Can you hear how badly he is hurting? Two times in succession: "Be merciful ... be merciful!" That is pleading, and in times of need God's people may feel free to do that: ask God for something two, three times in a row.

3. Psalm 57: When David Sat in the Cave

That is what David does here.

Verse 1b:
> For in you my soul takes refuge;
> in the shadow of your wings I will take refuge,
>   till the storms of destruction pass by.

Once again, this is David at his best. "I am not trusting in the few hundred gathered around me. I do not depend on my popularity among the Israelite army. I will not take my fate into my own hands, and walk ahead of you. I will undertake nothing, but wait upon you. Like a newborn bird hides under its mother's wings, so I hide under yours, O God, until the crisis is past. For the catastrophe that your people are now enduring is immense. But I know that through Hannah, you have promised a new time (1 Sam. 2:1–10). And your Word is the truth. Your promises never fail. Through Samuel you have promised to appoint me one day as shepherd over your flock Israel, and you will surely perform that promise. Until then, I will keep taking refuge under your wings."

With this same tender metaphor, David's great-grandfather Boaz had once welcomed David's great-grandmother Ruth as a woman who came to take refuge under the wings of the God of Israel (Ruth 2:12).

When a hero like David does not appear sturdy and stalwart, we need not be at all ashamed that before God we feel like teeny little birds who in their need for help love to crawl under his wings.

Verse 2:
> I cry out to God Most High,
>   to God who fulfills his purpose for me.

"I am facing powerful enemies, but I call upon the Most High for help, and who could oppose him? It has already been some years since Samuel came to anoint me in secret as king over Israel, but God's word will not return empty. Yahweh watches over his word to perform it. Therefore, I, David, need not keep reminding God. He will take care of it. I need not train these men here in the cave into a fleshly power to fight against the fleshly power of Saul. Yahweh is strong enough without our fist and muscle. Making me king is entirely Yahweh's business. And I trust that he will bring to the desired end in his time this matter that he began with me several years ago with Samuel's arrival in Bethlehem, even though I am sitting now like an outcast in this cave."

> Verse 3:
> **He will send from heaven and save me;**
> **he will put to shame him who tramples on me.**
> **God will send out his steadfast love and his**
> **faithfulness!**

"I have nothing but destitute refugees around me. They are oppressed, just as I am. The foundations in Israel have been destroyed, and we, poor righteous people, can do nothing here in the cave of Adullam (Ps. 11:3)." But God gave his Word through Hannah and Samuel, and perhaps the prophet Gad was with David in the cave of Adullam. Hannah had prophesied, "The adversaries of the LORD shall be broken to pieces" (1 Sam. 2:10).

"I am hoping in God's faithfulness to that Word. And I know that he will send us his 'loving-kindness and truth' (that is, his faithfulness) like two guardian angels, and they will protect us."

That is what God's faithful people need.

In the peril of our fight against the spirit of the age, amid all the crises affecting God's church in our day, and under the oppression by the wicked in the church of this age, those "bitterly distressed" need God's loving-kindness (his covenant keeping) and his truth (his faithfulness).

Otherwise, the church in our world is finished!

3. Psalm 57: When David Sat in the Cave

Verse 4:
My soul is in the midst of lions;
  who roar after human prey [ESV "I lie down amid fiery beasts"]—
the children of man, whose teeth are spears and arrows,
  whose tongues are sharp swords.

That is how perilous David's position was in the cave of Adullam! He was surrounded by bloodthirsty people. King Saul could have ripped David apart as a lion tears its prey. What other kind of prey was Saul hunting, if not human prey? That is how we have translated the second line. Later, however, men would walk from the region of the cave to inform Saul about where David was hiding (cf. 1 Sam. 23:19–24; 26:1). That was on top of everything else David was suffering—to be spied upon and betrayed while hiding in a cave. The men of Ziph were happy to oblige Saul in this regard (1 Sam. 23 and 26). So verse 4 is accurate to speak of "the children of man, whose teeth are spears and arrows." The mouth of these fellows could literally have cost David his life—to say nothing about the slander that Saul had ben spreading about David (cf. 1 Sam. 19:1).

We observed earlier in connection with other psalms that David was not the last one to discover lions hiding among his brothers—all Israelites were brothers, weren't they? The Lord Jesus would later call them "wolves" (Matt. 10:16).

Church history is full of this phenomenon.

Every age has known false brothers who could rip apart their faithful brothers and occasionally did so literally, with the rack. Similarly, there have always been within Christianity people "whose teeth are spears and arrows," whose tongue James rightly called "a fire, a world of unrighteousness. . . . It is a restless evil, full of deadly poison" (Jas. 3:6, 8).

Add to that, in our day, the printed word. What a flamethrower the press can be!

But if there has been One who had to drink this poisonous

cup down to the dregs, at the cost of his life, it was our Lord and Savior.

Verse 5:
Be exalted, O God, above the heavens!
Let your glory be over all the earth!

Now we know what David and his compatriots were busy doing. Poor, trampled troglodytes. They were driven from home and hearth, they were being chased by a king who was like a bloodhound, and they were surrounded by spies and troublemakers. How easily in such circumstances one could stare oneself blind at one's personal suffering and grief, and beseech God to pay attention to personal issues. What preacher does not discover in his own ministry that almost no chronically sick parishioner escapes the danger of becoming self-centered?

We must understand the petition from this vantage point.

Despite David's great personal suffering, his prayer is absolutely not self-centered but entirely theocentric. From his impoverished cave he extended his gaze to include heaven and earth. Here we see him as the future shepherd-king of Israel—the young lad who had made so glorious a confession to Goliath of his burning love for the honor of the God of Israel (cf. 1 Sam. 17:36–37) that he walked toward that lurching giant with nothing but a sling and a stone. This David lets us hear once again that for him there is nothing higher than the glory, the majesty of his God. He is standing up for God's honor as one genuinely anointed by Yahweh.

Saul and his gang were carrying on in Israel as if there were no God, but what would become of Yahweh's glory as the God who loves righteousness and justice and shows compassions to all who fear him? Wouldn't that glory be dragged through the mud if Yahweh did not intervene?

This explains the request of verse 5: "Be exalted!"

In this connection you must remember that when Israelite

3. Psalm 57: When David Sat in the Cave

judges announced their verdict, they would rise from their seat (Pss. 76:9; 82:1). "Be exalted, O God" is equivalent to saying, "Show your exaltedness by rendering a verdict concerning the oppressed in this cave and our persecutors. Let heaven and earth see that you are a God who loves justice."

"Let your glory be over all the earth." One can also render this as "over all the land ['*erets*]."

Where could God's glory shine more splendidly than in liberating Israel from the hands of Saul and the Philistines, and in restoring shalom or peace in the land?

At the same time, David's words extend even further.

David's prophetic view extended beyond the boundaries of the Old Testament, indeed, even beyond those of the New Testament, to the new earth, where the rod of all oppressors will be smashed, where all tears will be wiped away, and where the entire world will be full of the glory of Yahweh (Isa. 6:3; Rev. 21:23).

And all of that was prayed from a cave!

But in that underground cavern sat a David who clung to God's Word and delighted in God's promises (cf. Ps. 56:4, ". . . God, whose word I praise").

Meanwhile, a miracle occurred.

The walls of the cave buckled. The net that Saul kept stretched out had torn. The nervous collapse in Gath faded into the past as far as David was concerned. Suddenly he was living in the future, which he was looking to with such longing.

That is the miracle of faith. Faith functions like a pair of binoculars with which one brings the horizon of God's promises immediately before one's eyes. That is how David experienced through faith, already in the cave of Adullam, the day when Yahweh delivered him from his archenemy Saul (as later became apparent, through suicide at Gilboa) and gave him the royal crown (as later became apparent, when the men of Judah and Israel came to ask David to be their king). All of this happened without David himself stretching forth his own hand. At that point he was standing on that high plane of faith or of promise, while still entirely talking about his time in the cave in the past tense *during* his time in the cave!

Listen to this:

Verse 6:
They set a net for my steps;
    my soul was bowed down.
They dug a pit in my way,
    but they have fallen into it themselves.

Do you recognize this language of faith?

We too, believing in God's promises, can talk about a future eternal life already now in the present tense. This is a future melody, to be sure, but we can nevertheless say, "Whoever believes in the Son *has* eternal life" (John 3:36). That is how reliable the word is: "And this is the promise that he made to us—eternal life" (1 John 2:25).

Verse 7:
My heart is steadfast, O God,
    my heart is steadfast!
I will sing and make melody!

These are the words of a cave dweller who has been declared to be free as a bird! This man lived according to God's covenant among the ruins of Israel's life and was surrounded by bloodthirsty persecutors who could have ripped him apart. He lived amid a band of down-and-outers in a cave, with no other anchor than God's promise: "You will become king!" But even when there was not yet—from a human point of view—a trace of his kingship, he did not complain, "My heart is anxious, O God, my heart is anxious." Rather, he confessed his full trust in God.

3. Psalm 57: When David Sat in the Cave

Can you understand that this was a man after God's heart? He possessed what God loves to see in a person: unlimited trust in the love, faithfulness, and power of God, and constantly factoring that into his life and building his life practically on that basis.

How beautiful it is to the LORD when we continually praise him in the depths of our existence!

Verse 8:
> Awake, my heart [ESV "glory"]!
> Awake, O harp and lyre!
> I will awake the dawn!

Who knows how literally we should take this. Perhaps, early one morning, David stepped outside the cave, and at the mouth of the cave sang this psalm for the first time.

You could imagine this somewhat.

The glowing sunrise piercing the gray light of a new day, shining across the rocks and crevasses, the caves and caverns of the hill country of Judah, and there somewhere in that desolate wilderness could be heard: David singing, accompanying himself with beautiful chords on his harp. The men around him were listening with deep emotion. Oppressed believers. Distressed by creditors. Bitterly sorrowful. But wonderfully comforted by this new song of their beloved leader.

With all our radios, televisions, recorded and downloaded music, do we experience that zeal to praise God ourselves? David awakened himself early in the morning to do just that, perhaps as many as three times!

Verse 9:
> I will give thanks to you, O Lord, among the peoples;
>   I will sing praises to you among the nations.

Naturally, God's people sing God's praise always amid the peoples of the world. Nevertheless, we must not explain these words of David ("among the peoples" and "among the nations") as poetic exaggeration too quickly. For just as Solomon later praised Yahweh in the hearing of such rulers as Hiram, king of Tyre, and the queen of Sheba (1 Kgs. 5 and 10), so too David would one day praise Yahweh in the hearing of the diplomatic corps stationed in Jerusalem, praising him as the one who had called him, David, from tending sheep and had set him on Israel's throne. Wouldn't the credentialed emissaries stationed in the Israelite capital city have reported to their own people at home this royal praise for his God?

In the same way, it can be our calling, in appropriate ways and times, to praise our heavenly Father in the hearing of people of the world. For example, we do this when we sing together as a church in our public worship services. Such praise can be heard outside!

Verse 10:
For your steadfast love is great to the heavens,
    your faithfulness to the clouds.

Surely Israel's distress was still great. David's oppressors were still mighty. But there were promises. David had already been anointed to be the new king. Yahweh is very compassionate, which means that he is a God of his word! This was the dawning of a new day. Samuel's work had not been in vain. Yahweh had not abandoned Israel.

And now, three thousand years later, he isn't finished with Christianity either!

Verse 11:
Be exalted, O God, above the heavens!
    Let your glory be over all the earth!

Once more the petition rings out that we read earlier (v. 5) for God's intervention between the destitute refugees in the cave of Adullam and the wicked Saul. Once more the gaze of the cave-dwelling poet extends beyond the narrow walls of his cave to the expanse of heaven and earth.

This prayer rose through the clouds to reach the ears of the Mighty One of Jacob. He rose from his throne and showed his glory as the God of truth and justice.

David's kingship was the fulfillment of this wish. Israel's peace under Solomon's reign was the answer to this psalm. But these two events did not yet constitute a full response to this petition. Its scope was far too broad for that. That scope rose far above the little band of outcasts in the cave of Adullam. We should not too quickly explain the words *peoples* and *nations* in verse 9 as a kind of poetic exaggeration, and the same applies here with the expressions *the heavens* and *all the earth*. Heaven and earth are engaged in each other's history, and the glorious, blessed conclusion to their history is the dawning of divine glory over both that is here being requested. An Old Testament believer like David apparently knew about that already. We should not conceive of the faithful expectations of these brothers and sisters too narrowly. For example, through the peace offering, Israel was taught and assured about the promise of that beautiful future when perfect peace will exist between God and his people. According to this petition, David was looking for an earth filled with the glory of Yahweh.

In the future, however, God would arise one more time yet and definitively, in order to adjudicate once and for all the single great quarrel between all his oppressed children of all ages and their harsh oppressors.

We now know that he has given this judgment to David's great Son, our Lord Jesus Christ (John 5:22). Through him we who live so many centuries after David can see even better what an immense cause was being pleaded there in the cave of Adullam, when David called on God for help against Saul. Looking back, that was the cause of the Son of God (cf. Belgic Confession, art. 37). Those who, like David, are privileged to suffer on behalf of that cause can experience with him how caves can radiate in heavenly splendor.

Maybe this contains the secret of the praise of the Lord. Prosperity closes lips tightly. Luxury mutes the psalms. But caves, nets, pits, and campaigns of lies—all of these open mouths in praise, because those forms of oppression can impress upon God's people so deeply precisely who God and his Christ are, for all who take refuge in him.

Within the Christianity of our time, may our heavenly Father beget intercessors who pray, as David did in Psalm 57, on behalf of his scruffy homeless bunch—intercessors who join with the venture of the Most High and hope in his loving-kindness.

CHAPTER 4

Psalm 34: Praise and Wisdom from the Cave of the Oppressed

Who would ever sit in a cold cave singing psalms? Who would ever choose this kind of underground cavern for a classroom, for teaching the fear of the Lord to a band of desolate outcasts as pupils? And who would ever provide such instruction in poetic form? To top it all, who would ever go through the trouble of having the lines of that poem begin with the letters of the Hebrew alphabet in sequence, as a device for learning the poem by memory if desired?

That person was David, and that poem is Psalm 34.

But the joy and wisdom of this poem surpass all understanding because they proceed from the Holy Spirit. He supplied David with these lovely poetic words (2 Tim. 3:16; 2 Pet. 1:21). Before he could write them down, however, God had led David along such a difficult route that he finally almost went crazy from distress and suffered total nervous exhaustion. But then, on the basis of his rich experience, David could also relate who Yahweh is for a distressed human being. That is what he did in this psalm, initially before a motley crew of outcasts in the cave of Adullam. But God's Spirit preserved this poem in his Word, and innumerable subsequent Bible readers have been encouraged by this teaching psalm.

The Superscription

Indeed, a poor miserable human being—that was David's condition when he composed Psalm 34. The superscription reads, "Of David, when he changed his behavior before Abimelech, so that he drove him out, and he went away." In contrast to many commentators, we see no reason to doubt the suitability of this superscription. The name *Abimelech* need not occasion objection. Early on, commentators observed that "Abimelech" could well have been the title of Philistine kings (as "Pharaoh" was the title of Egyptian kings) and that this superscription could have had Achish in view, who was the *Abimelech* of Gath. We see behind this psalm, then, a David who has just narrowly escaped execution in the Philistine city of Gath. From 1 Samuel 22:1 we learn that David fled from there to the cave of Adullam. We believe that Psalm 34 originated there.

This means that Psalm 34 has the same historical background as Psalm 57, which we discussed in the preceding chapter. Seeing that we have already discussed the events in Gath that lay behind both psalms in connection with Psalm 56, we can be brief in discussing at this point the historical background of Psalm 34. You can read the narrative in 1 Samuel 21:10–22:2.

David was arrested in Gath as the renowned conqueror of Goliath, and there he was so overcome with stress that he stood foaming at the mouth with impotent rage, beating on the locked gates of Gath, seized with irrational fear in the presence of King Achish.

In connection with Psalm 56, we observed that David's behavior, in our opinion, was definitely not a trick to save his own life. No, at a given moment he was genuinely disoriented.

4. Psalm 34: Praise and Wisdom from the Cave of the Oppressed

The Hebrew text of 1 Samuel 21 does not require that we view this as David feigning insanity. And though that is how King Achish assessed the situation, it was an erroneous judgment on his part. And precisely through that error of King Achish, Yahweh saved David.

This seems to be the most suitable explanation of the events. With the traditional explanation, David comes to be viewed, to put it mildly, in a strange light. For then he supposedly would have saved himself with a clever trick and thereafter, in a couple of beautiful psalms like Psalms 56 and 34, praised Yahweh as the one who had saved him in such a surprising manner. If we are to see David as a clever actor, then we no longer know what to do with his authorship and the superscriptions to Psalm 34 and 56. This explains why many commentators acknowledge no connection whatever between the events in and after Gath, on the one hand, and these two psalms, on the other hand. Then what do you end up with? Timeless, generic religious truths. But if we accept that in Gath David momentarily lost his bearings, suffering severe stress and nervous exhaustion, the psalm opens up. Then in Psalm 34 we hear a man who can tell us from his experience what Yahweh can do for us! If you experience that kind of distress and have come to the end of your rope (and who hasn't had that experience? If not today, then perhaps tomorrow), then you know where you can turn to in the Word, for yourself and for your brother or sister.

Verses 1–22: God-Exalting Praise and Life-Ordering Wisdom

Psalm 34 is an acrostic psalm. Almost every line begins with a letter of the Hebrew alphabet in sequence. Psalms with this kind of artistic arrangement lack a clear grouping of ideas. For that reason, we wish to read through the psalm verse by verse.

Verse 1:
I will bless the LORD at all times;
   his praise shall continually be in my mouth.

Here speaks a man who, shortly before, was standing in Gath scratching his fingernails on the locked city gates, who must have been quite a sight with his dirty beard and wild looks. A man who now was no longer facing that acute mortal danger, though he was still an outcast who was being chased and who had lost everything, who had to spend his life in a cave together with other uprooted outcasts. We must remember this as we read this first verse.

This definitely was not someone who had nice things to say because he had everything his heart could have desired, but someone who had to do without everything a human heart could desire. He was a troglodyte. A caveman. Someone trampled underfoot. A homeless man. A man who had almost been driven crazy by his brothers in the church.

This man tells us that he not only wanted to praise Yahweh as long as he was breathing, but wanted to do so continually (cf. Phil. 4:4), even while he is experiencing such distress. And, as Luther says, according to H. Lamparter, to do so "not in the quiet isolation of a mystic, but in the church," even if this was a church living in a cave.

Job expressed that faith in his deepest misery (Job 1:21), as did all those Christians who at the burial of their loved ones read Psalm 103: "Bless Yahweh, O my soul . . ."

Verse 2:
My soul makes its boast in the LORD;
   let the humble hear and be glad.

Psalm 34 is really intended to make meek people joyful. But what kind of people are the meek? It seems obvious that in the first place David was thinking of the people sitting around him when he first sang Psalm 34, his fellow cave dwellers.

4. Psalm 34: Praise and Wisdom from the Cave of the Oppressed

When we discussed Psalm 57, we wondered what kind of people these were as well. They were definitely not troublemakers and quarrelsome people, but godly people. Many of them were fleeing from a harsh creditor. They experienced such oppression even though in the Torah of Moses Yahweh had explicitly forbidden Israelites from making life miserable for poor people!

By itself, however, this feature isn't characteristic of meek people, for not every poor person in the church or the world is meek simply because they are poor. In fact, the Bible speaks about rich meek people as well—recall Hannah and Abigail (1 Sam. 1 and 25). Even though we search for the meek most often among the poor, it is not their social position that is determinative, but their life attitude. Being meek is a question of a person's attitude toward God and his Word.

Notice again David's compatriots. These people had fled to David. Already that highlights a characteristic of the meek. They were poor, oppressed, underdogs, threadbare, and destitute, but they were refugees, not fist-clenchers, not partisans, not those who fight for their rights to the bitter end. They were the faithful who keep quiet amid all the noise in the territory of God's covenant. We encounter them in our day as well, and therefore in the Bible they are called the "quiet in the land" (Ps. 35:20).

The Hebrew describes them poignantly. The meek are the *'anawim*, "those bent over" (ESV "humble"). David's compatriots were bent over under their poverty and loss of rights, but at the same time in such circumstances they were bent over under the mighty hand of God that was pressing down upon Israel in their day. They were living at the close of the period of the judges, a time of judgment for the church! The meek were bent over under that reality. All the while their eyes were straining to see Yahweh act, the one who alone could help them. Once again, a characteristic of the meek: in your helplessness to be willing and able to wait for Yahweh's help.

In our revolutionary time today, when Christians are

also given to talking more and more emphatically about the rights of human beings and less and less about God's rights concerning us, it is precarious to ask what they understand regarding the life attitude of the meek who stand squarely opposed to the modern cry: "We are not going to take that!"

Have we possibly construed meekness too much as a question of character? That would fit rather well with the spirit of our age, which delights in psychologizing. The meek are then viewed as special characters. A meek person is a kind of soft figure, really, someone who takes everything at face value.

But that is not what David had in view. In fact, he himself was not that kind of person. David dared to face off with a lion and a bear, even with Goliath, a living brute. As a professional soldier, David was hardly a softy. The men around David in the cave really saw and felt the trampling of God's justice in Israel and the injustice perpetrated against them, but they did not do everything in their power to obtain the justice coming to them. They did not start a guerilla war against King Saul. If they were alive today, they would not be taking to the street with a placard or banner. They were not rebellious. They were *'anawim*, those bent over. That does not mean that we may not pursue our rights in a lawful manner among people and with God, but if we go no further than employing the suitable lawful means along with prayer, there will still be plenty of suffering to endure. This is what David's friends discovered. For them, there was no justice to be found in the Israel ruled by Saul. They did not protest against that, but they bent over under the situation and gave it over to Yahweh, and they were now waiting on him for their deliverance.

All things considered, these meek ones are the main characters in the Psalms. Someone has called Psalm 34 "a small catechism of the *'anawim*," but one might just as well call the entire Psalter the songbook and prayer book of the meek. In fact, the term *meek* is another name for the righteous, whom we discussed back in chapter 3 of the preceding volume on the Psalms.

4. Psalm 34: Praise and Wisdom from the Cave of the Oppressed

David wanted his psalm to make these meek ones happy and strong in their attitude. He had every reason to do so, as he would explain in greater detail later in this "catechism for the meek."

But first he writes of something else.

Verse 3:

**Oh, magnify the Lord with me,
and let us exalt his name together!**

To magnify Yahweh is to lift up Yahweh on high. To exalt his name is to lift up his great acts of power, for God's name is his power, his accomplishments, his acts of deliverance in the history of his people. "Let us humbly acknowledge and praise those acts in all their greatness," David is saying. "So let's not talk about Saul and those terrible creditors at home and those spies all around us, but let's talk about Yahweh and make him the focus of our thoughts!"

David was so wise to direct the thoughts of the outcasts surrounding him in praise to Yahweh. Singing psalms in the middle of their misery can supply God's children with such courage, just as we find in Psalm 42 of the 1773 Dutch Psalter: "But the Lord his deliverance will give. . . . In this confidence I shall live and sing of it in my song!" David arouses his fellow outcasts to this: "Magnify the Lord *with me!*" Did you catch the italicized words? Self-directed religion often suffers from an ego complex. People can twist the Christian faith into a religion of "me, myself, and I," continually focused on self, reading God's Word personalistically and individualistically as though it were simply a book "for me." With that attitude, people sing psalms about themselves. Many hymns pander to that spirit. Rather than flatly ripping various psalm lines out of their context and trying to apply them invariably to ourselves, we should first ask what Scripture is actually saying at that point. In terms of Psalm 34, we sing in the first place with *David* and about *David*. David's need and David's deliverance, that is the reason Yahweh is being praised here in the first place. David is asking, "Will *you* thank God with me for *my* deliverance?" And only then, from David's deliverance, can we so wonderfully learn to recognize God's saving power for our needs and fears.

Verse 4:
I sought the Lord, and he answered me
and delivered me from all my fears.

David was not exaggerating with these words. What David had experienced in recent times was terrifying. He first experienced the attempts on his life by his father-in-law: a deadly throw of the spear that barely missed him, and his house was surrounded. Then he fled, was separated from Samuel and Jonathan, was arrested in Gath, and heard the mocking of the Philistines: "We've got him now!" David's situation had been filled with mortal distress, so much so that his nerves were stretched to the point that they could break at any moment. He may just as well have been facing an execution squad! Weren't these "fears"?

But at this point David was focusing on Yahweh, for he would vigorously exalt him to the heights (v. 1). "I sought him," David said. Those who are meek understand this expression immediately. You seek after something precious not just with your hands but with all your heart and eyes. In that distressing period, David sought Yahweh intensely and pleaded with him for his saving intervention. We saw that in Psalm 56.

Then Yahweh "answered," not by means of a distinct message from heaven, but in the facts (in the Psalms, to "answer" usually means the same thing as to "save"). David's death sentence was already drawn up, so to speak, but Achish had refused to sign the papers, so it could not be implemented. For the Philistine ruler thought he was dealing with a madman, and in his world that was the kind of person one surely

4. Psalm 34: Praise and Wisdom from the Cave of the Oppressed

did not kill. By means of this error of judgment on the part of Achish, Yahweh saved David's life in the nick of time. "He delivered me from all my fears."

David now makes known this experience with Yahweh to his fellow cave dwellers to show them who Yahweh is for someone facing distress who takes refuge in him. He wants to show them the kind of fears from which Yahweh can deliver his people. From his own experiences with Yahweh, David creates a lesson for his hearers and readers. This explains the title of this chapter: praise and wisdom from the cave of the oppressed. David's praise of Yahweh had a didactic tone as well. David strikes this latter tone more emphatically in the next verse.

Verse 5:
**Those who look [continually] to him are radiant,
and their faces shall never be ashamed.**

That is what David wants to teach his audience first. With Yahweh you never fall down, at least if you look "continually" (that is actually what the text says) to him, and as long as you do not treat him as if he is merely one of *two* irons you have in the fire. For Yahweh is extremely sensitive when it comes to his honor. He refuses to share his redemptive honor with some shoddy idol that we have pasted together with our hands or in our minds.

For David, however, Yahweh was the only one from whom he expected help, and with such humble people Yahweh receives the honor coming to him. As a teacher of wisdom, David turned his deliverance into a proverb, a *mashal*: "Those who look to him are radiant with joy, and their faces are not red with embarrassment."

What's the proof? The very man who formulated this proverb! David himself. The man rejoicing in a cave. The man who is full of joy in Yahweh in the middle of a band of cave dwellers. For those who are not meek (thus, for the arrogant), this is incomprehensible and impossible language. But Paul, who also knew this joy, spoke of "the peace of God, which surpasses all understanding" (Phil. 4:7). The future is given to the meek, as Isaiah would one day declare and the Lord Jesus would one day proclaim (Isa. 61; Luke 4).

Verse 6:
This poor man cried, and the LORD heard him
and saved him out of all his troubles.

Do you see what David calls himself here? "This poor man." There is merely a hairsbreadth between the Hebrew words for poor (*'ani*) and for meek (*'anaw*). Both of them refer to someone bent over under his need, one who walks bent over from distress.

But David was also carrying a burden on his back. He had lost everything: his wife, his house, his friends Samuel and Jonathan, his job, even his church. David could not "go to church" any more. As far as his enemies are concerned, David complains in 1 Samuel 26:19, he has become a Gentile. And one doesn't simply get over the kind of nervous collapse he had experienced in Gath, certainly not if you have faced continual mortal danger along with your cave-dwelling band of declared outlaws. Remember in this connection that David's elderly father and mother, together with his brothers, had to flee on account of him, because Saul could have used them as hostages to force David to come out of hiding into the open. The fact that his father and mother had fled with him from Bethlehem must have put a lot of pressure on him (1 Sam. 22:1). No wonder that David calls himself a "poor man" and talks about his "troubles" (plural).

Nevertheless, those troubles were not restricted to the medical arena of his shattered nerves. Nor were they limited to the social arena (on account of the oppression of his compatriots). Perhaps most seriously, they were in the ecclesiastical sphere, due to the fact that people in Israel had abandoned the Word.

4. Psalm 34: Praise and Wisdom from the Cave of the Oppressed

It is striking that in the Bible, the word *trouble* is used frequently to refer to the situation into which Yahweh led Israel when it had forsaken his covenant (for this meaning of the word, see 2 Kgs. 19:3; Neh. 9:37; Ps. 25:22; and Ps. 77). David experienced such a time while he was composing Psalm 34, didn't he? Wasn't this near the conclusion of the period of the judges, and hadn't that been a period full of trouble because Israel had repeatedly forsaken Yahweh? And hadn't Yahweh begun to pour out his covenant curse upon his people for that reason? What was the Philistine domination over Israel during David's younger years if not the covenant curse that had been announced in Leviticus 26 and Deuteronomy 28–30? During such periods, the good people suffered along with the wicked people. You see that happening here with David and his friends, and later with godly people like Ezekiel and Daniel, who belonged to the captives of the first deportation.

With these observations we merely wish to indicate that we must not restrict David's "troubles" in this verse exclusively to the medical and social arenas. He is not speaking here primarily about generic human suffering, like distressing illnesses (asthma, nervous exhaustion) that believers and unbelievers alike share on this accursed earth; rather, he is talking about distress on account of Zion, sorrow on account of the Word being forsaken and on account of the persecution of the righteous under the bloody regime of the radical ruler Saul. David's complaint here comes from the same faith with which he had dared to confront Goliath and with which he had composed the most beautiful psalms. So we are not hearing simply an ordinary man—even though he is teaching us who are ordinary people the lesson of his troubles—but we are hearing King David, the anointed of Yahweh, a man who bore the special promises of the Spirit and who with his extra-sensitive heart and extra-sharp capacities of discernment must have suffered extra severely under the terrifying circumstances in Israel, where the most godly and upright had to take refuge in a cave. In such circumstances the church is far away. This is a time when God's most faithful children are so troubled that they flee away from the church.

What an encouragement lies here for us, ordinary people that we are, that David calls himself a "poor man." No one needs to think that God listens only to the kind of people who are like David, "heroes of faith" who dare to confront giants and can compose psalms, but doesn't listen to a man or woman who sometimes is utterly weak. Here our brother David acknowledges that he was not all that great and imposing a figure, but simply a poor man who could do nothing by himself and saw but one helper: Yahweh. This is how he came knocking on Yahweh's door. In great distress, but also in faith that Yahweh is almighty. At that point David showed that Yahweh listens in his highest heaven to the cry for help ascending from a cave.

Yahweh saves poor worms, Psalm 34 teaches!

But *how* did Yahweh deliver David? Of course, by means of the error in judgment made by King Achish, who mistakenly viewed David as an insane man and did not put him to death. But David spoke of troubles in the plural. How had Yahweh delivered him?

> Verse 7:
> **The angel of the Lord encamps
> around those who fear him, and delivers them.**

There is your answer: by means of the Angel of Yahweh!

To be sure, the article *the* is not in the Hebrew, so one could see this as referring to *an* angel. But can we say that an angel "encamps"? That is why we see this as a reference to the famous "Angel of Yahweh."

We are not always aware of it, but our Lord God is surrounded by millions of angels: "A thousand thousands served him, and ten thousand times ten thousand stood before him"

(Dan. 7:10). All of them are heavenly soldiers. Most of them naturally hold a lower rank, but among them there are rulers. For example, Michael is a ruler among the angels. Revelation 12 talks about "Michael and his angels." But over all these mighty heavenly armies, higher than rulers like Michael, stands the Angel of Yahweh. With this title, the Old Testament has in view a very special figure.

There is but one of this kind of exalted angel, the Angel of Yahweh. Though he is called an angel, he is more than a creature. Wherever this angel appears, Yahweh himself appears. Sometimes a story begins by speaking of the Angel of Yahweh and later shifts unnoticed to speaking about his activity as an activity of Yahweh himself. On one particular day, Joshua saw a man standing before him with a drawn sword, who said to him, "I am the commander of the army of the LORD." The same man commanded immediately thereafter, "Take off your sandals from your feet, for the place where you are standing is holy" (Josh. 5:14–15). The narrative continues in Joshua 6:2 by saying, "And the LORD said to Joshua. . . ." This Angel of Yahweh required from Joshua divine honor for himself, and his speaking was a speaking of Yahweh himself. Yahweh and this Angel are thus bound very closely together!

From the New Testament it appears that this Angel of Yahweh is the same as our Lord Jesus Christ. The Epistles to the Ephesians, the Colossians, and the Hebrews tell us impressive things about the exaltedness of our Lord as God's Son above all the angels of his Father! And he has not yet received the ultimate climax of his power and honor, which he will receive when we see him return on the clouds, thronged by his myriads of angels (Matt. 24:30–31; Col. 1:15–20).

That Christ, just as he will appear one day at his second coming, appeared during the Old Testament several times on behalf of Yahweh, with the power and authority that he will spread abroad at his return. One such example is when he said to Joshua, "See, I have given Jericho into your hand, with its king and mighty men of valor" (Josh. 6:2). And with divine ease the Ruler of the heavenly armies later made the walls of Jericho, several yards thick, collapse in a heap. Israel only needed to march around the city; the Angel of Yahweh did the work. From various Scripture passages we can learn how deeply this mighty Angel of Yahweh humbled himself centuries later. For although "he was in the form of God," he "did not count equality with God a thing to be grasped, but emptied himself, by taking the form of a servant, being born in the likeness of men" (Phil. 2:6–7).

His announcement of punishment in Judges 2:1–3 is an additional proof of his exaltedness. The people were weeping in distress when the Angel of Yahweh addressed them. There you can see immediately how foolish it is to conceive of this mighty Angel, whom we may now know as our Lord Jesus Christ, the Son of God, as a spineless figure who approves of everything, someone who is "our lovely Lord" who always speaks with "a sweet voice." Would such a thing be said about that Angel of Yahweh, who slaughtered the mighty army of the Midianites? Gideon and his three hundred men needed to do nothing but smash their jars and shout the name of Yahweh and of Gideon. Here as well the mighty Angel of Yahweh did the actual work (Judg. 6–7). In the time of Deborah, he set in motion the stars and the brook Kishon. Deborah sings of that fact in her song: "From heaven the stars fought, from their courses they fought against Sisera" (Judg. 5:20). And the Israelite city of Meroz was cursed by the Angel of Yahweh (Judg. 5:23). This is a cursing Angel of Yahweh! A cursing Christ!

Those powerful events of the fall of Jericho's walls, the destruction of the Midianites, and the battle of the stars against Sisera hadn't happened that long before David's time.

This divine military leader, the Angel of Yahweh, saw David as the one whom he had preserved thus far. He encamps—naturally with his army of angels—around those who fear him and he saves (pulls, draws) them out of their distress.

During that period the Israelites refused that protection.

They had rejected Yahweh as king and had ignored his Angel when they asked for a human king. They wanted a strong man who could go out ahead of the army (1 Sam. 8:20). Yahweh felt that he was being rejected.

But David was cut from a different cloth. David took seriously God's authority and faithfulness, and in that confidence he confronted a giant with a little stone and a sling. And look what Yahweh does when a meek person like David tells him that as a person he is at the end of his rope and is expecting everything from God alone! Then the Angel of Yahweh comes clothed with divine power to help him.

Here David turns that into something like a proverb. If we imagine that we can deliver ourselves, there remains no honor for Yahweh to enjoy. But if he has room to do that for us, as he did with people like David, then he does not stand around. Facing attempted murder and arrests is then not a hopeless situation, for Yahweh's mighty Angel protects the godly and saves them from danger.

In short, the following three verses are saying, go ahead and try it!

Verse 8:
Oh, taste and see that the Lord is good!
   Blessed is the man who takes refuge in him!

That was wise counsel from the cave of the oppressed. After all, Israel's greatest misery in that period was that king and people did not dare to take refuge in Yahweh! Saul did not dare to let Yahweh be God. Didn't he take matters into his own hands when Samuel didn't show up at Gilgal and his soldiers began to desert? On the other hand, it is so good to take refuge with Yahweh not only because he is so mighty but also because he is so good.

People, go ahead and try it. Just experience it. In Scripture, to "see" can mean to "experience," to "enjoy." Stand purposely still by Yahweh's goodness and protection in your life, or in the time and situation of the church. To restrict our attention to David: through David's calling and anointing, Yahweh had begun to take pity once again upon Israel, and in preparation for a new time! Did people see Yahweh's goodness in that?

> Verses 9–10:
> Oh, fear the LORD, you his saints,
>   for those who fear him have no lack!
> The young lions suffer want and hunger;
>   but those who seek the LORD lack no good thing.

Indeed, this is being sung by a cave dweller surrounded by a group of people who have lost practically everything. All of them were *'anawim*, people who walked bent over with distress. So the language David uses in these verses appears a bit exaggerated: "Have no lack!" One interpreter thinks he needs to make the rather mocking suggestion in this connection: "Why then do the godly so often call themselves *poor* and *miserable*?" He sees in Psalm 34 nothing less than an "undisguised sensual eudaemonism": whoever fears God suffers no lack (B. Duhm, *Die Psalmen*, 2nd ed. [Tübingen: Mohr, 1922], 58)!

This is indeed the language of exaggeration, characteristic of the didactic form used by Israelite wisdom teachers. What is David in these verses, but just such a teacher? In verses 17 and 19 he makes a couple more exaggerated declarations: The LORD delivers them out of *all* their troubles! We will say more about this unique, exaggerated way of talking when we come to those verses. Later, in connection with the book of Proverbs, we want to devote a separate chapter to this phenomenon.

The psalm interpreter we just mentioned would presumably not be the only one to add to lines like this a "Yes, but!" and, in so doing, show that he pays more attention to the exceptions than to the rule. The rule is this: Whoever seeks after Yahweh will never lack. Perhaps in order to understand David at this point, one needs to have barely escaped death several times, have landed in a cave in a quiet wilderness, and have given up his solitude when brothers and sisters arrived to live with him. Indeed, one needs to walk with Yahweh as David did in order to be able to understand rules like this, for David is here speaking with the audacious language of faith and the exaggerated language of a wisdom teacher. Occasionally, the light of faith places matters in a magical light. The wisdom teacher leaves aside for the moment the exceptions to his rules. In the spirit of these lines of the psalm, Christian fathers in the nineteenth century followed a meal of potatoes and potato water by leading their families in prayer with the words "Since many people are eating the bread of suffering, Thou has fed us full and well!" That's how God's children spoke to their heavenly Father in the Hunger Winter of 1945. Only in the fear of the LORD can you understand such language.

Verse 11:
Come, O children, listen to me;
I will teach you the fear of the LORD.

Is David suddenly changing his psalm into a children's sermon? Yes and no. There were indeed children in the cave with David (1 Sam. 22:1-2; 27:3; 30:1-3). Naturally, they too needed to learn to fear Yahweh, along with everything else a child needs to learn. Undoubtedly because he sought to extend Samuel's reformation, David was very interested in the teaching of the Word to the youth (2 Sam. 1:18). As we all know, among people who can be instructed, children are the ones who supply the most hope. Wise people who wish to spread their principles of living always seek to win the ear of the young people. So David is focusing on the youth here as well.

But at the same time, the words *children* or *sons* or *my son* are characteristic expressions for those who composed proverbs. They are used often in the book of Proverbs. The wisdom teachers certainly are not using them to refer only to young people, but children from age eight to eighty (cf. Prov. 1:8 and similar passages). This appears to be David's intention as well in these verses, for in verse 12 he proceeds calmly with "What man is there . . . ?" From this it is clear that he is directing his comments to men (and women). So here in verse 11, we should continue to think of all the refugees in the cave of Adullam—men, women, and children.

Someone, however, who speaks as a prophet and teacher to old and young with the term *children* naturally sees himself as a kind of "father" to them (cf. Judg. 17:10). A spiritual father, as Paul was to Timothy and Titus, and as Peter was to Mark (1 Tim. 1:1–2; 2 Tim. 1:2; 2:1; Titus 1:4; 1 Pet. 5:13). In this respect God's Word sounds its own melody. The teacher-pupil relationship is comparable to the father-child relationship.

On the one hand, this confronts the spirit of the French Revolution with its slogan "Freedom, *Equality*, and Fraternity." It would probably accuse David of "paternalism" because of the way he speaks. Admittedly, people are equal to one another in many respects: all of us must breathe to stay alive, all of us have red blood, all of us will one day appear before God's Son, and so forth. But in many other respects there is also inequality.

A father is not equal to his son. A father has received authority over his son, not the other way around. A father is older than his son. Their ages are unequal and, along with that, their life experience. Normally, the father has known God before his son did. The father presented his son for circumcision or baptism, thereby making an oath on behalf of his son to live in faithfulness to God and his Christ. If God wills, that son will one day come in turn to stand in the same position toward his own son. Then the first son will have authority, more experience, more knowledge of God and his service, more insight into Scripture. Here there is no question of paternalism but of creation ordinances.

How healthy this is for human living! For that intimate relationship—between father and son—is seen in the Bible as equivalent to the relationship between a teacher who instructs in the fear of Yahweh and his pupil. That is how David related as a "father" to the refugees in the cave as his "children."

Equality in the sense of the French Revolution did not exist between this "father" and his "children." Although they were all hunted outcasts, only David composed psalms, only he had been anointed king, and only he had been called to deliver his people. Consequently, there was obvious inequality in terms of calling and in concourse with Yahweh as well. David could teach them something about that.

God's order exists in this way so we may learn to know him. According to his arrangement, that proceeds "from father to son." First of all, of course, it proceeds from natural father to natural son. This responsibility remains greater than that of catechism teachers and school teachers. It is wonderful, however, if between those who teach in the fear of the LORD and their pupils there exists no old-fashioned academic distance but rather the warm bonds of the biblical father-son relationship. In this climate the revolutionary-democratic resistance against paternalism can hardly thrive.

Verse 12:
**What man is there who desires life
 and loves many days, that he may see good?**

David now begins his instruction. At this juncture, Psalm 34 becomes a didactic poem. The teacher immediately grabs the attention of his listeners with these questions. Their eyes would have opened wide! "What man is there who desires life?" Indeed, who in that cave would *not* have wanted that—when you've lost everything, when you're an outlaw, poor and miserable? This kind of question fixes one's attention.

With this David was referring of course to a good life, something we see from the next line: "and loves many days, that he may see good?" But what was a good life for an Israelite? Naturally, it was not spending your days in a cave—that was no "life" at all—but enjoying peace, sitting under your own vine and fig tree, eating the produce of your own field. It was not confronting hostile bands of robbers who steal wheat and wine from you and also not facing hardhearted creditors who come demanding either your money or your freedom. Israel could have enjoyed this kind of good life if she had kept the Torah. Yahweh had said, "If a person does them [my statutes and my rules], he shall live by them" (see the commentary on Lev. 18:5). "Keep my anti-Canaanite and anti-Egyptian statutes and ordinances. They will ensure your life." But what had Israel systematically done in David's time and the centuries before? They had broken Yahweh's prohibitions, despised his statutes, and brought down his covenant curse around their necks. At that point, Israel's society, cut off as it now was from its Sinaitic foundation, suffered political, economic, social, and religious decay. And the poor were victimized.

David grew up in a terrible time! At Saul's death the Philistines had penetrated the land as far as Gilboa, Jerusalem was still a Jebusite city, and Israel lived among Canaanites. David arose once more in the spirit of Joshua and Caleb. The period of the judges had intervened like a dark, useless interim period.

But listen now to Israel's new king. He is not yet sitting on the throne but in a cave, and yet he has been anointed and has his first subjects around him. What have people always hoped for with every new government? Improvement in their circumstances of living. "Now then," as David, already appointed king, points to the only path toward that hope being realized, "I will teach you to fear Yahweh, for only in that way will a person find happiness." This was primordial reformation language on David's part.

4. Psalm 34: Praise and Wisdom from the Cave of the Oppressed

Standing amid the ruins of Israelite life under Saul, he made the case to Israel and its young people that they could harbor future expectations only if they would return from the Baals to Yahweh. This lesson applies to Christianity as well, in its community living as well as in its personal living. The fear of Yahweh is a fountain of life, but the way of sin leads to death in every sphere of living (Prov. 12:28; 14:27). Death means decay, dissolution, defeat. But David is giving lessons in the life-giving fear of Yahweh. Taught by his bitter experiences, he sets before his "children" in the cave *how* they must fear Yahweh in the practicalities of life.

Verse 13–14:
Keep your tongue from evil
   and your lips from speaking deceit.
Turn away from evil and do good;
   seek peace and pursue it.

Those listening to David in the cave of Adullam suffered severely under wickedness in Israel, the rebellion against the God who had given the wonderful Torah. Instead of justice there was injustice. Instead of compassion, oppression. Instead of humbly walking with God, the arrogant disregarded him and his commandments.

Because of this, a serious danger threatened that "cave community," the danger that their hearts might be filled with a desire for revenge against their harsh oppressors, that their mouths might fall into sin through harsh speaking, and that strong men might prepare to retaliate, repaying harshness with harshness. Don't forget that David had one hundred people around him, among whom were heroes with whose help he could easily have mounted a guerilla campaign. He was after all still the popular conqueror of Goliath.

Here comes David with his counsel: "Defeat evil with good. Keep your tongue in check. Avoid evil." That is to say, forsake all rebelliousness, against both God and other people;

pursue a humble walk before Yahweh our God; and expect your salvation from him. Then you will seek peace as you respect God's order. There shall be no partisan war against King Saul, for then Israel would be afflicted even more severely. No fighting among brothers. Back off! Flee! Step aside for Saul. Bow down under injustice. Crawl into a cave.

We know how David himself had provided a good example in this regard. David had never initiated a fleshly campaign against Saul. Even when Saul lay twice at his feet, David refused to kill his mortal enemy out of respect for Saul's office as the anointed of Yahweh. In response to such a highly placed official, David did not take the law into his own hands. He waited humbly for God's time.

These poetic lines seem so simple, but they penetrate deeply into our lives. Only by avoiding every form of rebellion against God and his Word, and by respecting his order for human life, can these blessings come about. For that to happen, all of us, from eight to eighty years old, must know that we are "children" in the presence of David, our instructor in the fear of God.

Verse 15:
The eyes of the Lord are toward the righteous
and his ears toward their cry.

This is a wonderful promise, but are you that kind of righteous person? Presumably, many Christians think of something special in connection with this word. A brother here or a sister there might perhaps be called "righteous," but all those rows of people sitting in church on Sunday? In chapter 3 of the first volume on the Psalms, we discussed these righteous ones extensively and saw that in the Bible this is usually another word for Yahweh's godly or loyal covenant partners. In that chapter you can find a list of other biblical terms for these people: the upright, the faithful, saints, etc.

Such people were sitting with David in the cave. They

4. Psalm 34: Praise and Wisdom from the Cave of the Oppressed

were not sinless people—those don't exist. But they were men and women who heartily feared the God of Israel. Otherwise these heroes would have struck out with violence. Now they were bowed down under their oppression. They were "the meek" ("the bent-over ones," as the Hebrew puts it) and "the miserable ones" (which also means "those bowed down" in Hebrew).

What then does David say to his brothers? He pours oil on their wounds. He has restrained them from actions of reprisal and now speaks healing words with substantive comfort: "The eyes of the LORD are toward the righteous!" Were they perhaps thinking that he did not see them in the cave? Were they perhaps thinking that he did not notice the elderly Jesse when he, his wife, and sons departed Bethlehem to share with his son—anointed to be king yet declared an outlaw—the life of an outcast? Were they perhaps thinking that he did not see their oppressive creditors or their sorrow over the dismantling of God's and Samuel's reformational work? Did anyone think that this all had escaped God's notice? Just as a mother keeps her eyes on her little toddler, who faces constant danger, so Yahweh cannot lose sight of the righteous. Nothing escapes him. He hears them: "His ears are toward their cry." Mothers grasp this immediately. Especially if they have small children, they live day and night with their ears perked: "Did I hear something?" One peep from the little one, and she is alert. Her ears are like a radar, ready day and night to listen for any sound. That's how God's ears are perked day and night to hear the cry for help of his righteous ones.

Verse 16:
The face of the LORD is against those who do evil,
    to cut off the memory of them from the earth.

This is the reverse side of verse 15. God sees the righteous, but also the wicked.

Some have proposed to translate it this way: "The fury of

Yahweh is against those who do evil." It is obvious whom David has in view: Saul and his royal clique, who chased David as though he were a wild animal. Those God-forsaking creditors, who had distressed David's brothers so deeply that they fled to David out of pure misery. Men like Doeg, who had murdered twenty-five priests together with their families in Nob (1 Sam. 22:6–19; we will discuss this later in connection with Psalm 52, which was written after this murderous rampage). They did evil: they paid no regard to God and his Word.

They were the wicked in the church of that day. What did David and his friends do against these men? As we have observed several times, they did nothing. That is to say, David and his mighty men did not raise their swords against Saul and his men, in order to prevent a misbegotten fraternal fight in Israel. "Turn aside from evil," David had said. "No rebellion at any price!" *'Al tashkhet*: You must not destroy him, David! From a worldly perspective, David and his people did nothing. But they did in fact do something else. They reached for an instrument that carnal people in the church have always shrugged their shoulders at: they went to the supreme court, to the Judge of all the earth, immediately when David was arrested. We read that in Psalm 59, an imprecatory psalm of David when Saul had almost arrested him. There David did something, namely, ask Yahweh: "Kill them; Cast them down!" David himself had not done that, but he prayed that Yahweh would do it. David had every reason to do that. David's imprecatory psalm was definitely not motivated by personal revenge but was a prayer motivated by the interests of the country and of the entire people and kingdom of God.

By this we simply want to say, David *did* do something! He called upon Yahweh! Here in verse 16 he expresses his firm confidence, based in faith, that Yahweh would perform justice on behalf of his distressed people in the cave. David knew Yahweh well.

Yahweh fulfilled that expectation completely. In his own time, the moment arrived when he said, "Now it's finished."

4. Psalm 34: Praise and Wisdom from the Cave of the Oppressed 105

Without David ever stretching forth his hand, Saul fell on his own sword near Gilboa. More enemies of David would fall in battle on that day. The proposed translation "The fury of Yahweh is against those who do evil" would suit the text's context perfectly. "To cut off the memory of them from the earth." The people in the cave had shivered because of them, but Yahweh erased that frightening memory at Gilboa.

But David was someone who could wait for the day when Yahweh would bring his righteousness to light. Our Savior, however, said with some concern, "Nevertheless, when the Son of Man comes, will he find faith on earth?"—namely, God will surely obtain justice for his elect (Luke 18:8).

Verse 17:
**When the righteous cry for help, the Lord hears
and delivers them out of all their troubles.**

Wasn't David living proof of this? He said this to comfort his brothers and sisters who suffered under the forsaking of God and his Word among Israel, to arouse them to follow his example and especially to call to Yahweh! Then he would listen and save. Just look at David. Is "out of *all* their troubles" worded too boldly?

We will say more in connection with verse 19.

Verse 18:
**The Lord is near to the brokenhearted
and saves the crushed in spirit.**

Once again this is such a heart-warming word, but, whom is it for? Perhaps only for those Christians who dare not believe that God will be gracious to them? And those who are brokenhearted and crushed in spirit because they fear they will be lost eternally? Is David teaching here that God saves only such people who "go through hell"? We believe that Scripture is thinking of different people altogether when it speaks about "the brokenhearted" and "the crushed in spirit."

We want to go more deeply into these expressions, so let us first take note of the spiritual opposites of the "crushed in spirit." Their portrait will then become more clear in the process.

Hardness of heart and arrogance in spirit

In Zechariah 7 we find a description of the attitude adopted by the masses within Israel in response to the warnings of the "former prophets" to return to Yahweh. "But they refused to pay attention and turned a stubborn shoulder and stopped their ears that they might not hear. They made their hearts diamond-hard lest they should hear the law and the words that the Lord of hosts had sent by his Spirit through the former prophets" (Zech. 7:11–12). In response to the announcements of mighty judgment from the prophets, many Israelites had made their hearts as hard as a diamond. The books of the prophets are filled with talk about this hard, arrogant mentality in Israel.

When the ten tribes were severely afflicted by the attacks of the Assyrians, the Israelites did not yet see Yahweh's covenant curse in those attacks, but "in pride and arrogance of heart" they said, "The bricks have fallen, but we will build with dressed stones; the sycamores have been cut down, but we will put cedars in their place" (Isa. 9:10). If you can say that, then you are indeed as hard as a diamond. The Bible describes this elsewhere with other expressions: "an arrogant heart" (Ps. 101:5), "their heart is unfeeling like fat" (119:70), "arrogant in heart" (Prov. 16:5), "a proud heart" (21:4; cf. Isa 46:12), "a stubborn and rebellious heart" (Jer. 5:23), "impudent and stubborn," (Ezek. 2:4), "a stubborn heart" (3:7), and "a heart of stone" (11:19). Our Savior encountered this heart attitude in the church people of his time, so that he said with the words of Isaiah, "This people's heart has grown dull" (Matt. 13:15). He was also "grieved at [the Pharisees'] hardness of heart" (Mark 3:5).

4. Psalm 34: Praise and Wisdom from the Cave of the Oppressed

All these expressions show how, throughout the centuries, the attitude of the prevailing direction in Israel was opposed to the word of the prophets and completely insensitive to the thunderous blows that God had caused to fall upon Israel.

In response, the masses were, in a word, hard as a diamond.

Brokenhearted and crushed in spirit

But not all of Israel was like that.

There was always a remnant of people who walked humbly with Yahweh. In the Bible these were called "the brokenhearted" and "the crushed in spirit," clearly in contrast to their spiritual opponents: "those hard of heart," who went their own way in "arrogance of spirit" (cf. Prov. 16:18).

In Psalm 51 David sketches a self-portrait of a person who is "crushed in spirit." This is someone dealing with God and with his own sins (v. 4). We should not conclude from this, however, that the "brokenhearted" thought continually only about their own sins, for they were just as broken and crushed on account of the sins of God's church! That is evident, for example, in Psalm 147, which is set after the exile. The godly were bewildered: God's church was splintered across the wider Babylonian world empire. The temple had lain in ruins for seventy years. They had been destroyed. But now Yahweh proceeds to bind up their wounds (Ps. 147:3). "He heals the brokenhearted," that is, on account of the Babylonian captivity and the rubble that is Jerusalem.

That "brokenheartedness" and "being crushed in spirit" refers especially to pain for the sake of Israel and sadness for the sake of Zion, for the sake of God's people, something we see more clearly in the book of Isaiah:

> For thus says the One who is high and lifted up,
>   who inhabits eternity, whose name is Holy:
> "I dwell in the high and holy place,
>   and also with him who is of a contrite and lowly
>   spirit,

> to revive the spirit of the lowly,
>   and to revive the heart of the contrite.
> For I will not contend forever, nor will I always be
>   angry; . . .
> I will heal him;
>   I will lead him and restore comfort to him and his
>   mourners." (Isa. 57:15–16a, 18).

Here the phrase "of a contrite and lowly spirit" is another expression describing the "mourners" among God's people. Apparently, they are the ones who have not hardened their hearts like diamonds under God's quarrel with his vineyard (Isa. 5), but whose hearts have become contrite and humbled by the word of the prophets.

In Isaiah 61 as well, we hear the joyful message especially "to the poor . . . to bind up the brokenhearted, to proclaim liberty to the captives, and the opening of the prison to those who are bound" (Isa. 61:1). Later we see these humble ones in such people as Daniel, Ezra, Nehemiah, and Ezekiel, who were "brokenhearted" because Israel had been imprisoned for decades in the great Babylonian prison. The context of Isaiah 61 confirms that there is weeping here for the sake of the "ancient ruins" of Zion and "the ruined cities" of Judah.

But Yahweh looked down upon this kind of humble Israelite with sympathy, for "this is the one to whom I will look: he who is humble and contrite in spirit and trembles at my word" (Isa. 66:2). Isaiah 42 refers to the same kind of Israelite this way: "A *bruised reed* he will not break, and a *faintly burning wick* he will not quench" (Isa. 42:3; cf. Matt. 12:20, where the expressions refer to the "little children," those "who labor and are heavy laden" under the harsh religious yoke of the Pharisees, in connection with vv. 25–30).

We conclude that in the Bible the expressions "brokenhearted" and "crushed in spirit" are used interchangeably for the following synonymous expressions: the "humble," "those who hope in his loving-kindness," "the outcasts of Israel" (Ps.

147:2), "the lowly" (Isa. 57:15), "the captives," "those who are bound," "those who mourn in Zion" (Isa. 61:1, 3), "the contrite in spirit" who "tremble at my word" (Isa. 66:2), "the bruised reed," "the faintly burning wick" (Isa. 42:3), "little children," those "who labor and are heavy laden" (Matt. 11:25, 28).

Being "broken" and "crushed" was not some kind of characteristic experience of having had to travel a "hellish" route before coming to faith. The biblical class of the "brokenhearted" were sorrowful because they knew themselves intensely bound to God's people and were crushed on account of the desolate situation brought about by the sins of that people! They could be grieved by the question of whether God's people still had a future. Those wounds of the heart are what Yahweh healed.

In view of this meaning of the expressions in question, it seems evident that we should understand them in Psalm 34:18 in the same way. The cave of Adullam was full of "the brokenhearted" and "the crushed in spirit," and they were now being comforted by David with the assurance that Yahweh was near them and would certainly save them. Didn't David's compatriots legitimately resemble a "bruised reed" and a "faintly burning wick"? Weren't they those who "mourned"? What a tremendous salvation they experienced, then, when the report came that Saul had been defeated in battle and that David had become king! What a joyful message for those mourning in Zion when Yahweh made possible the return to Jerusalem from the Babylonian prison! What a blessed salvation our Lord Jesus Christ brought to those whose hearts had been broken under the religion of the Pharisees.

All those today who realize they are bound with all baptized Christians as the people of God must at times be "crushed in spirit" as they see so much ruin throughout the territory of "Zion" in this age. We will discuss this further in connection with Psalm 74. But Psalm 34:18 is a promise with which we may appeal to God as we beseech him not to withdraw his Word and Spirit from us and our children, even though the remnant within Christianity may possibly encounter a time of living as "cave churches." But the High and Exalted One can make the spirit of the humble and the heart of the contrite come alive (Isa. 57:15).

Verse 19:
**Many are the afflictions of the righteous,
but the Lord delivers him out of them all.**

There is no book in the entire world that is as honest and real as God's book. It proclaims to the righteous that they have God as a friend, even as a father and covenant partner. But for that reason the reality is not always a blossoming garden, since the godly suffer under the consequences of sin in the world. All of the godly known from the Bible knew adversity. In this respect, there is no suffering you can mention that the godly in the Bible did not experience: sickness, death, sorrow, childlessness, war, famine, unhappy marriages, poverty, exploitation. But in the context of this psalm, shouldn't we interpret the "afflictions" as referring especially to ecclesiastical distress, persecution for the sake of righteousness, oppression for the sake of faith? Concerning this cross-bearing in particular, it can always be said, "Many are the afflictions of the righteous."

But notice what David says next: "But the Lord delivers him out of them all." That is the same kind of rhetorical exaggeration we find in verse 17: the Lord "delivers them out of all their troubles." We also find the same kind in verse 20: "He keeps all his bones; not one of them is broken."

Some Christians begin immediately to talk about the exceptions to such poetic lines. "Yes, but," they observe, "aren't there still numerous adversities out of which God has *not* delivered the righteous? I know someone . . ." Indeed, they are right. God's Word speaks of women who died in childbirth: Rachel and the wife of Phinehas. Moses did not enter Canaan.

4. Psalm 34: Praise and Wisdom from the Cave of the Oppressed

Ezekiel became a widower. Hosea was married to an immoral wife. Hannah was severely afflicted. Jeremiah led a lonely life. Elijah sat in exhaustion under a tree. And David, the man behind Psalm 34, sat with a band of down-and-outers in a cave, and even afterward his life would remain full of adversity. He had to bury four sons. We could page through the entire Bible and find such people, who endured suffering common to humanity and endured suffering for the sake of righteousness, bearing their cross, something that happens only to the righteous. Can you then say, "Many are the afflictions of the righteous, but the LORD delivers him out of them all?" Yes, you can!

David is speaking here in the language of faith

We begin by observing that what we have here is the sturdy language of faith! David's first hearers in the cave understood him well. A child can use language like this when trying to impress other children: "My father can do everything!"

But is faith really allowed to speak this way?

May a man who has escaped from an execution squad and from various attempts on his life, together with others with whom he shares oppression, who have the divine promise that their protector will become king, boast once in a while in Yahweh and his great power? David, if you will, witnessed hundreds, thousands of acts of deliverance in the lives of so many of God's children. In order to place the rule of Yahweh's deliverance in full view, David allowed the exceptions to remain what they are—exceptions!

David is speaking pedagogically here

Moreover, David is instructing "children" (from eight to eighty years old) here (cf. v. 11). When it comes to experience in the fear of Yahweh, David is a "father," and in comparison to him, many parents are "children," that is students. Isn't it obvious that when David gives lessons in fearing Yahweh (v. 11), he establishes the rule?

And that rule goes like this: "God is our refuge and strength, a very present help in trouble" (Ps. 46:1). The examples of this are obvious in both Scripture and history.

How does David bring this rule to our attention? So that his hearers may learn to fear this God, David follows the wisdom of the rule "Exaggeration clarifies." A good teacher and a salesman know the effect of a little exaggeration. Someone who composes proverbs (and what else is David?) is silent about the exceptions when he formulates his principles of wisdom, since otherwise his words would not be provocative (Eccl. 12:11). "In all toil there is profit, but mere talk tends only to poverty," says the wise man (Prov. 14:23). In this spirit we motivate our children: "Do your best and you will succeed in the world!" At that point, we are speaking pedagogically, motivationally. Who would talk to his children at that moment about the obvious examples of people who despite their effort did *not* succeed? One must keep in mind the advice of Ecclesiastes 9:11 about "time and chance."

May David then offer such a lesson in Psalm 34? After all, he is busy as a teacher instructing "children," isn't he? He wants to admonish them to fear the Lord, doesn't he? Then you must talk this way. No one less than our Savior used this form of speaking, known as the *mashal*, when he taught, as we will see in our commentary on Proverbs.

Moreover, David had been delivered so wonderfully that he made that deliverance an example for his "children," an example of Yahweh's redemptive might, precisely to motivate them to trust Yahweh. The problem of Psalm 73—"Is Yahweh nearby?"—is simply not being discussed here, for David has discovered and experienced Yahweh's nearness!

Verse 20:
He keeps all his bones;
    not one of them is broken.

Yahweh is very economical when it comes to his children.

4. Psalm 34: Praise and Wisdom from the Cave of the Oppressed   113

"Precious in the sight of the LORD is the death of his saints" (Ps. 116:15). He doesn't let things get to the point of death, but if that should happen, however, even then he keeps watch over his deceased servants, as can be seen in the case of one no less than our Savior. God did not want his bones to be broken after he had died (John 19:32–36). Nor did our Savior undergo such a lengthy decay as ordinary corpses do in the cemetery (Acts 2:31).

David's intention here reminds us of our saying "Woe betide you!" We have the entire person in view. Holy Scripture can refer to the entire person when it uses words like *bone*, *soul*, and *body*. David may have been confused in Gath, but God saw to it that no one broke any of David's bones; in other words, his entire person was saved.

Verse 21:
Affliction will slay the wicked,
   and those who hate the righteous will be condemned.

The KJV says, "*Evil* shall slay the wicked." Good and evil are not simply moral entities, but they also constitute material good or evil for a person. Evil *is* evil for a person. Over the long run, it destroys him. The book of Proverbs especially illustrates this rule with multiple examples. This is why one cannot despise Yahweh's loyal covenant partners with impunity, for sooner or later Yahweh will arise and say, "What? Do you dare lay a finger on my covenant partner? By doing that, you are laying a finger on me, and I'll make you feel it!"

David encouraged his brothers with that comfort. They were suffering intense hatred, the kind Scripture identifies as existing between Cain and Abel, Esau and Jacob, Saul and David, the wicked and the righteous, those pretending to be godly and the upright, the Sanhedrin and the Lord Jesus—hatred in and because of the service of God. But their haters will pay for that. They "will be condemned" (v. 21b).

That was the comfort David extended and waited for with

his sword in its sheath, but with his prayer rising to God's throne! He was getting ready in faith for the time when Yahweh would adjudicate his appeal. That happened in Gilboa (1 Sam. 31).

> Verse 22:
> **The LORD redeems the life of his servants;**
> **none of those who take refuge in him will be condemned.**

When David's friends could finally return home and David ruled according to God's good laws, then Yahweh saved the "soul" ("life") of his servants. Things went better in every area of life.

In this way, Psalm 34 became an answered prayer.

Praise and wisdom from the cave of the oppressed—that's the title of this chapter dealing with Psalm 34. David knew our heavenly Father very well, for God had granted him deep insight into human living. If you don't view yourself as too grown up to listen like a child to the composer of this psalm, you will be motivated by David to devote more attention to tasting and seeing that our heavenly Father is good, and in so doing you can enjoy this abiding truth: "Blessed is the man who takes refuge in him!"

CHAPTER 5

Psalm 52: After the Mass Murder in the Priestly City of Nob

"Horrible! Now Saul has attacked Yahweh's *priests*! He killed almost eighty. The entire priestly city of Nob has been murdered! Including women and children! He even walked off with our livestock! I am the only one who survived the bloodbath!"

On a given day, Abiathar, the son of the Ahimelech the priest, stood before David with this dreadful news. Wherever this news spread throughout Israel, the godly shivered.

Where will this terror lead?

David answered this frightening question in Psalm 52.

The Historical Background

"To the choirmaster. A Maskil of David, when Doeg, the Edomite, came and told Saul, 'David has come to the house of Ahimelech.'" Here in the superscription we have the historical background to this psalm. We see no reason to doubt this.

You can read about this historical background to Psalm 52 in 1 Samuel 22:6–23. That Scripture passage grants us a penetrating glimpse into the heart and thought world of Saul and his accomplice, Doeg, to whom David directed this psalm.

Let's review this historical background.

Saul is sitting under a tamarisk tree at his residence in Gilboa. He is seated like a real military king, of course, with a spear in his hand. Around him stand his court officials. All of them are Benjamites, for Saul recruited all the top leaders of his government from his own tribe.

Nevertheless, he is sitting there filled with suspicion and self-pity.

"Hear now, people of Benjamin," he begins. "Will the son of Jesse"—he can't stand to mention David's name—"give every one of you fields and vineyards, will he make you all commanders of thousands and commanders of hundreds, that all of you have conspired against me? No one discloses to me when my son made a covenant with the son of Jesse. None of you is sorry for me or discloses to me that my son has stirred up my servant against me, to lie in wait, as at this day" (1 Sam. 22:7–8).

What a tone of self-pity and whining for a man with a spear in his hand. Notice how he thinks in terms of benefits! From this you can see how Saul had bound his court servants to himself. Hatred has blinded his eyes. Neither Jonathan nor David had ever lifted a finger against Saul, but he has concluded without any proof that Jonathan has "stirred up" David with the express purpose of laying a trap for Saul "as at this day"! Did David really have that large a following? According to Saul, he was lying somewhere waiting in ambush. These were distressful moments for the royal clique!

As everyone cowered in embarrassment not knowing how to answer the angry tyrant, Doeg spoke, the Edomite overseer of Saul's shepherds (1 Sam. 21:7). We have been told that when David came to Ahimelech, this Doeg "was in the

5. Psalm 52: After the Mass Murder in the Priestly City of Nob

presence of Yahweh." Outwardly the man had honored Yahweh. Like a real flatterer he adopted the recent verbiage of his master and reported that he had seen "the son of Jesse" in Nob, with "Ahimelech the son of Ahitub, and he inquired of the LORD for him and gave him provisions and gave him the sword of Goliath the Philistine" (1 Sam. 22:9-10).

This Doeg must have been very clever! By coming up with this information precisely at this moment, he showed that he was just the right guy for a royal court like Saul's. With this information he had put all the court personnel in his debt, for now Saul's attention was diverted, and at the same time he had supplied Saul with an object for his vengeance. Perhaps now an innocent priest was going to be the victim. This descendant of Esau seethed over the priests of the God of Jacob. He did whatever was needed to climb the ladder of prestige. At the same time, he confirmed the king's suspicion of David and Jonathan. His mention of the sword of Goliath in particular must have fortified Saul in his suspicion. Meanwhile, the sly Doeg could play the role of the loyal court official who kept no secrets from his master and to whom his palace colleagues owed a debt of gratitude.

For Saul, the proof was in. The "son of Jesse" has compatriots, not only in the royal household but also among the priestly circle. And Ahimelech is the chief conspirator in the plot. "Then the king sent to summon Ahimelech the priest, the son of Ahitub, and all his father's house, the priests who were at Nob, and all of them came to the king" (1 Sam. 22:11).

"And Saul said: 'Hear now, son of Ahitub.' And he answered, 'Here I am, my lord.' And Saul said to him, 'Why have you conspired against me, you and the son of Jesse, in that you have given him bread and a sword and have inquired of God for him, so that he has risen against me, to lie in wait, as at this day?'" (1 Sam. 22:12-13).

Now the priest had to plead for his life.

It was a sign of the harshness of Saul and Doeg that they remain unmoved by this moving plea. "Then Ahimelech answered the king, 'And who among all your servants is so faithful as David, who is the king's son-in-law, and captain over your bodyguard, and honored in your house? Is today the first time that I have inquired of God for him? No! Let not the king impute anything to his servant or to all the house of my father, for your servant has known nothing of all this, much or little'" (1 Sam. 22:14–15). Who is more loyal than someone who assists the king's trusted servant?

King Saul had no regard for justice as he listened to this plea. An investigation was not begun. Doeg had achieved his goal. The king rendered an immediate verdict: "You shall surely die, Ahimelech, you and all your father's house" (1 Sam. 22:16). Yahweh's enemy, the king of Amalek, was spared by Saul, while Yahweh's priests were murdered. Then the king commanded the soldiers of the guard, who were standing next to him:

> And the king said to the guard who stood about him, "Turn and kill the priests of the LORD, because their hand also is with David, and they knew that he fled and did not disclose it to me." But the servants of the king would not put out their hand to strike the priests of the LORD. Then the king said to Doeg, "You turn and strike the priests." And Doeg the Edomite turned and struck down the priests, and he killed on that day eighty-five persons who wore the linen ephod. And Nob, the city of the priests, he put to the sword; both man and woman, child and infant, ox, donkey and sheep, he put to the sword. (1 Sam. 22:17–19)

Remember that the descendants of Esau harbored hatred for generations against the descendants of Jacob (cf. Num. 20:14–21; 1 Kgs. 11:14; Ps. 137:7; Amos 1:11; Obad. 10).

A son of Ahimelech, the son of Ahitub, called Abiathar, escaped; he fled to David. When Abiathar reported to David that Saul—he, not merely Doeg, was the guilty one!—had killed the priests of Yahweh, David told Abiathar: "I knew on that day, when Doeg the Edomite was there, that he would surely tell Saul" (1 Sam. 22:22).

At that point, Psalm 52 was born in David's heart.

Verses 1–4: The mighty man accused

Verse 1:
Why do you boast of evil, O mighty man?
  The steadfast love of God endures all the day.

Immediately and to the point, David focuses attention on the mighty one. Who was he thinking of as he did this, Doeg or Saul? It is quite possible that he had both in mind at the same time, as well as other violent people of the sort.

He addresses them sarcastically as "O mighty man!" Imagine letting an Edomite loose on the priests of Yahweh! Or helping a murderous king find more victims! Eighty-five defenseless men slaughtered! Putting women and children, yes, even infants, to the sword! Not just any man "dares" to do that. Murdering an entire priestly city—indeed, that is work for "real men"!

And you boast about that? You think you're a brave king and a successful courtier? You are thinking in terms of earthly might and forgetting that God still exists. We, the powerless spectators in this bloodbath, strengthen ourselves in the loving-kindness or covenant faithfulness of Yahweh, the God of Israel, on whose priests you have dared to lay a hand. One day he will render justice.

David has gotten to the point in this opening line and formulated the core of the psalm. The "mighty man" with his violence is contrasted with God and his faithfulness. Saul and Doeg are acting in human strength; David and the godly are acting in God's strength.

The superscription to this psalm is correct to speak of "a *maskil* of David." This alludes to a poem that gives *insight*—insight through the light of the Word. That is what this psalm can provide, for church history knows multitudes of "mighty men" and "violent men" like Saul and Doeg. Church leaders who looked out for themselves, purchased favors with fields, and rewarded loyalty with vineyards. The politics of the Good Ol' Boys' Club and rewarding people with positions of honor are, unfortunately, not things you would find only in the world. The "Saul character," the one who goes out before us and fights *our* battles (1 Sam. 8:20), is all too familiar. As Reformed commentator J. C. Sikkel put it,

> Saul's passion, his banal carnal serving of himself at the cost of everybody and everyone, constituted his style of government. For Saul, everything had a material price. Everything is for sale, must be bought, and must be able to be sold. . . . Saul's system of government is mighty. Fields and vineyards, advantage and prestige, benefits of jobs and posts, and the name of a man awarded by the arbitrariness and favor of the mighty dispenser—they do many mighty things.
>
> But how ignoble this rule of Saul was in Israel!
>
> How ignoble it is today. Especially where the name of the Lord is known!
>
> Of course this style of government is mighty. Mighty through fleshly power. But also mighty in perverting character. In trampling underfoot virtue and honor and a good name. In oppressing and corrupting what lives from the true fountain of grace and righteousness. In providing Satan an advantage and in multiplying the lies. In mocking the honor and the name of the living God, and of Jesus Christ whom he has sent.
>
> Praise God, Christ lives!
>
> Therefore there is yet another system of living and

5. Psalm 52: After the Mass Murder in the Priestly City of Nob

acting than the system of Saul. There is a system sung about by David in Psalm 101. (*Naar Gods hart*, 2 vols. [Watergraafsmeer: Sikkel-Comité, 1921–22], 1:190)

Read Psalm 101 against this somber background! There the godly David sings about his "government program": "*I* will ponder the way of the blameless. . . . *I* will know nothing of evil. . . . Whoever has a haughty look and an arrogant heart *I* will not endure. . . . *I* will look with favor on the faithful in the land, that they may dwell with *me*; he who walks in the way that is blameless shall minister to *me*. No one who practices deceit shall dwell in *my* house; no one who utters lies shall continue before *my* eyes." One shouldn't read this psalm as a timeless description, separate from its concrete situation, or without having Saul's government in view, a government that is the direct opposite of what Psalm 101 is showing us.

Returning to Psalm 52 as a teaching psalm, we can learn here what attitude a righteous person needs to adopt while enduring Saul's style of governing, which uses traitors like Doeg.

Verse 2:
Your tongue plots destruction,
   like a sharp razor, you worker of deceit.

Doeg was slyly plotting precisely at the moment he came to Saul with his destructive report! "You plot destruction," David says. If it is true that Doeg was the chief among Saul's advisers, he likely had often sown destruction with his tongue. In that case, Mitchell Dahood's translation is quite suitable: "Why *at all times* do you harbor pernicious thoughts? . . . artist of deceit!" (*Psalms II* [Garden City, NY: Doubleday, 1968], 11 [emphasis added]).

David's response, then, is spiritual—especially in terms of what he does not say.

Suppose that as an anointed king and former military leader with a gang around you, you had received the kind of message that Abiathar brought to David. It would boil inside you and make your hands shake. These were difficult moments for David, as he sought to keep his position and his calling in mind! How easily he could have arisen as an avenging judge! But he did not do that. He prayed to God to avenge Saul's conduct but kept his sword sheathed. We don't hear him hurling insults. Nor do we see him give a broad analysis of the crimes of Saul and Doeg, partly because he wanted to compose this psalm as a teaching psalm for similar situations. In that case, what was more important than the particularities was the foundational orientation, and one tends then to use somewhat more stereotypical language. But he has unmasked his fellow churchgoer (Doeg and he had met in *God's house*!) who was a destructive person feigning piety. People like that can exist among God's people. David was accusing his opponents before God's face. Wasn't his characterization of Doeg's tongue as "a sharp razor" exactly correct? After all, that tongue had caused eighty-five priests with their wives, children, and even their infants to lose their lives!

With poetic lines such as these, Psalm 52 gives us insight into the circumstances and relationships within Christianity, for this Doeg and this Saul were not the last ones to act in this way. Here we let J. C. Sikkel speak once more:

> Especially in sacred territory, Satan has forged and invented his instrument whereby he grabs hold of the sacred. In this manner he finds entrance for the fleshly domination of power, for the fleshly doctrine of power with its own method of discipline. Then come the servants to join the ranks, who, with beautiful ideas of self-deception perhaps, put themselves in service to the fleshly regime that uses fleshly violence. Unconsciously, but also consciously, they cooperate more and more with pursuing their ego, and with unrighteousness, which corrupts character, which makes the

lie serviceable, which slams the conscience shut, which suppresses every sense of truth and righteousness and humanness, becoming blindly serviceable to the godless system. In the end, every sacrifice is made for the party, for the domination of human power, for their own ego. In this way there arises the damnable ones who seize the innocent and the sacred, who delight in destroying their victims chosen from among those who live faithfully before God.

This continues until the day the righteous Judge will avenge all that innocent blood when the time arrives for the self-manifestation of the Lamb of God who was slain, to whom has been given, not because of his fist but because of his blood, all authority in heaven and on earth. (*Naar Gods hart*, 1:194–95)

According to verse 5, this appears to have been David's hope.

Verses 3–4:
You love evil more than good,
    and lying more than speaking what is right.
You love all words that devour,
    O deceitful tongue.

People have cited these verses as proof that the superscription to Psalm 52 is incorrect, for Doeg told the truth, after all! Wasn't it the case that David had been with Abimelech, and that the latter had given him provisions and the sword of Goliath? The question, however, is this: what *is* truth? According to the pagan Greek meaning of the word, Doeg did indeed speak the "truth": he did no violence to the facts, but disclosed them without hiding anything. And if it really happened and it corresponds with the reality, then along the lines of ancient Greek thought, one is speaking the truth. They spoke of *alētheia*, the nonhidden. Being faithful to the truth, in this climate of thinking, is to collect the "bare" facts, the "honest" facts, if necessary, to tell the raw reality. In Scripture, however, *truth* is another word for faithfulness both toward God and toward one's neighbor. Thus, the Bible recognizes all kinds of supposed lies: of Samuel (1 Sam. 16), mandated by the Lord himself, and of the midwives of Pharaoh (Exod. 1). Note what the Lord Jesus says concerning Jairus's daughter: "The child is not dead but sleeping" (Mark 5:39). He draws a veil over the reality for the sake of his neighbor. Consider 1 Corinthians 13:7 as well: love "covers all things" (ESV "bears all things"). The concept of "truth" in the sense of "honesty with respect to the facts" subjects God and the neighbor to the facts. But God says to love him above all and to love your neighbor as yourself. The ninth commandment does not involve simply "lying," but says that you may not drive your neighbor away from his place and that you may not sabotage his legal protection (this was the view of B. Holwerda in his seminary lectures on Joshua 2).

Weren't David, Ahimelech, Abiathar, and the priests of Nob toppled in a terrible manner through Doeg? That is why, according to biblical standards, this man was a genuine liar, even though his report corresponded perfectly with the facts. He had refused to speak righteousness and had adopted a posture that was noncovenantal. He would have been truthful (such a thing is possible in the Bible) if he had remained silent. But now his speaking about Ahimelech to the blinded, bloodthirsty Saul, though it conformed to the facts, was in the Bible's light lying and deceitful. Anyone who has read Moses regarding the ninth commandment (see the commentary on Deut. 24:16–26:16) will have no difficulty with David's manner of speaking in Psalm 52.

David knew Doeg: "You love . . . [a] deceitful tongue!"

Verses 5–7: "May God break you down forever!"

> Verse 5:
> But God will break you down forever;
>   he will snatch and tear you from your tent;
>   he will uproot you from the land of the living.

Harsh language? Just what we would expect from the Old Testament? Bereft of love for one's enemies? We don't plan to discuss these and similar objections against the imprecatory psalms again. We refer the reader to our discussion in connection with Psalm 59. For that matter, one can translate the line above in two ways: as a prayer for God's curse ("God, *may you* . . .") or as an announcement of God's curse ("God *shall* . . .").

Before anyone expresses their objections, they would do well first to realize how awful Saul's and Doeg's actions were. In that regard one shouldn't think primarily of the abominable mass murder of the women and children of Nob, though this bloodbath is in itself repulsive. A cry for the death penalty—and isn't this what David is doing?—is truly understandable in connection with that deed. But Saul and Doeg had not only assaulted innocent people; by murdering the priests, they had attacked the servants of God himself! These were important servants. For Israel, priests were essential for their life!

If we come away from the book of Leviticus with one impressive lesson, it is the lesson of God's holiness. In the presence of everything that hints of sin or death, Yahweh is simply a consuming fire. We could compare God's holiness to high-voltage electricity. Such cables are often identified with warnings: "High Voltage! Caution!" Touching one of them is inevitably fatal, which is why they need to be isolated and set apart from human traffic and contact. In this way you can partly imagine how impossible it was for sinful, mortal Israelites to engage with the holy God unprotected. His holiness would be fatal for them if it weren't isolated. In order to protect Israel against his divine wrath and aversion toward sin and death, Yahweh had provided the tribe of Levi to render service as an "isolation zone" between Yahweh and Israel. Then Israel was protected. To return to the metaphor of high-voltage electricity: the tribe of Levi served as a transformer, so to speak, between the holy God and his sinful people. That is why the Levitical priest stood between God and Israel. He was the means of approach. Without his intervention a fatal "short circuit" would exist between God's consuming holiness and sinful people.

Now consider how awful Saul's deed was.

He not only murdered an entire city population—we could also say, an entire congregation of God's church—but he also removed the protection of Levi, leaving himself unprotected before a holy God! David understood this when he composed the poetic lines above. This deed simply had to result in Saul's destruction! He was subject to destruction for this act alone, not to mention Hannah's prophecy, Yahweh's promise to David, and Saul's earlier arrogance. In these phenomena, David had a sufficient promissory foundation for making requests like the ones we are now discussing.

In this respect as well, Psalm 52 is a didactic poem. If petitions like this, prayed against figures like Doeg and Saul, were impermissible (rather than obligatory), and if such requests were displeasing to God, then poems like Psalms 52 and 59 would not have been included in God's Word for his people to sing. Indeed, our Savior did pray, "Father, forgive them, for they know not what they do" (Luke 23:34; cf. Acts 3:17; 1 Cor. 2:8). But can you say that Saul did not know what he was doing? "Kill the priests of Yahweh," he had commanded, and his guards refused to follow his order! (1 Sam. 22:17). And David was not the last one whose petitions of this kind are included in Scripture. With dying lips, as he was being stoned in the forecourt of the house of Yahweh, the godly Zechariah, the son of Jehoida, said, "May Yahweh see and avenge!" (2 Chr. 24:22).

5. Psalm 52: After the Mass Murder in the Priestly City of Nob

Verses 6–7:
The righteous shall see and fear,
 and shall laugh at him, saying,
"See the man who would not make
 God his refuge,
but trusted in the abundance of his riches
 and sought refuge in his own destruction!"

Naturally, the righteous shivered when the news of the mass murder in the priestly city of Nob went through the land. People such as the elderly Samuel, Prince Jonathan, the farmer Abigail, the prophets of Naioth, as well as the hundreds of refugees surrounding David—in short, the entire remnant of that time trembled at the report of the bloodbath that the king had wrought.

But what could the godly do for David, now that Saul was unwilling to retreat from such dreadful repressive measures? Psalm 11 could possibly have been written during this time, with its lament, "For behold, the wicked bend the bow; they have fitted their arrow to the string to shoot in the dark at the upright in heart; if the foundations are destroyed, what can the righteous do?" (vv. 2–3).

In view of the lines of Psalm 52 cited above, however, David was certain that in his own time Yahweh would arise to bestow on him the promised kingship. At the same time David appears to have foreseen that Yahweh would do this by meting out severe punishment against wicked people such as Doeg and Saul. At that point another period would dawn for the godly, one when, with holy fear for Yahweh's display of righteousness, and together with holy joy, they would laugh on account of the defeat of mass murderers such as Saul and Doeg. All of Israel's godly remnant would be able to write this "In Memoriam" in connection with the death of those who murdered the priests: "See the man who would not make God his refuge, but trusted in the abundance of his riches and sought refuge in his own destruction!"—or, as Dahood has translated it, "relied on his perniciousness" (*Psalms II*, 11).

So David was composing their epitaph in advance!

David was giving expression to the assurance of his faith here to the ears of poor Abiathar and the other refugees. For his words directly contradicted the facts at hand. As we have observed rather often with David, his trust in God's promises could lead him to speak about those future deliverances as though Yahweh had already performed them. "Stay with me; do not be afraid, for he who seeks my life seeks your life. With me you shall be in safekeeping" (1 Sam. 22:23).

We know how David was not put to shame for this faith that he expresses in Psalm 52. Doeg's fall is not reported in Scripture. He could well have perished with Saul at Gilboa.

From David we can learn to take notice of such events. In church history there have been more "Sauls" and "Doegs" who have perished. The wicked pay no attention to that (Ps. 28:5), but the righteous do. As we can learn from this psalm, they look on this with appropriate joy! They do this, for example, when they received the obituary announcement of Queen Athaliah following her sixty-six year-long tyranny (2 Kgs. 11), and when Jeremiah and his group got news of the prophet Hananiah. Jeremiah had been directly contradicted by this false prophet, but within two months, Hananiah was a corpse (cf. Jer. 28:1, 17)! This was how Daniel experienced the defeat of the men who had seen to his stay in the lions' den (Dan. 6). Mordecai saw his archenemy Haman hanging on the gallows (Esth. 7). The church in Jerusalem knew that an angel of the Lord had killed her enemy Herod (Acts 12:23).

Psalm 52 teaches us to take notice of such acts of God.

Verses 8–9: "But I am like a green olive tree"

Verses 8–9:
But I am like a green olive tree
  in the house of God.
I trust in the steadfast love of God
  forever and ever.
I will thank you forever,
  because you have done it.
I will wait for your name, for it is good,
  in the presence of the godly.

To feel the power of David's imagery, you need to know something about olive trees. Experts tell us that the olive tree, with its wide crown and perpetually green leaves, must have been the picture par excellence of prosperity (cf. Jer. 11:16). It grows slowly and can get very old. It actually is impossible to uproot, since an old stump continues to bring forth new shoots (Ps. 128). Weren't there olive trees in the forecourt of the sanctuary?

David takes this image of prosperity, power, and hopefulness and compares it to this moment when Saul seemed to be at the apex of his unbridled power and David was a poor hunted troglodyte, to whom the single survivor of the priestly bloodbath in Nob had fled! Viewed according to the flesh, Saul's position is invincible and David's position is hopeless. Nevertheless, David dared to say about himself, "But I am like a green olive tree!" Once again, that is the powerful language of his faith, which explains why he is the man after God's heart. Completely renouncing earthly power—in which Saul and Doeg took delight—David depended entirely on God's power and his faithfulness. In direct contradiction to the showmanship of those hostile bullies, David confessed clearly in the hearing of his fellow refugees that he was expecting a wonderful future from God and his loving-kindness, for which he would praise Yahweh. With the binoculars of his faith, David brought directly into view, despite his desolate situation, the future of God's promises, so that with the courage of that faith he could talk about that future deliverance as if Yahweh had already accomplished it: "Because you have done it!" Done what? Yahweh has judged Saul and has made David king.

When our power in the kingdom of God has been reduced to zero and we can do nothing more, then with this *maskil* of David we can receive insight through the light of the Word in our situation: God himself makes his Word true, and his promises for the remnant will not fail in our day as well.

Let us consider it a great joy to be verdant olive trees in God's house, just as in his distress David experienced great joy from the fact that no "Saul" would take him away from God's house (the church). In the midst of death and decay, God's people possess the promises of eternal life. Like David, let us always praise him, for our Father has a right to our praise. Together with his Son and Spirit, he alone ultimately accomplishes everything.

In short: wait on his name! That is what Psalm 52 teaches. And David literally did it for several years. Wait. Patiently, but with both eyes focused on God's promises. That is the bottom line for believing Christians in this day as well, in light of the inconspicuous persecution and oppression inside the world of the church. In his *Treasury of David*, Charles Spurgeon concluded his exposition of this psalm with these words: "Men must not too much fluster us; our strength is to sit still. Let the mighty ones boast, we will wait on the Lord; and if their haste brings them present honour, our patience will have its turn by-and-by, and bring us the honour which excelleth."

Chapter 6

Psalm 74: Weeping for God's Church

Have you ever lain awake for hours at night because of the church? Have you ever gone to the doctor with stomach troubles because of the church? Have you ever had sadness over the church?

You are not the first one to have been weighed down on account of the church. We already hear this complaint in the Psalter. Indeed, we hear it often. The "laments of Zion" constitute a long series: Psalms 44, 74, 77, 79, 80, 89, 90, and 102.

We are going to be reading several of them with you in the next chapters in order to learn the right way to complain when we mourn over the church: not in the arrogant mentality of the inflexible Maccabees and their later sympathizers, but in the humble spirit of the Asaphites.

We begin with Psalm 74.

Not a Bleak Psalm for Old Testament Times But a Genuine Didactic Poem for Our Time

What are we actually to make of Scripture passages like Psalm

74 in our day? What are we to make of a lament about the destruction of a temple 2,500 years ago, especially a temple whose worship became obsolete and disappeared almost 2,000 years ago (Matt. 27:51; Luke 19:43–44; Heb. 8:13)? Is such a lament still relevant for Christians today? One celebrated commentator has declared this psalm to be as impoverished as Psalm 73 is rich, since it lacks any expression of awareness of guilt, or of a life of faith, or of the certainty of victory. Others declare this psalm to have very little religious significance for us today.

We could, of course, reject such opinions indignantly, but that does not yet prove that the song does have religious importance for us. Many would shrink back from making judgments like those above. But if we ourselves are at a loss about how we should appreciate this psalm (apart from singing a few select verses from it), then are we that far removed, at least in heart, from the view of such commentators? If we enjoy a few of its stanzas merely because we have pried them away from the entire psalm or because the words sound so nice as to excite a religious heart, then aren't we employing the same standard as those critics, namely, that of religious sentiment?

The custom of singing selected stanzas of psalms has generally not helped very much for singing the psalms as covenant songs that have been composed in specific historical circumstances. Guided by a subjectivist, pietistic spirit, people have often sung the psalms for the sake of how edifying their versification and melodies sound. This let them easily spiritualize and individualize various matters. But are we then acting any differently than those who think that a psalm like Psalm 74 has little "religious" relevance for us?

For the sake of understanding the Psalms, we would do well to wipe clean our fogged-over reading glasses. In fact, the future of modern Christianity, of the people of God in our day, could depend, more than we realize, on the continued existence of people who, as they pray, pour out their laments about the "Zion" of our day. The One to whom they pray has included psalms like Psalm 74 in his Word for a reason, and as "a *didactic poem* of Asaph," no less!

The relevance of such psalms becomes evident only when we read them in terms of their historical background and only when we then compare that situation with the situation in which we live today as Christians. Then we will see that the superscription to our psalm is perfectly accurate: "A didactic poem [ESV "Maskil"] of Asaph," such that believers in our day can learn fundamental lessons for discerning the times.

Historical background: the destruction of Jerusalem by the Babylonians

On January 15, 588 BC, Nebuchadnezzar reached Jerusalem "with his entire army." Apparently planning to force Jerusalem to surrender through starvation, the Babylonians constructed a siege wall around the city (2 Kgs. 25:1). A terrible siege began that would last a year and a half, with a brief interruption (Jer. 37), from January 15, 588, until July 19, 586.

Yahweh was pleased to destroy and eradicate Judah (Deut. 28:63). At the end of the siege, famished fathers and mothers were not handing over to one another the flesh of their own children to eat, but keeping it for themselves, as Yahweh had threatened through Moses (Deut. 28:54–57). Some of the pampered and spoiled women who had sauntered so proudly and elegantly through Jerusalem were boiling their own children (Lam. 2:10; 4:10). "The children beg for food, but no one gives to them" (4:4). Nursing infants died at their mothers' breast (2:12). "My priests and elders perished in the city, while they sought food to revive their strength. . . . Those who once feasted on delicacies perish in the streets" (1:19; 4:5).

After an eighteen-month siege, the Babylonian troops succeeded in making a breach in the wall, enabling them to enter Jerusalem. What happened next is described with pens dipped in tears, in three places—most briefly in Chronicles, more extensively in Kings, and most completely in Lamentations. Provoked by the lengthy siege, the Babylonian soldiers moved through the streets murdering and plundering. Neither infant nor elderly, neither priest nor prophet was spared (2 Chr. 36:17; Lam. 2:20; 4:16; 5:12). Women and girls were assaulted (Lam. 5:11). Owners of upscale houses had to watch helplessly as their expensive possessions were plundered and set on fire (2:5). Rulers dangled from trees with ropes around their necks (5:12).

King Zedekiah, who fled shortly before the fall of the city, was arrested near Jericho and brought to the headquarters of Nebuchadnezzar at Ribla. There the supreme ruler pronounced sentence on the disloyal vassal for having broken his vassal oath so faithlessly (2 Chr. 36:13; Ezek. 17:13–24). First, Zedekiah had to look on while his sons were executed before his eyes. For just like their father, they had been included in the vassal treaty with Nebuchadnezzar, and therefore they too came under the curse sanctions of the supreme ruler. Then, Zedekiah's eyes were plucked out. Perhaps by Nebuchadnezzar himself, for kings usually implemented that punishment with their own hands. Next, he was bound and brought to Babylon. The Lamentations moan, "The breath of our nostrils, the LORD's anointed, was captured in their pits, of whom we said, 'Under his shadow we shall live among the nations'" (Lam. 4:20). Several prominent leaders from ecclesiastical and political groups were put to death (2 Kgs. 25:18–21; Jer. 52:24–27).

The destruction of Jerusalem occurred only a month after the fall of the city. Four weeks after the walls were breached, Nebuchadnezzar razed the city to the ground (2 Kgs. 25; Jer. 39:2; 52:6, 12). Walls, palaces, and strongholds were torn down to save Nebuchadnezzar from having to make a third siege. Then the most terrible thing happened. Those pagan soldiers climbed up Mount Zion and invaded Yahweh's temple. But we should not forget about the raids or the announcement that all Jerusalem's citizens should prepare to be transported to Babylon! The people had to say goodbye to their homes, their city, village, and birthplace. They wondered whether

6. Psalm 74: Weeping for God's Church

this exile would be permanent. All of this occurred under the watchful eyes of the heavily armed Babylonian soldiers.

In our opinion, these events form the historical background of Psalms 74 and 79. Some have assigned these psalms to the time of the Maccabees and the destruction of the temple in 168 BC, but it seems to us that the psalm fits better in the framework of the events narrated above, which occurred around 586 BC.

We discern in the background of our psalm the picture of devastated Judah as portrayed by the poets of the Lamentations: quiet streets, empty of pilgrim traffic. Abandoned gates, where no old men sat any longer. All its majesty had departed. Mount Zion was deserted. Jackals prowled there during the night (Lam. 1:4, 6–7; 5:15, 18).

In those same years when the Lamentations were sung for the first time, a godly man, Asaph, brought his sorrow over God's church into the presence of Yahweh, with what we now have as Psalm 74.

He did this to teach the brotherhood how to lament.

An author from the generation of the choral prophets of Asaph

For the psalm-singing church, Asaph has always been a familiar name. David appointed the Levite Asaph as the leader of the temple singers (1 Chr. 16:5). Other leaders included the Levites Heman and Ethan (6:33, 44). After the death of their famous father, Asaph's sons continued their musical labor for centuries. We encounter sons of Asaph from the time of Solomon until after the captivity. When Zerubbabel returns with a number of Judeans from Babylon to Jerusalem, the family of Asaph was in his group. Ezra speaks of 128, Nehemiah of 148 people (Ezra 2:41; Neh. 7:44).

When we encounter the phrase "Of Asaph" in the superscription to a psalm, we need not think exclusively of the man Asaph who lived in David's time, for it is very possible that one of his descendants is being identified. In Israel, the name Asaph became a family name or a group name, so that "Asaph" was really understood to mean "the sons of Asaph."

When Asaph and his brothers accepted their office as singers following their appointment, they did so with a (premier?) performance of Psalm 105 (cf. 1 Chr. 16:7–36). We can learn a few things about the task of "Asaph" from this.

That task was first of all the singing of God's praise. In connection with important events in Israelite life, the Asaphites sang God's praise: for example, after a victory (2 Chr. 20), at the dedication of a wall of Jerusalem after the captivity (Neh. 12), and especially in the ordinary temple worship. As far as that worship went, these Levitical singers had a larger repertoire than just the refrain "For he is good, for his lovingkindness endures forever." According to Ezra 3:10–11, though, this refrain was a specialty of the sons of Asaph.

Secondly, included in Asaph's task was prophesying. Often in the history of Israel, the "sons of Asaph" prophesied. They sang their prophecies. When the ark was brought into Jerusalem, the sons of Asaph not only sang in praise to Yahweh what we now call Psalm 105, but they also prophetically illuminated the new situation in the kingdom of God. They did so with the words "The world is established; it shall never be moved" (1 Chr. 16:30). This world was the Israelite world, whose establishment Yahweh had begun at Horeb. As genuine seers, the sons of Asaph were given to discern, in clear historical perspective, the new situation that existed after the ark had been brought into Jerusalem (1 Chr. 16:7–36).

The sons of Asaph often combined both of these tasks—singing praise and prophesying. They sang as they prophesied, and they prophesied in a poetic manner. "David and the chiefs of the service also set apart for the service the sons of Asaph, and of Heman, and of Jeduthun, who prophesied with lyres, with harps, and with cymbals" (1 Chr. 25:1). From Asaph himself we read that he "*prophesied* under the direction of the king" (1 Chr. 25:2). And we read of Jeduthun, "who prophesied with the lyre in thanksgiving and praise to the LORD" (1 Chr. 25:3). The singer Heman was also called "the king's seer, according to the promise of God" (1 Chr. 25:5). Concerning David's contemporary, Asaph, we read not only that he prophesied but also that he was called "Asaph the seer" (2 Chr. 29:30), just as Jehuthun was called "the king's seer" (2 Chr. 35:15).

The sons of Asaph also did more than just sing psalms. They also composed psalms. Their poetic artistry was in service to prophecy. An example of this kind of prophesying "son of Asaph" is the Levite Jahaziel, who prophesied in a distressing situation during the reign of King Jehoshaphat, "The battle is not yours but God's" (2 Chr. 20:14-17). No wonder, then, that psalms whose superscription speaks "of Asaph" (Pss. 50; 74–83) cause us to think of the books of the Prophets. It was the "sons of Asaph" who in the course of history frequently illuminated Israel's situation from the Word of God.

In this way, after the awful eruption of Yahweh's wrath upon Judah and Jerusalem around 586 BC, someone from this famous family cast the catastrophe of his time in a poetic manner in the light of God's Word. We know this poem now as Psalm 74, a didactic poem of Asaph.

A didactic poem

In our Bibles Psalm 74 has the superscription "A didactic poem [Heb. *maskil*] of Asaph." The Hebrew word derives from a verb that means "to have understanding," "to have insight," and "to give others insight." When we investigate how this word is used, we see that often it has to do with providing insight from God's Word for a particular situation—when people want to show forth God's deeds, when they want to understand, or have others understand, that Yahweh has done something. "They shall *wisely consider* of his doing" (Ps. 64:9, KJV). "That they may see and know, may consider and understand together, that the hand of the LORD has done this" (Isa.

41:20; cf. Deut. 32:29; Neh. 8:13; Prov. 16:20; Ps. 106:7; Isa. 44:18; Jer. 9:24; Amos 5:13; Dan. 9:22; 12:10). The gift of this understanding was encountered frequently among the sons of Asaph.

That is why we prefer translating *maskil* as "didactic poem." Some have proposed translating *maskil* as "a pious meditation" or "an artful poem," but considering the activity of the sons of Asaph within Israel's history (prophesying while singing and composing psalms) and the association between the Hebrew words *maskil* and *sakal*, the phrase "didactic poem" strikes us as an excellent superscription to this psalm. It could also be translated somewhat more freely: "a poem offering insight."

This superscription fits Psalm 74 perfectly. During the Babylonian threat and subsequent attack, many inhabitants of Judah were utterly lacking the requisite insight into the cause and background of the situation: Yahweh's wrath because they had forsaken the covenant! The book of Jeremiah inveighs in many passages against the harsh, arrogant mentality characterizing most people in Judah at that time. In that situation, someone from the "sons of Asaph" composed a *maskil*, a prophetic psalm that could supply insight into the situation and teach the attitude that was discerning with respect to godly living before Yahweh. Perhaps the composer (like the poets who composed the Lamentations) harbored the hope that he would be able to lead his brothers and sisters to better discernment with this psalm.

Insight deepened, for our time as well

What must we who live more than 2,500 years later do with a lament like Psalm 74? As already mentioned, one commentator could find in it no expressions of any particular faith commitment and instead found it a spiritually impoverished psalm. People may well indignantly dismiss such declarations, as we observed, but meanwhile they in fact confirm them by practically never singing the psalm. Does this song,

6. Psalm 74: Weeping for God's Church

then, have little to say that has religious value? When it comes down to it, are we ourselves at a loss what to do with a lament about the destruction of a temple that occurred 2,500 years ago? Do we rescue ourselves from these difficulties at all by saying "that's just how things were in the Old Testament," thus declaring this psalm to be obsolete and without any application for us? One could pose these questions in connection with other psalms of lament over Zion, like Psalms 44, 77, 79, 80, 89, and 102.

To find an answer, we must be clearly aware that Jerusalem was no ordinary city, and its destruction was no ordinary destruction. Nebuchadnezzar came as God's servant (Jer. 27:6) to execute God's curse upon his unfaithful covenant partner Judah. The psalms in question, therefore, are not political "dirges," but ecclesiastical lamentations. They lament the covenant curse that has fallen upon God's people. They constitute concrete humbling under the smiting hand of God, a humbling cast in poetry and written down in black and white.

What can these lamentations teach us?

The basic principle for understanding these psalms is this: read them as songs in which God's people sing about how they live in God's covenant! All the psalms are distinguished from the religious ditties of the masses primarily in that the psalmists are honoring God's covenant in every poetic line. But how many baptized Christians still know that they continue to stand in a covenant relationship with God? After all, in their baptism they received the sign and seal of God's covenant. Whether all those baptized Christians one day inherit "the blessed earth" or undergo God's full covenant wrath as covenant breakers is an altogether separate question! But they are nonetheless in a covenant relationship and stand under the sanctions of blessing and curse that are part of God's covenant, and to an even more powerful degree than Israel was formerly, under the Horeb covenant. Baptized Christians now live in the much richer new covenant, with its better promises, better High Priest, better Surety and Mediator, but—as a consequence—also more severe threats of curse (Heb. 7–8; 10:29; 12:25, 29). God the Holy Spirit included the nations of the West and the East, highly privileged with the promise of the gospel, including Christ's blood, which results in the forgiveness of our sins, and Christ's Spirit, who cleanses our hearts and lives. But what is the response of the masses of baptized Christians to this gospel? And to God and his Christ? In recent centuries, haven't people within Christianity been increasingly falling away? When we discussed Psalm 46, we spoke of the world crisis of our age and how our time is a time of judgment. The devastation occurring in the realm of Christianity is indescribable.

But if you simply don't see it, as happens with Christians who are so "broad minded" that they "appreciate" everything religious and have no conception of the terrible covenant apostasy within modern Christianity, then how could you ever sense the need to crack open this lament about the ecclesiastical ruins? The same goes for those Christians who do recognize the apostasy but live too self-sufficiently to really suffer because of the crisis within Christianity. They would actually have to agree with the liberal commentator who insisted that Psalm 74 has little to tell us of any religious importance.

But those Christians who are united through "one Lord, one faith, one baptism, one God and Father of all" (Eph. 4:5–6) with all of Christianity can lament with Psalm 102:14: "For your servants hold her stones [of Zion, of the ruined temple] dear and have pity on her dust." And they agree with Calvin's comment on this verse: "But no desolation ought to prevent us from loving the very stones and dust of the Church." Such Christians confess, "This song has something of burning relevance to say to us." For they find in this song the teaching model, even for our day, of a God-pleasing "prayer for the needs of Christendom," as one ancient Reformed liturgical prayer is entitled.

6. Psalm 74: Weeping for God's Church

Verses 1–11: Lament about Yahweh's Covenant Curse

Verse 1:
O God, why do you cast us off forever?
   Why does your anger smoke against the sheep of
      your pasture?

In this first verse we already see what a genuine didactic poem Psalm 74 is: a poem filled with insight through the light of the Word. But then we must know the spirit of the time in which the psalmist was speaking and against which he is rising to oppose: a spirit of blindness and shamelessness under the smiting hand of God. In what follows we will review a number of Scripture passages from the books of Isaiah and Jeremiah, passages that can be understood properly only when read in their context, but even apart from their contexts they serve to provide an impression of the spirit of the age against which Psalm 74 is directed.

Yahweh had already been severely disciplining his people for about one hundred years, first by means of the Assyrian invasions and more recently by means of the Babylonian captivity. Nevertheless, most of the people of Judah failed to recognize God's hand at work in these events. The masses saw only "political developments." Approximately one hundred years before the destruction of Jerusalem, during the Assyrian world domination, Isaiah had tried in vain to remove the blindfold from the church in Judah. The prophet had to lament, however: "They do not regard the deeds of the Lord, or see the work of his hands" (Isa. 5:12). "The people did not turn to him who struck them, nor inquire of the Lord of hosts" (9:13). "But you did not look to him who did it, or see him who planned it long ago. In that day the Lord God of hosts called for weeping and mourning, for baldness and wearing sackcloth; and behold, joy and gladness, killing oxen and slaughtering sheep, eating flesh and drinking wine. 'Let us eat and drink, for tomorrow we die'" (22:11–3). "O LORD, your hand is lifted up, but they do not see it" (26:11). This is how Isaiah had prophesied about one hundred years before Psalm 74.

A relatively short time before, in the years preceding the attacks of the Babylonians and the destruction of Jerusalem and the temple, Jeremiah had in fact prophesied in the same spirit as Isaiah, among a generation just as shameless. Here are a few citations from his prophecy: "In vain have I struck your children; they took no correction" (Jer. 2:30; cf. vv. 19, 35). "Therefore the showers have been withheld, and the spring rain has not come; yet you have the forehead of a whore; you refuse to be ashamed" (Jer. 3:3; cf. v. 13). "You have struck them down, but they felt no anguish; you have consumed them, but they refused to take correction. They have made their faces harder than rock; they have refused to repent" (Jer. 5:3). "Were they ashamed when they committed abomination? No, they were not at all ashamed; they did not know how to blush" (Jer. 6:15; cf. 8:12). "They have turned to me their back and not their face. And though I have taught them persistently, they have not listened to receive instruction" (Jer. 32:33; cf. ch. 36). Even the poor who were not led away to Babylon hardened themselves in their shameless attitude: "They have not humbled themselves even to this day, nor have they feared" (Jer. 44:10; cf. Ezek. 3:7; Mic. 6:9; Hag. 2:17).

Only a remnant looked up from the Babylonians, who were perpetrating injustice, to God, who was using this world power to strike his people. To this remnant belonged not only godly men like Jeremiah but also his secretary Baruch, Daniel and his friends, Ezekiel, and the poets who wrote the Lamentations, as well as the Asaphite composer of Psalm 74. He had seen Yahweh's burning anger in the catastrophes that Judah was undergoing.

Literally, he began his poem with the words "Why is your nose smoking . . . ?" In so doing, Asaph was echoing the sacred language of Moses and the prophets about God's nose (Exod. 15:8; Deut. 33:10; 2 Sam. 22:9, 16 [= Ps. 18:8, 15]; Isa. 65:5). In connection with God's wrath, David spoke in Psalm 18 about "the blowing of the breath of his nose." Just like David and the Prophets, Asaph was not at all afflicted with that prudish transcendental nonsense that is inclined to correct for us the revelational words of God about his face, hands, feet, nose, sorrow, and sadness, with the assistance of lofty words like *anthropomorphism* and *anthropopathism* (see the commentary on Gen. 6:7).

As a good seer, Asaph saw very clearly that Yahweh is *snorting* at us (this word perhaps best conveys the Hebrew expression of a smoking nose [cf. 2 Sam. 22:9]). Like someone who was genuinely humble, he was not pondering about retracting his personal solidarity with Israel's guilt, or about doubting God's right to be angry. The Christianity of our time, estranged as it is from God, refuses to "take it" when God comes to visit her with his strict discipline, just as the masses in the days of Isaiah and Jeremiah refused to "take it." But Asaph humbled himself under the mighty hand of God (cf. 1 Pet. 5:6).

So his question, "Why are you angry?," is not asking the reason for God's anger but is an expression of Asaph's surprise. Can the Shepherd of Israel keep doing this to the sheep of his pasture? At this point we are hearing the "loneliness of faith," along with the composer of the Lamentations, who at the same time confessed, "For the Lord will not cast off forever, but, though he cause grief, he will have compassion according to the abundance of his steadfast love; for he does not afflict from his heart or grieve the children of men" (Lam. 3:31–33; cf. Isa. 8:17). This explains why the psalmist, in order to soften Yahweh, holds up before him: "Lord, we remain your sheep, right?" Other Asaphite psalms of petition seek to attract Yahweh's attention with the same moving imagery (cf. Pss. 77:20; 79:13; 80:1).

Verse 2:
Remember your congregation, which you have purchased
of old,
which you have redeemed to be the tribe of your
heritage!
Remember Mount Zion, where you have dwelt.

Did Yahweh really want to break this ancient bond of love that existed between him and Israel? In order to restrain him from doing that, the psalmist reminds Yahweh of the days "of old" (Heb. *qedem*). Scripture often uses this word to refer to Israel's "prehistory," which spanned from Abraham until the entrance into Canaan (cf. Ps. 44:1, from exodus to entrance; Isa. 51:9–10, exodus; Lam. 2:17, Horeb; Mic. 7:20, Abraham and Jacob).

During that period Yahweh, as Israel's Maker, had for the first time created Israel (Ps. 100:3; Isa. 44:2; 54:5; Hos. 8:14). From two people who were as good as dead—Abraham and Sarah—he had called the people of Israel into existence (Heb. 11:11–12). "Is not he your father, who created you?" (Deut. 32:6; cf. Exod. 15:16). Israel can properly be called a creation of Yahweh.

When Pharaoh attempted to own the life of Israel, Yahweh requisitioned the slaves living in Goshen for himself. Yahweh placed other nations in the care of angels, but he claimed Israel for himself (Exod. 5:1; 6:5–6; Deut. 32:8–9; Pss. 77:15; 78:35). In this way, Israel became Yahweh's inheritance or treasure.

Indeed, hadn't Yahweh himself dwelled among Israel in a tent from Horeb to the time of David, and in the temple on Mount Zion from the time of David until Psalm 74 was composed? God had bound himself to Israel with firm bonds!

What a great work God had performed, namely, the creation of an Israelite world! The foundation of this world occurred in the days "of old," which the psalmist would presently recite. The completion of that great work of God came

6. Psalm 74: Weeping for God's Church

about when Yahweh came to dwell among Israel on Mount Zion in the temple of Solomon. With that event in mind, David had the Asaphites sing for the procession of the ark to Jerusalem, "The [Israelite] world is established; it shall never be moved" (1 Chr. 16:30).

Did Yahweh now want to forget that work entirely? "Remember!" the psalmist cries out to Yahweh. "No, Yahweh, don't forget Israel, your own creation! How could you release your claim on Israel from of old? How could you surrender your inheritance and your own treasure forever? Will you then surrender your ancient plan to dwell among your people? Your Israel, already chosen in Abraham before the foundation of the world, 'before Horeb'—will you now abandon and forget her forever?"

From the beginning of the didactic poem we can learn what we must remind our heavenly Father about in times of judgment: his historic deeds of redemption, especially his foundational deliverances. For us this is the proclamation of the gospel in formerly pagan Europe. That is the foundation on which all subsequent deliverances depend (1 Pet. 2:9–10; Eph. 5:8). This work of the Spirit signifies for us a powerful basis for pleading when we want to make intercession "for the needs of all Christendom."

Verse 3:
Direct your steps to the perpetual ruins;
  the enemy has destroyed everything in the sanctuary!

Did Yahweh have in mind once again the great work that he did in the days "of old"? Then he must quickly look at it. Quickly, for the poet says, "Pick up your feet!" Someone walking fast lifts his feet higher than someone who is just strolling.

What did our Asaphite discover to be the worst? The premature death of many children and infants in Jerusalem? The other distress that the siege of Jerusalem had brought upon the Jerusalem citizenry? That so many fine homes were destroyed or that King Zedekiah had his eyes plucked out? The deportation to Babylon? No, all of that faded in comparison to his pain in connection with the destruction of God's house. "The enemy has destroyed everything in the sanctuary!"

In the next verses he recalls those terrible scenes that played out with the destruction of the temple. For whom is he doing that? For those who had not witnessed those scenes? For his brothers in Judah? No, for Yahweh! Did Yahweh really know just how much havoc the Babylonians had wreaked? Well, our psalmist will help him remember.

> Verses 4–8:
> **Your foes have roared in the midst of your meeting place;**
>   **they set up their own signs for signs.**
> **They were like those who swing axes**
>   **in a forest of trees.**
> **And all its carved wood**
>   **they broke down with hatchets and hammers.**
> **They set your sanctuary on fire;**
>   **they profaned the dwelling place of your name,**
>   **bringing it down to the ground.**
> **They said to themselves, "We will utterly subdue them";**
>   **they burned all the meeting places of God in the land.**

Had Yahweh witnessed that sacrilege? Had he heard the soldiers howling like animals in the sacred forecourt where the sons of Asaph had sung God's praise? Had he seen how the pagans had ransacked the temple? Like woodchoppers in a forest, they had torn down the beautiful copper pillars of Jachin and Boaz with their artistic capitals, their copper braiding with ninety-six pomegranates (Jer. 52:23). They had stolen all the large and small precious utensils from God's house: the copper sea, the pegs, the pots, scales, spoons, knives, cooking pans, and everything made of gold and silver. Then came the worst of all: they set God's house on fire! The red glow above Mount Zion told everyone in the Judean countryside that the temple of Yahweh was going up in flames. Had the psalmist witnessed it with his own eyes? His description sounds a lot like an eyewitness account in any case.

But hadn't Yahweh already been making known for a long time through his prophets that he, the Holy One, would not continue dwelling among his unholy people? Hadn't Ezekiel already seen Yahweh depart from the temple in a vision? He had seen "the glory of Yahweh" depart from the temple in a kind of royal wagon. Although he departed with hesitation—because even for God this was a momentous deed—nonetheless Yahweh finally left (Ezek. 10:18–19).

Over against that, the psalmist posited this: "But what about your Name, then?" After all, wasn't the sanctuary "the dwelling of your Name"? Wasn't this heap of rubble the house "of which you have said, 'My name shall be there'"? (1 Kgs. 8:29). In verses 10, 18, and 21–22 he reaches for this argument once more.

But aren't we also facing totally destructive enemies? Or aren't rationalism and neo-Gnosticism real enemies of God's people? Aren't those enemies howling together with humanism and Scripture criticism "in the territory of the covenant," just as the pagans formerly bellowed in the temple? Don't these spiritual movements smash the faith of many into smithereens? Hasn't evolutionism raised up its torches as symbols of victory everywhere, including in our own schools? Hasn't it undermined the Word of truth and downgraded us from being children of God to being little dust balls blown about by the ancient winds of evolution, terrified midgets in a hostile universe filled with nothing more than natural forces. The Babylonians stole the sacred temple utensils, set the house of God on fire, and took the church of Judah along into captivity. The modern enemies we have mentioned aren't doing anything different, are they? They are stealing God's holy Word from us, breaking down God's house (which is now Christ's church), and leading many of God's people into the captivity of nihilism, a philosophy that has led so many to despair.

In all of this shouldn't we first of all notice God's anger, as Asaph and the composers of the Lamentations saw behind the defeats of Judah? Could God be breaking down the walls of his vineyard, so that various idols and false teachings can come in and ravage the Western church (see the commentary on Ps. 80:11–13)? But then intercessors may derive confidence from this didactic poem of Asaph, that they may similarly call for help from our heavenly Father. "Lord, do you see what devastation the enemy has wreaked in your house," that is, in the Christian church?

Verse 9:
We do not see our signs;
   there is no longer any prophet,
   and there is none among us who knows how long.

Here as well our Asaphite tasted God's wrath. Through Moses Yahweh had spoken so generously: If Israel would not seek divine revelation from magicians, soothsayers, and necromancers, he would provide new, faithful prophets regularly (see the commentary on Deut. 18:16–18). But what had Israel done? She had sought her consolation from soothsayers who "chirp" and spiritists who "mutter" (Isa. 8:19). In the time when he composed Psalm 74, Asaph would have known of necromancers and fortune-tellers among the people of Judah. King Manasseh had employed them (2 Chr. 33:6).

Then Yahweh came with his judgment of a famine of the Word (cf. 1 Sam. 3:1). Ezekiel had announced the catastrophe to come: "They seek a vision from the prophet, while the law perishes from the priest and counsel from the elders" (Ezek. 7:26). When Asaph composed his psalm, this catastrophe had occurred: Jerusalem's "king and princes are among the nations; the law is no more, and her prophets find no vision from the LORD" (Lam. 2:9). The prophecies of Jeremiah had also come to an end.

Were the prophecies of Ezekiel and Jeremiah unknown?

Jeremiah had written his prophecies in a book and published them, hadn't he? (Jer. 36). He had proclaimed that after seventy years Babylon's domination would end, hadn't he? (cf. Jer. 15:11–12; 27:7; 29:10; Dan. 9:2; 2 Chr. 36:21). Indeed, but another part of the judgment of their age was that God's people heard such prophets but did not understand them (Isa. 6:10). The prophecy had occasioned a blinding and hardening among many, so that Asaph was rendering the idea of the masses when he wrote, "There is none among us who knows how long." Even though Jeremiah's disciples knew well enough, how few of them were there?

The situation of the church in Judah was indeed pathetic: Asaph no longer saw any prophecy or "signs." Many think this refers to the "signs" of Yahweh's gracious presence among Israel: his temple, his altars, his Sabbath, his priests and prophets. If we translate it as "we see no signs before us," then we see this as referring to miraculous signs from Yahweh. In that case, the psalmist is lamenting not only about the lack of prophecy, but also about the painful absence of (miraculous) signs of Yahweh's redemptive intervention, which Israel had been permitted to enjoy so often in former times of distress. This explanation fits well with verse 11: "Why do you hold back your hand, your right hand?"

People note that nowadays the Bible is the most widely printed book in the world, but is God's Word understood? Having the Bible is something different from understanding the Bible. And are people in the church speaking and living close to the Word? Or are people everywhere "casting off restraint" because there is no longer any prophecy? (cf. Prov. 29:18).

Verse 10:
How long, O God, is the foe to scoff?
   Is the enemy to revile your name forever?

The poet must have known how sensitive Yahweh was

about his name. Now there was no longer any righteousness among Israel that he could use to move Yahweh to intervene, so the psalmist takes refuge in the ultimate basis for pleading, something that was at the same time one of the strongest weapons in the arsenal of prayer: "But your name, Lord Yahweh?" In Scripture, this term refers to God's fame, the reputation that Yahweh had built throughout the centuries by means of his great deeds of grace and judgment. God's name is God's power and the fame accruing to that power, his great deeds and the rumor of them among the nations, the remembrance of him (the way people talk about him).

Remember that the psalmist is still focusing on God and oriented toward God. Should people in Babylon be saying, "Oh, the famous God of Israel is not what he used to be. He can't stand up against our god, Marduk!" What a reproach that would be to Yahweh's glorious name! How long must that go on?

Here we have the crowning argument if you're going to plead for "Zion"!

Daniel also prayed in this same manner:

> Now therefore, O our God, listen to the prayer of your servant and to his pleas for mercy, and *for your own sake*, O Lord, make your face to shine upon your sanctuary, which is desolate. O my God, incline your ear and hear. Open your eyes and see our desolations, and the city that is called *by your name*. For we do not present our pleas before you because of our righteousness, but because of your great mercy. (Dan. 9:17–18)

This argument was what succeeded in moving Yahweh to "rise up" for his people and deliver them from the Babylonian captivity. Ezekiel, however, had to remind Israel emphatically:

> It is not for your sake, O house of Israel, that I am about to act, but for the sake of my holy name, which

you have profaned among the nations to which you came. And I will vindicate the holiness of my great name, which has been profaned among the nations, and which you have profaned among them. And the nations will know that I am the LORD, declares the Lord GOD, when through you I vindicate my holiness before their eyes. (Ezek. 36:22–23)

That is also how Yahweh heard and listened to Psalm 74:10.

Verse 11:
Why do you hold back your hand, your right hand?
    Take it from the fold of your garment and destroy them!

It was with that right hand that God had formerly done such "mighty saving deeds" (cf. Ps. 20:6). With that hand he had led Israel out of Egypt into Canaan and there provided her with many victories (Pss. 44:3; 60:5; 78:54; 80:15). People in Israel had sung so often, "The right hand of the LORD exalts, the right hand of the LORD does valiantly!" (Ps. 118:16). Why is that right hand no longer active? That was why those tragic catastrophes could have happened in Judah. This explains the psalmist's petition: "Take it from the fold of your garment and destroy them [those who blaspheme your name]!"

This petition probably sounds more stately in our ears than the poet really intended. You need to realize that when it came to clothing in the ancient Near East, what was worn above the belt or waist area—called "the fold of your garment" here—performed the same service as our pants pockets. Unemployed men today stand, looking around, with their hands in their pants pockets; Israelite men did the same thing, but with their hands in the folds of their garments. In modern language, the psalmist intended something like this: "Lord, don't stand idly by looking around with your hands in your pockets; do something and destroy those taunting enemies!"

We too have every reason to make this lament. "Lord God, if things keep going this way, nothing will be left of your work among the great evangelized nations of the West. Do not withdraw your Word and Spirit from us!"

What confident language that Asaphite dared to use toward the LORD. But he was not the only one to do so. Moses dared to ask the Almighty, "O Lord, why have you done evil to this people?" (Exod. 5:22). We read in Isaiah 63 similarly bold language: "Look down from heaven and see, from your holy and beautiful habitation. Where are your zeal and your might? The stirring of your inner parts and your compassion are held back from me. . . . O LORD, why do you make us wander from your ways and harden our heart, so that we fear you not?" (Isa. 63:15, 17). The composer of Psalm 83 dared to tell Yahweh, "Do not keep silence!" (v. 1). The composer of Psalm 10, "Why, O LORD, do you stand far away? Why do you hide yourself in times of trouble?" (v. 1). Psalm 13, "How long, O LORD? Will you forget me forever? How long will you hide your face from me?" (v. 1). Psalm 44, "You have sold your people for a trifle. . . . Awake! Why are you sleeping, O Lord? Rouse yourself! Do not reject us forever! Why do you hide your face? Why do you forget our affliction and oppression?" (vv. 12, 23–24).

According to traditional religious standards, those words are not bold and confident language but impertinent and insolent talk toward God. But God saw to it that his Word included the confident expression of Psalm 74, "Take your hand from the fold of your garment [your pocket]," and he included this expression so that we would follow its example.

Verses 12–17: Recalling the Historical Background of the Covenant Relationship

The Asaphite who composed Psalm 74 was a genuine kindred spirit of the composers of the Lamentations. In part 1 of his psalm (vv. 1–11), we heard the tone of Lamentations 2: "My eyes are spent with weeping; my stomach churns; my bile is poured out to the ground because of the destruction of the daughter of my people. . . . Look, O LORD, and see! With whom have you dealt thus?" (vv. 11, 20). But he will beseech Yahweh to rise up for his people for the sake of his own name (Ps. 74:22). That will be part 3 of the psalm (vv. 18–23). However, before he lifts up his petition, in part 2 he sets forth the basis for his plea. In this middle portion his thoughts return to the days "of old" (cf. v. 2) and to the miracles that Yahweh did for Israel. Since then, has his arm shortened? This is how he comforts himself with God's almighty power in the face of his own impotence.

At the same time this second section constitutes a courageous confession!

From Jeremiah 44 we know that after the catastrophe of 586 BC, many contemporaries of the psalmist had complained that they should not have stopped sacrificing to the queen of heaven! "For then we had plenty of food, and prospered, and saw no disaster. But since we left off making offerings to the queen of heaven and pouring out drink offerings to her, we have lacked everything and have been consumed by the sword and by famine" (cf. Jer. 44:15–19). These people of Judah had not humbled themselves before God even after the destruction of Jerusalem (Jer. 44:10). Against that arrogant spirit of rebellion (cf. Jer. 40:7–43:7), our Asaphite confessed in Psalm 74, "Yet God is my King from of old!" Read against the background of Jeremiah 40–44, this middle section of Psalm 74 is using confessional language, in direct opposition to the spirit of the age. No wonder someone has written that if this psalm had no superscription, and if the name of its composer had not been mentioned, we would have ascribed this song to none other than Jeremiah. In fact, Asaph is contending here against the same spirit in the church of his day as Jeremiah and Ezekiel had fulminated against for their entire ministry.

Verse 12:
Yet God my King is from of old,
   working salvation in the midst of the earth.

This verse has something of a topical ring that echoes the middle section of the psalm. Did some people in Judah want to resume sacrificing to "the queen of heaven" (Jer. 44)? Were others completely disheartened as they stared themselves blind at the power of Nebuchadnezzar, who had destroyed Jerusalem and deported the people of Judah? Were others still relying on the pharaoh of Egypt (Jer. 41:16–43:13; 44:26–30)? Our psalmist confesses *God* as "my King." We should not read this as a strictly personal expression. The poet was functioning here as the mouthpiece of the entire believing remnant in Judah, people who still acknowledged Yahweh as Israel's suzerain, and he was speaking of "*my* King" as the spokesperson for all these brothers and sisters.

We encounter this line of speaking in Lamentations 1 as well, which was written at roughly the same time as Psalm 74. This poet identifies himself with Jerusalem down through the centuries, speaking in the name of that city as a historical entity and using the first-person singular (cf. Lam. 1:12–22). In the following chapter we will return to discuss this manner of speaking, whereby an individual becomes a mouthpiece for an entire people, in connection with the petition of Psalm 79:8: "Do not remember against us our former iniquities."

What then does this psalmist confess about Israel's suzerain, in contrast with the human "great kings" of his day, like Nebuchadnezzar and the pharaohs? First, that Yahweh has been Israel's suzerain for such a long time; second, that he had already accomplished so much that was salutary. He is holding this before God! The poet is now laying the basis for his plea in verses 18–23. You can sense his unexpressed thought: Will Yahweh now be willing to intervene to liberate us?

Just as in verse 2, the psalmist's thoughts return to the days "of old" (*qedem*), the "prehistory" after which Yahweh created Israel as a nation (v. 2) and, by establishing the Horeb covenant, declared himself to be Israel's suzerain and Israel to be his vassal (see the commentary on Exod. 19–24). Israel had often sung about this event of Yahweh becoming king (Deut. 33:2; Judg. 5:4–5; Ps. 68:7–8; Hab. 3:3). There at Horeb, however, Yahweh not only sanctified and set apart Israel to be his kingdom, he also placed Israel under his royal protection (Exod. 19:5–6). Like a real suzerain, similar to the custom of human suzerains, Yahweh had taken upon himself as a covenant obligation the protection of his vassal Israel: "The LORD will cause your enemies who rise against you to be defeated before you" (Deut. 28:7). As long as Israel remained faithful, Yahweh was obligated to help her on account of his promise. In an emergency, political vassals could send emissaries to their suzerain. By means of praying and pleading, Israel had to remind Yahweh of his promise to help. Psalm 44 is a fine example of faithful Israel making an appeal, in the midst of a crisis situation, to Yahweh's obligation of protection as Israel's suzerain.

But in the time of Psalm 74, Israel was living in captivity precisely because of her unfaithfulness. Was the psalmist simply throwing up a random plea to Yahweh? Or is his psalm an example of hoping for God's return, concerning which Yahweh had spoken through Moses (Lev. 26:40–42)? Even if Yahweh had to visit Israel's unrighteousness with the most extreme kind of punishment, namely, captivity, he promised never to allow the people to disappear altogether from the earth. If a remnant would repent and humble themselves, then Yahweh would remember his covenant with Abraham: "Then I will remember my covenant with Jacob, and I will remember my covenant with Isaac and my covenant with Abraham, and I will remember the land" (Lev. 26:40–42). Notice the reverse historical order: from the end (Jacob) back to the beginning (Abraham). For this reason we talked in our Leviticus commentary about God's "way back," namely, the way from his punishing of them on account of their breaking the

Horeb covenant to his remembering of the underlying Abrahamic covenant.

So then, there was a remnant who repented and humbled themselves, wasn't there? Our psalm is proof of that. Besides this Asaphite there were more people "mourning in Zion." Recall such humble believers as the composers of the Lamentations, or Jeremiah, Baruch, Gedaliah, Daniel and his friends, Ezekiel, the authors of Psalms 79 and 102. Yahweh would be able to travel his way back, after all (Lev. 26:40–42)!

Notice how covenantally our Asaphite poet clothes his appeal to Israel's great king. In verse 2 he expressed a brief recollection of the historical connection. By establishing this covenant, God had become Israel's suzerain. Why then hadn't he demonstrated this toward the Babylonian attackers? Formerly he had rescued so brilliantly. In verse 20 the psalmist calls out to the suzerain: "Have regard for the covenant!"

The psalmist is going to embroider upon this theme of verse 12 in verses 13–17. The examples of Yahweh's liberating power that he provides in these verses occurred in the days "of old" (*qedem*; cf. v. 2), beginning with the liberation out of Egypt, followed by the miracles during the trek through the wilderness. How powerfully Yahweh had rescued his vassal Israel as her suzerain during these times, so that forty years later people were still talking about it in Jericho at Rahab's inn (Josh. 2:10–11). Yahweh was responsible for creating world news: he had set his people free "in the midst of the earth."

The poet is now going to hold before Yahweh these ancient deeds of power.

> Verses 13–14:
> **You divided the sea by your might;**
> > **you broke the heads of the sea monsters on the waters.**
> **You crushed the heads of Leviathan;**
> > **you gave him as food for the creatures of the wilderness.**

6. Psalm 74: Weeping for God's Church

Here the psalmist is speaking poetically about Israel's trek through the Red Sea. He adorns his language by bringing on stage a couple of monsters from the Semitic stories of the gods. According to these myths, when the world came into existence—these pagans no longer acknowledged a divine work of creation—the gods had to wage a fierce contest with precosmic water monsters: powerful serpents and multiple-headed dragons. They were known as Leviathan, Rahab, and Tannin. We recognize in these narratives a few mutilated remnants of truth, fragments of the revelation concerning God's work on the third day, of separating the seas and the land.

These legendary monsters are mentioned, however, in various passages of Scripture: Job 3:8; 9:13; 26:12; 40:15-20; Psalms 74:14; 87:4; 89:10; 104:26; Isaiah 27:1; 30:7; and 51:9. Of course the authors of these Scripture passages put no credence in the existence of these monsters. They used them merely for poetic decoration, empty containers that had lost their original pagan content. Our language has many examples of this as well, doesn't it? When we speak of a "gigantic" effort or a "titanic" struggle, we aren't confessing our faith in the Giants and the Titans, figures in Greek mythology, are we? Who would think that with the word "chaos" people are referring to a primordial flood in enmity against God, and who still believes in Mars, the god of war, when he mentions the month of March? In the same way, the Israelite poets use the names Rahab and Leviathan as poetic ornaments to sing the glory of Yahweh.

They did that in their own unencumbered way.

Of course, they occasionally bring up these names when they are talking about Yahweh's work of creation (Job 9:13; 26:12). But more often these names surface when the context speaks of certain world powers. In Isaiah 27:1 the "Big Three" of that time are compared to the legendary monsters mentioned. "In that day the LORD with his hard and great and strong sword will punish Leviathan the fleeing serpent [Assyria, lying alongside the racing Tigris], Leviathan the twisting serpent [Babylon, lying around the winding Euphrates], and he will slay the dragon that is in the sea [Egypt]" (cf. v. 13a; Ezek. 29:3–5; 32:2). *Tannin* is the Hebrew word for dragon, and *Leviathan* means "crocodile." Perhaps people called Egypt *Tannin* because in ancient times the Nile was full of crocodiles. This "sacred" animal, with its breathtaking appearance, its voraciousness, and its fearlessness, captured the imagination of the ancient Easterner (cf. Job 41). The animal could reach eighteen feet in length, and its colossal mouth contained no fewer than seventy teeth. Throughout the course of many centuries, imperialist Egypt had behaved in the same way toward the nations in Canaan: like a real *Tannin*, a predatory monster. Other Scripture passages portray Egypt as *Rahab* (Ps. 87:4; Isa. 30:7; 51:9). So just as we still speak of the German eagle and the Dutch lion and the Russian bear, in the world of the Bible people spoke about the Babylonian crocodile (Leviathan) and the Egyptian dragon (Tannin). Although, as we learned from Isaiah 27:1, the usage was not always consistent. People could refer to the Assyrian Leviathan as well as the Babylonian Leviathan. We ourselves are familiar with the American eagle as well as the German eagle. The book of Daniel also compares world powers with "beasts" (Dan. 7; cf. Rev. 13).

The psalmist is praying for Judah in an absolutely hopeless situation. It had been overrun by the Babylonian Leviathan (Isa. 27:1). Jeremiah lamented during the same time when the Asaphite sang Psalm 74: "Nebuchadnezzar the king of Babylon has devoured me; he has crushed me; he has made me an empty vessel; he has swallowed me like a monster [*Tannin*, the same word used in Ps. 74:13b]; he has filled his stomach with my delicacies; he has rinsed me out" (Jer. 51:34). Judah's fate appeared to have been sealed permanently.

In this desperate situation the poet sought to use a corresponding distress in Israel's past in order to move Yahweh to a corresponding rescue. In this context, only one fact became the focus: the liberation out of the fatal choke hold of the Egyptian Tannin or Leviathan that had tried to slay Israel. How forcefully Yahweh had crushed these Egyptian dragon heads for Israel when he parted the Red Sea for his people! But when Pharaoh and his army were crossing the dried-up seabed, Yahweh pulverized the heads of that monster and crushed that Leviathan. Vultures, jackals, and dogs had a feast of Pharaoh and his people, together with the corpses of the Egyptian soldiers that washed up, and they cleaned them to the bone. On the beaches of the Red Sea it would have been just like it was later with Jezebel, of whom "they found no more of her than the skull and the feet and the palms of her hands" (2 Kgs. 9:35). In this way Yahweh showed his supreme power over the Egyptian Leviathan at that time. If only he were willing to do the same thing now against the murderous Babylonian Leviathan! "Why do you hold back your hand" (v. 11)?

Verse 15:
You split open springs and brooks;
   you dried up ever-flowing streams.

In the wilderness as well, Yahweh delivered Israel from many a distressing situation. When Israel feared dying from thirst, God made water come forth from the rock (Exod. 17:5–6; cf. Num. 20:11; Ps. 78:15–16; 105:41; Isa. 48:21). When the "ever-flowing streams" of the Jordan River looked like they would obstruct Israel's entrance into Canaan, Yahweh made the river dry up for a short time (v. 15). Naturally, for the Creator of sun and moon, summer and winter, day and night, these feats represented no difficulty whatsoever. What would be too miraculous for the One who had determined the measure and the boundary of the earth?

Verses 16–17:
Yours is the day, yours also the night;
   you have established the heavenly lights and the sun.

> You have fixed all the boundaries of the earth;
> you have made summer and winter.

Was the poet thinking here of the deliverance that God had given to Joshua (Josh. 3)? If necessary, God can even "make the sun stop" in order to save his people (Josh. 10). The Asaphite knew that Yahweh was still just as powerful. He *can* save us from the choke hold of the Babylonian Leviathan, for he is after all the Creator of the ends of the earth (cf. Isa. 40:12–31).

With great emphasis the psalmist is directing himself toward Yahweh in this second section of his psalm. Seven times he uses the pronoun *you*. "You, Suzerain of Israel, you are the one who . . ." The emphasis lies not on the miraculous deeds but on "you." The greatest miracle was not the miraculous deeds that the psalmist was recounting but the miraculous compassion and favor of Israel's King.

Pleading the prologue of God's work

This middle section of Psalm 74 contains a didactic poem as well.

From it, we can learn how to pray for all the needs of Christendom. One of the primary lessons of the psalm comes from part 2 (vv. 12–17): an appeal to God's historic deeds of deliverance in particular, especially the foundational deeds. In the old covenant those were "the days of old": the calling of Abraham, the liberation out of Egypt, and the event at Horeb along with everything that accompanied that. Now in the new covenant, the foundational deeds are the death of our Lord Jesus Christ and his exaltation to God's right hand, together with pagan nations being called to the light of the gospel (Eph. 5:8; 1 Pet. 2:9–10). Earnestly appeal to God with the following words: "Remember this, O LORD!" (Ps. 74:18).

Perhaps today, behind all the destructions that have occurred in the arena of God's covenant, we can see more clearly than was possible under the old covenant that Satan has been busily at work (Eph. 6:11–12). Remarkable, isn't it, that in Revelation 12 he is portrayed as "a great red dragon, with seven heads and ten horns" (Rev. 12:3)? He stood before the Israelite church when she had to bring forth the infant Jesus (v. 4). In Revelation 13 John sees the anti-Christian violence in the world, together with the false doctrines that destroy the church, appearing in the form of beasts, monsters with multiple heads, new Leviathans and Tannins.

With an eye on these satanic monsters, the apostle Paul urged the Ephesians: "praying at all times in the Spirit, with all prayer and supplication . . ." (Eph. 6:18; cf. v. 12). Psalm 74 can teach us how the church of Christ may appeal to her great king that he honor his covenantal obligation of protection: "You are the one who . . ." Remind him especially and primarily of the foundational history undergirding the covenant relationship.

Verses 18–23: Pleading to the Suzerain Yahweh for His Intervention

A brief review

In part 1 (vv. 1–11) the psalmist painted for us the curse of God's covenant, as Israel's suzerain had executed that in those days upon his disloyal vassal, Judah.

In part 2 (vv. 12–17) he reminded Yahweh of the historical prologue, the prehistory of the covenant relationship between Yahweh and Israel. At the same time he directed Yahweh's attention to how magnificently he had fulfilled his suzerain obligation of protection toward his vassal, Israel.

In part 3 (vv. 18–23) we will read his actual plea. Supported by the historical prologue of the covenant relationship, the disloyal vassal, Judah, who was being punished, was beseeching Yahweh through the mouth of the Asaphite for his suzerain intervention, especially for the sake of his own name.

Verse 18:
Remember this, O LORD**, how the enemy scoffs,**
   and a foolish people reviles your name.

We must understand the phrase "your name" to also refer to Yahweh's fame, his *reputation*, the renown that had gone forth from him before the church and the world. The destruction of city and temple and the deportation of Judah to Babylon were surely events that occasioned the taunting of Yahweh, events that brought reproach to his name. The pagans were thinking that he was unable to protect his city and temple against the Babylonians and their gods. Moreover, his name was being despised by "a foolish people." To whom is this referring?

Proceeding on the basis of the Hebrew parallelism in verse 18, one could expect a synonymous expression for "the enemy," perhaps the Babylonians. But Moses once called Israel a "foolish and senseless people" (Deut. 32:6). In the time of the Asaphite, Jeremiah had stated, "They are stupid children; they have no understanding" (Jer. 4:22; cf. 5:21). Rather than accepting Yahweh's ultimatum through Jeremiah, the majority of the people of Judah had refused to humble themselves before Yahweh to the end. Even in Babylon, Ezekiel still had to summon people to contrition. Could our psalmist have been thinking here of the foolish way many of his countrymen continued to despise Yahweh even after the catastrophe of 586 BC? If so, then as a real intercessor, he was interceding for his shameless brotherhood by reminding Yahweh about his name.

In the midst of modern Christianity as well, such a "foolish people" is living in such a way that they haughtily despise the name of God (or the fame of God's great deeds through Jesus Christ) and build their hope on the gods of this age, all of them just like the classic idols invented by human brains. Aren't these people then *enemies* who are mocking the name of our God in our day? Although the things done by God's

6. Psalm 74: Weeping for God's Church

loyal people may have led the LORD's enemies to blaspheme (cf. 2 Sam. 12:14), nevertheless, as these people look upon the dishonoring of God's name, they may with Asaph appeal to him: "Remember this, O LORD, how the enemy scoffs!"

> Verse 19:
> **Do not deliver the soul of your dove to the wild beasts;
> do not forget the life of your poor forever.**

Do you know of any animal more defenseless than a dove? Do you know of any clearer contrast than that between a predator and a turtledove? Asaph thought that, as a wild animal seizes a turtledove in its claws, Babylon had slain Judah. How could Yahweh even look at that? Had Yahweh forgotten his "poor ones"? Such a "worm" like Jacob, such a people like Israel! (Isa. 41:14). The Psalter uses the phrase "poor ones" to refer most often to the poor or the weak or the contrite of spirit—people like the poet himself, who bowed under Yahweh's smiting hand and acknowledged his right to discipline, brothers like Jeremiah and his followers, the poets who composed the Lamentations, Daniel and his friends, Ezekiel and his group. Would Yahweh forget those people forever?

> Verse 20:
> **Have regard for the covenant,
> for the dark places of the land are full of the habitations of violence.**

An appeal to God's faithfulness to his covenant has always been one of the most powerful means to move God's fatherly heart. Show him that he is the God of the oath and of the covenant for his people.

But God's covenant lay trampled underfoot, didn't it? By her unfaithfulness, Israel had violated the covenant and for that reason, like an insulted suzerain, Yahweh had visited his covenant wrath upon Israel, hadn't he? Indeed, but Asaph and his cohorts humbled themselves under God's smiting hand, and Yahweh had promised that he would remember his faithful remnant in the land of their captivity, hadn't he? (Lev. 26:40–42; see our discussion of Ps. 74:12). Hadn't Solomon prayed in advance, in connection with the dedication of the temple, concerning a situation like this one in Psalm 74 (1 Kgs. 8:46–51)? The covenant of which the psalmist is here reminding Yahweh must have been the covenant with Abraham, a covenant Yahweh had promised to remember even if Israel were to break the Horeb covenant (Lev. 26:40–42).

Meanwhile, our Asaphite was not the only one who sought the face of Yahweh during the years when the temple lay destroyed and Judah lived in captivity. Daniel, Ezra, Nehemiah, and the composer of Psalms 79 and 106 prayed for the restoration of the church (Ezra 9; Neh. 9; Dan. 9). It is striking that in their prayers of confession for the sake of covenant renewal, these intercessors all cited the historical prologue of the covenant relationship, the prehistory of Yahweh's benefits. This prehistory played a role not only with the establishment of a covenant or with the accusation of a disloyal covenant partner, but also with making intercession for restoration of the covenant that had been violated.

If in our day you want to make intercession for all the needs of Christendom, take a lesson from this didactic poem of Asaph, and remind our God and Father especially of his covenant, no longer established through the blood of animals, as in the time of Psalm 74, but through the blood of God's Son himself.

What a basis for pleading we have—that new covenant!

In this verse the psalmist is also rehearsing his distress about the caves in which murder was committed in his day. We probably will not be guilty of impermissible spiritualizing if we interpret this verse as referring to "the dark places" where souls are murdered in our day. In the temples of God-denying science, immature faith is destroyed. Powerful political idols

6. Psalm 74: Weeping for God's Church

draw many away from the true God. Ecumenism darkens many eyes to the cleft between truth and falsehood and between the righteous and the wicked. A modern "Maccabean" spirit of resistance closes the eyes of many to God's hand of discipline upon both church and world. Just as it did at the end of the Middle Ages when the covenant was forsaken—study the paintings of Hieronymous Bosch—doubt has become pervasive: Does God exist? Many children of Christianity sense that every anchor is slipping away, and they experience despair as the dominant factor in their lives.

In this situation, let us not pray irrationally, unhistorically, for a "revival" (from what, and to what?), but let us plead on the basis of God's covenant and hold before his eyes the historical prologue of his covenant with prior Christian nations, the prehistory of his benefits that he showered upon our ancestors!

Verse 21:
**Let not the downtrodden turn back in shame;
let the poor and needy praise your name.**

By now, the godly had hung their harps on the willows in Babylon, and they wept as they thought of Zion in ruins. They could not sing psalms there. "How shall we sing Yahweh's song?" (Ps. 137). In Jerusalem itself, where otherwise the psalms rang out, foxes were wandering across the desolate Mount Zion (Lam. 5:18).

Give us something to praise you for once again!

Verse 22:
**Arise, O God, defend your cause;
remember how the foolish scoff at you all the day!**

Didn't God have a dispute with those arrogant temple destroyers, who were now mocking God as being inferior to their idols? Was Yahweh remembering that reproach clearly?

Why then was he not standing up for his own name?

What reproach is heaped on our God and Father in our world, day after day, from the ranks of apostate Christianity! In spoken or written language, his name or fame is trampled underfoot abominably. Do we ever pray, "Remember that reproach"? God is more powerful than all the modern spirits put together, isn't he? He is the Holy Spirit, who can grant a return to God and his covenant, isn't he? If only he would stand up in our day as he did in the sixteenth century, when he showed so many new glimpses of his favor among us.

Verse 23:
**Do not forget the clamor of your foes,
   the uproar of those who rise against you, which goes
      up continually!**

This is how the miserable and poor believers like Asaph, Jeremiah, the composers of the Lamentations, and Daniel pleaded for divine compassion with respect to the need of the church of Judah: for the sake of God's name and on the basis of God's covenant. And God has decided to answer that appeal to his name, this prayer. As we observed in connection with verse 10, however, Ezekiel had to proclaim emphatically that Yahweh intervened not for the sake of Israel but "for the sake of my holy name" (Ezek. 36:22). At that point Yahweh stood up, and at that point he conducted his judicial dispute, and at that point he avenged the reproach done by his enemies. And at that point the people of Judah who returned praised God's name: "Then they said among the nations, 'The Lord has done great things for them!'" (Ps. 126:2).

In the Netherlands he did great things through the Réveil in the nineteenth century, things that brought many thousands of people from their refined humanistic religion to God's covenant and words. At the beginning of these movements of return, the godly were thinking of Psalm 74 as well.

May the Spirit of these petitions awaken in the church of

our day many prayers like Psalm 74: intercessory prayers for covenant renewal, which is something different than a religious "revival." In today's contest of spirits, let us call upon God for help in the manner of the Asaphite, and remind our Father of his name! "Lord God, listen to the foul cursing against you and your Word that arises from the midst of a foolish people." Can people endlessly bring shame upon God and his truth?

Who knows but that God may one day grant us to return.

For "this is the one to whom I will look: he who is humble and contrite in spirit and trembles at my word" (Isa. 66:2). He demonstrated that by answering Psalm 74 in the return from the Babylonian captivity.

The Contrite Spirit of Psalm 74 Contrasted with the Arrogant Spirit of Resistance of the Maccabees

We have been reading Psalm 74 against the background of the destruction of the temple by the Babylonians in 586 BC. But critical commentaries, especially the older ones, place the origin of this psalm in the time of the Maccabees. Granted, people in these circles believe less and less that the psalms originated during the Maccabean period, especially for reasons deriving from the study of antiquities. To us, however, this dating of the psalm is obstructed especially by the deep difference between the humble spirit from which the Asaphite is speaking and the arrogant "resistance spirit" from which the Maccabees lived. We believe it is dangerous to take Psalms 74 and 79 upon our lips with a Maccabean mentality.

Psalm 74 is thoroughly *anti*-Maccabean!

The Maccabees

In the beginning of the second century BC, the Syrian king Antiochus IV Ephiphanes ruled over Palestine. This ruler wanted to destroy the Jewish people entirely by imposing

Hellenistic culture upon them. In December 168 BC, he desecrated the temple. He had a pig, which for Israel was an unclean animal (Lev. 11:4, 7; Deut. 14:8), sacrificed on a small Greek altar to the Greek god Zeus. He imposed the death penalty for observing both the Sabbath and the command regarding circumcision. Everywhere in Jewish territory, pagan altars were built and sacrifices to pagan gods were required.

Against all of this there arose a revolt among the Jews, especially due to agitation by the priest Mattathias, the father of the famous Judas Maccabeus. In the apocryphal books of the Maccabees you can read about the struggle that the Maccabean family waged to obtain Jewish religious freedom and political independence.

We are not denying that Psalm 74 could have been an instructive and comforting psalm for some believers during that time, but the claim that it was a characteristic product of the time and spirit of the Maccabees is something we want to oppose with vigor, because the spirit of Psalm 74 is squarely opposed to that of the books of the Maccabees.

We draw your attention to the following points of difference.

"God is with us!"

First, we have read how Asaph spoke of Yahweh in Psalm 74 as an angry God who looked idly on, "with his hand in his bosom," as his own house lay in ruins, apparently deaf to the reproach that people were bringing on his name. The psalmist pleaded with Yahweh to intervene and not to remain aloof. The writer of the books of the Maccabees and his heroes proceed, however, from the axiom that of course God can never forsake the Jews. For them this is a kind of absolute saving promise. The notion that God can look idly on as the pagans overrun his people and his dwelling apparently never occurred to them. "Therefore he never withdraws his mercy from us. Although he disciplines us with calamities, he does not forsake his own people" (2 Macc. 6:16, NRSV). Did you hear that? He does not forsake his own people! The writer is saying that people need to remember that the punishments he is narrating in his work "were designed not to destroy but to discipline our people" (2 Macc. 6:12).

In this respect, the Maccabees had their predecessors in Israel (cf. Num. 14:39–45; 1 Sam. 4). The composer of Psalm 74 saw clearly that in his day God was in fact not *with* but *against* his people. The Maccabees, however, thought they could lift up Psalm 46 in every time and situation: God is with us! In 2 Maccabees 15 we read the following about the famous Judas: "But Maccabeus did not cease to trust with all confidence that he would get help from the Lord. He exhorted his troops not to fear the attack of the Gentiles, but to keep in mind the former times when help had come to them from heaven, and *so to look for the victory that the Almighty would give them*" (2 Macc. 15:7–8; cf. 1 Macc. 4:30; 2 Macc. 15:7–10). But Hophni and Phinehas (1 Sam. 4); Zedekiah, the son of Chenaanah (1 Kgs. 22:24); Pashur, the son of Immer (Jer. 20); the prophet Hananiah (Jer. 28); Ahab; and Zedekiah (Jer. 29) all had lived from this same arrogant spirit or attitude. "In all circumstances, God is with us!" For these Israelites this was a truth for all time and from which we may proceed in "faith" in all circumstances. After all, God really couldn't abandon his people, could he? That was simply inconceivable! Who said so? The false prophets mentioned above, with their timeless paradigm: "Once God's people, always God's people! Once in God's favor, always in God's favor! Once God is among you, he will always be among you! Once you've enjoyed his goodness, you'll always enjoy his goodness!"

When we discussed Psalm 46 in the preceding volume, we saw how dangerous it is for God's people simply to claim the slogan "God is with us!" in all circumstances, so we can spot here the deep cleft between Psalm 74 and the books of the Maccabees. Here we have the essential contrast between living according to the Word that is always addressed within particular situations, versus living according to certain "truths" that are for all time. Conditional promises and threats (cf. Lev. 26:3, 14, "*If* you . . .") versus unconditional pledges of nothing but salvation. Paying attention to the deeds of Yahweh versus being blinded toward the work of his hands. Being humbled under his smiting hand versus being hardened under that hand. Humility versus pride. Contrition that occasionally fears that God is forgetting his entire church and is looking upon her with his hands in his pocket (Ps. 74:11) versus sovereign, autonomous religious individuals who stand pat for *their* church and swear by "the work of their own hands." Having an eye for God's judgments (Ps. 74:1–11) versus philosophical driveling about the benefit of adversities (2 Macc. 6:12; cf. the Stoics). Living with the living God, who blessed his people with the exodus from Egypt (Ps. 74:12–15) and punished them with the Babylonian captivity (Ps. 74:1–11), versus living with an image of a dead deity, an imaginary conception of God. But Yahweh can relate to his people as one who "turn[s] to be their enemy" (Isa. 63:10). The self-invented god of the harsh Zealot religion can never be angry toward his people, because he is always with his people. He is completely safe and innocuous for his worshipers, who then also never complain to him or plead with him in the way that Asaph did toward Yahweh in Psalm 74.

BLINDED TO THE CAUSE OF YAHWEH'S ANGER

Second, we are struck by the fact that the writer of Maccabees hardly seems to have an eye for the causes underlying the troubles the Jews were facing at that time. There is no clear and concrete reference to Israel's apostasy from Yahweh. Perhaps the author does speak here and there about God's wrath, but he does so in a way that is very passionless and unhistorical, as though Yahweh were a capricious God who, just like the pagan gods, suddenly erupts in rage for no apparent reason. There are formulations that do appear to go in a somewhat better direction (2 Macc. 5:17; 7:18), but these are set in the context of generic and unhistorical comments about "the sins." This causes a deep difference in attitude.

The Maccabees simply refuse to accept the fact that "our holy place, our beauty, and our glory have been laid waste" (1 Macc. 2:12). They refuse to bow down, but continue to stand firm. Psalm 74, by contrast, looks up, from human beings to Yahweh, who is bringing about Israel's adversity. "I will lay your cities waste and will make your sanctuaries desolate" (Lev. 26:31–39; cf. Deut. 28:49–68). "Asaph" was willing to bow down under that divine Word. In his day he watched this divinely threatened curse come to be fulfilled—a person needs to *be willing* to see that!—and according to his psalm, he appeared to be willing to bow down under that fulfilled curse.

THE MACHO ZEALOT FIGHTER AS THE FOCUS OF ATTENTION

Third, as we have seen, Psalm 74, no less than the books of Kings and Chronicles, devotes some attention to the heroic resistance King Zedekiah and his army offered during the eighteen-month siege by the Babylonians. Asaph, however, didn't focus on the lionlike soldier in Judah's army any more than the composers of the Lamentations had; instead, he focused on Yahweh, whose fury against his people was smoking hot. In this respect we find an entirely different atmosphere in the books of the Maccabees. It is striking how often in these books people talk about "*our* holy place" or "*the* holy place," and how seldom they talk, as Asaph did in Psalm 74, about "*your* holy place." Thus the Maccabees and their followers talk continually about "*our* religion," "*our* law," "*the* religion of our fathers," "*the* law" (as an independent entity), and as we saw in connection with the temple itself, "*our* pride," "*our* jewel" (cf. 1 Macc. 2:12; 3:43, 58).

It seems as though they regarded the kingdom of God as their own private business. They are "embittered" about the measures taken by the pagans, or "fly into a rage" about them (cf. 1 Macc. 2:44), or feel *they* have been wronged (1 Macc.

10:74). The Maccabees are constantly portrayed as the macho, principled defenders of "*our* religion" and "*our* law." *They* are the ones who stand tall for the law (cf. 1 Macc. 2:64). "*We* will not obey the king's words by turning aside from *our* religion to the right hand or to the left" (1 Macc. 2:22). "*They* gladly fought for Israel" (1 Macc. 3:2). "Let us restore the ruins of our people, and fight for our people and the sanctuary" (1 Macc. 3:43).

It is very noteworthy that the book of 1 Maccabees narrates the story almost as though it were a world chronicle. The Maccabees trusted entirely in their own powers. Prayers played no significant role; results were attributed not to miracles but to personal wisdom and energy.

The boasting of the Maccabees and their followers occurred within this harsh, zealot-like resistance posture, according to this apocryphal book. "His [Judas Maccabeus's] fame reached the king, and the Gentiles talked of the battles of Judas" (1 Macc. 3:26; cf. 5:63; 6:44; 9:10; 14:4–5; 16:23). The man Judas Maccabeus was called "the savior of Israel" (1 Macc. 9:21). His brother Simon did not take second place in this regard, given his saying "You yourselves know what great things my brothers and I and the house of my father have done for the laws and the sanctuary; you know also the wars and the difficulties that my brothers and I have seen" (1 Macc. 13:3). He had an imposing monument erected on the grave of his father and brothers (1 Macc. 13:27–30). Martyr stories played an important role as well (2 Macc. 6:18–7:42; 14:37–46).

This puts the books of the Maccabees more in line with what Scripture loathes so strongly—paying homage to great "Sauls"—in contrast to what Scripture prefers to see: the humble, believing attitude of contrition like David, who defended *Yahweh* and *his* divine rights by trusting not in military powers but in God. Such people boast not in their own fighting and standing up against someone but rather in the name of Yahweh.

6. Psalm 74: Weeping for God's Church

There is a big difference between the rage, the indignation, and the offense of the Maccabees, on the one hand, and the holy zeal for God's house with David, Hezekiah, Josiah, and Asaph, on the other hand. The former "stood up" for "our" holy place. The latter wept on account of God's sanctuary. In Psalm 74 Asaph prayed to Yahweh as Israel's suzerain and pleaded on the basis of his covenant; the Maccabees relied on treaties with the Romans, made and established with a certain degree of political shrewdness (1 Macc. 12:1).

Spiritual opposites

How could anyone ever explain Psalm 74 as being a product of the spirit of the Maccabees? Asaph and Daniel are the spiritual opposites of the boastful Maccabees! The godly of that time—just like those in our age—probably read Psalm 74 as a quiet polemic, a Scriptural didactic poem, against the fleshly, nationalistic spirit of resistance of the macho Maccabees, who refused to take it when in times of judgment God released enemies upon his people. The principled person stands up in vigorous protest against such unmitigated injustice, against the flagrant violation of the rights of religious people. The inflexible person fights against every violation people commit against "our" law and against "the religion of our fathers."

What a deep chasm there is between an Asaphite and a Maccabean!

CHAPTER 7

Psalm 79:8: Do Not Remember against Us the Iniquities of Former Generations

What do we have to do with the sins of our ancestors? Have you ever heard it said during a worship service, "Lord, do not reckon to us the self-directed piety of our medieval ancestors?" The modern churchgoer has no sense at all of being responsible for that piety. Who is afraid that God would punish children today for the religious and social injustice of former generations? Well, at least one person would be: the writer of Psalm 79, if he were alive today.

His psalm displays many similarities with Psalm 74. Both arise with the singing prophetic family of Asaph. Both lament the destruction of the temple by the Babylonians. Nevertheless, there are differences of accent. Whereas Psalm 74 brings up the destruction of the temple more extensively, Psalm 79 recalls more of the suffering of the population of Judah. As for the rest, the substantive agreement is so large that we may refer the reader to our discussion of Psalm 74 in the previous chapter. One petition is unique to Psalm 79, however, and we want to focus on that in this chapter: "Do not remember against us the iniquities of former generations" (v. 8a, ESV mg.).

These words tell us that in our day this Asaphite would certainly have felt intensely responsible for the ecclesiastical sins and the injustice of Christianity when it blossomed and dominated medieval society. For he prayed that Yahweh would not reckon to the generation living around 586 BC the sin of it ancestors. He not only felt that he was implicated in the guilt of his contemporaries, but he also took into account the accumulated wrath that previous generations in Israel had aroused.

We are afraid that many Christians do not share this concern of Asaph, despite the crisis of our time. First, they hardly sense their connectedness with former generations in the Christian church. Second, as a result of this ahistorical orientation, they are not at all afraid of God's accumulated wrath. Third, they read Scripture far too much through defective spectacles, fogged over by a perspective that is alien to Scripture, namely, individualism. This is why Psalm 79:8 remains an incomprehensible Scripture verse and a forgotten lesson in the school of prayer.

This reading impediment constitutes a hindrance for understanding not only Psalm 79, however, but also other prayers in Holy Scripture that similarly induce us to confess the sins of our fathers before the Lord, like Psalm 106, Ezra 9, Nehemiah 9, and Daniel 9. That is why we want to make an exploratory expedition through the Bible to see how God's Spirit never sees us apart from our ancestors, nor from our contemporaries, nor from our descendants. May this deepen our insight into our position before God as modern Christians, and lead us to imitate Asaph in self-conscious solidarity with our ancestors as we pray, "Do not remember against us the iniquities of former generations!"

7. Psalm 79:8: Do Not Remember against Us

God's People Is Not the Sum of Its Individuals But a Historical Body Encompassing Many Generations

The word *individual* belongs to the family of the Latin verb that means "divide" (cf. the word *division*, meaning a part of an army). An *in*-dividual is then the last and smallest, the unit of the human race that cannot be divided any further, comparable to what people in the natural sciences call an atom. Nowadays this word, which was originally a scholarly term, is used by everybody, and people talk about "individual this" and "individual that." Among the great multitude of faceless humanity, the view has taken root that such things really exist: the individual, the isolated person, the last indivisible and irreducible entity of the human race.

In many respects, modern Europeans and Americans think individualistically, taking the separate individual as their starting point. From youth onward these moderns possess a certain proficiency for construing the individual person separately from the contexts in which God has placed him. This individualistic way of thinking has played awful tricks on Western Christianity in the service of God. Anyone who sees humanity as a grand pile of dried, loose grains of sand easily falls into a religion of the ego, where the church especially serves to satisfy the religious needs of the individual. The ministry of the Word must be "personal," and the hymns sung most frequently place the pious individual with his personal experiences and desires at the center.

If, however, we wish to understand prayers like Psalm 79:8, Psalm 106, Ezra 9, Nehemiah 9, and Daniel 9, we'll have to thoroughly clean up the scientific fantasy of a so-called individual and the accompanying religion of the ego. God simply has not created people who are totally separated from their fellow human beings. Every person has a father and a mother—whether one is happy with them or not—and even an orphan has a family tree, even if no one can identify it. Through one's father and mother, every person is somehow firmly connected to the entire human race. Each one is thoroughly intertwined in the human race and, in many respects, determined by that intertwining. A person can have her father's eyes, the musicality of her mother, and the wandering nature of her grandfather.

This notion that every person is bound with innumerable bonds to one's fellow human beings has eroded significantly in our world. People feel the bond with their ancestors far less than the people in the Bible did. As a result of this individualistic orientation, many modern people live ahistorically. People say that some Arabs can still list their ancestors going back twelve generations, but who today knows the names of all of his eight great-grandparents, even though he may well have sat on his great-grandmother's lap! How many are interested nowadays in the history of their country, their city, and their race?

People in the Bible were much more aware that they were children of their parents and thereby members of the house of their father or grandfather. They were aware that this house in turn was part of the tribe and that this tribe was again part of an entire people or nation. So more than we do today, people in the past knew they were related to a larger human entity. This was equally true whether they looked back (ancestors) or looked around (contemporaries) or looked ahead (descendants).

We want to investigate this matter in Scripture.

The biblical notion of community

All Israelites belonged to the "offspring of Abraham" (John 8:33; Ps. 105:6). But most often in Scripture they are called "the children of Israel," simply "Israel," or occasionally "Jacob." Regular readers of the Bible are so accustomed to these phrases that they perhaps no longer realize that the patriarch Israel had the same name as his children. We usually think that the name Israel itself refers first of all to Father Israel's descendants. Scripture sees the bond between Father

Jacob and his descendants as being so close that it uses the same name to refer to both the man and his posterity. This is why the psalmist can complain, "They have devoured *Jacob*" (Ps. 79:7), when he has Jacob's *posterity* in view (cf. Ps. 24:6; Isa. 40:27). Jacob and Israel are the names of both persons and a people. In the Bible's understanding there is no sharp contrast here. On the contrary, this use of names points to an intimate historical unity.

We encounter this with the name of Jacob's sons too: Ephraim, Judah, and Joseph are also names not just of persons, but of tribes. The bond between the tribal head and the tribe is so close, however, that both receive the same name. In fact, Scripture views the Israelites so strongly as a unity that it sometimes describes the entire people as a wounded man (Isa. 1:5–7), or a woman, the daughter of Zion, a mourning widow (Lam. 1), an unfaithful wife (Ezek. 16), or a barren woman (Isa. 54).

The Israelites were so strongly aware of this unity that spanned the centuries that they would talk of themselves with the first-person singular pronoun. You would likely say, "We English speakers," but an Israelite spoke of his people as an "I." We will cite a few examples of this.

In Numbers 20:14–21 we read that Moses sent messengers to the king of Edom with this message:

> "Thus says *your brother* Israel: . . . Please let us pass through your land." . . . But Edom said to *him*, "You shall not pass through, lest *I* come out with the sword against you." And *the people of Israel* said to *him*, "*We* will go up by the highway, and if we drink of your water, *I* and *my* livestock, then *I* will pay for it. Let *me* only pass through on foot, nothing more." But *he* said, "You shall not pass through." And Edom came out against them with a large army and with a strong force. Thus *Edom* refused to give Israel passage through *his* territory, so Israel turned away from *him*.

Here we see a remarkable alternation between singular and plural!

In Psalm 44 we encounter the same alternation: "Through *you we* push down our foes. . . . For not in *my* bow do *I* trust, nor can *my* sword save *me*. But you have saved *us* from *our* foes and have put to shame those who hate *us*" (Ps. 44:5–7). We encounter the same manner of speaking in Psalm 65: "When iniquities prevail against *me*, you atone for *our* transgressions" (Ps. 65:3; cf. Exod. 17:3; Isa. 12). In Jeremiah 31:18–19 Ephraim, the kingdom of the ten tribes being led away, complains in the first-person singular, "You have disciplined *me*, and *I* was disciplined, like an untrained calf; bring *me* back that *I* may be restored, for you are the Lord *my* God." Yahweh then speaks about Ephraim as his "dear son" and "darling child," and also about "he" and "him."

In connection with these Scripture passages, one could speak of personification, but we are nonetheless dealing with more than a stylistic technique here. Such formulations show how thoroughly engrained the notion was within Israel that they constituted not the sum of pious individuals but a tight unity firmly bound together with each other by their common ancestry and especially by their common covenant with Yahweh. We'll return to that in a moment.

However, the Israelites did not merely understand themselves as a historical unity, the one Israel united through the centuries; rather, they were in turn also addressed this way by Yahweh. In Jeremiah 26:4–5 Yahweh threatens, "If you will not listen to me, to walk in my law that I have set before *you*, and to listen to the words of my servants the prophets whom I send to *you* urgently, though *you* have not listened . . ." Here Yahweh apparently has in mind all the prophets whom he has sent, from Joshua to Jeremiah. Yahweh says that he sent them "to *you*," but "*you*" did not listen. These people addressed as "you" must have been Jeremiah's audience with their ancestors. Jeremiah's contemporaries evidently could not separate themselves individualistically or distance themselves from their ancestors. This was in part because they were united in attitude, united in rejecting the prophets.

The Lord Jesus spoke to the Pharisees and scribes in the same way. These people were persecuting the Lord Jesus on account of the Word, demonstrating that they were united in spirit with their prophet-persecuting ancestors. Perhaps because of our individualistic way of thinking, we would separate fathers and sons from each other and say, "This is what the fathers did (and not the sons), and that is what the sons did." But the Savior directly addressed these sons of the prophet persecutors concerning "the blood of Zechariah the son of Barachiah, whom *you* [Pharisees and scribes, together with your ancestors] murdered between the sanctuary and the altar" (Matt. 23:35). Here as well, the shared attitude is decisive, but we will return to this later.

Perhaps we can see the close connection between ancestors and descendants in the broad use of the word *son* as well. In the Bible distant descendants are called one's "son." Read the genealogies, where sometimes entire generations are skipped, and grandchildren and great-grandchildren are called a person's "sons." Our Savior is called the "son of David."

Let's not dismiss this Israelite notion of community with the evolutionist argument that we are dealing here with typical remnants of a tribal notion that was overcome long ago, one that arose among nomadic peoples. It could well be that these ancient peoples comprehended better than modern people that God did not create individuals.

There is yet another factor, however, that makes it clear that the Israelites realized they were closely connected to each other. That factor is the history of Israel. True enough, being connected in historical events in general can forge unity among people, but Israel's historical connection was unique: the Almighty had chosen Israel as his own people, had established covenants with Israel, and had often saved Israel in glorious ways. Israel's history was thus really a history of redemption. Therefore Scripture speaks continuously about

Israel as a unity. The Israelites were closely connected to their ancestors and descendants by means of God's covenant, in blessing and curse, down through the centuries.

In the following section we will use various examples from Scripture to show how close a connection existed in Israel in terms of Yahweh's blessings. In the section after that, we will do the same thing in terms of Yahweh's curse in response to Israel's forsaking of the covenant. From this exploratory expedition through the Bible we will come full circle back to our starting point: "Do not remember against us the iniquities of former generations" (Ps. 79:8).

Solidarity in Terms of Blessing

God continually dealt with his people as a strong, tightly knit unity when he visited blessing or curse upon them. He sent those not to people as such—for he had not created such beings—but always as mutually related people, whether as members of a house, as citizens of a city, or as members of one nation.

You with your house and your city

When the great flood came, God rescued not the individual Noah but rather this righteous man together with his wife, his sons, and his sons' wives (Gen. 7:13). In the same way, he spared out of wicked Sodom not only the individual Lot but also his wife and daughters and, had they wished, also his sons-in-law (Gen. 19:12–16). This way of acting seems to have become self-evident in Israel. Thus the spies swore that they would preserve the life of not only Rahab personally but also "your father and your mother, your brothers, and all your father's household" (Josh. 2:12–20; cf. 6:25; Judg. 1:25). Nor did Yahweh deal individualistically with King Zedekiah. Jeremiah had to tell the king, "Thus says the LORD, the God of hosts, the God of Israel: If you will surrender to the officials of the king of Babylon, then your life shall be spared, and this city shall not be burned with fire, and you and your house shall live" (Jer. 38:17). Shortly thereafter, the Babylonian commander Nebuzaradan did not look at Jeremiah as a religious "individual," completely separate from the national catastrophe; he told the godly Jeremiah that this catastrophe had come "because you [plural] have sinned against Yahweh" (Jer. 40:3).

God's covenant with Abraham and his posterity

The powerful example, naturally, is the covenant that God established not only with the individual Abraham but with his entire family (Gen. 17:23). As sign and seal of that, Abraham had to be circumcised, as well as "every male among you . . . whether born in your house or bought with your money from any foreigner who is not of your offspring" (Gen. 17:10, 12). Circumcision had to be performed on the male reproductive organ—a poignant proof that God was not entering into his covenant only with Abraham personally: at the same time, he was including all who would be born along the route of procreation from his covenant partner Abraham and his slaves. Circumcision was not simply a seal of God's promises from his side, but also an oath of fidelity from man's side, a declaration of loyalty under oath that an Israelite father made on behalf of his son whom he was circumcising (Gen. 17:9–14). Yahweh threatened Moses with death when he failed to honor his oath of fidelity that had been pledged by his father Amram by failing to circumcise his son (Exod. 4:24–26). This language is different from that of modern individualistic Christians, who can occasionally be heard saying, "We will allow our children to decide freely!" As if children of baptized generations could ever be "free" before God!

This foundational blessing of a shared identity as a people, included together in covenant with God, forged Israel together into a unique unity, and one far greater and deeper than that of an ancient Eastern sense of tribal identity. After all, it is questionable whether it is correct to identify this as characteristic of a "primitive" nomadic culture. American children can come home elated after history class, exclaiming, "Mother, *we* won the Revolutionary War!" A child today can feel proudly connected to his eighteenth-century ancestors! Modern mothers will also meet such an exclamation with an approving smile in return.

Passover: God led us out of Egypt

People in Israel used this first-person plural form annually, when they celebrated the Passover meal to commemorate the deliverance from Egypt. When one of the children, who had not experienced this event with his own eyes and feet, asked his father, "What do you mean by this service?" then the Israelite father, who similarly had not experienced this event himself with his own eyes and feet, was supposed to reply, "It is the sacrifice of the LORD's Passover, for he passed over the houses of the people of Israel in Egypt, when he struck the Egyptians but spared *our* houses" (Exod. 12:24–27). Indeed, such a father who probably had never been in Egypt himself was supposed to tell his child, "It is because of what the LORD did for *me* when *I* came out of Egypt" (Exod. 13:8; cf. 13:14). He was even allowed to say, "*We* were Pharaoh's slaves in Egypt. And the LORD brought *us* out of Egypt with a mighty hand. And the LORD showed signs and wonders, great and grievous, against Egypt and against Pharaoh and all his household, before *our* eyes. And he brought *us* out from there, that he might bring *us* in and give *us* the land that he swore to give to *our* fathers" (Deut. 6:20–22; cf. 29:16; Amos 3:1–2).

God dried up the Jordan for you

Scripture speaks about the trek through the Jordan River in the same manner. According to individualistic thinking, the only people who experienced the trek were those who walked with their own feet across the dry riverbed. But Scripture sees

7. Psalm 79:8: Do Not Remember against Us

within this generation also subsequent generations walking across the Jordan riverbed. A person from each tribe had to take a stone from the dry riverbed, and with those twelve stones Joshua built a monument at Gilgal. If later a child were to ask his father, "What do these stones mean?" then the Israelite father was supposed to answer, "*Israel* passed over this Jordan on dry ground. For the LORD your God dried up the waters of the Jordan *for you* until *you* passed over, as the LORD your God did to the Red Sea, which he dried up *for us* until *we* passed over, so that all the peoples of the earth may know that the hand of the LORD is mighty, that you may fear the LORD your God forever" (Josh. 4:21–24).

Descendants blessed on account of their ancestors

Scripture also shows examples of families and persons on whom God's blessing rested because of their God-fearing ancestor. At great risk to his life, Jonathan chose the side of persecuted David (1 Sam. 19:1–3) and made David swear to him, "Do not cut off your steadfast love from my house" (1 Sam. 20:15, 17). After this, didn't that house often profit from their forefather Jonathan's loyalty to David? The crippled son of Jonathan, Mephibosheth, who was presumably not an impressive figure, "ate always at the king's table" (2 Sam. 4:4; 9:13). Rather than executing this man as a possible threat to the Davidic dynasty, David swore to him, "Do not fear, for I will show you kindness *for the sake of your father Jonathan*" (2 Sam. 9:7; cf. 16:5–13; 19:28). The list of the generations of Saul's house in 1 Chronicles 8:29–38 could never have been written apart from David's faithfulness to his oaths toward Saul and Jonathan. In the same way, Yahweh dealt with Hezekiah and protected Jerusalem "for my own sake and *for the sake of my servant David*" (2 Kgs. 19:34; cf. 8:19).

This was not something unique to the Old Testament, for after Zaccheus had been converted, the Lord Jesus told him, "Today salvation has come to this house" (Luke 19:8–9). And when the Philippian jailer asked Paul and Silas, "What must

I do to be saved?" they replied, "Believe in the Lord Jesus, and you will be saved, *you and your household*" (Acts 16:30–31).

Life relationships taken into account in connection with blessing

These examples show how God works when he blesses: not individualistically, but always in terms of the relationships in which people are living. And when he came with his curse, he acted in the same way. We want to adduce some examples of that in the following section.

Solidarity in Terms of Curse

When Yahweh established the Horeb covenant, he gave Israel this command: "You shall not make for yourself a carved image.... For I the LORD your God am a jealous God, visiting the iniquity of the fathers on the children to the third and the fourth generation of those who hate me, but showing steadfast love to thousands of those who love me and keep my commandments" (Exod. 20:4–6). As we shall see, this did not mean that Yahweh would never consider the personal conduct of the children of idol-worshiping and image-serving Israelite parents. Yahweh is not like that, as we learn from Ezekiel 18:20. The second commandment hardly excludes God from paying attention to the personal behavior of the children of those who violate his covenant or from evaluating what those children themselves are doing.

Royal families under God's judgment

There is no clearer explanation of the second commandment than the history of the punishment of the house of Jeroboam. Yahweh was deeply offended by Jeroboam's calf worship at Dan and Bethel. "Therefore behold, I will bring harm upon the house of Jeroboam and will cut off from Jeroboam every male, both bond and free in Israel, and will burn up the house of Jeroboam, as a man burns up dung until it is all gone" (1 Kgs. 14:10). From that time on, an inherited curse lay upon the royal house of Jeroboam. Baasha executed this divine judgment. "And as soon as he was king, he killed all the house of Jeroboam" (1 Kgs. 15:29-30). But weren't innocent people killed then too? Didn't the descendants die because of an undeserved fate that hung over this royal house? No, for Scripture says emphatically, "And this thing became sin to *the house* of Jeroboam, so as to cut it off and to destroy it from the face of the earth" (1 Kgs. 13:34). Yahweh made an exception for the only good person in Jeroboam's house: "And all Israel shall mourn for him and bury him, for he only of Jeroboam shall come to the grave, because in him there is found something pleasing to the LORD, the God of Israel, in the house of Jeroboam" (1 Kgs. 14:13).

The same thing happened with the house of Baasha. He also received the message that God would sweep away his house in the same humiliating way he had swept away Jeroboam's house, because Baasha "walked in the way of Jeroboam" (1 Kgs. 15:33–16:7). His son Elah was murdered, not only because of the "inherited curse" upon the house of his father, but because he had offended Yahweh just as deeply as his father, Baasha, had (1 Kgs. 16:3).

The house of Ahab was also exterminated, together with his imperial nobles, confidants, and priests (1 Kgs. 22:22; 2 Kgs. 9; 10:11). Did this happen because a particular fate hung over Ahab's house? No; it happened because they hated Yahweh *in the same way that Ahab had*. That entire house was wicked (cf. 2 Kgs. 3:2-3; 8:26; 11:1).

These are a few examples in connection with the second commandment.

More examples of assigned collective guilt

With respect to other kinds of evil too, Yahweh did not punish individualistically. The Pharaoh of Egypt had taken Sarai, Abraham's wife, into his house, but he did not receive individual punishment because of that, since "the LORD afflicted Pharaoh and *his house* with great plagues because of Sarai, Abram's wife" (Gen. 12:17).

Later Abimelech, the king of Gerar, did the same thing. Misled by Abraham's words, "She is my sister" (Gen. 20:2), Abimelech received a divine warning beforehand, but in case he should ignore it and not return Sarah to her husband, Yahweh threatened him: "You shall surely die, you and *all who are yours*" (v. 7). Abimelech's communal identity was so strong that he accused Abraham, "How have I sinned against you, that you have brought on me *and my kingdom* a great sin?" (v. 9). In fact, Yahweh had already begun to punish, for "the LORD had closed all the wombs of the house of Abimelech because of Sarah, Abraham's wife" (v. 18). But when Sarah was returned to Abraham, "God healed Abimelech, and also healed his wife and female slaves so that they bore children" (v. 17).

In Israel people would not have seen anything unrighteous in this manner of acting, for people dealt with each other in the same way. During the period of the judges, a gang of Danites stole the god and priest of a certain Micah. Tearfully the man who had lost his business of providing self-directed religion complained, "What have I left?" (a question you can hear Christians asking when they are robbed of or lose their self-directed religion). But the Danites respond, "Do not let your voice be heard among us, lest angry fellows fall upon you, and you lose your life with the lives of your household" (Judg. 18:25). This Micah was not individualistically separated from his household.

In a cowardly manner, Joab, David's general, fatally stabbed Saul's general, Abner. Did David at that point declare merely his own personal innocence of this murder in some kind of individualistic manner, and did he view this as an individualistic act on the part of Joab? Not at all, for David said:

> *I and my kingdom* are forever guiltless before the LORD

for the blood of Abner the son of Ner. May it fall upon the head of Joab and upon *all his father's house*, and may the house of Joab never be without one who has a discharge or who is leprous or who holds a spindle or who falls by the sword or who lacks bread! (2 Sam. 3:28–29)

David was so arrogant that he ordered a census of the people, for which he received as punishment from Yahweh the choice from among three things that would not affect him alone: "three years of famine . . . in your land," "flee[ing] three months before your foes," or "three days' pestilence in your land" (2 Sam. 24:13). When David chose the last one, "the LORD sent a pestilence on Israel . . . and there died of the people from Dan to Beersheba 70,000 men" (v. 15). Joab had also issued this warning: "Why should it be a cause of guilt for Israel?" (1 Chr. 21:3). Later David perceived how his people had suffered because of his sin, but even then he still declared something that for our individualistic mind-set sounds hard to take: "It is I who have sinned and done great evil. But these sheep, what have they done? Please let your hand, O LORD my God, be against me and against *my father's house*. But do not let the plague be on your people" (v. 17).

Jeremiah also spoke from this concept of communal solidarity. He warned the princes and the people who wanted to kill him: "But as for me, behold, I am in your hands. Do with me as seems good and right to you. Only know for certain that if you put me to death, you will bring innocent blood upon *yourselves* and upon *this city* and *its inhabitants*" (Jer. 26:14–15).

These examples were certainly not unique to the Old Testament, as a few episodes from the New Testament prove. Ananias sold a field and deceived the Holy Spirit by withholding some of its proceeds. As punishment for that, not only did he himself die, but his wife, Sapphira, died as well (Acts 5:1–11). Severe abuses existed in the Christian church in Corinth. Paul declared the church as a community to be guilty and dared to add, "That is why many of you are weak and ill, and some have died" (1 Cor. 11:30).

Life relationships affected by punishments

The Scripture passages cited above may have made it clear that according to all of Scripture, when God disciplines, he definitely does not do so in an individualistic fashion; instead, he always treats people in terms of the relationships in which they live, whether house, family, or even city and nation. As we saw, these life relationships are often affected by divine punishments.

But how do we square this with "the soul who sins shall die" (Ezek. 18:20)?

In Ezekiel 18:20 we read, "The soul who sins shall die. The son shall not suffer for the iniquity of the father, nor the father suffer for the iniquity of the son. The righteousness of the righteous shall be upon himself, and the wickedness of the wicked shall be upon himself." How do we square this with the cited examples of communal sharing in blessing and curse? Can we spot here in Ezekiel a certain progress from the more primitive times, with their lower stage of religion, to a more developed time, with a deeper sense of justice and a resulting higher stage of religion? We can hardly answer this question in the affirmative, if only because in the New Testament we encountered the same mode of action.

Evolutionistic theologians have argued that Ezekiel was one of the discoverers of the "individuals." After he was active, these people argue, "the Israelite religion" was supposedly more "personally" colored than before his time. If they were right, we would have outgrown all those Scripture passages we studied above. But we don't believe this at all. Rather than using individualistic categories to condemn the clear biblical examples of solidarity in relationships both within and outside of Israel, we should learn to think about this matter biblically; on the basis of this biblical instruction, we should condemn this mistaken way of thinking! Further study shows that Ezekiel 18:20–21 hardly constitutes a breaking point for this biblical understanding of communal identity.

United in mind, therefore united in punishment

As we saw, in Holy Scripture a person is not viewed, either by God or by others, "by himself," and a group of people is not seen as a collection of separate individuals. In this context we have spoken several times about a notion of communal identity. The Israelite was aware, in both blessing and curse, of being bound to his fellow Israelites, not only his contemporaries but also those fellow Israelites of previous generations. To clarify this sharing in a communal identity in terms of good and evil, people have used the illustration of a tree. When a tree falls, its branches fall along with it; they cannot be protected from the fall as isolated individuals. The connectedness of the branches with the tree entails this. But does this mean, according to Scripture—with Ezekiel as perhaps the exception—that a person is *automatically* blessed and punished in terms of this communal identity? Do the "branches" simply belong to the "tree" of house, city, or nation? Not at all. The quiet assumption from which the biblical notion of communal identity proceeds is this: an entire house, an entire family, an entire city, or an entire nation is of one mind, of one heart, of one sentiment—*unless the opposite is the case!*

If children repent of their fathers' sins, or if some repent of their nation's sins, then Yahweh deals with them in terms of Ezekiel 18. This repenting remnant occasionally may still have to suffer along with the guilty masses, despite having received special promises, but we will come back to this in a moment. As a rule, Scripture proceeds from the fact that a person is of one heart and of one mind with his family, city, and nation. We saw this in the examples of communal punishment above. They did not at all exclude the possibility of a person's own participation in the evil that was committed. Pharaoh's rulers themselves drew the Pharaoh's attention to the pretty wife of

Abraham (Gen. 12:14–15). It is possible that Achan was assisted by his children in hiding his rather sizeable loot in his tent (Josh. 7:21). David cursed Joab together with his entire family because of the murder of Abner. He was observing here a family feud (2 Sam. 3:20). Ananias was not the only one who died because of his deception: his wife Sapphira also fell dead at Peter's feet. But she had known what her husband was doing! (Acts 5:2). In these examples we repeatedly deal with a communal punishment of people who are of one mind and of one sentiment.

The biblical notion of communal identity simply proceeds from that unity of sentiment, at least as long as the opposite is not the case. For it could be that a person or various people repent of the evil in the community to which they belong(ed). And then God would not put such godly ones who humble themselves into the same category with all of the impenitent wicked ones. The books of the Prophets show clearly that in times of judgment of an entire people, Yahweh was aware of anyone who repented before him. He then placed this remnant in a position of exemption! In the midst of the pronouncements of the most severe judgments upon *the people*, this Shear-jashub (Isa. 7), or remnant-that-repents, got to hear the most wonderful promises *as the remnant*. This is all the more proof that God doesn't lump everyone together in the same class of people, not even in times when his wrath burns. In these times when he punishes his people, he does not neglect to make or observe distinctions among them. In the preaching of judgment and even in the situation of judgment itself, the remnant receives a hopeful position of exemption.

"Is there injustice on God's part? By no means!" (Rom. 9:14).

One for many—individuals for all

In several of the examples mentioned earlier, we meet a stimulating phenomenon: occasionally an individual represents the entire group. Individuals act as though they are

7. Psalm 79:8: Do Not Remember against Us

the entire nation or the entire family, and their deeds are decisive for their entire group. Abraham ratified God's covenant for the sake of his entire house (Gen. 17). Because of her actions toward the spies, Rahab rescued the life of her entire family (Josh. 2). Achan's sacrilege brought his entire house, and almost his entire nation, into his destruction (Josh. 7:1, 11–12). Joshua spoke on behalf of his wife and children: "But as for me and my house, we will serve the LORD" (Josh. 24:15). Through his timely capitulation to Babylon, King Zedekiah could have spared his entire house and city (Jer. 38:17). The Philippian jailor's decision brought salvation to his entire house (Acts 16:31–34). Righteous men like Noah and Lot were responsible for their wives and children escaping divine judgments.

So we see that Scripture does not show us merely a man and his house, a king and his people as unbroken entities; it simultaneously shows us that such a unity was often represented by one or more individuals: a father, a king, a prophet, a champion. Someone once illustrated this with the metaphor of a symphony orchestra. Occasionally a musical theme is expressed by a single instrument. But at that moment, the instrument represents all the instruments of the entire orchestra. At that moment, this single instrument *is* the orchestra. In a certain sense, Achan was that for Israel. On the basis of this idea, the author of the book of Joshua writes, "But *the people of Israel* broke faith in regard to the devoted things, for *Achan* . . . took some of the devoted things. And the anger of the LORD burned against *the people of Israel*" (Josh. 7:1). Yahweh's reprimand to Joshua not to lie on the ground makes it clear that Yahweh looked at that single man, Achan, as representing all Israel, as though the nation were concentrated in that man. "*Israel* has sinned; *they* have transgressed my covenant that I commanded *them*; *they* have taken some of the devoted things; *they* have stolen and lied and put them among *their* own belongings. Therefore *the people of Israel* cannot stand before their enemies. *They* turn their backs before their enemies, because *they* have become devoted for destruction" (Josh. 7:11–12).

From the viewpoint of our Western individualistic thinking, such Scripture passages are incomprehensible. Anyone who views humanity as a pile of loose pebbles will protest in his heart against such Scripture passages. It is remarkable, though, that objections to such relationships of solidarity are often more loudly expressed when it comes to God's punishments than to his blessings. Seldom does one hear people criticize the fact that the family of the godly man Noah profited from the rescue that God granted the righteous Noah (Gen. 6:9). And as far as God was concerned, the sons-in-law of Lot could have been spared (Gen. 19:12; cf. Josh. 2:12–20; 6:25 [Rahab's family]; Judg. 1:25). Indeed, after all, all children of believers share with their parents in the promise, which has priority, and the threats of God's covenant. But when the situation involves connectedness in punishment, then many individualistic Christians frown, even though the notion that one person or several individuals "are" the community is nowadays not entirely excluded (as we see, for example, in sports, where the masses see their nation incarnated in a particular team and encourage the team with a chant such as "U-S-A! U-S-A!").

The Levites represented all the Israelite firstborn before Yahweh (Num. 3:12; 8:16). In the same way one can say that the elders at the gate of Bethlehem "were" the entire city populace (Ruth 4:9, 11). Occasionally a few righteous people could be so united with the entire nation that, when it wanted to do evil, they didn't say, "*You* are about to . . . ," but "*We* are about to bring great disaster upon *ourselves*" (Jer. 26:19). Or they complained, "For the wound of the daughter of my people is my heart wounded" (Jer. 8:21). Or they themselves confessed sins on behalf of Israel by saying, "Hear the prayer of your servant that I now pray before you day and night for the people of Israel your servants, confessing the sins of the people of Israel, which we have sinned against you. Even I and my father's house have sinned" (Neh. 1:6). A similar confession of guilt in Psalm 79 formed the introduction to this section. Later we will cite other passages as well.

God never views people as being separate from each other!

That is why it was not strange for Isaiah to say about the servant of Yahweh (and, behind him, the Servant of Yahweh), "But he was pierced for our transgressions; he was crushed for our iniquities; upon him was the chastisement that brought us peace, and with his wounds we are healed" (Isa. 53:5).

One for many—individuals for all.

Who would not think here of Adam?

Certainly, the relationship of Adam and his first transgression to us is unique. But we can learn from it for our current discussion.

Adam "was" the entire human race. We were in him. He was our representative with God, our head, in a juridical sense. In the same way, according to Scripture, that is the structure of the human race and we simply have to accept it. The human race looks more like a cluster of grapes, full of distinct grapes that are nevertheless bound to each other, rather than a pile of loose grains of sand that lie alongside each other but are not bound to each other. We are bound so tightly to the first man Adam that the Holy Spirit says, "Just as sin came into the world through one man, and death through sin, and so death spread to all men *because all sinned*" (Rom. 5:12).

The arrogant natural human heart and the fallen natural human understanding resist these words. They say, "How am *I* actually implicated in the sin of Adam?" But this objection is fundamentally not only unfounded but also ungrateful. Earlier we pointed to the phenomenon that no one protests when God rescues both the righteous Noah and Lot as well as their house, and spares both Rahab as well as her family—and continues to want to have a covenant with us and our children!

By virtue of one and the same structure of the human race, in Adam we are all guilty and liable to death, and only if we believe in the *one Man* Jesus can we be saved through him. If people were to stand alongside one another so loosely connected, in a juridical sense as well, as individualistic thinking suggests, then a separate Christ would have had to suffer and die for each individual. The angelic world has a different structure. In that world there is no marriage, no gender difference, no procreation. But God has "made from one man every nation of mankind" (Acts 17:26). We were all born from one father and one mother, and God has maintained this structure of humanity despite the entrance of sin. He condemned all of us in that one individual, Adam. Many people refuse to believe this. But once again, let's not forget that that very same structure of the human race makes it possible for many, very many, an innumerable many people to be saved through one Man, Jesus of Nazareth, the Son of God. In him God granted us a new Head, who came to make good what the first head had failed to do (Rom. 5:12–21; 1 Cor. 15:22). He is now the Firstborn of all who have fallen asleep but will arise as certainly as he did (1 Cor. 15:20, 23). For Jesus Christ is bound with us so intimately that in Scripture his church is sometimes called his body (Rom. 12:5; 1 Cor. 6:15; 10:17; 12:12–31; Eph. 1:23; 4:12; Col. 1:18, 24). When Saul persecuted Christians, he heard Christ say, "Saul, Saul, why are you persecuting *me*? (Acts 9:4).

Our Relationship to the Misdeeds of Former Generations of the Church

What do we have to do with the sins of our ancestors? We began this chapter with that question. Who is concerned about God visiting upon our generation both its own sins and also the sins of former generations? Where today are those sins being confessed along with Psalm 79: "Lord, do not remember against us the iniquities of former generations"? This alarming situation gave us the boldness to show how deeply Psalm

79:8 is rooted in all of Scripture. We will need to speak as those who speak "the oracles of God" (1 Pet. 4:11) when we talk about God's people again. This is why we cited so many examples from Holy Scripture and explained how these examples speak of God's people not as the sum of individuals, but as a historical entity that encompasses many generations. They are mutually connected by means of bonds of solidarity, both with respect to God's blessing and with respect to God's curse.

For many people, the view of this Scriptural reality has been distorted by an individualistic manner of thinking and the egoistical religion that flows from it, and also by insensitivity and blindness toward God's deeds of judgment in our own day. The spirit from which the outcasts were speaking in Ezekiel 18:2 is very much alive: "The fathers have eaten sour grapes, and the children's teeth are set on edge." Many Christians seem blinded to the reality of God's accumulated wrath, and perhaps for that reason they don't know what to do with Psalm 79:8. This psalmist was afraid of the surplus of wrath that Israel had accumulated with Yahweh, and that is why he pleaded, "Do no remember against us the iniquities of former generations!"

Accumulated wrath

In large families children occasionally start the day a bit out of sorts. A patient father and mother will not immediately apply severe punishment, but will initially limit their response to warnings. But sometimes these warnings don't help. The child's crankiness continues throughout the morning into the afternoon. Throughout such days, irritation builds up in the heart of the father and mother. Their anger festers. Then a particular misbehavior is the last straw, and a forceful unloading of anger follows. Is that due only to the final act of misbehavior? No, this last incident unleashes the anger that had been accumulating during the entire day, as it filled with the child's mischief. It was the final straw.

The same can happen between God and his people.

Our heavenly Father is patient. He does not always punish immediately. Sometimes he allows his wrath to accumulate. On their part, people "are storing up" that wrath, as Paul puts it in Romans 2:5. A person can gather with God a storehouse not only of righteousness but also of wrath! One paraphrase of Romans 2:5 puts it this way: "Every refusal and avoidance of God adds fuel to the fire" (*The Message*).

That's how things often went in Israel's history.

There were many times when God saved up his wrath and Israel heaped up an accumulation of wrath for "the day of wrath," even though, as we saw above, that wrath was poured out not on the innocent children descended from guilty ancestors but on the sons who continued walking in the wicked path of their ancestors.

Next we turn to several examples that illustrate this truth.

THE GODLY KING JOSIAH

When Josiah began to rule, Judah was still encumbered with the religious misdeeds of Josiah's grandfather, Manasseh, and his father, Amon. During their reigns, both they and the people had forsaken Yahweh. And then Josiah began to cleanse the land and the temple (2 Chr. 34:1–8; "cleanse" is a wonderful verb that expresses what we call reformation or church renewal). It was then that people discovered "the book of the law of Yahweh," which Shaphan read to the king. "And when the king heard the words of the Law, he tore his clothes" and said, "Great is the wrath of the LORD that is poured out on us, because our fathers have not kept the word of the LORD, to do according to all that is written in this book" (2 Chr. 34:19, 21).

So Josiah had an eye for the fact that, as he put it, "our fathers" had accumulated with Yahweh a surplus of wrath. He feared that this accumulated wrath could be unleashed upon his generation at any time. The prophetess Huldah had told him, on behalf of Yahweh, that Yahweh's accumulated wrath would not be quenched (2 Chr. 34:25).

7. Psalm 79:8: Do Not Remember against Us

From this history, however, we learn to see Yahweh's accumulated wrath, and at the same time we receive confirmation of the general rule according to which we saw him respond: as with the parents, so with the children, unless the latter conduct themselves differently. For as soon as Josiah humbled himself and adopted a different posture toward God from that of his father and grandfather, Yahweh sent his word to him:

> Because your heart was tender and you humbled yourself before God when you heard his words against this place and its inhabitants, and you have humbled yourself before me and have torn your clothes and wept before me, I also have heard you, declares the LORD. Behold, I will gather you to your fathers, and you shall be gathered to your grave in peace, and your eyes shall not see all the disaster that I will bring upon this place and its inhabitants. (2 Chr. 34:27–28).

Yahweh refrained from pouring out his wrath for a few more years. It was only under Josiah's wicked son, Jehoiakim—who fell once again into the wickedness of his grandfather and great-grandfather—that Yahweh began to unleash his accumulated anger (2 Chr. 36:5–8).

Concerning this accumulating of wrath, Yahweh spoke through Isaiah: "Behold, it is written before me: 'I will not keep silent, but I will repay; I will indeed repay into their lap both your iniquities and your fathers' iniquities together'" (Isa. 65:6–7).

JEREMIAH'S PROPHECIES

Here, too, we encounter remarkable words about "the surplus of wrath" that Judah "had accumulated with Yahweh for the day of wrath," as Paul would later express it. We are referring to the following citations from the book of Jeremiah.

When Judah asked Jeremiah to explain his reasons for his prophecies of judgment, he had to reply, "Because your fathers have forsaken me . . . and because you have done worse than your fathers" (Jer. 16:10–12). Once again we have a proof that solidarity with ancestors in curse presupposes solidarity in sin and guilt. In that instance, Yahweh is a God who "repay[s] the guilt of fathers to their children after them" (32:18).

In Jeremiah 32 Yahweh complains that for centuries he has been insulted by his people: "The children of Israel have done nothing but provoke me to anger by the work of their hands, declares the LORD. This city has aroused my anger and wrath, from the day it was built to this day." Pay attention to those final words: "to this day"! What follows becomes all the more clear, then:

> So that I will remove it from my sight because of all the evil of the children of Israel and the children of Judah that they did to provoke me to anger—their kings and their officials, their priests and their prophets [note the plural!], the men of Judah and the inhabitants of Jerusalem. They have turned to me their back and not their face. And though I have taught them persistently, they have not listened to receive instruction. (vv. 30–33)

During those years and centuries, Yahweh's wrath was accumulating.

When Nebuchadnezzar came and that wrath descended in its fullness and most of the people of Judah were transported to Babylon, a small remnant stayed behind in the land. But even this remnant continued hanging on to pagan idols (Jer. 44:1–8). For our discussion, it is instructive to hear how Yahweh addressed these impenitent people of Judah about the sins of their fathers:

> Have you forgotten the evil of your fathers, the evil of the kings [plural!] of Judah, the evil of their wives, your own evil, and the evil of your wives, which they committed in the land of Judah and in the streets of

Jerusalem? They [you yourselves and your fathers] have not humbled themselves even to this day, nor have they feared, nor walked in my law and my statutes that I set before you and before your fathers. Therefore [by virtue of the rule: as with father, so with children] thus says the LORD of hosts, the God of Israel: Behold, I will set my face against you for harm, to cut off all Judah. (Jer. 44:9–11)

Notice the connection between "we and our fathers" in Jeremiah 44:17. The "we" in this Scripture passage consistently includes the preceding generations.

IN THIS CONTEXT EZEKIEL 20 IS INSTRUCTIVE

The prophet receives a visit from a committee of elders who represent the captives in Babylon and want to consult Yahweh through Ezekiel. He provides these men with a prophetic mandate: "Let them know the abominations of their fathers" (Ezek. 20:4). And this is what Ezekiel does next. He brings up this word from Yahweh: "Nor did they [the fathers] forsake the idols of Egypt" (v. 8). That is why Yahweh had been accumulating his wrath. Even though in the wilderness it was already great, only for the sake of his name did God refrain from destroying Israel (v. 14). The sons of this generation were just like their fathers: "The children rebelled against me" (v. 21). Subsequent generations blasphemed Yahweh as well (v. 27). Therefore Ezekiel had to ask, on behalf of Yahweh, "Will you defile yourselves after the manner of your fathers and go whoring after their detestable things?" (v. 30). Since the general rule "as with the father, so with the son" applied in this situation, the wrath that Yahweh had accumulated against the fathers was poured out upon the children, because these children imitated the sins of their fathers (Ezek. 20:33–38). "With wrath poured out [thus, no longer being accumulated] I will be king over you" (v. 33; cf. Lam. 2:17; 5:7).

These Scripture passages show that God's wrath can grow throughout the years, and even centuries, until people have saved up a surplus balance of wrath with him, something that makes the godly tremble. Indeed, precisely those righteous ones, who themselves walk blamelessly before God, confess the sins of their ancestors and contemporaries with a sense of solidarity in their historical guilt.

The idea of solidarity in historical culpability

One of those who feared the "accumulation of wrath" that Israel had banked with Yahweh was the poet of Psalm 79. This explains his petition: "Do not remember against *us* the iniquities of former generations!" This righteous person acknowledged solidarity in the historical culpability of the church. And he did so despite his personal righteousness! We encounter this phenomenon with the "best" among Israel. They confessed the iniquity of the fathers as their own, although personally they feared Yahweh intensely.

We refer you to the following Scripture passages.

THE RIGHTEOUS INTERCESSOR ON BEHALF OF A WICKED PEOPLE

In Leviticus 26 we read, "But if they confess their iniquity and the iniquity of their fathers . . . then I will remember my covenant with Jacob, and I will remember my covenant with Isaac and my covenant with Abraham" (vv. 40, 42; cf. Neh. 1:9). Didn't the poet of Psalm 79, just like the one who composed Psalm 74, hope in "God's way back"? Moses had pictured that in the future, in connection with the people's deep humbling in a crisis of divine judgment (see our earlier comments on Ps. 74:11). Even so, this poet must have feared Yahweh intensely. Personally he would have had no part in the unrighteousness of his forefathers, or would surely have broken away from that iniquity, but he is nonetheless the one who prays that Yahweh would not reckon this wickedness to the generation now living.

7. Psalm 79:8: Do Not Remember against Us

Scripture gives us more examples of godly people who despite personal righteousness nonetheless confessed the unrighteousness of the forefathers as their own. These intercessors had very little need for distancing themselves individualistically from their sinning ancestors, and we have already observed and discussed how, on occasion, individuals functioned as though they represented the entire people. This poet served as a mouthpiece of the entire people, continuing a wonderful tradition.

King David

When Yahweh had delivered David from the grasp of Saul and of all his enemies, David sang in his song of thanksgiving, "The LORD has rewarded me according to my righteousness, according to my cleanness in his sight" (2 Sam. 22:25; cf. vv. 21–24, equivalent to Ps. 18:20–23). But despite this declared personal righteousness and blamelessness before Yahweh, we read the following declaration about the ark from this very same David: "*We* did not seek it in the days of Saul" (1 Chr. 13:3). The godly David says this, the man who had lain awake on account of the ark (Ps. 132). Modern Christians perhaps would say something like "*They* did not seek it in the days of Saul," but humble David does not isolate himself individualistically. He says, "*We* . . ."

King Hezekiah

"He did what was right in the eyes of the LORD, according to all that David his father had done" (2 Chr. 29:2). Scripture devotes three chapters to Hezekiah's righteousness. But he nevertheless did not separate himself from his unfaithful ancestors; he did not adopt a posture that said, "I did not do that, but my father, Ahaz, did." No, it was this godly Hezekiah who confessed, "Our fathers have been unfaithful and have done what was evil in the sight of the LORD our God. . . . Behold, our fathers have fallen by the sword, and our sons and our daughters and our wives are in captivity for this" (2 Chr.

29:6, 9; cf. 28:17, 21). Hezekiah had a sin offering brought for the royal house (29:21).

King Josiah

This great-grandson of Hezekiah "did what was right in the eyes of the LORD, and walked in the ways of David his father; and he did not turn aside to the right hand or to the left" (2 Chr. 34:2). Once again we have an example of someone who himself was a righteous man but nevertheless understood that he was in solidarity with his wicked fathers (Manasseh and Amon) and his own contemporaries, both in Judah and in Israel. We saw earlier how he tore his clothes when Shaphan read to him from the book of the law that had been rediscovered. At that point Josiah acknowledged, "Great is the wrath of the LORD that is poured out on us, because our fathers have not kept the word of the LORD" (2 Chr. 34:19, 21). Josiah had an eye for the accumulated wrath of Yahweh and his participation in the historical culpability of the church.

The prophet Jeremiah

This godly man also served as the mouthpiece of his sinful nation. Rather than distancing himself personally, he was the man who confessed, "Let *us* lie down in *our* shame, and let *our* dishonor cover *us*. For *we* have sinned against the LORD our God, *we and our fathers*, from our youth [cf. Jer. 2:2] even to this day, and *we* have not obeyed the voice of the LORD our God" (3:25; cf. 32:23; 44:9).

In Jeremiah 14:20 the prophet confesses, "We acknowledge our wickedness, O LORD, and the iniquity of our fathers, for we have sinned against you." But Yahweh replied that any possible repentance on the part of Israel would be too late, because he was ready to visit his wrath on the Judah of Jeremiah's day "because of what Manasseh the son of Hezekiah, king of Judah, did in Jerusalem" (15:4). He poured out accumulated wrath on a generation that persisted in the sins of the fathers. This wrath is mentioned in Jeremiah 16:10–12 as well, where Yahweh instructs his servant how to respond if people asked him, why all those prophecies of disaster? Jeremiah was supposed to reply, "Because your fathers have forsaken me . . . and because you have done worse than your fathers" (vv. 11–12).

When the night of captivity had fallen and God had poured out his burning anger upon Judah and Jerusalem, there were righteous ones who confessed the sins of their fathers and of their contemporaries using the first-person plural: Daniel, the composers of the Lamentations, and the authors of Psalms 106 and 79.

Daniel

Read Daniel's moving intercessory prayer in chapter 9 in its entirety; we can cite only a few parts of it here:

> O Lord, the great and awesome God, . . . we have sinned and done wrong and acted wickedly and rebelled, turning aside from your commandments and rules. We have not listened to your servants the prophets, who spoke in your name to our kings, our princes, and our fathers, and to all the people of the land. To you, O Lord, belongs righteousness, but to us open shame, . . . to our kings, to our princes, and to our fathers, because we have sinned against you. (vv. 4–8)

This is what godly Daniel confessed, and the Bible book that bears his name is filled with examples of his obedience. This godly man included himself completely with his guilty ancestors by confessing, "*We* have sinned, *we* have done wickedly!" (v. 15).

The composers of Lamentations

These writers as well sang their laments from an intense solidarity with historic Jerusalem. The author of Lamentations

1 serves as the mouthpiece of this city by letting her speak in the first-person singular. In Lamentations 3 this confession resounds: "We have transgressed and rebelled" (v. 42). In Lamentations 4 we read the confession, "This was for the sins of her prophets and the iniquities of her priests, who shed in the midst of her the blood of the righteous" (v. 13). If we fail to hear the sounds of a confession of historical culpability there, then we certainly hear them in these words from Lamentations 5:7: "Our fathers sinned, and are no more; and we bear their iniquities."

Psalm 106

"Both we and our fathers have sinned; we have committed iniquity; we have done wickedness" (Ps. 106:6). The psalmist then turns immediately to confess to God guilt for iniquities from Egypt to the Babylonian captivity! "Our fathers, when they were in Egypt, did not consider your wondrous works" (v. 7). Indeed, this godly intercessor felt that he was involved during the Babylonian captivity with Israel's sins in the wilderness (vv. 13–33), in the period of the judges (vv. 34–36), and in the period of the kings (vv. 36–39). His psalm is one comprehensive confession of the historical guilt of the church, including some sins that had been committed more than five hundred years before his time!

After the return from captivity, did a "Glory, hallelujah!" victorious attitude dominate among the returning captives? There was joy, to be sure (Ps. 126), but the centuries-old misdeeds of the church that had led to the captivity did not end up in the dustbin of forgetfulness with faithful men like Ezra and Nehemiah. When they once again were confronted with the sin of God's people, they confessed once again those historical misdeeds.

Ezra

Shocked at the mixed marriages among the captives who had returned, this godly priest confessed, "O my God, I am ashamed and blush to lift my face to you, my God, for our iniquities have risen higher than our heads, and our guilt has mounted up to the heavens. From the days of our fathers to this day we have been in great guilt[,] . . . we, our kings, and our priests" (Ezra 9:6–7).

Ezra did not separate himself from his fathers and their sins either, but even though he personally feared the Lord intensely, he realized that he was a member of a sinful nation, and he confessed, "*We* have forsaken your commandments" (v. 10).

Nehemiah

In Nehemiah 1 we read a prayer in which Nehemiah asks Yahweh to hear "the prayer of your servant that I now pray before you day and night for the people of Israel your servants, confessing the sins of the people of Israel, which we have sinned against you. Even I and my father's house have sinned" (v. 6). But especially his prayer in Nehemiah 9 shows how this righteous man realized that he too was a member of a sinful line of generations. Looking at the catastrophe that Judah had suffered since the invasion of the Assyrians until Nehemiah's own time, this godly man confesses, in solidarity with all who had experienced Yahweh's punishments, "Yet you have been righteous in all that has come upon us, for you have dealt faithfully and we have acted wickedly. Our kings, our princes, our priests, and our fathers have not kept your law" (Neh. 9:33–34). In verse 37 he speaks about "the kings whom you have set over us because of our sins."

Here you have nine examples of people who each feared Yahweh from the heart. For them, the rule "As with the fathers, so with the sons" did not apply. Kings like Hezekiah and Josiah clearly broke with the sins of their fathers. Nevertheless, they confessed those sins while serving as mouthpieces for God's people. They were the righteous intercessors among a wicked people. And as we have seen, they spoke not only using the third-person plural, but also using the first-person plural time and again.

Above, we have seen examples from Scripture where one functioned in place of many or a few in place of everyone. When Achan stole, God's wrath burned against the Israelites (Josh. 7:1). Would God's wrath have been quieted after the captivity in a corresponding manner? Would Yahweh have accepted the confession of guilt of those individuals as valid for everyone, and permitted Israel to return to her homeland in part on account of this interceding remnant, just as God gave Abijam "a lamp in Jerusalem" for David's sake (1 Kgs. 15:4), and delivered Israel out of Egypt in remembrance of his covenant with Abraham (Exod. 2:24), and would have spared Sodom for the sake of one more righteous person (Gen. 18)?

Our relationship to the misdeeds of our Christian ancestors

In light of the discussion above, Psalm 79:8, the verse that serves as the title of this chapter, needs little commentary: "Do not remember against us the iniquities of former generations!" This petition shows us that the psalmist was an intimate compatriot of intercessors like the authors of the Lamentations, Psalm 106, Daniel, Ezra, and Nehemiah—all of whom confessed before God in the same century, faced with the same crisis of divine judgment, the same historical misdeeds of the church. Our psalmist considered himself not a religious individualist but someone personally implicated in the sins of his ancestors.

Unfortunately, ideas like those we have discussed in this chapter in terms of Psalm 79:8 and the rest of Scripture go squarely contrary to the thinking and action of a Christianity that has been severely infected with the virus of revolution and the viruses of individualism and ahistorical orientation. Solidarity in privileges and in culpabilities, accountability of one generation for another, the authority of fathers and mothers over their children, also with respect to God's covenant and words—these are things that many Christians can hardly handle. Any love for the history of their own family, of their city, of their land, and of the Christianity of which they are a part seems impossible for them. They are unhistorical, shallow people.

The apostle Peter, however, once wrote, "But do not overlook this one fact, beloved, that with the Lord one day is as a thousand years, and a thousand years as one day" (2 Pet. 3:8). What does that mean? For the Lord, it was but one day ago that the events of the Middle Ages occurred, and the sins and wickedness of our fathers are still red-hot to him!

Who takes account of that anymore?

Who fears for himself and for his children and his grandchildren that the accumulated wrath of God will be poured out on account of the sins of Christians from the Middle Ages, or from the sixteenth and seventeenth centuries, and every century since, sins from more than five hundred years ago? Who is still afraid of God's anger that our ancestors have accumulated through their rationalism (twisting God's Word into scholastic notions) and mysticism (twisting God's Word into mere "experiences")? These are the religious "sins of the fathers" (cf. the second commandment)! Even more, who is still afraid of God's wrath on account of "our" social injustice toward African peoples (slave trade, colonialism, cultural imperialism) and toward our own brothers (child labor, oppressing widows, orphans, and workers throughout Western society)? Or do people suppose they can distance themselves from such sinful ancestors and their wickedness through some kind of "Declaration of Independence" or similar means?

We must not only return to a Scripture mode of speaking about human beings, so that we can be armed against various ancient and modern Gnostic "soul-religion" and against the rising tsunami of Eastern mysticism, but we must also return to the biblical teaching about the structure of the human race. In this way we can escape the snare of various forms of unhistorical "personality religion" and egocentric religion, expressions of religion that are as blind to God's historical deeds of salvation as they are to our historical culpabilities. Because of this blindness, people do not fear God's accumulated wrath. They fail to observe his outstretched hand or his already smiting hand, refusing to intercede with an appeal to God's name and mercy, since they lack any sense of guilt. Such a hardened, arrogant posture can make the circumstances of our Christian religion only more serious and call down judgments that are even more severe. Zealot-like "zeal" for God and a Maccabean-like activism, apart from insight into the situation, can make God's wrath in such a situation only greater.

May God grant in his favor in our time that there may still be those who pray the petition of Psalm 79:8—godly people who know that they are implicated by the sins of the fathers. May there arise from the deepest parts of Christianity a moaning intercession to the God and Father of our Lord Jesus Christ, who has been insulted by so many people: "Do not remember against us the iniquities of former generations; let your compassion come speedily to meet us!"

Chapter 8

Psalm 88: In the Last Stage of a Fatal Illness

Psalm 88 is perhaps the saddest of all the psalms. Can you find one with a more sorrowful sound or such a disconsolate ending? In published Bibles where the last verse of this psalm ends up being printed on the bottom of the page, we tend to turn the page automatically as we look for an expected comforting conclusion, like we find with other psalms of lament. Take Psalm 130, for example; it begins, "Out of the depths I cry to you, O Lord!," but then everything ends well: "O Israel, hope in the Lord! . . . He will redeem Israel from all his iniquities." Psalm 88, however, ends with "darkness" (v. 18) and this final word characterizes the entire psalm. We are listening to a dying man pray here! Every line breathes the air of death, so to speak.

What is such a somber psalm doing in God's Word?

A Didactic Poem of Heman the Ezrahite

What is such a somber psalm, where we can discover not even a flicker of joy, doing in God's Word, which is so often called the Good News? The superscription supplies the answer to this question. This somber song is contained in Holy Scripture for our instruction. Psalm 88 is a "didactic psalm" (Heb. *maskil*). We have already encountered this word in the heading to Psalm 74. The purpose of such psalms is to teach us how to evaluate particular situations according to God's Word, which explains their classification as didactic poems. They provide insight by the light of the Word. In Psalm 88 this involves the hopeless situation of a man who is deathly ill.

Psalm 88 is therefore a didactic poem for deathbeds.

It can teach us important wisdom for such sad days. To mention but one issue: at such a time, how can we approach God? With what attitude? With what tone? With what words? With what arguments can we lend force to our petitions? Psalm 88 teaches us evangelical wisdom about these things. Isn't it liberating to learn from Heman that God does not desire any kind of triumphalistic faith from us when we go to meet our end? When God's children walk through the valley of the shadow of death, our heavenly Father requires no heroism of faith. On the contrary, this psalm shows that he is satisfied when in their sorrow and collapse, his children do little more than moan in his ear. In fact, what is Psalm 88 but the moans of a dying man in God's ear? Our heavenly Father certainly did not disapprove of this lament of Heman, or else God's Spirit wouldn't have included this lament in Holy Scripture. Rather than providing a certain kind of deathbed piety, can't this didactic poem bring about evangelical relaxation, both on one's deathbed and around it?

Who was Heman, the author of this psalm?

People have supposed that this was Heman the sage, who was surpassed in understanding and knowledge only by Solomon (1 Kgs. 4:31). True, this Heman is called a Zerahite, a son of Zerah, in 1 Chronicles 2:6, but by switching the first two Hebrew letters, this word could be Ezrahite. Psalm 88 would

8. Psalm 88: In the Last Stage of a Fatal Illness

then be a prayer amid the life-threatening crisis of one of the wisest men. This would increase the value of the psalm as a didactic psalm even more.

There was another Heman, however, whom others have identified in this context, namely, the Heman mentioned in 1 Chronicles 6:33–38; 15:17, 19; 16:41–42; 25:1, 4, 6; 2 Chronicles 5:12; 29:14; and 35:15. This Heman was a grandson of Samuel and a great-grandson of Hannah the prophetess. David appointed him, along with Asaph and Ethan, as a leader of the church choir in the temple. These were especially called to lift up songs of thanksgiving: they belonged to "those chosen and expressly named to give thanks to the LORD, for his steadfast love endures forever" (1 Chr. 16:41). This Heman, who was then a contemporary of Solomon (2 Chr. 5:12), was also called "the king's seer in the words of God" (1 Chr. 25:5 KJV). It is rather inviting to see this Heman as the author of Psalm 88. In this case, a person whose office it was to put Yahweh's loving-kindness into song would have left us a teaching poem for the prayers of God's people at the time of death.

It is difficult to determine with certainty which of these two Hemans we must see as the author of Psalm 88. Some exegetes think that in Scripture there is not two but only one Heman: a wise singer. One thing is certain, however: whether Psalm 88 comes from the hand of a very wise man, or from a prophetic singer, or from a very wise singer, the psalm comes not simply from a skilled person but from a gifted brother who was "carried along by the Holy Spirit" (2 Pet. 1:21). This poem, written or dictated by a dying man, was so pleasing to God that he preserved it in his Word for his people, in service to those who are extremely ill, so they may pray this prayer in their hour of death.

Verses 1–9: "I stretch out my hands toward you"

> Verses 1–2:
> O Lord, God of my salvation;
>   I cry out day and night before you.
> Let my prayer come before you;
>   incline your ear to my cry!

The opening verses are determinative for the entire psalm. It may well be one of the most somber in the Psalter, prayed by a man who was lying at the edge of his grave, but he does not yet bid God farewell. He does not shake his clenched fist as he shouts a curse at heaven (cf. Job 2:9), but he spreads forth his hands to pray. In all his distress Heman keeps clinging to God. Psalm 88 is being sung on the foundation of God's covenant with Israel.

In his mortal crisis Heman turns to Yahweh. In fact, this divine name constitutes the key to the entire psalm, for in those four Hebrew letters, YHWH, God supplied Israel in a nutshell his entire gospel promise. When a believing Israelite heard the name Yahweh, he heard the beloved sounds "Savior," "Helper," "Lifegiver", "I am with you." In addition, Heman calls him "God of my salvation," and salvation means liberation. People have also translated this as "my Savior." This is the same God whom we now know as the God and Father of our Lord Jesus Christ.

To him, Heman cried out day and night: "Incline your ear!"

You see the broken man with his arms lifted up—that was one of the Israelite postures for praying. Early in the morning he begins (v. 13), and in the evening he still has his hands raised upward (v. 1).

In these opening verses Heman's psalm is a genuine teaching psalm. He does not conceal the fact that he is in a heap of trouble. He does not place that trouble in a falsely pious light. Nor does he call into doubt Yahweh's power to save. This is not to deny the existence of temptations in the

8. Psalm 88: In the Last Stage of a Fatal Illness

life of God's children, nor is it to argue that those tempted are always people of little faith or even unbelievers. Our Savior was acquainted with severe temptations by the devil, and yet our Lord was the greatest believer. The "accuser of our brothers" (Rev. 12:10) can bring the human heart into such confusion that it sometimes doubts the forgiveness of sins—and sometimes even doubts God's existence. But this is not the rule, as some believers seem to think. They fearfully wonder, Will I have to endure severe temptations on my deathbed? For them, Psalm 88 is a comforting teaching psalm. Heman knew what it is to suffer, but apparently he knew nothing about suffering temptations. His trust in God was unshaken. Yahweh was the God of his salvation. Psalm 88 ends with the word "darkness," to be sure, but the light that was ignited by his opening words penetrates all the way through.

Heman's address teaches us also that he continued to hope in deliverance by Yahweh. Did that poor man lying on his sickbed receive deliverance? Did Heman get better, and did he then write this psalm? Or did he call Yahweh "God of my salvation" on account of his expectation of the resurrection of the dead and the life of the coming age (for Old Testament believers did indeed know about these)? Since we do not know the outcome in Heman's case, we did not dare to place Psalms 30 and 88 alongside each other as two prayers of people who were mortally ill, one who did get better (Ps. 30) and one who did not (Ps. 88).

It is certain, however, that Psalm 88 transports us into the situation of a believing man who is looking death in the face. Through his teaching poem, this mortally ill brother arouses the church facing extreme crisis not to direct rebellious shouts to heaven but to express our laments as humble prayers before God, accompanied with the request to the Supreme Majesty that he incline his ears to those prayers.

Verses 3–6:
For my soul is full of troubles,
    and my life draws near to Sheol.
I am counted among those who go down to the pit;
    I am a man who has no strength,
like one whose bed is [ESV "like one set loose"] among the dead,
    like the slain that lie in the grave,
like those whom you remember no more,
    for they are cut off from your hand.
You have put me in the depths of the pit,
    in the regions dark and deep.

Here again we encounter the broad meaning that the words *life* and *death* can have in the Bible (cf. our discussion of Ps. 30). Just like David in Psalm 30, so too Heman in Psalm 88 was not "dead" in the strictly biological sense of the word, which usually refers to the heart and brain no longer functioning. In that sense, Heman was still alive, but as far as his feelings were concerned, he was already among the dead. For Heman was deathly sick, "full of troubles" (v. 3), languishing in distress (v. 9), forsaken by his entire group of friends (v. 8), "helpless" (v. 15), destroyed by assaults (v. 16). The godly Israelite called such an existence "not being alive"; Heman called that being already in the grip of death.

Heman used poignant expressions for that. "I am counted among those who go down to the pit" (v. 4). He sees his name already included in the citizen registry of Sheol, the realm of the dead. There is his bed (v. 5). We have chosen this translation of the difficult language of verse 5, because we encounter this metaphor rather often in Scripture (Ps. 139:8; cf. Job 17:13; Prov. 7:27). In terms of his experience, Heman is already residing in the remotest regions of the underworld. His life's journey is ending (v. 5). He has no more strength (v. 4). According to Heman and the biblical view of life, when you are that badly off as a human being, then you are not really living any longer.

Anyone who knows the visage of someone terminally ill will find this biblical manner of speaking more accurate than our Western scientific definition: as long as someone's heart and brain are still functioning, he is still alive. Anyone who sees a terminally ill person lying in bed, deathly weak, sunken, indeed, sometimes emaciated, a gasping and moaning heap of human misery, can readily understand that David and Heman sighed: I am already dwelling in the embrace of the realm of the dead! Don't we come close to saying this with our own expressions like "He's got one foot in the grave"?

Verse 7:
**Your wrath lies heavy upon me,
and you overwhelm me with all your waves.**

In our time of such advanced scientific medicine, the first question at every sickbed is, What's wrong with this patient? What is his sickness and what organs are affected? Heman writes a psalm about sickness, however, without ever mentioning anything that resembles illness. Not a word about those causes of sickness that we talk about so much: bacteria, viruses, vascular constriction. Nor does he talk about the progress of his disease. In short, he supplies hardly any description of illness. How would he have indicated that? There was hardly any medical expertise in those days. On the basis of the complaint in verse 15, "Afflicted and close to death from my youth up," some have thought that he suffered from leprosy. This translation, however, is not the only possible one, as we will see when we discuss that verse. Moreover, when we discussed Leviticus 13–14 in our commentary, we dealt with the false view that biblical leprosy was an incurable and terrible disease that left those suffering from it terribly deformed. Biblical leprosy could come and go. People didn't die from it. Heman was not suffering from that kind of leprosy. But because he mentions nothing more about his illness, we are left guessing. One could suppose just as accurately that he was in the final stage of cancer, tuberculosis, or one of numerous other illnesses.

Apparently the name of his illness did not interest Heman all that much, either. Whereas we would be very interested in knowing the answer to the question, What's wrong with that sick person?, Heman asked instead, What is God doing with me? In this respect Psalm 88 can be for us an indispensable teaching psalm. It's fine that today we know more than Heman did three thousand years ago in terms of pathology and bacteriology. But don't we risk letting the factual explanations of the sciences captivate all our attention? Who continues to pay attention to God's hand? Do very many people get any further than "Well, he has something wrong with his lungs," and "she has something wrong with her liver"? Of course, we need not call such facts into question, but let's not look down, on that basis, on "primitive" Heman, who didn't know exactly what was wrong with him. The question becomes, Who penetrates further, the modern agnostic who with certain scientific nearsightedness looks no further than the sickness, or Heman, who in his sickness also sees God's hand? As Christians, we run the risk of exchanging the living God, who rules over everything, for an intellectual deity or an imaginary god, one who bothers only with "religion" whereas the rest of life is guided by various autonomous natural laws. Then, in days of sickness, we no longer take into consideration the concrete hand of our heavenly Father, as Heman took him into account, not only in his illness but also in everything flowing from that: *God* is overwhelming me!

God's all-guiding hand

He observed God's all-guiding hand behind his thoroughly desperate situation: "You have put me in the depths of the pit" (v. 6). Heman didn't lie down powerlessly because his lungs or liver "accidentally" quit working. He looked deeper: "You overwhelm me with all your waves" (v. 7). Notice how pervasive this is: "you," "your hand," "your wrath," etc. Even in the absence of his trusted friends, Heman spotted God's hand: "You have caused my companions to shun me" (v. 8; cf. v. 18). The same applied to his external appearance, which presumably was somewhat loathsome: "You have made me a horror to them" (v. 8). In this way as well, Psalm 88 is a genuinely didactic psalm.

In our civilized society people expend immense effort to ease pain and soften suffering. Nevertheless, everyday there are innumerable masses who lie in agony like Heman, whose most bitter crisis of having to die cannot be relieved by any doctor. So what must they do then? Complain? Of course, but how? Some complain about themselves, that they have ended up with such a weak heart, or such a bad kidney. Others curse or moan about something or other. When we consider the entirety of suffering humanity, then believers like Heman are presumably in the minority by far. Even for the godly King Asa, the physicians were accorded more esteem at a given moment than Yahweh (2 Chr. 16:12). The terminally ill Heman, however, saw that he was dealing with God in every facet of his situation.

God's wrath in Heman's illness

Heman talks about God's wrath at various points in the psalm: "Your wrath lies heavy upon me" (v. 7). "Why do you cast my soul away?" (v. 14). "I suffer your terrors" (v. 15). "Your wrath has swept over me" (v. 16).

Was there, then, a particular sin in Heman's life that was the cause of his sickness? We read nothing about that. Nor do we hear him confess any guilt for sin. Just like with Psalm 30, we think it is better therefore to think of a general experience of God's people. We live our existence with "mortal bodies" (Rom. 8:11) and a "body of death" (7:24), a collection of decaying powers. Such ideas played themselves out in the heart of Paul and continue to do so for many believers throughout their lives, not to mention when death taps us on the shoulder and says, "Your life is coming to an end!"

That's what was going on with Heman; he was thinking, "Now I'm going to die!" At that point a lot of thoughts go through a person's head and heart. At that point even the most callous individual sings a bit more softly. The most faithful believer, who throughout life has clung to God's promises of the forgiveness of sins and eternal life, often gets to see a fast-forwarded movie of his life that was filled with weaknesses and sins, and of his defective walk in the ways of the Lord. The *cause* of our existence ending in death can make a deep impression on a Christian at that point: "Oh, how much I have sinned throughout my life!" Various theological and religious arguments evaporate at that point, and the person who is dying acknowledges God's right to be angry with him, precisely because God had given him so much grace through his Word and Spirit. For that reason, in connection with Scripture passages like the one we're discussing we must think not first of our fall in Adam, since for God's people that has been dealt with in Christ, but of our grieving of the Spirit of Christ, whom God has given to us. That sinning against grace is what accuses us most deeply. But even though that is indeed the reason for fearing God's wrath, the cause of death in the world lies in our solidarity with His Royal Highness Adam (Rom. 5:12–21).

Nowhere does God's Word gloss over the terribleness of death. In the New Testament, Paul calls death the last enemy, which will finally be dethroned when Christ returns (1 Cor. 15:50–57). Nor does he speak lightly about it, but sighs in the face of death (2 Cor. 5:4). Believers also face the universal human judgment that must befall them on account of their solidarity with Adam's sin. Although they hate death, this feeling is not decisive among God's children. For them, death is not something catastrophic, but in a certain sense it is something incidental. Their death in solidarity with Christ lies in the past, in the time of Pontius Pilate's governorship, and in Christ God has granted them eternal life. Nevertheless, Scripture nowhere speaks about death with great fanfare.

"Flesh and blood cannot inherit the kingdom of God" (1 Cor. 15:50). That distressed Heman: "I know that nothing good dwells in me, that is, in my flesh" (Rom. 7:18). And then to have to appear before the holy God, who is angry with sin! That makes a dying child of God think about what he deserves.

> Verse 8:
> You have caused my companions to shun me;
>   you have made me a horror to them.
> I am shut in so that I cannot escape.

Some illnesses can so consume the victim that in the end there is nothing left of a formerly robust person but an emaciated wretch of skin and bones. Could this have been the case with Heman? Healthy people sometimes need to get control of themselves before entering the sickroom. Did Heman look so wretched because of his illness that his friends hardly dared to visit him? Or could he no longer endure their visits because he was too weak? Here as well he acknowledged the hand of God that had isolated Heman's trusted friends (or acquaintances) from him. The godly Israelite called this kind of living without fellowship no life at all; it was instead entering the vestibule of death.

A feeling of severe constriction has overtaken Heman. "I am shut in so that I cannot escape," he moans. Job knew this feeling as well: "He has walled up my way, so that I cannot pass, and he has set darkness upon my paths" (Job 19:8; cf. 3:23; Lam. 3:7).

> Verse 9:
>   My eye grows dim through sorrow.
> Every day I call upon you, O Lord;
>   I spread out my hands to you.

There is a religiosity that would require a person to look

with a peaceful smile at bystanders while his body is wracked with pain, fever shoots through his veins, and he feels mortally ill. We do not find Heman practicing this religiosity. This gifted brother declares honestly that he has it very rough and that he has moaned, wailed, and cried out to God. Heman did not merely acquiesce to the fact that he was probably going to die. No Christian need be ashamed if, in a similar situation, they are overwhelmed by desperation and have the feeling of seeing no escape anywhere. That is one of the comforts hidden in Psalm 88.

Verses 10–12: Prayers Clothed with Reasons Seeking an Outcome

> Verses 10–12:
> Do you work wonders for the dead?
>   Do the departed rise up to praise you?
> Is your steadfast love declared in the grave,
>   or your faithfulness in Abaddon?
> Are your wonders known in the darkness,
>   or your righteousness in the land of forgetfulness?

Heman believed that the dead are really dead.

Of course, not in the sense that there will be no resurrection of the dead, as people in the church of Corinth argued (1 Cor. 15:12). Or as Hymenaeus and Philetus were arguing, "that the resurrection has already happened" (2 Tim. 2:17–18). They would have viewed this allegedly biblical teaching as something spiritual. According to them, the deeper meaning would have been a resurrection "from within" a person. Such things are still claimed. But then people use the expression to mean that the dead are really dead, that they remain dead. That after death there is nothing more, that a person never comes back, that a person will not rise either to eternal life or to eternal destruction. Heman did not believe that, of

8. Psalm 88: In the Last Stage of a Fatal Illness

course. Together with all the saints in the Old Testament, he undoubtedly confessed, "I expect the resurrection of the dead and the life of the coming age." As we have seen, the ancient Israelite church lived from this promise (cf. the commentary on Ps. 16 and the general comments on Lev. 1–7). Let no one misunderstand us on this point.

But Heman believed, along with the Preacher: "the dead know nothing" (Eccl. 9:5). Until the return of Jesus Christ, they rest "in the grave," "in Abaddon" (Ps. 88:11), "in the land of forgetfulness" (v. 12), where people forget themselves and are forgotten by others (cf. Job 14:21; 21:21; Eccl. 9:5).

In light of the foregoing verses, this was a source of deep sorrow for our brother, not in the first place because of the various sweet things he would leave behind, like his trusted friends (vv. 8, 18), but most of all because there, in the realm of the dead, he would no longer be able to practice his life's calling—praising Yahweh! Undoubtedly, Heman the sage could have said this, but what if our psalm came from Heman the singer? Then these lines of the psalm speak even more strongly, for Heman the singer was called, together with Asaph and Ethan, to sing in the temple worship: "Give thanks to Yahweh, for his steadfast love endures forever" (1 Chr. 16:41–42). What wouldn't Heman be able to proclaim any longer if he were to die? The steadfast love of Yahweh! This apparently was Heman's most beloved desire: singing that steadfast love (Ps. 88:13). But to do that, he had to be alive! "The dead do not praise the LORD, nor do any who go down into silence. But we will bless the LORD" (Ps. 115:17–18).

Just as we saw David doing in Psalm 30, Heman is laying this issue before Yahweh as an argument for extending the life of the one praying (see our comments on Ps. 30, where we discuss the same argument that Heman sets before Yahweh here).

Heman viewed his situation, according to these verses, not as hopeless. He wanted to remain living yet for a time! In that respect, his didactic poem speaks with liberating language: even this godly man was hardly longing to die!

Verses 13–18: Not a Happy Ending

> Verses 13–18:
> **But I, O Lord, cry to you;**
> **in the morning my prayer comes before you.**
> **O Lord, why do you cast my soul away?**
> **Why do you hide your face from me?**
> **Afflicted and close to death from my youth up,**
> **I suffer your terrors; I am helpless.**
> **Your wrath has swept over me;**
> **your dreadful assaults destroy me.**
> **They surround me like a flood all day long;**
> **they close in on me together.**
> **You have caused my beloved and my friend to shun me;**
> **my companions have become darkness.**

This is how Heman concludes his teaching poem, not with a nice ending that smooths everything over, but with an accumulation of complaints. And so he puts a period after the word *darkness*. Some have translated this last verse this way: "My preeminent friend is the darkness." One could entitle this psalm "A Psalm out of the Darkness."

But this conclusion to Psalm 88 is also part of its teaching as a genuinely didactic poem.

There is a kind of religion, not in accordance with the Word, that wants us to sing in every circumstance: "Joy, joy, joy, joy, down in my heart—for Jesus has died for me!" And then there are the "gospel" funeral songs that talk about joyfully facing death and the grave.

In view of the conclusion to his psalm, the dying poet, Heman, was hardly "joyful all the time." He cried out to heaven, "Why?" (v. 14). He felt that he had been forsaken by

8. Psalm 88: In the Last Stage of a Fatal Illness

Yahweh and abandoned (v. 14). Why had Yahweh permitted that wheel of torture to roll over him (v. 15)? Heman cries out that it is "dreadful" (v. 16), that he is swimming in a pool of troubles that God has caused to flow over him (v. 17). And then that loneliness! No friend to comfort him, even if only by being there (v. 18). This is quite different language from "My heart is always joyful!"

Of course we would not want to contradict the apostle Paul, who taught that the kingdom of God consists of "joy in the Holy Spirit" (Rom. 14:17). Nor would we detract from his exhortation "Rejoice in the Lord always; again I will say, rejoice" (Phil. 4:4; cf. 1:25; 2:17–18). But we want to warn against people reading such Scripture passages as supratemporal religious propositions or as laws that are valid always and everywhere. Paul made his comments in the epistles to the Romans and the Philippians in the context of his life's struggle against Judaizers and legalists who were attempting to bring the newly converted Gentile Christians under another religious yoke. These poor folk had barely been freed from the darkness of the kingdom of Satan, when these Judaizers threatened to lock them up in a gloomy religious prison. Legalism, and especially Judaism, rob us of our Christian joy. At that point the apostle wrote to the Philippians, who were being threatened by the gloom-dealing Judaism, "Rejoice in the Lord always!" We must read this exhortation situatedly, in terms of its historical context!

In no way are we denying that many children of God, through the grace of the Holy Spirit and through their faith in God's promises, can greet death with joy. The question is simply this: What is the route to such joy? Without turning Psalm 88 into a law, we can learn from Heman this liberating lesson: We need not prescribe for one another as a rule of life the slogan of "joy, joy, joy, joy, down in my heart!" Heman's teaching poem ends in deep darkness. When a person realizes that the time has come to depart from all flesh, then days come like those Heman experienced, according to Psalm 88:

full of horrors, torments, bitterness, and darkness. And all of this comes despite our trust in God's promises and our expectation of the life of the coming age! For although the last verse ends with "darkness," it always constitutes a part of Heman's conversation with Yahweh. He does not become an atheist. Therefore he asked, why? (v. 14), and therefore we find, in the light of Psalm 88, that many so-called Christian hymns have a strongly Gnostic, world-despising odor and lay religious burdens on people that even an inspired Bible writer like Heman could not bear.

Let us be glad that God's Spirit has placed Psalm 88, gloomy as it is, in his Word. It is a teaching poem that presents God's children with the following: On the rock solid foundation of God's covenant, such struggles can take place in the life of God's faithful children like Heman for the preserving of "all the joy of living."

Our heavenly Father did not blame Heman for this.

Let us not turn this experience of Heman, however, into a rule valid for all time and all people. Scripture tells us, after all, about deathbeds like that of Jacob, who confessed, "I wait for your salvation, O Lord" (Gen. 49:18), and afterward drew up his feet and gave up his spirit. Jacob died just like his father and grandfather, having lived a "long and full life." We don't know how old Heman was, but apparently he had not yet lived a "full life." Could his sorrow, like that of Hezekiah, have been caused by a realization like the following: "I said, In the middle of my days I must depart; I am consigned to the gates of Sheol for the rest of my years" (Isa. 38:10)?

Nevertheless, Heman certainly knew the torah of Moses, with its endlessly repeated promises: God will make this earth a place of delight once more! We intentionally remind the reader of this so we can stand forcefully against the Marcionite-Gnostic spirit that would be able to use Psalm 88 as a crowbar to separate the "gloomy" Old Testament from the "more joyful" New Testament. In principle nothing has changed after Psalm 88, not even through the coming of Jesus

8. Psalm 88: In the Last Stage of a Fatal Illness

Christ. Adam and Eve already knew the promise of eternal life. The difference between the Old and New Testaments is not the difference between darkness and light but between less and more light.

Naturally, as we read Psalm 88, we cannot omit reference to Romans 8: "For I consider that the sufferings of this present time are not worth comparing with the glory that is to be revealed to us" (Rom. 8:18). In principle Heman knew this as well, which is why we do not replace Psalm 88 with Romans 8. On the contrary, Heman's teaching poem can instruct us about how difficult God's children can (and may!) have it when, in the face of death, swept away by a terrible illness, they need to hold fast to these triumphant words of Paul. Excruciating pain and a visage that is repulsive even to friends can "surround" a child of God "like a flood all day long" (Ps. 88:17).

But the Spirit comes to strengthen us in our weakness!

He has already done this in part by placing Psalm 88 in the Scripture. He uses this psalm to teach us that even in the deep weakness from which Heman was speaking, God does not abandon us to our fate. The path is not the same for everyone, nor is it equally long for everyone, but experience confirms the Word: the path does not necessarily end with the severe farewell struggle of Psalm 88, but rather with the abiding confession of Romans 8:31–32: "What then shall we say to these things? If God is for us, who can be against us? He who did not spare his own Son but gave him up for us all, how will he not also with him graciously give us all things?"

Chapter 9

Psalm 90: Not a Psalm for New Year's Eve

Is Psalm 90 truly a psalm for New Year's Eve? It is often used, almost overused, in that context. Many Christians see this psalm as aptly portraying a mood that overcomes them on the last day of the year, when you reflect on the brevity of life and the transitoriness of human beings. That is when they like to open the Bible to Psalm 90 to use the psalm or parts of it for meditating sentimentally along with the opening line of the hymn: "Hours and days and years and ages swift as moving shadows flee."

How did people reach this point?

They have reached the point of pressing God's Word forcefully into the service of popular cultural traditions!—the point of domesticating such a powerful psalm, of transforming an explicitly historically situated prayer into a timeless perspective, of reducing a prayer about a time of judgment to a meditation useful for any and every time.

Psalm 90 is "a prayer of Moses, the man of God." This superscription is the key to the psalm.

Psalm 90 must be read in terms of its historical situatedness.

The Superscription: "A prayer of Moses, the man of God"

Yahweh, Israel's God and our God, is not only merciful and gracious but also patient, with great lovingkindness and faithfulness. That is what Moses, the composer of Psalm 90, heard from Yahweh's own mouth (Exod. 34:6). But there can come an end even to that gracious God's great patience. That is what Israel discovered in the wilderness.

What happened there?

The historical background

Yahweh had preserved Israel from certain extermination in Egypt. The mighty Pharaoh, who at that time ruled a world empire, was holding Israel captive. The Israelites' "cry for rescue from slavery came up to God. And God heard their groaning, and God remembered his covenant with Abraham, with Isaac, and with Jacob" (Exod. 2:23–24). He granted freedom and hope to the slave laborers who were being worked to death by promising them the land of Canaan. A land "flowing with milk and honey," where they would finally receive rest each under his own vine and his own fig tree (1 Kgs. 4:25; Mic. 4:4). Yahweh would be king, and the entire Israelite world or society would rest on the foundation of the Horeb covenant and its redemptive ordinances, about which God himself had said, "If a person does them, he shall live by them" (Lev. 18:5; cf. Ezek. 20:11, 13, 21).

Didn't Yahweh have the right at that point to see joyful faces and devoted people? But what did he get instead? Endless murmuring. It already began before the Red Sea: "Is it because there are no graves in Egypt that you have taken us away to die in the wilderness?" (Exod. 14:11). Three days after the unparalleled miracle of Israel's passage on dry ground through the sea, they murmured again against Moses: "What shall we drink?" (Exod. 15:24). In the wilderness of Sin: If only they had died near the flesh pots in Egypt! There at least

9. Psalm 90: Not a Psalm for New Year's Eve

they had enough to eat! (Exod. 16:3). At Rephidim Moses was at the end of his rope: "What shall I do with this people? They are almost ready to stone me" (Exod. 17:4), because there was no water. Indeed, Israel had the temerity to call God's entire covenant with Abraham into question and to subject all his demonstrations of faithfulness to debate, by throwing out the question "Is Yahweh among us or not?" (Exod. 17:7).

Yahweh patiently bore with all of this.

Yahweh did not punish his people before the one-year stay at Horeb. But thereafter he surely did! When he accepted royal rule over Israel, had arranged for the tabernacle as his royal tent, and had established a covenant with Israel, he refused to allow such crass denigration and undermining of his promises and deeds to go unpunished any longer. At that point he lets the word "provoke" slip (Num. 14:11, 23; 16:30 KJV). This shows progression not only in Israel's wickedness but also in Yahweh's punishment. After the sin with the golden calf, Yahweh wants to exterminate Israel and begin afresh with Moses, but in response to Moses's fervent plea, Yahweh exercises patience once more. But at Taberah Yahweh reduces the outlying parts of the camp to ashes (Num. 11:1–3). At Kibroth-hattaavah they cry out for meat. Yahweh provides meat. Many eat so much that they die (Num. 11:4–35). At Hazeroth God's anger touches Moses's own sister. Miriam is punished with leprosy because of her rebellion against Moses (Num. 12). The nadir is reached when ten of the twelve spies who were sent out return and sow doubt among Israel about God's power to bring them into Canaan according to his promise.

This was more than enough for Yahweh.

To begin with, these weren't simply ordinary people who had gone to look at Canaan, but twelve princes (Num. 13:2). That made the matter more serious. But which land had they gone out to explore? The promised land! The land that had already been granted by God to Israel by virtue of his promise! How often had Yahweh said, "I have given it to you!," namely, in promise form, as part of God's promissory speech (read Gen. 15:18; 28:4; 35:12; cf. Exod. 20:12; Num. 32:9; 33:53; Deut. 5:16; 9:23; 12:1; Josh. 2:9, 14; 6:16; 18:3).

But what conclusion did ten of the twelve commissioned princes reach in their, shall we say, majority report? "[The land] flows with milk and honey, and this is its fruit. However, the people who dwell in the land are strong, and the cities are fortified and very large. . . . And there we saw the Nephilim (the sons of Anak, who come from the Nephilim), and we seemed to ourselves like grasshoppers, and so we seemed to them" (Num. 13:27–28, 33).

You hear not a single word about God and his promise! That was the worst feature of this report. The entire matter was seen purely from the human vantage point. For that reason God's promise was shoved aside as unable to be fulfilled. This was sheer unbelief, crass despising and negation of God's covenant and redemptive deeds, pure distrust of God and his word, as if Yahweh had not bound himself by oath to give Israel the land of Canaan—indeed, as if they did not already possess it, by virtue of God's promise! This report, then, was nothing less than a kick against God's lovely promise. These leading figures in Israel's ecclesiastical life were despising the gospel. According to them, the gospel could not be true. And because princes were the ones making this claim, in the eyes of the people the gospel was perhaps even more unbelievable.

Joshua and Caleb were fighting a losing battle. If they said that Yahweh would bring them into the land and they did need to take the land because he would give it to them, that would only make the Israelites more angry, and Joshua and Caleb might be stoned.

At that point Yahweh's patience was exhausted. At that point practically the entire church of that time put their faith in the words of the ten spies who were sowing doubt, and for the umpteenth time they fell into murmuring: "Why is the LORD bringing us into this land, to fall by the sword? Our wives and our little ones will become a prey. Would it not be better for us to go back to Egypt?" (Num. 14:3). At that point Yahweh responded to this apex of distrust and provocation by saying, "They don't want to enter Canaan? Good, I won't let them enter! Turn around! Would they prefer to die in this wilderness? Fine, they'll die in this wilderness! All the young men who were counted among the warriors who were to have conquered Canaan were no longer counted worthy. Their corpses would fall in the wilderness. Just as they preferred!" For every day of spying, Israel would spend one year wandering in the desert, "until the last of your dead bodies lies in the wilderness" (Num. 14:33; see the commentary on Num. 13–14).

And so they died away, in swarms.

The ten princes went first. They "died by plague before Yahweh" (Num. 14:37) because they had undermined the promise by their talk. Next came those of military age, men who were twenty and older. Moses must have seen a lot of such men die in the wilderness. Israel left behind a trail of graves in the wilderness as their punishment. This was proof of Yahweh's renowned anger at Israel's betrayal and denigration of the gospel or the promise. It was wrath that had been saved up (Num. 14:11, 27; and see our discussion of Ps. 79:8). The age of the mighty men was a bit more than one hundred, given the ages of Moses (120 years, Deut. 34:7), Aaron (123 years, Num. 33:39), and Joshua (110 years, Josh. 24:29); this was shortened under God's wrath, so that the very mighty men lived "only" eighty years and the mighty men seventy years. The ordinary average Israelite no longer reached the higher ages.

There you have the background of Psalm 90: a church that, on account of despising the promise, was dying off under the wrath of God. Thus, Psalm 90 isn't simply a psalm about the transitoriness of humanity and the brevity of human life. Psalm 90 isn't lamenting the fact that all people must die. Pagan songs lament that as well. But rather, as A. Janse notes, this psalm laments the fact that God's people died under his wrath against them.

Don't lose sight of that as you read Psalm 90. Don't turn this historically situated appeal to God, an intercession on Israel's behalf arising from a particular need in history, into a universal timeless perspective.

Moses composed psalms too

As for the composer, in the Psalter only Psalm 90 is explicitly identified as a song of Moses. Nevertheless, Moses may well have been one of the greatest Israelite psalm composers. That fact is evident not only from this majestic psalm but also from demonstrations of his extraordinary poetic skills in Exodus 15:1–21, Deuteronomy 31:19–20, and especially Deuteronomy 32 (see the commentary on this song).

Moses is identified here as "the man of God." This title is used to identify prophets as well (Judg. 13:6, 8; 1 Sam. 2:27; 9:6–10; 1 Kgs. 12:22; 13:1–31; 17:18, 24; 2 Kgs. 1:9–14). In 1 Chronicles 23:14 we read of "Moses, the man of God." Moses was a prophet. In Deuteronomy 18:15 he spoke about "a prophet like me." David was also a "man of God (2 Chr. 8:14).

We turn now to reading Psalm 90.

Verses 1–17: "We are brought to an end by your anger"

> Verse 1:
> **Lord, you have been our refuge [cf. ESV mg.]**
>   **in all generations.**

Though Moses was raised in Egypt, he knew what mountains were. When he looked after the sheep of his father-in-law in Midian, he walked every day in a large mountainous region. The Sinai peninsula featured colorful granite masses and desolate valleys. The mountain that has been considered to be Sinai or Horeb since the early centuries of Christianity is an impressive mass of red granite. It would be natural that such a mountainous region with its caverns and caves would offer a place of refuge for various desert animals. Said more delicately, as it is in the verse above, it was a safe "refuge."

Somewhere in the desert between Egypt and Canaan, amid the majestic mountains, Psalm 90 was lifted up to God as a prayer of Moses, the man of God. The poet addresses Yahweh in verse 1 as "Lord" (with small letters). In the Old Testament this is often the translation of *'adōn*, or "ruler" of heaven and earth. He is identifying that Lord with an image from his surroundings: a "refuge," a safe mountain cavern.

The person praying is probably more than one hundred years old. He apparently has seen various generations come and go. Now he is making intercession for his people, but he is not losing sight of the generations already past. Perhaps because of his age, he increasingly senses his bond with his ancestors and contemporaries, who together constitute the one Israel, and he lays before God the need of that people which spans the centuries. Pause to notice that he persistently speaks in the first-person plural. This intercessor is a mouthpiece for God's people (see our discussion of Ps. 79:8).

We paraphrase this first verse of Psalm 90 as follows:

> Lord, we have been wandering for so long now. Despite all his wealth, our father Abraham was still a guest and sojourner, and he had to buy a place to bury his wife Sarah. Isaac and Jacob were also guests in Canaan, guests in Paddan-Aram, and guests in Egypt. There they often faced serious danger. And as far as we and our parents are concerned: we were slaves. Without rights. Oppressed. Worked to death. How many of our newborn baby boys were drowned in the Nile? But you, O Ruler, have been a refuge for us from generation to generation. We could always take refuge with you. Not only we who live in "this great and terrifying wilderness," but our ancestors Abraham, Isaac, and Jacob took refuge with you centuries ago. For you

are the Eternal One, and your eternal arms surround us (Deut. 33:27).

Verse 2:
Before the mountains were brought forth,
    or ever you had formed the earth and the world,
    from everlasting to everlasting you are God.

Indeed, the granite mountain clefts were centuries old. How long had they dominated the landscape? The Israelites spoke of "the everlasting hills" (Gen. 49:26) and of "the eternal mountains" (Hab. 3:6). But Yahweh was there before these eternal mountains. He was already there at the time water covered these giants. But then Yahweh sounded his voice and the mountains rose up, the valleys sank down, and the water flowed away (Ps. 104:6–8). Who was the God who called mountains and valleys into existence in this superhuman way? Yahweh was already there at that point. For he is God from eternity to eternity: from the temporal horizon past to the temporal horizon coming.

What a contrast there is between this eternally living God and the Israelite people dying off in the wilderness under his judgment!

Verse 3:
You return the mortal one to dust
    and say, "Return, O children of man!"

What is left of a person a few years after his burial? Dust. Moses uses a word that recalls something that is pulverized, crushed to smithereens! The King James Version renders it as "Thou turnest man to destruction." The word we are translating as "the mortal one" (*'enosh*) identifies the person as a weak, fragile, and mortal creature. We read the same thing in Psalm 8: "What is man that you are mindful of him, and the son of man that you care for him?" (v. 4). At one moment he stands before you healthy, and the next moment he is destroyed (see our discussion of the name Enosh in our commentary on Gen. 4:26).

Moses saw this in a poignant way.

How many had he seen buried in the wilderness by now? This had been going on for years. Those buried first had long ago become dust—literally, become pulverized. "You are dust, and to dust you shall return!" (Gen. 3:19). How many thousands of years ago was it when Yahweh pronounced this sentence upon Adam? As far as Moses was concerned, it sounded forth every day in the wilderness: "Return again, you children of men, to the earth (*'adamah*) from which you were taken" (cf. Gen. 3:19).

Verse 4:
For a thousand years in your sight
   are but as yesterday when it is past,
   or as a watch in the night.

Occasionally we ask, "Yesterday? What kind of day was that again?" In terms of our experience, days can fly past. For God, a thousand years are like a night watch for an Israelite: one-third of a night. If you're sleeping, it passes just like that. In the same way, entire periods of world history are just moments for God.

But even this verse is not a universal truth! It begins with the little word *for* and thus connects verse 4 to verse 3. There the punishment of Kadesh was narrated in poetic form: "You will die in the wilderness!" Then comes verse 4: "*For* a thousand years in your sight are but as yesterday"—let alone one or two years, or even three! The trek from Egypt to Horeb may well have been a long time ago for the ordinary Israelite, but for Yahweh, Israel's treachery ever since Egypt had happened no more than a minute ago! Yahweh was still angry about that: "*For* a thousand years . . ."—so he doesn't forget after just a few decades!

This is a verse that makes us tremble.

For the Lord, the Middle Ages happened as though it were only yesterday. The apostasy of those centuries? For him, it happened not even a day ago. The iniquities of us and of our fathers, like the slave trade? It's still fresh in his memory.

The kinds of words Moses writes here may well drive us to pray the prayer of Psalm 79:8 that we discussed previously: "Do not remember against us the iniquities of former generations" (cf. ESV mg.)

Verses 5–6:
> You sweep them away as with a flood; they are like a dream,
>   like grass that is renewed in the morning:
> in the morning it flourishes and is renewed;
>   in the evening it fades and withers.

Being swept away . . . How often had Moses the shepherd stood looking at a raging mountain stream, swollen by a Near Eastern torrential downpour, as it destroyed trees and bushes with breathtaking force and swept them away in the raging current? (cf. Matt. 7:24–25). Now he is watching human lives being swept away, as Israel leaves behind a trail of graves. The number of those who had been brought from Egypt is becoming increasingly more sparse. Every stop along the way became, as time passed, a cemetery. The people are nothing more than the short-lived Near Eastern wild flower: in the morning it is still fresh, and in the evening it is withered. Like a nap in the morning, after you've already been awake. Dying "before your time," the Preacher would say (Eccl. 7:17).

All of this happened, not because of the inevitable brevity of life, but because Israel had provoked Yahweh. They had despised his promise, despised Canaan, and had not dared to move forward with Yahweh. Despite all his signs and wonders, they had not yet trusted him.

No, Moses surely did not view this massive death as

something normal. So many people dying at such a record pace isn't something that just happens by itself. This is not something we can attribute to the universal human judgment of mortality. There was more going on here. Here people were simply being swept away! In that, Moses saw God's punishing hand. "*You* sweep them away." God had nominated all the men of Israel, at least the soldiers older than twenty, to die within forty years. That is what Moses was seeing behind the unusually high numbers of those who died in those years. Paul saw a similar "lesson" in the many cases of death in the church of Corinth (1 Cor. 11:30–32). Moses did not view the many cases of death as normal.

Verse 7:
For we are brought to an end by your anger;
    by your wrath we are dismayed.

Notice the use of "we" here! A praying Moses is still speaking here, not a moralistic preacher declaring universal truths. This is not a lesson that is perpetually applicable to all people. And thankfully not! God's Word speaks about, and from within, the constantly changing circumstances in which God and his people have enjoyed mutual interaction in the course of history. Never static, always dynamic. All times are not alike, after all. Moreover, God is not always working in the same way with his church. Sometimes he saves up his wrath for a long time, as he did before Horeb. At such times he puts up with his people and with great patience tolerates their complaining about meat and water. We have just been discussing this. In other times it seems as though Yahweh is unwilling to put up with any iniquity on the part of his people.

But Psalm 90 is historically situated after Horeb. That fact lends to the psalm not only an enormous enriching of its meaning, but also an enormous increase in responsibility before Yahweh. After that, Kadesh happened. When Moses prays our psalm, he does so under the curse of the terrible fact that Israel was being chased away from the gate of the promised land to live again in the wilderness, in order to die there at an increased pace. *This* church during *this* time was indeed perishing under God's wrath. This was one of the generations in church history to which the word of Jeremiah is applicable: this was "the generation of his wrath"—a saying that happily does not apply at all times (Jer. 7:29).

Just as we read verse 7 in terms of its historical situatedness, we must read verse 8 in the same way.

Verse 8:
You have set our iniquities before you,
    our secret sins in the light of your presence.

Here we have no general declaration about a perpetual activity of God. There are times when Yahweh "does not deal with us according to our sins, nor repay us according to our iniquities" (Ps. 103:10). But Psalm 90 was prayed for the first time when Yahweh did do that: "You have set our iniquities before you." At this point he did repay sins, although not completely according to the measure of Israel's iniquities (Ps. 103). In that connection Moses seemed to be aware of "our secret sins," which God views as more wicked than we often do. Was Moses also thinking here of the "intentional" sins that occur "secretly" before others but not before God? (For more on "intentional" and "unintentional" sins, see the commentary on Lev. 4)

Meanwhile, this verse is a striking illustration of the characterization of Moses given in Numbers 12:3: "Now the man Moses was very meek, more than all people who were on the face of the earth." There were four men who did not participate with the ten spies in sowing doubt and who prophesied against badmouthing the promise of God: Joshua, Caleb, Aaron, and Moses, who did so at the risk of being stoned (Num. 14:5–10). Despite this, in Psalm 90 Moses does not separate himself as an innocent individual, apart from his culpable fellow Israelites; rather, he uses the first-person plural to demonstrate that he is a humble confessor of everyone's shared guilt: "*our* iniquities . . . *our* secret sins."

"Moses was very meek." Such righteous people understand that it is not always appropriate to sing Psalm 103: "As far as the east is from the west, so far does he remove our transgressions from us" (v. 12). Moses discerned the time and realized that now was the time for lament.

> Verse 9:
> For all our days pass away under your wrath;
> we bring our years to an end like a sigh.

We must not forget who the speaker is in this verse. Moses could lament, along with Israel after Kadesh, "All our days pass away under your wrath, we bring our years to an end like a sigh." That's how it was during those particular forty years when the largest part of God's church at that time experienced his judgment of the shortening of life and premature death. This lament is also historically situated. Fortunately, this lament need not be uttered always and everywhere and by every generation of God's people. Moses had good reason for doing so. Every day he saw a freshly dug grave or a sickbed that would become a deathbed, all of which drummed into Israel that God was angry with them. That is how Moses and his older contemporaries lived out their years: led out of Egypt but not into Canaan, an ecclesiastical life with no sign of fresh life, disappointing, fruitless times, when they were walking around and around in the same circle until people realized all of a sudden that their own life was past. Gone like a sigh.

Oh, how the lifespans had been shortened!

> Verse 10:
> The years of our life are seventy,
> or even by reason of strength eighty;

> yet their span is but toil and trouble;
> they are soon gone, and we fly away.

For Moses, seventy or eighty years was a short time. His own father, Amram, became 137 years old (Exod. 6:20). He himself became 120 (Deut. 34:7), Aaron reached 123 (Num. 33:39), while Miriam, who was older than Aaron, apparently died shortly before Aaron did, having reached approximately the same age (Num. 20:1, 29). Moses's servant, Joshua, reached 110 (Josh. 24:29). Apparently, these people were not the only ones who surpassed the hundred-year mark (Josh. 24:31).

After the Kadesh episode the Israelites in general did not get any older than seventy or eighty. That means that in Moses's eyes, they died in the strength of their lives. For him, together with Joshua and Aaron and Miriam, this was middle age. So the Israelites died before their time (Eccl. 7:17; Isa. 38:10; 65:20). The average Israelite lived, after the Kadesh episode, forty years fewer than Moses and the other people mentioned. The ages were shortened under the wrath of God. The generations living when Psalm 90 was written died, not "old and full of days," but relatively speaking, in the peak of their lives.

Israel's anguish reached still more deeply, however. "What was once the source of our pride," Moses laments, "has become toil and trouble." (Recall the translation of the ASV: "Yet is their pride but labor and sorrow." We could also translate it this way: "adversity and calamity." But what did he mean by "their pride"?

If we read the psalm as a universally religious song applicable to all people, we might think of everything in a person's life he could be proud of. But Psalm 90 is not a universally religious timeless song for New Year's Eve. Therefore, we must not dilute the words *their pride* into something that characterizes the life of every person. The word *their* refers to that short, fleeting life of the Israelites of that time who were living under God's judgment after the Kadesh episode. The word

9. Psalm 90: Not a Psalm for New Year's Eve

pride refers to something Moses and the Israelites of that time were proud of. We think it is most plausible that this is a reference not to various universally human things but rather to the glorious exodus from Egypt, and the "foundation of the [Israelite] world" at Horeb. These were majestic events. Behold all that Yahweh had done for Israel! He had knocked a world empire to pieces. He had temporarily dried up a sea. He had provided an entire nation with food in the wilderness. He had announced himself as King at Horeb. He had established a new covenant. He had arranged for his royal tent and announced ordinances and rights that were so good that Yahweh himself said about them, "If a person does them, he shall live by them" (Lev. 18:5). Shouldn't we recall these facts first as we hear Moses talk in verse 10 about those proud years?

But what must Moses now conclude, to his sorrow? That everything which in those years of the exodus and Horeb was their pride had now (as he is writing Psalm 90) become "toil and trouble." The word for *toil* here (*'awen*) is rendered elsewhere with the word *delusion* (Isa. 41:29), and occasionally it refers to an idol (Isa. 66:3). If we recall these meanings of *'awen* in this line in verse 10, then we prefer the rendering "delusion" or "vanity" over "toil." Moses is complaining in this verse that at the time Psalm 90 was written, the entire promised and initiated work of God, from the exodus out of Egypt to the entrance into Canaan—"their pride"—was, so to speak, in vain. We speak similarly when we occasionally say, "It's all for nothing." That is what Moses is sighing: "What once made us so joyful has now become a disaster [*'awen*]."

Continue to remember: Psalm 90 is referring to a time of judgment!

In Egypt Yahweh's judgment passed by the Israelite houses marked with blood when he put to death the firstborn (Exod. 12:12–13, 29). Now, however, Moses is watching Yahweh's word being fulfilled daily: "But as for you, your dead bodies shall fall in this wilderness. And your children shall be shepherds in the wilderness forty years and shall suffer for your faithlessness, until the last of your dead bodies lies in the wilderness . . . and you shall know my displeasure" (Num. 14:32, 34). It had been Israel's "pride," the apex of her existence as a people, that Yahweh had come so near with his pleasure, but now they were experiencing his displeasure.

But had the Israelites realized this? Did they see themselves as living under the wrath of God? Moses doubted that!

> Verse 11:
> **Who considers the power of your anger,
> and your wrath according to the fear of you?**

Who among those around Moses knew the power of God's anger? In Scripture, *knowing* is a matter of the heart. Who had an eye for Yahweh's outrage against Israel? Or had people simply become accustomed to it, viewing it simply as their fate? Were they blind to Yahweh's hand? Did people know the meaning of "my displeasure" (Num. 14:34)? Later on, Isaiah asked the same question: "To whom has the arm of the LORD been revealed?" (Isa. 53:1). After all, this may be expected from people who fear Yahweh. Later, in his farewell song, Moses mentioned this matter again: "For they are a nation void of counsel, and there is no understanding in them" (Deut. 32:28). Nevertheless, Moses was praying for that wisdom.

> Verse 12:
> **So teach us to number our days
> that we may get a heart of wisdom.**

Moses prays that we may have an eye open to the situation in which we are living. A wise person, after all, is someone who fears Yahweh and thereby knows his situation and understands his time, so that he knows what he must do and what he must refrain from doing. In a time like that of Psalm 90, getting a heart of wisdom consisted of paying attention to the deeds of Yahweh and humbling oneself under his mighty hand. In later times as well, Israel lacked this wisdom (see our commentary on Ps. 74:1). How fervently Moses wanted to see Israel counting the days, as Yahweh was counting them during that time: "a year for each day" (Num. 14:34). And how fervently Moses wanted to hear Israelites praying from that attitude of the heart.

Verse 13:
Return, O LORD! How long?
Have pity on your servants!

Yahweh had turned away from Israel.

At Kadesh he had said, "According to the number of the days in which you spied out the land, forty days, a year for each day, you shall bear your iniquity forty years, and you shall know [or: so that you may know] my displeasure" (Num. 14:34).

This kind of language is far different from the kind of reasoning about God that talks of him being present always, everywhere, in the same way. Such theorizing about God would insist that what Moses says here is "actually" not true, because "of course" God never forsakes his church. Moses may be correct from a human vantage point, but "down deep" it's not true, because "in the proper sense" we cannot talk of someone "returning" who "in reality" was never absent.

We intentionally used quotation marks in the preceding paragraph, to show the Gnostic character of this kind of theologizing. Early on, Gnosticism, which from its very beginning has always been averse to the Old Testament, spoke arrogantly of the "simple faith" that still held on to the literal sense of Scripture, in contrast to the Gnostic theological-scientific "higher" and "deeper" knowledge of Scripture. Already in the apostolic era, Gnosticism tried to form a bridge from the historicality of the gospel to the eternal-universal, from the concrete to the abstract, from myth to reason.

But Scripture—and we hear this message formulated

explicitly from the mouth of Moses here in Psalm 90—teaches us not to theorize about God, but to deal personally with the living God who occasionally does indeed turn away from his church and abandons her to her own fate. This is how Moses talks about Yahweh, who after forty years and two generations had interrupted his redemptive work—begun famously in Egypt and crowned gloriously at Horeb—for the time being. When Moses wrote Psalm 90, Yahweh had withdrawn for years already (cf. v. 15: "as many years as we have seen evil"). That was no backward "simple faith" but a hard fact.

In these circumstances, Moses pleaded: "Yahweh, have pity on your servants!" Or as the King James Version puts it, "Let it repent thee concerning thy servants." This is how Moses knew Yahweh already at this point, namely, as a God who "relents over disaster" (Joel 2:13). "How long must it continue? Each day another burial. Turn back, Yahweh, let us no longer wander around in circles. Have you no pity for us? For years now we've been living in a dark night of your wrath, punishment, and destruction. O God, let morning now dawn upon us, rather than this night. Light instead of darkness. Life instead of death."

Verse 14:
Satisfy us in the morning with your steadfast love,
   that we may rejoice and be glad all our days.

Could Moses be alluding here to that unforgettable morning when manna lay on the desert ground for the first time? Only days before, he had faced the virtually insoluble problem of providing food for the entire people in the wilderness. But then the new morning dawned, and "there was on the face of the wilderness a fine, flake-like thing, fine as frost on the ground" (Exod. 16:14). From that day forward, Yahweh had satisfied his people every morning with manna. Was Moses referring to that when he prayed, "Satisfy us in the morning with your steadfast love"? In any case, he prayed to Yahweh for a new time, for a heartwarming indication of Yahweh returning to his people that would penetrate the oppressive situation on a given morning. He prayed for a proof that Yahweh had returned, so the mourning clothes and tears over a loved one who had died prematurely would be replaced by the tears of joy at the dawning of a new time, a time when Yahweh would satisfy his people with steadfast love (cf. Deut. 33:23).

Verse 15:
Make us glad for as many days as you have afflicted us,
    and for as many years as we have seen evil.

How long now had there been a damper on Israel's life? How many years had been filled with sickness, death, destruction, brevity, aimless wandering, pointless activity? In such times, we are inclined to look at the people and to complain about the circumstances. Moses, however, talked of the "days . . . *you* have afflicted us."

This is proof of wisdom acquired through the fear of the LORD. That is what Moses prayed for in verse 12. That petition for Yahweh to reverse the order once again was intensely moving. No longer years of calamity according to the days that Israel had spied out Canaan, but years of well-being according to the days that you have afflicted us. If only Yahweh would do that: grant just as many years of joy as he had sent days of affliction!

Verse 16:
Let your work be shown to your servants,
    and your glorious power to their children.

Moses is referring, of course, to the work that Yahweh had begun when he called Abraham from the Ur of the Chaldeans and made him expand into a great nation. The work that he had continued when he rescued this nation out of Egypt and made it into his kingdom at Sinai. All of that now called for the necessary result of inheriting the promised land of Canaan. By asking that Yahweh's work *be shown* to his servants, Moses was referring to his redeeming work instead of his afflicting work.

It is remarkable that even someone as great in the kingdom of God as Moses had to beseech God concerning his "work." Even this "man of God" could do his best for the church of his day, but if Yahweh did not return, all of Moses's efforts would avail nothing, and all his attempts at effecting a revival, assuming that he had undertaken such efforts, would have been without result. Yahweh had to do it—Moses saw that clearly. Yahweh had to cease doing nothing.

Such situations can reoccur. In times when God opposes his church and has forsaken her, there is nothing that fervently faithful labor, comprehensive activity, diligent study, huge sacrifices, well-run organizations, open discussions, and intense arguing can do to change the decrepit situation. If God does not get to work, all human efforts in such times help not at all. God must be willing to make work of his promises. People cannot automatically count on that in times of (promised!) judgments and punishments. For then the fundamental question is, does Yahweh take pleasure in working salvation? He does not always do so, even though we are his people through and through. At that point only one instrument helps: praying like Moses did in Psalm 90.

At least the older generations had seen God's glory, in Egypt and at Sinai. But what did the Israelite young people see in the recent years of wandering throughout the wilderness? They had grown up in a church whose life went around and around in the same circle. What a depressing business! Moses is praying for the young people. "Let our boys and girls see your glory once again through the fulfilling of the promise that started it all: inheriting Canaan. Grant our children the rest that you promised Abraham long ago. Each with his own vine and his own fig tree. No desert as dwelling place, but a land flowing with milk and honey."

If only Yahweh would make "work" of that!

Verse 17:
Let the favor of the Lord our God be upon us,
and establish the work of our hands upon us;
yes, establish the work of our hands!

"From now on, do not let your wrath rest upon us, but shine upon us with your lovingkindness. Then our work can thrive and take root and bear fruit again as well." With this last remark, we can recall the animal husbandry of the Israelites and the trade skills (technical knowledge and capabilities) they taught their children to prepare them for settling in Canaan (Num. 20:19; Exod. 36:8–38). But one could also recall the work that a man like Moses performed for this people: beginning with his "academic" training in Egypt and his dealing with Pharaoh, leading this people for forty years, and not least of all, his literary efforts connected with the production of the Torah, the foundation of Holy Scripture.

Moses prayed that God would "establish" all this work, make it endure, so that it would not sink away in a morass of vanity and uselessness, but that something would come from it all.

The composer of the Torah is praying here for fruit to come from his work.

A Review of Psalm 90

So, here we have no sentimental psalm for New Year's Eve.

We have a prayer of Moses, the man of God. Thus the question is legitimate: Did God hear this prayer? Most certainly!

It is sad, though, to read that Moses himself, who had prayed so fervently for love to be shown to Israel rather than wrath and the dominion of death, did not see the glimmer of such an earnestly expected dawn in advance. At Meribah the children sinned in the same way their parents had sinned earlier: "Why have you brought us out of Egypt?" But now God did not punish them! We said earlier: those times did occur! (cf. Num. 23:8; Isa. 28:23–29). But Moses did not treat Yahweh as holy in the sight of the Israelites. He portrayed him as a God of punishment instead of the God of provision (see the commentary on Num. 20:2–13). At that point, he was not allowed to enter God's sanctuary of Canaan.

Yahweh turned away from his burning wrath at that point. There were also times when he did that. Among Joshua and his younger contemporaries, Yahweh showed his glory and work once again. He displayed his lovingkindness and compassion to that generation. Then joy came once more to Israel, as did the dawn for which Moses had prayed. God's "work," pleaded for by the poet of Psalm 90, was seen in the drying up of the Jordan, the fall of Jericho, and the apportioning of the inherited land. When, after forty years of wandering, these Israelites were sitting each under his own vine and fig tree, they could witness in that blessing the love of Yahweh their God for Israel.

As far as the work of Moses's hands was concerned, he had to leave it behind unfinished, but the foundation of Holy Scripture, with regard to the human side to this great work, stands under his name. In this regard, Yahweh heard Moses's petition in Psalm 90:17! Moses appears to have spent forty unprofitable years in Midian waiting for God to call him. Another forty years appear to have been just as unprofitable for Moses, spent between Kadesh and Canaan. But how gloriously Yahweh heard his prayer, "Establish the work of our hands upon us, yes, establish the work of our hands!"

What an impressive work Moses brought about!

Fortunately it is not always and everywhere the time for taking Psalm 90 on our lips. People need to beware of Gnostic thinking, which always wants to melt down the gold of God's historical Word into a collection of eternally valid truths.

9. Psalm 90: Not a Psalm for New Year's Eve

The historical context of Psalm 90 is this: Israel was disappearing under God's wrath because she had despised the promise of God given to her at that time. The wrath of God was being brought down on account of despising the gospel!

Didn't that rage rest upon Europe as well? Read the chronicles of war and watch the documentaries and visit the mass graves of World Wars I and II in the light of this psalm!

"The generation of his wrath" (Jer. 7:29).

"We are brought to an end by your anger" (Ps. 90:7).

By reflecting on those periods from the twentieth century, people who belong to Christianity, the people of God of this era, can unfortunately echo Moses: "Who considers the power of your anger, and your wrath [upon Christendom]?"

Nevertheless, a serious psalm like this one can also lift us up.

For what did Moses do in that terrible time of ecclesiastical and national apostasy and decline, as he saw countless graves and gravestones? He called out to the Lord, the *'adon*. He prayed for Israel's posterity, for her children and her young people.

As we have seen, that prayer was heard.

May the God and Father of our Lord Jesus Christ have compassion on many young people within modern Christianity, and unless he sends his Son upon the clouds, also on the Christianity of the next century.

CHAPTER 10

Psalm 104: How Numerous Are Your Works, O Yahweh. You Have Done Them All with Wisdom

The Israelites were for the most part farmers. Most of the men left the city gates early every morning to work their land, and returned at nightfall by entering through the city gates. All that time they enjoyed the freedom of nature. Those who stayed behind—women and children, the aged and craftsmen—also lived for the most part under the open sky. Due to the subtropical climate of Palestine, Saul could sleep at night on the flat roof of Samuel's house (1 Sam. 9:26), whereas Jacob spent the night outside in the field (Gen. 28:11). So the Israelites were really people of the outdoors.

This brought them much closer to nature than the modern Western city dweller who spends most of his life indoors. As a result, the Israelites had a better ear and eye for the preaching of nature than today's average city dweller. Just look at how much attention the psalmists pay to events in heaven and on earth, on mountains and in valleys. In Psalms 8, 29, 33, 65, 67, 104, 147, 148, and others, they praised God as Creator.

Creation Psalms

Psalms like those just mentioned are called nature psalms. This is not a particularly biblical name. We can hardly scrap the word *nature* from our dictionaries, but the so-called nature psalms never use the word. Nor, in fact, does the entire Old Testament. Nature is an abstract concept, and neither Israel nor her neighbors could embrace that notion. Scripture speaks much more concretely about "heaven and earth," "the earth and its fullness," "the world and those who dwell therein," "the sea and everything in it," and the like.

When we read Psalm 104 in a moment, we will see that the Israelite had an entirely different perspective on what we Westerners call nature. For the Israelite, "the earth and its fullness" did not constitute a gigantic super-automaton from which everything emerged, without any divine assistance, automatically or according to autonomous natural laws: flora and fauna, babies and rain, light and darkness.

That is why we prefer the classification "creation psalms."

Purpose

What purpose did the poets have when they composed the creation psalms? Undoubtedly, in the first place they wanted to sing of the glory of the Creator and his creation, to express deep amazement for the power and majesty of Yahweh. But that does not exhaust their purpose. The psalmists give expression to that amazement in an Israelite manner in a Canaanite world, and frequently as the pious remnant living among a Canaanized Israel.

The world surrounding Israel venerated the creature above the Creator. Sun, moon, and stars, as well as rain and fertility, were venerated as gods. Instead of rooting out these abominations, the Israelites themselves often served the rain god Baal and bowed down before the entire "host of heaven" (2 Kgs. 17:16; 21:3–9; 23:4–5). Archaeology has supplied us with many examples of Egyptian, Assyrian, Babylonian, and

Canaanite prayers and psalms, some of which are directed to the sun god or the moon god. Jeremiah saw people in Jerusalem offering sacrifices on their rooftops to the sun, moon, and stars. Entire families were involved: "The children gather wood, the fathers kindle fire, and the women knead dough, to make cakes for the queen of heaven" (Jer. 7:18). That is the world in which Israel sang her creation psalms.

In our discussion of the creation story in the commentary on Genesis, we referred to the possibility that this narrative had a polemic purpose as well and was composed in opposition to the spirit of Canaanitism that constantly threatened God's people. We should consider the same possibility in connection with Israel's creation psalms. In these psalms the godly not only praised Yahweh's honor, but also contended for Yahweh's honor. The purpose of these psalms, then, is twofold: to sing the praises of and to confess Yahweh as Creator. But this confession refers to the deepest sense of the word: standing up for the truth at those points where the spirit of the age raises objection and where such confession is often accompanied by suffering. That is what the godly remnant in Israel did with this kind of psalm. When many in Israel had gone over to the rain god Baal, or were bowed prostrate to the sun and the moon, then the righteous person confessed in direct opposition to public opinion: "By the word of the Lord the heavens were made, and by the breath of his mouth all their host" (Ps. 33:6). "Let them praise the name of the Lord! For he commanded and they were created" (Ps. 148:5). Sun, moon, and stars are the "work of [God's] fingers" (Ps. 8:3). The creation psalms must have sounded like genuine fight songs in many eras of Israelite church history. And should we not take them upon our lips in our generation of atheistic technocracy, with the same purpose of praising our God and Father in amazement and of confessing him polemically as the Almighty Creator of heaven and earth?

"O Yahweh my God, you are very great!"

Psalm 104 is therefore not a song about nature, for the psalmists never recognized that concept which is alien to the Bible, as we observed. So is he then singing in praise of the creation? We do indeed classify Psalm 104 among the creation psalms, but upon closer inspection we see that it is a song not to the creature but to the Creator. Psalm 104 is a poem about Yahweh, the God of Israel, especially about his majesty and splendor that radiate throughout heaven and earth (v. 1).

The theme

"Yahweh my God, you are very great!" (v. 1). With that the psalm opens, and that is also the theme of this meditation (v. 34) that the poet has developed into a psalm overflowing with praise of Yahweh's greatness. Except that such greatness was identified not with the forgiveness of sins or God's faithfulness to his Word, as Psalms 103 and 105 do, but rather with the work of God's creation and maintenance of our earth, or with his enormous housekeeping.

A divine housekeeping

God's housekeeping—that is what Psalm 104 is actually about. We read about a divine household manager, a king who has clothed himself with majesty and splendor (v. 1). His royal robe is the light (v. 2). His tent covering is the heavens (v. 2). Yahweh stretches that out just as easily as an Israelite stretches out his own tent covering (v. 2; cf. Isa. 40:22; Zech. 12:1). And just as the Israelite occasionally added another room to his house (Elisha lived in this kind of attic room in the Shunammite's home, 2 Kgs. 4:10; cf. 1 Kgs. 17:19, 23), Yahweh also turns his upper heavens into an attic (the same word that the Shunammite used) "on the waters," upon the clouds (Ps. 104:3; cf. 18:11–12; 68:5; Ezek. 1).

Indeed, that is poetic language. You can hardly compare a tent to upper "chambers," but this poetic language portrays a powerful reality: the divine housekeeping. Servants—the winds and the flashes of lightning—walk through this house (Ps 104:4). It has a timepiece: the moon (v. 19). It has lamps that provide light: the sun (v. 19). Order and regularity govern this house, which is necessary for good housekeeping. There are fixed times for this and fixed times for that (vv. 19–23).

Moreover, God's housekeeping is immeasurably great. A number of things belong to it: the mountains and valleys, the oceans and fields, the forests and the heavenly bodies, the animals in countless species, and all people as well. What a tremendous amount of food is consumed every day in this house. All the animals must eat and drink regularly. But the mountain bluffs, which cannot drink water from the streams, are drenched (Ps. 104:13). "Man's heart" must be strengthened with bread (v. 15). The mighty cedars of Lebanon need food (v. 16). But so do the birds in those trees, and the storks nesting in the cypress trees (v. 17; ESV "fir trees") share in God's housekeeping. So too do the mountain goats in the heights, the rock badgers hiding among the rocks, and the roaring predatory animals in the jungle (vv. 18–22). All of them are members of God's household.

Anyone who knows what one husband and wife spend on the effort, care, love, and wisdom required to provide housekeeping for fewer than ten people, and on the care of a pet, will, if he fears God and reflects on God's cosmic housekeeping, agree heartily with Psalm 104: "Yahweh my God, you are very great!"

The structure of Psalm 104

Psalm 104 is one of the larger psalms, but when we consider its enormous subject, we can hardly say that it is long. In only eighty-one lines the psalmist sings of God's greatness in all his creation: heaven and earth, the world of people and of animals, the plant kingdom and the realm of the stars. Don't you think that is a masterful sample of poetic artistry? This is partly because the psalmist has structured his poem in such a clear way. Once you get hold of the key to that structure, you will see how beautifully this psalm is organized.

That key is this: what Genesis 1 proclaims to us in a narrative manner, Psalm 104 proclaims to us in a poetic manner. In Psalm 104 you hear the poetic echo of Genesis 1. This includes even the psalm's arrangement. The psalmist has structured his song of praise about the Yahweh's creational greatness according to the creation sequence in Genesis 1. Let's lay these arrangements alongside each other.

Genesis 1 alongside Psalm 104

How does Genesis 1 end? With the creation of humanity as vice-gerent over everything God had made: plants and animals, birds and fish (cf. Ps. 8). But what happened before that? The story of God's care, something he continues to have, for people and animals to be able to live on this earth. For as Genesis 1 tells us, God did not leave the earth desolate but saw to it that people and animals could live on the earth. Light served human existence in particular (vv. 3–5). Dew and rain made the land fruitful for man (vv. 6–8). God created grains and fruit trees especially in service to man (vv. 9–13, 29). Lights in the sky served as indicators for man of days, months, and years (vv. 14–19). Yahweh prepared everything especially for his vice-gerent, humanity.

When we look now at Psalm 104, we see that the poet has arranged his description of God's greatness according to the six creation days of Genesis 1, and we see that he shines his full light on Yahweh's immense goodness toward humanity and animals. The overview on the facing page can perhaps show more clearly the correspondence between these sequences.

Naturally, these remarkable parallels do not exclude the unique character of both Scripture passages. Genesis 1 narrates that Yahweh made heaven and earth and how he did that. But Psalm 104 remains a piece of poetry that is obviously constructed according to the sequence of the six creation days, though with poetic freedom. In that connection, the

10. Psalm 104: How Numerous Are Your Works, O Yahweh

GENESIS 1

First creation day
The light.

Second creation day
The firmament or the heavens.
Waters above and beneath the firmament.

Third creation day
Separation between the dry land (the earth) and the waters under the heaven (the seas).
Green herbs.
Seed-bearing plants.
Fruit trees.

Fourth creation day
The lights in the sky, sun, moon, and stars, to give light and to differentiate between day and night, and for fixed times, days, and years.

Fifth creation day
The great sea monsters and every swarming living being with which the waters teem, and various winged birds.

Sixth creation day
Cattle, creeping and wild animals. Human beings as rulers over fish, birds, cattle, and every creeping animal.

Seventh day
Yahweh rested from all of his creation work.

PSALM 104

Psalm 104:2a
He covers himself with light.

Psalm 104:2b-4
The heavens.
The rain clouds.
The wind and lightning.

Psalm 104:5-18
He sets a boundary that they may not pass, so that they might not again cover the earth. He makes the streams flow and quenches the thirst of all the animals of the field.
Birds among the branches.
Grass, green plants, wheat, vines, olive trees, cedars, and cypress trees.

Psalm 104:19-23
The fixed times (moon) and fixed time of the sun's setting. Night and day, light and darkness. The night for predatory animals. The day for man's work.

Psalm 104:24-26
The sea with its innumerable teeming swarms, the ships and Leviathan (legendary sea monster).

Psalm 104:27-30
Everything depends on God for food and life.

Psalm 104:31
Yahweh rejoices over his works.

psalm speaks, for example, about the animals before speaking about sun, moon, and stars, and before bringing humanity on stage in verses 15 and 23. For the psalmist is talking about the finished creation, and Genesis 1 is talking about the creation work itself. These and other small details detract in no way, however, from the clear structure of Psalm 104. The psalmist praises Yahweh's greatness following the order of the creation days, complete with God's joy in his creation on the seventh day.

A psalm of praise

To praise is to tell proudly what someone has done. Psalm 104 praises God by telling proudly of the immense power and goodness and wisdom with which God made the heavens and the earth. The psalmist includes the work of providence or sustaining God's creation work, as we shall see. But everything that he gathers together testifies of Yahweh's greatness:

Verse 1:
Bless the Lord, O my soul!
   O Lord my God, you are very great!
You are clothed with splendor and majesty.

The first day: "Let there be light"

On the first day God created light. This explains why the psalmist begins his meditation with that initial work of creation: the light! The ancient Israelites did not yet know about our modern devices for illumination; they knew what jet-black darkness is. That is why they valued, perhaps more than we do, the greatness of God's power and goodness in his daily renewed blessing of daylight. In that phenomenon, the poetic eye of the psalmist saw something like the royal robe of Yahweh:

Verse 2a:
   Covering yourself with light as with a garment.

Literally he is saying that God *wraps* himself in the light. With this form of expression he comes close to those Scripture passages that hold before us the fact that every day God creates light (present tense) (cf. Amos 4:13; Isa. 45:7; Jer. 10:12).

"Heavenly Father, you are very great!" May the inestimable enjoyment of the daylight regularly lift our hearts to that praise, for in comparison to God's provision of light, the most-modern devices we have are nothing.

The second day: "Let there be firmament"

On the second creation day, God made a separation between the water on the earth and the millions of tons of water in what we now call the atmosphere and what in the language of everyday experience Scripture calls the firmament or heaven (Gen. 1:6–8). That heaven supplied the psalmist's pen with these words:

Verses 2b–4
> Stretching out the heavens like a tent.
> He lays the beams of his chambers on the waters;
> he makes the clouds his chariot;
>> he rides on the wings of the wind;
> he makes his messengers winds,
>> his ministers a flaming fire.

Don't Yahweh's "splendor and majesty" (v. 1) come to powerful expression in this as well? How many tons of water are poured down on a region in a sudden rainstorm? With divine pleasure Yahweh manages that immense household above our heads. For him, that mighty heavenly dome is nothing more than a piece of tent covering is for a Bedouin. Here as well the poet employs the present tense: God did not stretch out that covering just once, at creation, but he continues to do so. From those warehouses above our head, Yahweh pours rainwater down upon the earth (v. 13).

The Canaanites assigned rain and wind, clouds and lightning, to the domain of Baal. By confessing Yahweh as Lord of the firmament, the godly Israelite was speaking polemical language. In this respect, Psalm 104 remains "profitable for teaching, for reproof, for correction, and for training in righteousness" (2 Tim. 3:16). With the help of present-tense participles, which form the warp and woof of so many psalms, the psalmist praises the God and Father of our Lord Jesus Christ as the Lord of the firmament, the God whose hand we know to be present behind every weather map. Every low pressure and high pressure center is under his rule. Doesn't Psalm 104 speak polemical language against the spirit of our age, as well, an age that omits any mention of God's name in meteorology?

The third day: "Let the dry ground appear"

On the third day God made the first separation between water and dry land, a miracle for which God's people have praised him throughout the centuries—with Psalm 104, for example.

> Verses 5–9:
> He set the earth on its foundations,
>   so that it should never be moved.
> You covered it with the deep as with a garment;
>   the waters stood above the mountains.
> At your rebuke they fled;
>   at the sound of your thunder they took to flight.
> The mountains rose, the valleys sank down
>   to the place that you appointed for them.
> You set a boundary that they may not pass,
>   so that they might not again cover the earth.

This is how people who lived in the world of the Bible spoke about the earth: like a flat saucer that has been placed on pillars (mountains) in the waters under the earth, "so that it should never be moved" (v. 5). We will return to this biblical way of talking when we have finished reading Psalm 104. As a modern person living in the twenty-first century, don't grin too quickly at this kind of language. Don't bring on stage too quickly the term *worldview* in order to maybe save face for those who wrote the Bible, for we ourselves could easily lose face in that respect.

What a miracle: The earth is established!

Fine, we know now that the earth is an immense globe that turns on its own axis and also moves around the sun with amazing speed in an orbit of millions of miles; even more, together with our entire solar system it forms a path through God's universe. But then shouldn't we praise God's greatness even more on account of the fact that he has established the globe? He sees to it that this enormous planet, which moves in multiple ways simultaneously, is "never moved"!

Continental reclamation

Singing praise to Yahweh: that is something the psalmist arouses even further by recalling the time when the oceans still covered our earth. "You covered it with the deep as with a garment" (v. 6a). The water stood higher even than the mountains (v. 6b) until, on the third creation day, Yahweh separated the continents and oceans from each other. The tone in Genesis 1 is rather sober: "And God said, 'Let the waters under the heavens be gathered together into one place, and let the dry land appear.' And it was so. God called the dry land Earth, and the waters that were gathered together he called Seas. And God saw that it was good" (vv. 9–10). Psalm 104 expresses it even more strongly. Not only did God say, "Let the waters be gathered," but with his thunderous voice he threatened them so that they would flow away from the land and mountains (v. 7).

How much, then, does God deserve our praise on account of these enormous realities. Who knows the power of the water? What an effort it has taken to drain the Netherlands, from the time of the Romans to the building of the Delta Works! God chased the oceans, so that they fled, merely with his voice. Think of Psalm 104 when you fly over the ocean: our entire earth once looked like that!

The Almighty deserves our praise all the more because he dried up the earth a second time. During the flood, the water again stood higher than the mountains, when for one year God removed the boundaries of the sea that he had established. At that time Yahweh repeated the miracle of the third creation day. Christian geologists have suggested the possibility that at that time events occurred like those Psalm 104:8 describes: "The mountains rose, the valleys sank down." Surely the maps of the continents and oceans had to be significantly redrawn after the flood. In view of its structure, however, Psalm 104 is referring first of all not to the flood but to the events on the third creation day.

Mythical conceptions?

Expositors of Scripture who have been influenced by evolutionism hear in verse 6 the echo of an ancient Near Eastern myth according to which God supposedly waged a life-and-death struggle with the monsters of chaos at the time of creation. We have here a poignant sample of the way in which theologians who are under the pressure of evolutionism twist and reverse the facts. Psalm 104 offers no echo of a myth, at least not substantively, except perhaps in a few matters of style; rather, the myth in question sounds forth an echo of the truth, just as the pagan flood stories contain twisted remnants of truth. The truth of Scripture, however, is not the highest rung on the ladder of pagan lies, as evolutionism suggests; pagan myths are the lie's perch that has been constructed on remnants of truth. God's Word is not an evolved myth, but myths are corrupted remnants of the Word.

The water will not return

Now those oceans will stay where God directed them to go! This is yet another testimony of Yahweh's greatness, for which the psalmist wants to see praise offered to him. Psalm 104 is not the only Scripture passage where we observe that the boundaries of the "Great Sea," as the Mediterranean Sea is called, always made a deep impression on the Israelites. Despite the Netherlands' own centuries-long national struggle against the water, we perhaps do not take enough notice of the divine work in fixing the coastlines along continents. The earth contains more than twice the amount of water as land; the ratio is approximately 3:7. If the water that is now held together in the form of ice over Greenland and the North Pole were to melt, the sea levels would rise more than 160 feet. The Father of our Lord Jesus Christ holds back all those bodies of water from swarming across the land. He keeps in check the oceans on the earth's surface that are sometimes miles deep. Christians who are familiar with the globe can therefore regularly praise their heavenly Father: "You set a boundary that they may not pass, so that they might not again cover the earth" (v. 9; cf. Gen. 8:21; Job 38:10–11; Prov. 8:29; Jer. 5:22).

God turned those tamed waters into a blessing:

Verses 10–13:
You make springs gush forth in the valleys;
    they flow between the hills;
they give drink to every beast of the field;
    the wild donkeys quench their thirst.
Beside them the birds of the heavens dwell;
    they sing among the branches.
From your lofty abode you water the mountains;
    the earth is satisfied with the fruit of your work.

Every piece of creation is a portrait of God's greatness in all of that incomprehensibly immense housekeeping on earth! God not only cares for the streams that eventually become rivers; he also sees to it that they provide the animals with something to drink (v. 11).

And the rain? "Baal takes care of that," said the Canaanized Israelites. But the psalmist sticks with the Torah and praises Yahweh for the rain: "From your lofty abode you water the mountains" (v. 13). For the one who discerns clearly, this is polemical language directed against the worship of Baal and Astarte that was all too prevalent. Judges 2:6–3:4 is a complaint about that terrible evil! Without that fundamental chapter, the Prophets and Writings that follow cannot be understood correctly. This is a warning for modern Christianity. In a world where we say "it rains," and God's name is silenced in connection with any discussion of the weather, believers can bring to him the appropriate praise by singing in their gatherings not only verses about the forgiveness of sins but also a praise song like Psalm 104. Perhaps we might also be able to echo the Torah: "The LORD God caused it to rain" (cf. Gen. 2:5).

The provision of food for man, animal, and plant

"And God said, 'Let the earth sprout vegetation, plants yielding seed, and fruit trees bearing fruit'" (Gen. 1:11). The poetic echo of this immense event is heard in Psalm 104 as well. Anyone familiar with what it takes to feed all the mouths in a family every day can be profoundly amazed by the power of God, who feeds all the animals, all the people, and even all the trees. For that work, which Yahweh began on the third creation day, the psalmist praises him as follows.

> Verses 14–18:
> You cause the grass to grow for the livestock
>   and plants for man to cultivate,
> that he may bring forth food from the earth
>   and wine to gladden the heart of man,
> oil to make his face shine
>   and bread to strengthen man's heart.

> The trees of the LORD are watered abundantly,
> the cedars of Lebanon that he planted.
> In them the birds build their nests;
> the stork has her home in the fir trees.
> The high mountains are for the wild goats;
> the rocks are a refuge for the rock badgers.

Hunger is not the rule here on earth, but rather what the psalmist says: God daily opens wide his hand and satisfies his creatures with good (Ps. 104:28). "The LORD is good to all, and his mercy is over all that he has made" (145:9; cf. 136:25). The Savior referred to that as well: God "makes his sun rise on the evil and on the good, and sends rain on the just and on the unjust" (Matt. 5:45). A drinking donkey is really tasting God's goodness without knowing it (Ps. 104:11). But even "the trees of Yahweh" can drink their fill. Fruit trees drank from artificially dug canals (Ps. 1; Prov. 21:1), but who pays attention to the cedars of Lebanon and the innumerable other giants in the forest? Yahweh does! They are dear to his heart, for he himself planted them (Ps. 104:16).

This psalm, especially verses 14–16, tingles with a sense of the joy of living. Wine makes a person glad, and who supplies the wine? Yahweh (v. 15)! The psalmist saw Yahweh's goodness in the healthy and oil-glistening faces of the people around him (v. 15). Joy echoed from the animal world as well. Birds sing among the branches, and maybe the poet once saw badgers in the mountain bluffs around the Dead Sea. Without saying the word, the psalmist praises the goodness with which God daily supplies people and animals with what they need: food, drink, and some joy.

The fourth day: "And God said, 'Let there be lights in the expanse of the heavens'"

On the fourth day, God created the great lights in the heavens, "to separate the day from the night." He said, "And let them be for signs and for seasons, and for days and years, and let them be lights in the expanse of the heavens to give light upon the earth" (Gen. 1:14–15).

We hear an echo of that in our psalm.

> Verses 19–23:
> **He made the moon to mark the seasons;**
> **the sun knows its time for setting.**
> **You make darkness, and it is night,**
> **when all the beasts of the forest creep about.**
> **The young lions roar for their prey,**
> **seeking their food from God.**
> **When the sun rises, they steal away**
> **and lie down in their dens.**
> **Man goes out to his work**
> **and to his labor until the evening.**

The psalmist continues embroidering upon his theme: the majesty and splendor of Yahweh (Ps. 104:1). He made the sun and the moon! In the world around Israel, these were venerated as gods. Anyone who called them ordinary creatures was confessing his faith in a dangerous way during many times throughout Israelite church history. We will return to this below. Our world has sunk even deeper, for it no longer acknowledges God at all and views sun, moon, and stars entirely independently of God and his Word. Therefore, when Christians sing Psalm 104 today, they are lifting up a polemical praise song that goes directly against the spirit of our age. "I believe in God the Father Almighty, Creator of heaven and earth"—anyone who confesses that sees God's greatness in the daily descent of darkness. "*It* is getting dark," we say, using a rather unchristian expression, but the psalmist dots his i's and crosses his t's with his formulation that "*you* make darkness, and it is night."

Psalm 104 knows nothing of a "nature" that is autonomous and automatic.

The miracle of the ordinary

As we have already remarked, many today understand nature to be a kind of gigantic robot from which everything just comes "by itself," apart from any divine guidance: wood and minerals, food, even children. People inevitably harbor the notion that heaven and earth simply continue. Sickness? That comes from bacteria. Harvest? It grows by itself. Rain and wind? Matters of high- and low-pressure centers. Along with the word *nature* a virtually ineradicable, presumably scientific assumption has crept unnoticed into our daily mode of speaking, according to which the creation in fact exists apart from God. Natural laws are not phenomena upon which, thanks to God's faithfulness, we can depend; rather, they are events that come into existence more or less automatically and with a certain amount of regularity.

In Psalm 104, however, we enter an entirely different climate, as we have already observed. It is the longest creation psalm, but you'll find the word *nature* nowhere in the psalm. The psalm is squarely opposed to the unbelief that characterizes so many of the modern natural sciences. If we can learn one thing from this psalm, then it is to praise God for the miracle of the ordinary. In this psalm, streams don't just flow by themselves, but Yahweh sends them along their course (v. 10). Grass doesn't just grow by itself on the mountain bluffs, but Yahweh causes it to sprout (v. 14). Nothing in the world owes its existence to independent natural laws, but everything comes from the hand of Yahweh. We people live by the word of Yahweh (see the commentary on Deut. 8:3). Whether we think of trees or storks, the coney or the wild donkey, sea creatures or the sun and moon, everything owes its existence and continuation to Yahweh's hand, Yahweh's face, and Yahweh's Spirit (Ps. 104:27–30).

Here we are inhabiting a climate entirely different from that of natural science books that nowhere mention God's name with respect, unlike older science books.

The fifth and sixth creation days: animals and man

On the fifth day God said, "'Let the waters swarm with swarms of living creatures, and let birds fly above the earth across the expanse of the heavens.' So God created the great sea creatures and every living creature that moves, with which the waters swarm, according to their kinds, and every winged bird according to its kind. And God saw that it was good" (Gen. 1:20–21).

And on the sixth day God said, "Let the earth bring forth living creatures according to their kinds—livestock and creeping things and beasts of the earth according to their kinds. . . . Let us make man in our image, after our likeness. And let them have dominion over the fish of the sea and over the birds of the heavens and over the livestock and over all the earth and over every creeping thing that creeps on the earth" (Gen. 1:24, 26).

We hear the echo of that in Psalm 104.

Verses 24–30:
O Lord, how manifold are your works!
    In wisdom have you made them all;
    the earth is full of your creatures.
Here is the sea, great and wide,
    which teems with creatures innumerable,
    living things both small and great.
There go the ships,
    and Leviathan, which you formed to play in it.
These all look to you,
    to give them their food in due season.
When you give it to them, they gather it up;
    when you open your hand, they are filled with good
        things.
When you hide your face, they are dismayed;
    when you take away their breath, they die
    and return to their dust.

> **When you send forth your Spirit, they are created,**
> **and you renew the face of the ground.**

The underwater world testifies to Yahweh's greatness as well. The modern ichthyologist, or fish expert, knows far more about that world than our poet did. And yet we've only begun to explore the flora and fauna in the deeper regions of the oceans with our most advanced equipment for deep-sea photography and deep-sea diving. The phrase "teems with creatures innumerable" in verse 25 will simply increase in profundity.

The psalmist also mentions the legendary Leviathan. Among the Canaanites this was a power that opposed the deity, but for the psalmist is was a kind of sea creature that, for Israel's God, was little more than a toy (v. 26).

That entire animal world is deeply dependent on Yahweh. "These all look to you" (v. 27), not only for food but first of all for their life's breath. For that, human beings and animals are entirely dependent on God's hand and God's face (vv. 28–29). And to this, Moses added dependence on God's word (see the commentary on Deut. 8:3). This absolute dependence is expressed nowhere as powerfully as here. Intermediate causes are excluded entirely from view. From one moment to the next, all people and animals receive their breath from God. "When you hide your face, they are dismayed; when you take away their breath, they die and return to their dust" (v. 29). God could permit every living being to die in one moment (Job 34:14–15). "The Spirit of God has made me, and the breath of the Almighty gives me life" (Job 33:4). According to Psalm 104, this applies to all human beings and to all animals, so that we can speak of the one "breath of the spirit of life" in people and animals. But the reverse is also true? "When you send forth your Spirit, they are created, and you renew the face of the ground" (v. 30). In the springtime the land of Palestine undergoes a genuine facelift.

Creating, after Genesis 1

You might have been struck by the fact that the author of Psalm 104:30 easily used the verb *create* for the new growth that God calls into existence in springtime. We refer to this with the term *providence*, a term of suspiciously pagan origin. The work of God's upholding or providence is something so unimaginably great that Scripture uses the same words for this as for that initial foundational miracle: the creation of heaven and earth. We encounter this word usage elsewhere in Scripture (cf. Isa. 45:7; 65:17–18; Jer. 31:22; Amos 4:13; Ps. 51:10). Is it possible that Christianity passed the first stage en route to its later "God is dead" theology when it introduced the distinction between creation and providence? Once humanity grew up and matured, what people used to call God's *upholding* has become more and more a question of human organizing and human intervention.

"In wisdom have you made them all" (v. 24)

In addition to being almighty and good, our heavenly Father is also all wise. The psalmist may certainly not have studied modern natural sciences, but he nonetheless has an eye for the purposefulness in God's creation. Take the heavenly bodies, which were created first of all to shine indispensable light upon the earth but also simultaneously to set the heavenly clocks and calendars for fixed times (v. 19). Our clocks and calendars are set in reference to them. Just see what wisdom God implemented for establishing regularity in the world: the nighttime for predatory animals and the daytime for people. People in Israel didn't know about around-the-clock manufacturing. But our all-wise Maker knew better than anyone else that we need periodic rest, which he made to coincide with the times of darkness. The objections people have to working nights prove God's wisdom. And we are speaking at this point only about the heavenly bodies, but where is God's wisdom *absent*?

This earth, which is under the curse, displays brilliant

harmony in various areas. Consider how God has made one creature dependent on another creature. Streams do not flow for no purpose, since they quench the thirst of the animals (vv. 10–11). Trees provide birds with living space (v. 12). Rain does not fall purposelessly from the sky, but moistens the mountain bluffs so that grain and grass can grow there (v. 13). That grass in turn becomes wonderful food for the animals, and the grain becomes food for people (v. 14). For thousands of years wine has been an instrument of enjoyment (v. 15). Trees attract storks, and the bare rocks supply exactly what the mountain goats and badgers need (vv. 17–18). Fish feel at home in the sea (v. 25). Everything has its companion—human beings, animals, and plants.

The seventh day: God's day of rest

"And on the seventh day God finished his work that he had done, and he rested on the seventh day from all his work that he had done" (Gen. 2:2). With divine joy Yahweh "saw everything that he had made, and behold, it was very good" (Gen 1:31). We hear the echo of that divine joy in our psalm, as well.

Verse 31:
May the glory of the Lord endure forever;
  may the Lord rejoice in his works,

This is how the psalmist participates in God's joy. Even the volcanoes testify to Yahweh's greatness:

Verse 32:
who looks on the earth and it trembles,
  who touches the mountains and they smoke!

In a time when atheism presumes to be able to appeal to arguments drawn from the natural sciences, may the Spirit who inspired this psalm turn us away from speaking about

God's works of creation like "the men of Ashdod," and fill the mouths of many Christians with praise like that of Psalm 104. With or without people joining him, the psalmist says emphatically:

> Verses 33–34:
> I will sing to the LORD as long as I live;
>   I will sing praise to my God while I have being.
> May my meditation be pleasing to him,
>   for I rejoice in the LORD.

God's Spirit incorporated his meditation in Scripture because Yahweh was pleased with it!

"Let sinners be consumed from the earth"

The ending of Psalm 104 is unique.

> Verse 35:
> Let sinners be consumed from the earth,
>   and let the wicked be no more!
> Bless the LORD, O my soul!
> Praise the LORD!

You will not find this kind of ending in any pagan psalm. Israel's pagan neighbors knew only of the monotonous always-and-forever-turning cycle of their fertility religions, all of which were decorated in terms of streams of summer and winter, the dry season and the wet season. Theirs was a cyclical religion of a fertility god repeatedly dying and rising. But on the basis of the Torah of Moses, Israel was hoping for the great future when the head of the serpent would be destroyed and all nations would share in the blessing given to Abraham (Gen. 3:15; 12:3). Moreover, the Torah protected believing Israel from the pagan notion of a fundamentally evil creation. That is why the psalmists could compose such joyful psalms about God's good creation. Psalm 104 might devote more attention to God's splendor in creation than to its "bondage to corruption" (Rom. 8:21), even though the poet also knew about "sinners" and "the wicked" in Israel, and about God's curse upon the earth (Gen. 3:17–19; Rom. 8:21–22). But he believed Yahweh's promises of a paradisal living together between Yahweh and his people (e.g., by means of the tabernacle and the peace offerings). The prophets have repeated and clarified that promise (Isa. 2:1–5; 11:1–10; 25:6–12; 32:1–8; Hos. 2:15; Amos 9:11). In our discussion of Psalm 16, we saw that Old Testament believers already knew that before he restored this paradisal fellowship, God would judge the world. The psalmist concludes his meditation by referring to this final judgment and this second paradise.

His closing words testify of his longing for the last day: may God's good earth soon be freed from Satan's partners and, along that route, be filled with peace. This explains his joyful ending: "Bless Yahweh, O my soul! Praise Yahweh!"

Review of Psalm 104 and Several Other Psalms

We shall now take the time to provide a brief reflection concerning several sections of Psalm 104. At the same time we can give attention to other psalms that similarly praise Yahweh as the Creator of heaven and earth.

Is Psalm 104 speaking from a naïve "biblical worldview"?

Yahweh stretches "out the heavens like a tent. . . . He lays the beams of his chambers on the waters. . . . He set the earth on its foundations" (Ps. 104:2, 3, 5; cf. 24:1–2). People have said that these and similar expressions are characteristic descriptions of the "biblical worldview" (a universe consisting of three stories: heaven, earth, underworld). On the basis of the arrogant evolutionistic science, they have characterized this "worldview" condescendingly as "primitive," "naïve," "obsolete," and "dating from an early stage of development."

In so doing, people completely lose sight, however, of the fact that Holy Scripture is using the language of ordinary experience to describe visible phenomena, as we have remarked. But what is the difference between this and what we ourselves do, in fact, 450 years after Copernicus? Our calendars continue to indicate the sun*rise* and the sun*set*, don't they? No one thinks us strange if we talk about precipitation that "came down in buckets," do they? Why then should we look down on the saints in the Bible who talked about "windows" and "floodgates" in the sky that someone opened? Who would think it strange for a modern air traveler to say that, looking down from cruising altitude, Ireland looks like a green saucer in the middle of the sea? Is such a person talking any differently than the Israelites? Witnesses of an atomic explosion may explain the power of the explosion by saying, without blushing, "The earth seemed to shake on its foundations." Does this mean such people have a "primitive worldview"? Why then are the Israelites alleged to have such a worldview when they use the same language of ordinary experience, while modern journalists are not accused of naïveté?

Moreover, people are using a word that is far too weighty when, simply on the basis of such ordinary expressions like those we cited above, they speak almost solemnly of "the biblical world*view*"! As if that were exhausted by the well-known descriptions about a universe consisting of three stories and a sky with "floodgates" and an earth with "foundations"! People are forgetting entirely that Holy Scripture also speaks about an invisible reality that is just as real as the visible reality. For example, it speaks not only about the visible Aramean horses and chariots around Dothan but also about the invisible fiery horses and chariots that only Elisha's servant could see surrounding his master (2 Kgs. 6:15–18). On our freeways we see no angels, but they are indeed present to protect us (Ps. 91; cf. Acts 12:7–10; 2 Cor. 4:17–18; Col. 1:15–16). This invisible world lies beyond the sciences' field of investigation, which is occupied with "all that is done under heaven" (Eccl. 1:13). But where does an evolutionistic science acquire the right simply to set aside the biblical data about the invisible reality so that it can arrogantly conclude, on the basis of the Bible's language of ordinary experience concerning the visible world, that the biblical worldview is supposedly "primitive"?

The following two facts, then, we have intentionally not placed in the foreground, but neither do we wish to leave them unmentioned.

Underestimating antiquity

In many respects modern scientific thinking is caught in the spell of evolutionism. Because of this, to its own shame (and soon, its own injury), it can seriously underestimate the capacity and understanding of people who lived in Bible times.

Here we can mention but a few examples. In the sixth century BC the school of Pythagoras taught that the earth was a sphere, and in the fourth century BC, Eudoxus concluded on the basis of the spherical shape of the earth that the heavens existed in the same spherical shape (referring to our solar system) and that the heavenly bodies moved in a circular orbit. In the third century BC Eratosthenes calculated the circumference of the earth by means of a triangular measurement performed simultaneously at Alexandria and Syene in Egypt. It is well-known that the length of his measurement was approximately 4.5% larger than the measurement produced with modern technology. We should recall that—as we see from this Greek measurement occurring in Egypt—in antiquity the relationships between nations were numerous (cf. 1 Kgs. 10:24). Moses (fifteenth century BC) and Daniel (sixth century BC) were acquainted with the science of their time (Dan. 1:4; 2:48; Acts 7:22). The library of Carthage, destroyed in 146 BC, must have held about 500,000 volumes.

In the light of this data, people would minimally display some wisdom if they talked less boldly about a "primitive" worldview held by those in Bible times. Who knows precisely what a Moses, a Solomon, and a Daniel knew? The myth of evolutionism and the widely implemented specialization within the modern sciences presumably obstruct a realistic vision of the status of human capacity and knowledge in antiquity.

WHO IS ACTUALLY SPEAKING NAÏVELY?

A second remarkable fact is the reports that reach us from the world of the natural sciences. We understand that people have used the results of the natural sciences to call Scripture's way of speaking naïve and primitive, but it is becoming increasingly clear that those same results are themselves becoming obsolete and outdated. In the near future, words like *primitive* and *naïve* will potentially become applicable to the self-conceited critics of Holy Scripture. The worldview of the natural sciences, from which so far the modern criticism of Scripture has drawn its impulses, is itself obsolete. It dominated from about 1600 to 1900 and is now perishing. And with it, the basis supplied by the natural sciences for modern criticism of Scripture is also disappearing!

A free(ing) atmosphere

All of Psalm 104 "tingles with a sense of the joy of living," we remarked earlier in connection with verses 14–16. Wine sparkles, faces glow with health, birds sing in the trees, and mountain goats scamper among the rocky bluffs. The psalmist sang of Yahweh's creation work from a vibrant sense that the Torah provided to the believing Israelites. When we realize in what sort of world this psalm was sung, we also discover what a profound liberation the gospel of the Torah brought to Israel and what a wonderful basis it offered the godly for singing joyfully about the Creator.

THE FEARFUL SENSE AMONG ISRAEL'S PAGAN NEIGHBORS

One thousand years before Abraham, the world of the

10. Psalm 104: How Numerous Are Your Works, O Yahweh

ancient Near East had attained a stage of civilization more developed than many people realize. People knew a lot about mathematics and astronomy. An impressive body of literature existed at that time, including wisdom books and "psalms." Goldsmiths produced jewelry that a modern woman would enjoying wearing. Merchant enterprises were familiar with forms of credit and used invoices for goods brought by caravans that had traveled distances in excess of 1,200 miles (2,000 kilometers). Through Greek culture, our own culture continues to be influenced by that ancient Near Eastern civilization.

Nevertheless, these civilized peoples lived in continuous dread because they were victims of one of most heartless religions the world has ever known. The world of the gods that the Babylonians every day supposed dwelled above them could not be trusted one bit: whimsical, fickle beings, both toward each other as well as toward human wretches. They were full of mischief and devoid of everything Scripture calls holiness. The miserable pagans felt like little more than toys of the gods and the spirits, objects of harassment by higher powers against which they could somewhat defend themselves only with solemn religion and sorcery. If someone accidentally came into conflict with the whims of some deity or other, then he had committed sin. This explains the many open-ended confessions of guilt that we find in Babylonian literature: better to have the deity fill in the amount of the debt. According to the Babylonian story, the flood came over the earth without any indication of the reasons. Every New Year's Day the despots in heaven determined people's fateful destinies in the coming year. Our New Year's Day celebration is thus hardly a Scriptural practice.

The miserable Babylonians and Canaanites, however, not only had a world of whimsical deities above them; they also sensed that they were surrounded by an entire swarm of spirits who spied on them day and night. Do not suppose that people could have locked their door and prevented these spirits from entering, for they could come inside anywhere and everywhere. Then you were in real trouble. Your livestock languished. Or a mother expecting a baby could not give birth, because the female demon Lamashtu had obstructed the delivery or killed the newborn baby. People would ascribe fever, toothache, and broken bones to these tormentors. Certain spirits were especially assigned to children. Just imagine the worry of mothers. In Palestine archaeologists have unearthed many beads and objects that mothers presumably fastened around their children's necks as amulets.

Living in darkness

Can you grasp what a fearful sense of living filled the pagan world around Israel? Every hour of the day, people felt like they were harassed, spied upon, or threatened. Spitting or relieving oneself in a river that happened to be "divine" was a serious crime.

People had only one means at their disposal for resisting this world of gods and spirits: solemn religion. These gods and spirits had a weakness for that, and it explains why the neighboring nations around Israel sought to ensure their lives by various sacred actions, oath formulas, sacrifices, amulets, prayers—all of which had to be performed precisely, according to the rules. Archaeologists have discovered numerous sculptures of livers, probably teaching aids for instruction in reading human organs. Nebuchadnezzar also looked at livers and shook arrows before setting the date for a military expedition (Ezek. 21:21). Priests, charmers, and astrologers were the experts called in to get the good powers on one's side and to avert the evil powers. Even our distant ancestors in Northwest Europe lived in terror in the face of evil forces, sacred trees, and sacred stones. What word describes this kind of living better than the word *darkness* (Eph. 5:8)?

Echoing the liberation music of the Torah

What a completely different atmosphere we breathe with Psalm 104! Already in the opening lines we inhale the pure

10. Psalm 104: How Numerous Are Your Works, O Yahweh

mountain air of pure truth. There is not one word about capricious gods and spying tree spirits and river spirits. There is no trace of denigrating creation. On the contrary, the composer of Psalm 104 sang the opposite: "May Yahweh rejoice in his works!" (v. 31). That language is quite different from that of a deity squarely opposed to this world.

Psalm 104 is singing in the light of the Torah! What does the Torah teach us about Yahweh? That he alone is God, and that sun, moon, and stars are creatures and nothing more. That he has made us human beings not to be slaves in a bad world of gods and spirits, but to be his vice-gerents, for whom he remains, even after their rebellion, a God of love, faithfulness, and compassion. The pagans couldn't trust their gods one bit. Yahweh bound himself to Noah, Abraham, and Israel. Like a reliable great king, he supplied his treaties engraved on stone. In black and white, we would say. In duplicate (Exod. 20). Nowhere in the Torah do we read about oath formulas or stories about half-gods and half-humans. No examining livers, but exactly the opposite: powerful prohibitions of everything that tended toward sorcery and necromancy. These were abominable sins in God's holy eyes! In addition, in the entire Torah we find no trace of enmity between God and his creation. Why should a human being have to be afraid of that? After all, Yahweh had created it. Evil was embedded not in the creation but in the human heart. The Torah thus cut off at their root, in principle, all forms of asceticism and every posture of tragedy. In this way the Torah liberated Israel from fear of gods and spirits; fear of sun, moon, and stars; fear of enchantments; and fear of the dead.

What, then, is the Psalter?

The Psalter is, as we saw earlier, the echo of the liberation music of the Torah and of the instruction of the Prophets. In the Psalms we hear, in a certain sense, the answer of God's people to God's Word in the Torah.

We hear that echo in Psalm 104 as well.

The evangelical atmosphere

Psalm 104 is without doubt a wonderful sample of the evangelical sense of life that Israel could share if she lived according to the Torah. We hear an entirely different tone in this psalm than in similar pagan songs. Those songs appear to cringe before the gods, but our psalmist speaks directly to "my God" and says, "I rejoice in Yahweh" (vv. 1, 34). Our poet experiences no fear of nature; why would he? His God, Yahweh, was Creator and at the same time Covenant Partner. The Torah of Moses has delivered the godly Israelite from the pagan myths about the semidivine "creation." Psalm 104 does not see the chariots of Baal in the clouds; it sees the chariots of Yahweh (v. 3). The lightning flashes are not messengers of Baal but of Yahweh (v. 4). The mighty sea, viewed by the Canaanites as a living being (the god Yam), for which the Israelite also harbored deep respect, was held within specific boundaries by Israel's Covenant Partner (vv. 6–9). Even the legendary sea monster, Leviathan, appears in this psalm simply as God's playful creature (v. 26). Our psalm talks about the moon, which in the entire ancient Near East was venerated as a god, as a calendar in service to people (v. 19a). The sun, which was similarly deified everywhere else, keeps its daily schedule as one of Yahweh's obedient subjects (v. 19b).

Do we not hear an evangelical kind of talk about God's creation in Psalm 104? Away, then, with that dread of a deified sun, moon, stars, and seas. The psalmist mentions rejoicing in Yahweh no fewer than six times (vv. 1, 15, 31, 33–35). Afraid of God's good creation? The psalmist expresses deep appreciation for creation. Listen to his enthusiasm about the light (v. 2), clouds and winds (vv. 3–4), the water (v. 10), birds, grass, wheat, bread, wine, cedar wood, beautiful animals like mountain goats, and heavenly lamps and chronometers. This is the gospel in the face of the frightened sense of living that characterizes our time as well! But we will say more about that in a moment.

Other creation psalms speak with similar liberation music.

Psalm 8 and the Majesty of Human Beings

Psalm 8 also speaks on the basis of the gospel found in the Law of Moses. To be sure, Psalm 8 is no song either in praise of humanity or in praise of nature, but first all in praise of God, the liberator of Israel. God's greatness is the focus. As is often the case in the Psalms, the theme is announced at the beginning: "O Yahweh, our Lord, how majestic is your name in all the earth" (v. 1). This declaration is repeated in the last verse (v. 9). Within this framework the psalmist talks about the greatness of the human being. Do you think for a moment that this human being is a slave of capricious gods and sneaky spirits? David has been set free from that: "You have made him a little lower than the heavenly beings, and crowned him with glory and honor" (v. 5).

Note this:

> You have given him dominion over the works of your hands;
> you have put all things under his feet,
> all sheep and oxen,
> and also the beasts of the field,
> the birds of the heavens, and the fish of the sea,
> whatever passes along the paths of the seas.
>
> (vv. 6–8)

We perhaps would be inclined to illustrate human greatness by pointing to our immense technological capacity: mining and shipbuilding, blast furnaces and tools, chemicals and space travel. All of this demonstrates the royal splendor with which God has crowned us.

Don't you hear in Psalm 8 the very same liberating Mosaic talk about man? David was freed from the fear of gods and spirits under which he watched Philistines and Canaanites bow.

Meanwhile a deep crevasse lies between Psalm 8 and various kinds of humanistic talk about man. David acknowledged that God had made man almost divine: "You have made him a little lower than the heavenly beings. . . . You have given him dominion . . . ; you have put all things under his feet." All human greatness is received greatness. David was talking about that with humility, in the context of the greatness of God. Having begun with God's greatness (vv. 1–3), he arrives at the glory that we human beings have received from God (vv. 4–8), only to end again with the majesty of God (v. 9). Having been instructed by the Torah and standing on the foundation of Horeb, godly Israel knew that such a human being is great only when he knows his place with respect to God. When people forget that, they always end up living in the very same fear and humiliation from which the Spirit of Christ had delivered their ancestors by the gospel. Then that ancient hopeless dread of our ancestors returns with the advice "Let us eat and drink, for tomorrow we die" (1 Cor. 15:32). The philosophies of desperation gripping apostate Christianity in our age echo a cry similar to "Let the mountains fall upon us and the hills cover us" (cf. Luke 23:30; Rev. 6:16), philosophies that remarkably display increasing interest in, of all things, horoscopes! The return of superstitious respect for the stars!

"He commanded and they were created"

What was the purpose of the creation psalms? As we remarked earlier, in the first place they praised the greatness of the Creator and his work, and in the second place they contended for the honor of the Creator. That also applies to those lines of the psalm that talk about God's creation work itself.

Surely Israel knew something of the creation stories circulating among her neighbors. The names of the gods varied, but at bottom those stories all said the same thing. They told of all the life-and-death struggles between different gods. In Babylon people viewed the water as the original element of the universe. At the same time, people viewed this water as an eternal evil power. (Recall that people suffered because of the flooding of the Euphrates and Tigris Rivers.) Water was a kind of hostile enemy deity. Pagans in the ancient Near East believed in this kind of evil primal element all through the centuries. According to them, the creation contained evil elements from its very beginning. These evil elements were "production mistakes" for which we human beings bear no guilt, but which we must bear as our fate. These are notions that are alive and well in our own day, as we will see in a moment.

But the Torah taught what actually happened when the world was created. There were no gods wrestling with each other, but a certain Yahweh, who gave a command seven times: "And God said . . ." And seven times he indicated that he found what he had made to be good.

The resonance of this instruction echoes through the Psalter:

> By the word of the LORD the heavens were made,
>   and by the breath of his mouth all their host. . . .
> For he spoke, and it came to be;
>   he commanded, and it stood firm.   (Ps. 33:6, 9)

> Praise him, sun and moon,
>   praise him, all you shining stars! . . .
> Let them praise the name of the LORD!
>   For he commanded and they were created.
>   (Ps. 148:3, 5)

Of course, here as well we hear first of all the praise of God and profound amazement for Yahweh's power and wisdom. But the psalmists were giving expression to this in a Canaanite world, perhaps among a Canaanized Israel. Squarely opposed to the spirit of many eras in Israelite church history, the psalmists confessed in lines like those cited above that Yahweh is the Creator of heaven and earth.

People were supposed to mention the idols as infrequently as possible (Exod. 23:13; Ps. 16:4). But if we know the world surrounding Israel even a little bit, and we recall Israel's constant yearning for the idols of her pagan neighbors, then silence about particular phenomena spoke volumes. There is not a word about a supposed "eternal water" functioning as an evil force of chaos, not a word about the bodies of gods hacked in pieces, and similar niceties; rather, with playful enjoyment, Yahweh created heaven and earth. To do that, he needed to speak but a word and it came into existence. Such poetic lines must have sounded, in many periods of Israel's history, like genuine fight songs on the lips of the faithful remnant. Lifting up "the high praises of God," but in the context of executing "punishments on the peoples" (Ps. 149:6–7). So then, what do you think about the tenor in our age of atheistic technocracy, one that in its own way views heaven and earth as separate from the God of the Bible, and surprisingly, at the same time succumbs to such a tragic sense of living?

The Creator is also the Lord of history

"Let sinners be consumed from the earth, and let the wicked be no more!" (Ps. 104:35). With that future expectation the psalmist ends his song praising the Creator and his work. He didn't view creation as something going around in an eternal cycle; rather, he saw it in the light of a redeemed future, when there will no longer be any wicked people walking upon God's earth.

With this language he was again saying something uniquely biblical.

Cyclical religion

Just as Israel must have had some knowledge about the religion of her pagan neighbors, so too her neighbors in turn must have had some acquaintance with Yahweh, the God of Israel. How surprised they must have been, then, to discover that this God was a God of stories, histories, redemptive facts! The pagan world, of course, had its own stories about the gods, like scandals involving the tryst between a god and a young girl, from which a demigod was later born. But at this point we aren't referring to those stories. What had those gods done for their worshipers three, five, ten, or fifteen centuries ago? What could their worshipers tell about that? Nothing. Pagan religion moves constantly in a cyclical fashion. Often pagan religion venerates nature and its cycle of rising, shining, and then declining. The sun is their god, or the rain, or the luscious, fertile land that each year supplies food to man and beast. But forming a history? Pursuing a goal? Making known a plan? Opening up a future? Not at all. Whether you choose German, Greek, or Semitic pagans, their entire religion is a desperately repetitive religion with a constant annual cycle: there is a dry summer; people pray for rain; the rain god couples with the goddess of fertility; their union produces new fruitfulness; a new harvest comes; the rain god dies; the sweltering summer occasions deep concern; autumn arrives; the rain god awakens once again; etc., etc., etc. To this cyclical model we owe, in the final analysis, our own so-called church year (see the commentary on Ps. 29:11, "'Christian' Cyclical Piety," pp. 289–91).

God's Word is a history book

Paganism does nothing other than constantly revolve in a circle, but Yahweh, the God and Father of our Lord Jesus Christ, is the Creator of heaven and earth and also the God who had already promised Adam a new earth in the future. He is the God of the flood, the Covenant Partner of Israel, who already talked about the Pentecost dispensation with Abraham. He is the God who beat Egypt to a pulp and laid Canaan open for Israel. The Torah taught Israel to look back as well as to look ahead, and because of this, Israel possessed a historical understanding.

From beginning to end, God's Word is a history book, something entirely different from the so-called sacred books like the Qur'an or those of the Buddhists. The God of the Scriptures makes history with his people and can be truly known only from his actions!

The pagan world was absolutely unaccustomed to this, and to the extent that paganism returns, Christianity will gradually become unaccustomed to it as well. Among pagans, talking about the gods invariably came down to pinning their reasoning and their perspectives on nothing, and such talk was simply timeless, "pious" hot air. In our day those who populate departments of theology hollow out God's actions in order to fill the remaining void with—can you guess?—perspectives! In opposition to this dehistoricizing of God's work of redeeming humanity, the ancient church confessed the truth in the twelve articles of the Apostles' Creed, with its substantive claims about God the Father and his creating work, and God the Son and his historically situated life history and work of salvation ("under Pontius Pilate").

The Echo in the Historical Psalms

Just as there are creation psalms, which also speak about God's history with Israel, so too there are historical psalms, which point to Yahweh's actions in heaven and upon earth (cf. Pss. 18; 24; 66; 68; 105; 107; 135; 136).

We conclude this section with a brief look at Psalm 74, a psalm of lament in connection with the ruins of the temple, at a low point in Israel's history. This psalmist encouraged himself precisely with what we are discussing in this section: the close connection between creation and history. Internalizing the deliverance from Egypt, the psalmist praises Yahweh as the great Creator of heaven and earth:

> Yet God my King is from of old,
>   working salvation in the midst of the earth.
> You divided the sea by your might;
>   you broke the heads of the sea monsters on the
>   waters.

You crushed the heads of Leviathan;
> you gave him as food for the creatures of the
> wilderness.

You split open springs and brooks;
> you dried up ever-flowing streams.

Yours is the day, yours also the night;
> you have established the heavenly lights and the
> sun.

You have fixed all the boundaries of the earth;
> you have made summer and winter.

(Ps. 74:12–17)

Sun and moon: not gods, but lamps and clocks

"He made the moon to mark the seasons; the sun knows its time for setting" (Ps. 104:19). We will come back to these poetic lines in a moment. When we hear them first in the Canaanite world and then in our own world, we will notice more clearly the confessional tone of those lines.

PRAYING TO THE HEAVENLY BODIES

From the earliest times, the peoples of the ancient Near East showed profound religious reverence for what Scripture often calls: "the entire host of heaven," sun, moon, and stars.

People everywhere perceived the sun to be a god or goddess. In Egypt, they called it Ra, in Babylon, it was called Shamash, and in Canaan, Shemesh (cf. the place name Beth-shemesh, 1 Sam. 6:12; was an ancient temple to the sun god located there at one time?). This sun god supposedly controlled all life on earth. At the same time he was the supreme judge, who on his daily journey along the sky saw everything and therefore knew everything. In Egypt, Assyria, and Babylon, people even sang "psalms" in honor of the sun god. To give you a sense of that, we have included something from an Egyptian prayer to the sun god and then from an Assyrian prayer.

The Egyptian song has achieved some recognition because

of its indisputable similarity to Psalm 104, at least in terms of structure and content. Just like the composer of our psalm, the Egyptian "psalmist," Akhenaten, takes a walk through the entire creation. But whereas Psalm 104 praises Yahweh for everything that grows on the earth, the pagan Akhenaten honors the sun (Aten) as the almighty creating deity. Here are several lines from his psalm, which is even longer than Psalm 104 (cited from *Ancient Near Eastern Texts Relating to the Old Testament*, ed. James B. Pritchard, 3rd ed. [Princeton: Princeton University Press, 1969], 370):

> When thou settest in the western horizon,
> The land is in darkness, in the manner of death.
> They sleep in a room, with heads wrapped up,
> Nor sees one eye the other. . . .
> Every lion is come forth from his den;
> All creeping things, they sting. . . .
> At daybreak, when thou arisest on the horizon,
> When thou shinest as the Aton by day,
> Thou drivest away the darkness and givest thy rays.
> The Two Lands are in festivity every day,
> Awake and standing upon (their) feet,
> For thou hast raised them up.
> Washing their bodies, taking (their) clothing,
> Their arms are (raised) in praise at thy appearance.
> All the world, they do their work.
> All beasts are content with the pasturage;
> Trees and plants are flourishing.
> The birds which fly from their nests, . . .
> How manifold it is, what thou has made!
> They are hidden from the face (of man).
> O sole god, like whom there is not other!
> Thou didst create the world according to thy desire,
> Whilst thou wert alone. . . .

If the composer of Psalm 104 did obtain any stimulation

from the pagan psalm literature—something that is quite possible, but very difficult to prove—then this would fortify the polemical motive of his psalm.

The monumental work of James B. Pritchard mentioned above contains pages full of prayers and hymns (in English translation) that the Egyptians, Sumerians, Assyrians, and Syrians directed toward the sun god and the moon god. The moon occupied an important place in ancient Semitic religions as well. The cities of Ur and Haran, from which Abraham came (Gen. 11:31–32; 12:4), were important centers of worship of the moon god Sin, who was called "the guide of the caravans." You will find below several lines from a prayer to the moon, found on clay tablets in the library of the Assyrian king Ashurbanipal, a contemporary of Judah's kings, Manasseh and Amon (cited from *Ancient Near Eastern Texts*, 386):

> O Namrasit [a name for the moon god], unequaled in
>   power, whose designs no one can conceive,
> I have spread out for thee a pure incense-offering of
>   the night; I have poured out for thee the best
>   sweet drink.
> I am kneeling; I tarry (thus); I seek after thee. . . .
> May my god and my goddess, who for many days
>   have been angry with me,
> In truth and justice be favorable to me; may my road
>   be propitious; may my path be straight.

Would Ahaz and his grandsons, Manasseh and Amon, also have prayed something like "O Moon, I lie before you upon my knees"? Scripture tells us that Ahaz would go to the roof of his palace to worship the Lord Sun in the daytime and Mistress Moon at night (2 Kgs. 23:12). We read that Manasseh "worshiped all the host of heaven and served them" (2 Kgs. 21:3; cf. v. 5; 17:16, 19). It is possible that during the festivals people carried an image of the sun god through Jerusalem by chariot (2 Kgs. 23:11; cf. Jer. 8:2; 19:13; Zeph. 1:5; Acts

7:42), even the women's fashions of that world reflected this idolatry, for women often wore a little moon on their necks (cf. Isa. 3:18). A hundred years later entire families were busy baking sacrificial cakes for "the queen of heaven" (Jer. 7:18). All of this happened despite Yahweh's solemn warning issued against this Canaanite practice, already before Israel's entrance into Canaan! (Deut. 4:5, 19; 17:3).

"The heavens declare the glory of God"

Throughout these centuries Yahweh preserved a remnant, to which the psalmist belonged. These godly people adhered to the Torah, from which they understood that sun, moon, and stars proclaim God's glory and are not gods but the work of God's fingers (Pss. 8; 19; 102).

Psalm 8. Psalm 8 is a "nocturne" composed by David under the impression of the shining Near Eastern starry sky. But he did not look up like a Canaanized Israelite; instead, he looked through the spectacles of the Word, as Calvin put it, and was liberated from fear of the starry sky. David did not lie prostrate before the stars. He was brought back to the ancient, divinely revealed knowledge from the time of Adam and Eve, which acknowledged that God had made the sun, moon, and stars in service to man and not the other way around. In these lines you can savor once again that liberated sense of life that the Torah discloses:

> When I look at your heavens, the work of your fingers,
> the moon and the stars, which you have set in
> place . . . (Ps. 8:3)

Psalm 19. Is Psalm 19 a more or less unfortunate combination of one psalm that sang about the Torah and another that praised Yahweh as Creator? Some have argued that, but for a biblical way of thinking, the references to the Torah talking about Yahweh and to the firmament with its history do not constitute the contradiction that people have wanted to use to cut Psalm 19 into two parts. The God who showed the way for the sun, moon, and stars was the same one who showed Israel the way (*torah* means "guide"). With a unified voice, Psalm 19 sings something that is thoroughly Scriptural when it confesses with praise,

> The heavens declare the glory of God,
> and the sky above proclaims his handiwork.
> (Ps. 19:1)

Psalms 33 and 95. Here we have wonderful examples of psalms that praise Yahweh as Creator and as the Lord of history.

> By the word of the LORD the heavens were made,
> and by the breath of his mouth all their host.
> (Ps. 33:6)

> For all the gods of the peoples are worthless idols,
> but the LORD made the heavens. (Ps. 96:5)

Psalm 102. Psalm 102 is the prayer of a distressed person who succumbed to the church's distress in the Babylonian captivity and poured out his lament before Yahweh. Meditating on that piece of history, the psalmist firmly grasps hold of Yahweh's almighty power as Creator:

> Of old you laid the foundation of the earth,
> and the heavens are the work of your hands.
> (Ps. 102:25)

Compare this with what we read in Psalm 136:

> Give thanks to the Lord of lords . . .
> to him who by understanding made the heavens, . . .
> to him who made the great lights. (vv. 3, 5, 7)

Psalm 147. Once again we have a psalm that praises Yahweh both as Creator and as the great king of Israel who allowed his vassal people to return from Babylon to Jerusalem. The psalmist places both the gathering of Israel's deported ones and his caring for the clouds, rain, ice, and such things on the same level as divine miracles:

> He determines the number of the stars;
> > he gives to all of them their names.
> Great is our Lord, and abundant in power;
> > his understanding is beyond measure.
> > > (Ps. 147:4–5)

Compare this with Psalm 148:

> Praise him, sun and moon,
> > praise him, all you shining stars!
> Praise him, you highest heavens,
> > and you waters above the heavens!
> Let them praise the name of the LORD!
> > For he commanded and they were created.
> And he established them forever and ever;
> > he gave a decree, and it shall not pass away. . . .
> Let them praise the name of the LORD,
> > for his name alone is exalted;
> his majesty is above earth and heaven.   (vv. 3–6, 13)

"The sea is his, for he made it"

Except for the Phoenicians, the ancient Semitic peoples were not attracted to seafaring. That surprises no one who recalls the kind of boats people used at that time to travel the Mediterranean Sea. Granted, Paul traveled with 276 people in one ship, but the apostle also shipwrecked three times and was adrift at sea for a night and a day (2 Cor. 11:25; cf. Acts 27:14–15). What did people use a thousand years earlier for sea travel? In Paul's time people sailed without the use of

10. Psalm 104: How Numerous Are Your Works, O Yahweh

a compass, orienting themselves by the coastline, while ship travel stopped altogether during the winter (Acts 27:12). If there is any place where a person feels small and helpless, it's in the presence of the ocean.

Nevertheless, the Israelites looked at "the mighty waters" differently than did their pagan neighbors, who deified the sea. The inhabitants of ancient Ugarit viewed the wintery roughness of the sea as the struggle among the gods for dominion over the earth. It is very significant in this context that the Hebrew word for sea (*yam*) is also the name of a god. But thanks to the instruction of the Law, the sea was demythologized for Israel, who knew Yahweh as the Creator of the sea with everything in it. Israel confessed that on the third day God had created the sea and dry land and that except during the year of the flood, he kept one separate from the other. We heard the poet of Psalm 104 praise Yahweh for this constant divine display of power with regard to the oceans.

In this world filled with fear of the sea and with stories of gods and raging chaotic waters and a divine sea, tiny Israel praised Yahweh with polemical zeal as the one who had made the sea! As the composer of Psalm 95 put it:

> For the LORD is a great God. . . .
> The sea is his, for he made it. (vv. 3, 5)

Rather than being instilled with pagan fear, the sea could occasionally be of great comfort to the believing Israelite precisely because he realized that nature was not a neutral arena but something to be entirely integrated with his acknowledgment of Yahweh as Israel's Creator and Great King. Psalm 146 offers this jubilation:

> Blessed is he whose help is the God of Jacob,
>   whose hope is in the LORD his God,
> who made heaven and earth,
>   the sea, and all that is in them. (vv. 5–6)

The Creator of the sea can help! To Israel's way of thinking, the most convincing proof of Yahweh's supremacy over the sea was undoubtedly the crossing through the Red Sea, of which the psalms have preserved a lively recollection:

> When the waters saw you, O God,
>   when the waters saw you, they were afraid;
>   indeed, the deep trembled. . . .
> Your way was through the sea,
>   your path through the great waters. . . .
> You led your people like a flock
>   by the hand of Moses and Aaron.
>   (Ps. 77:16, 19–20)

> He divided the sea and let them pass through it,
>   and made the waters stand like a heap.   (78:13)

> He rebuked the Red Sea, and it became dry,
>   and he led them through the deep as through a
>   desert.   (106:9)

> The sea looked and fled. . . .
> What ails you, O sea, that you flee?   (114:3, 5)

> Give thanks to the LORD, for he is good,
>   for his steadfast love endures forever. . . .
> [Give thanks] to him who alone does great wonders,
>   . . .
> to him who divided the Red Sea in two, . . .
> and made Israel pass through the midst of it, . . .
> but overthrew Pharaoh and his host in the Red Sea.
>   (136:1, 4, 13, 14, 15)

This was how godly Israel talked about the sea: never as a mere natural phenomenon, but as the arena for Israel's heavenly Covenant Partner to display his might. May the enormously increased knowledge of nature lead us Christians all the more to praise God and to rely on his steadfast love, even as the psalms cited above stimulate us to that response. Today, thanks to television and deep-sea photography, masses of people get a glimpse of the ocean depths. May this expanded knowledge of God's almighty power not testify against us when the Lord Jesus returns. For the sea itself can render a person inexcusable and guilty before God (cf. Rom. 1:20). The coastlines themselves drawn on our maps teach us:

> Whatever the LORD pleases, he does,
> in heaven and on earth,
> in the seas and all deeps. (Ps. 135:6)

> Mightier than the thunders of many waters,
> mightier than the waves of the sea,
> the LORD on high is mighty! (93:4)

The creation psalms make the good confession in a fearful atmosphere

THE BLOOD OF MARTYRS?

Some godly believers have probably sealed the confession contained in the creation psalms with their blood. King Manasseh, who built altars for the worship of the starry hosts, filled Jerusalem with the blood of martyrs (2 Kgs. 21:16). Certainly people of Judah were among them, people who adhered to the ancient truth that Yahweh had created heaven, earth, the sea, and everything in them. According to one Jewish tradition, Isaiah was sawn into pieces around that time (cf. Heb. 11:37). In any case, prophets lifted up their voices against Manasseh's abominable idolatries (2 Kgs. 21:10–15).

At some periods in church history, anyone who sang the psalms we cited above risked his life. For of course you could not counteract the veneration of heavenly bodies any more profoundly than by confessing that they are not gods but the work of God's hands, creatures, in service to human beings.

But is it not heavily overlaid with polemic?

Still, you might be inclined to argue that the psalmists never give any indication that they are polemicizing. That is true, but one who discerns well only needs a small, suggestive hint—at least, that goes for the discerning Israelite who was well acquainted with the service of Baal and Astarte, together with the veneration of heavenly bodies. It is remarkable that Scripture speaks to us about this in such a sober manner. Perhaps we were mistaken in telling you about those idolatrous hymns. Perhaps it is better for us to remain children when it comes to wickedness. In a similar way, the apostles nowhere explain for us any of the Gnostic systems against which they are polemicizing, except briefly, as in 1 John 4, for example, where it is called the spirit of the antichrist! And in 1 Timothy 4 we read about the doctrine of demons, devils, and evil spirits. Irenaeus assures us that the apostles were polemicizing against Gnostic ideas. In the same way, the psalmists were apparently hesitant to teach us doctrines about the Egyptian, Canaanite, and Babylonian idolatries. We thought it would be helpful, however, and would make reading the psalms more concrete if we told you a few details that were undoubtedly well known to the Israelite reader of that time, but probably not so well known to the Christian reader today, details about the religious situation within which the creation psalms were sung and confessed.

Obsolete?

Nowadays we no longer witness the worship of the sun, moon, or sea. We do see the mighty triumph of the natural sciences. Via television we have seen astronauts walk on the moon. We've learned to use light-years for explaining the measurement of distances in the universe. We know that by comparison, the sun is a "dwarf," "only" 105 times larger than the earth. People have seen stars that are 63,000 times larger than the earth and have a luminosity of approximately 100,000 times that of our sun. But the books and magazines that tell us these things are dead silent about the Creator. They rob God of his honor as Creator in order to give that honor instead to the idea of evolution. For that reason, the creation psalms summon us, not with less but with much more seriousness, to give thanks "to him . . . who by understanding made the heavens" (Ps. 136:5). Let us sing often, both at home and in our worship services: "Great is our Lord and mighty in power, his understanding is without limit!" We know a little bit about the impressive works the psalm is singing: "the work of your fingers" (Ps. 8:3). Sirius is 560,000 times farther away from us than the sun. If this star were just as far away as the sun, however, its heat would boil all the oceans on earth, and all the water and every living thing upon earth would disappear. But don't be afraid: "And he established them forever and ever; he gave a decree, and it shall not pass away" (Ps. 148:6). That is a verse young people might want to write inside their science textbooks! Manasseh had not sunk so low that he failed to acknowledge that there were divine beings, even though he falsely saw the sun, moon, and stars as gods. But our world no longer acknowledges any God at all, and views the starry galaxies as autonomous and independent entities. So we must sing our psalms in direct contradiction to the spirit of our age: "The name of the LORD . . . alone is exalted; his majesty is above earth and heaven" (Ps. 148:13).

That becomes in our time genuine liberation music!

DO NOT BE AFRAID; HOLD ON TO GOD'S FATHERLY HAND!

The gospel proclaimed by the Law of Moses was profoundly liberating for Israel, setting her free from fear—fear of gods, fear of spirits, fear of moon and stars, fear of the sea, fear of magic and of the dead. God's Word is a Word of salvation, and salvation literally means deliverance!

In the New Testament period as well, there has dominated throughout the world a sense of thoroughgoing dread toward that strange world that was so immense and so dark.

The monster of Gnosticism attempted to snare the Christian church in that sense of dread. The Gnostic of that time complained—actually, just as people in our own time complain—about being "trapped" or "cast about" in this dirty world. According to such a Gnostic, a person's soul was an exile living in a body.

These are nothing but the sounds of fate and determinism!

Because the Gnostic could not deal with his existence, he either fled into abstinence from food, drink, and sexuality, or surrendered to them without restraint. In that world the apostle Paul brought the liberating teaching of the Torah when he preached that it was absolutely a demonic teaching to suggest that this world was evil, and that food, drink, sexuality, and everything else belonging to our physical existence was inherently inferior (1 Tim. 4). Believers, who have come to acknowledge the truth, know better. Timothy had to proclaim these things faithfully—things he had learned in his youth from the Torah (2 Tim. 3:15)—and had to fight boldly against the old wives' tales about abstaining from this dirty world (1 Tim. 4:7).

After being suppressed somewhat in the centuries between Paul and us, this paganism is surfacing again in our generation, with its fearful attitude toward life. Modern man feels alone and frightened, a tiny accidental atom cast into the immeasurable stream of evolution that has already been flowing for billions of years. What those evil powers of the stars and the gods were for the ancient pagan, the laws of causality, thought to be similarly powerful and inexplicable accidents, are for modern man. Many flee into unrestrained lawless sexuality and to various forms of narcotics in order to forget their "imprisonment."

But even for today there exists no other or better means of healing for all the sickly Gnostic mythologizing of the Christian faith that is undermining God's Word, and for all the Gnostic notions of determinism and the sense of dread, than a simple, believing reading of Moses, the Prophets, the

Psalms, and the Apostolic Writings—and then reading them especially against the background of the paganism of older and more recent times that has never ceased to threaten, distress, and choke God's people throughout the centuries. For what is Gnosticism at bottom but paganism?

Do not be afraid! Hold fast to God's liberating Word. This earth, with everything in it and around it, together with every form of causality and evolution, lies in God's fatherly hand. Sing about that by using his creation psalms. Stand still with Psalm 104. Dare to live by the provision from God's hand as the possession of Jesus Christ in life and in death. Eternal life is preserved for you in Christ as an unfading inheritance. So you need not despair, for you have a living hope (1 Pet. 1:3).

"O Yahweh my God, you are very great!" (Ps. 104:1).

Chapter 11

Psalm 111: I Will Give Thanks to Yahweh![1]

"Hallelujah, I will give thanks to Yahweh with my whole heart," sings the poet who composed Psalm 111. Would you like to join along? Then we will walk through his psalm of praise verse by verse and see what we can learn from it when we too want to give thanks to God.

Naturally, you can do that anywhere: when you stroll, when you're driving your car, together as a family in your family prayers. Then we are praising him as a relatively small group. But the psalmist says:

> Verse 1:
> **Praise the Lord!**
> **I will give thanks to the Lord with my whole heart,**
>   in the company of the upright, in the congregation.

We would say, "in the church," for our church services are just such assemblies. From this we learn how important

---

1. [*Translator's note:* This chapter, authored by F. van Deursen, did not appear in the Dutch original, and has been added to this translated volume.]

Scripture says our congregational singing really is. It's wonderful if you regularly place your money in the offering plate, but Psalm 50 says, "Offer God your praise!" Now then, if you can still sing, join along. You might not have a very beautiful voice, or you might have a voice weakened with age, but that doesn't matter as long as you praise him, in song or in speech, with a heart that is flowing forth completely toward him.

For we don't sing his praise for ourselves first of all, to stimulate a warm religious feeling (although that can be a result); we do it primarily for him, our heavenly Father! When you recall that praising God means boasting of his deeds, his accomplishments, and his work, then it is easy to praise him:

Verse 2:
Great are the works of the Lord,
    studied by all who delight in them.

The most gifted researcher can devote his whole life to studying a tiny part of God's creation and at the end admit that he has only just begun. Where and when are we not able to praise Yahweh? When we are looking at a flower or a tiger, at a fly's leg or the rings of Saturn, we must always acknowledge, "Our God is so great!"

Do our Christian educators ever point this out to their students? Whether you are learning a language or the properties of various metals, whether biology or mathematics, history or geography, you are always dealing with what God has created.

Everywhere in the world you can see the sun, moon, and stars. You can see clouds drifting across the sky. You can hear the thunder, feel the rain, see the animals, marvel at newborn babies. Paul wrote that God's "invisible attributes, namely, his eternal power and divine nature, have been clearly perceived, ever since the creation of the world, in the things that have been made" (Rom. 1:20). Unfortunately, millions willfully close their eyes to this. But let us say with the poet of Psalm 111 instead, "I will praise Yahweh with my whole heart, for everything that I see from his hand is replete with divine majesty!"

Verse 3:
Full of splendor and majesty is his work,
   and his righteousness endures forever.

What natural scientists tell us about God's microworld, and what the astronomers tell us about God's macroworld, is majestic. All of us know something of the unimaginable distances in the universe, and we know that our earth is minuscule compared to other heavenly bodies. Indeed, "full of splendor and majesty is his work"—say it loudly!

But fortunately, God not only permits us here on earth to live in a global display of power and glory, he permits us to see his eternal righteousness as well. In the Bible that is another word for his faithfulness—his faithfulness to himself, his faithfulness to his creation, his faithfulness to Noah. God is no despot, no brute, no whimsical, fickle tormentor. No, if there is one thing the Supreme Majesty loves, it is justice.

God has never been guilty of abuse of power, nor has he ever compelled anyone by means of abusing justice. He did not do this even in our redemption. Jesus's crucifixion bore witness not only to supreme love but also to supreme justice. That is why we praise God for his righteousness and move from his work of creation to his work of reconciliation.

Verse 4a:
He has caused his wondrous works to be remembered.

The most wonderful monument of his miracles is Holy Scripture. As we read Scripture daily, we are constantly reminded of what God has done: the miracles of creation, the flood, the Egyptian plagues, the collapsing walls of Jericho, the sun standing still for Joshua and deliverance from Babylon. And the miracle of all miracles is the incarnation of God's

Son who was born of the virgin Mary and his suffering, dying, and rising; his exaltation at God's right hand; the outpouring of the Holy Spirit; and then the spread of the gospel from Jerusalem to Rome in twenty-five miraculous years.

And soon we will experience the already-promised miracles of Jesus's return, the raising with a new body of all those believers who have fallen asleep, the final defeat of Satan, the last judgment, the destruction of death, and the new earth as a place of perpetual delight.

God has done, has promised, and has eternally fixed all of this and much more in the greatest monument of all his miraculous acts: the Bible, Holy Scripture, the Holy Spirit's Book.

And what is he, then, according to his Book?

Verse 4b:
The Lord is gracious and merciful.

He can make and break us. He can pulverize us. He could have condemned us eternally, but he came with his Son, who took away the sin of the world on the cross. The poet of Psalm 111 did not know that at the time, but we are privileged to see even more clearly how gracious and merciful God is. He preferred to surrender his Son to suffering and death rather than see us lost for eternity! Our guilt may be ever so great, but for those of us who confess him, his grace and mercy are always far greater!

Speaking of praising God, what Christian who has any understanding of his sin would not sing heartily with Psalm 103, "Praise him who will graciously forgive all your trespasses, no matter how many they be"?

Verse 5a mentions something about him that is just as wonderful and lovely:

He provides food for those who fear him.

The psalmist was particularly thinking of the miracle that

11. Psalm 111: I Will Give Thanks to Yahweh!

for forty years Israel needed merely to scoop up her food from the ground six days a week, with a double portion available on Fridays. But what do you think about those of us who live in the wealthy West? How often has your wife or your mother had to tell you, "Husband and children, today I have nothing for you to eat, and I don't know where we're going to get food"? Have you never heard this? Then that shows you how well God cares for us.

Verse 5b:
He remembers his covenant forever.

Isn't that something we must praise him for time and again? Our salvation depends neither on our accomplishments or disposition, nor on God's good mood. But he has bound himself to us contractually—for his covenant is also a contract. Naturally, he has obligated us in his covenant to obey his covenant demands. But the emphasis here lies on the fact that on his end, he has taken upon himself enormous obligations toward us.

Of course, he took these upon himself out of free grace and in sovereignty, but the fact remains that he did that! In this way, to say it reverently, he has obligated himself contractually, so that if we confess our sins with a contrite spirit, he will forgive us for those sins and grant us eternal life. Receiving forgiveness is a covenant promise. And when we die, he will continue to remember his covenant, that he has promised us the resurrection from the dead!

In verse 6 we read of how God promised the land of Canaan to Israel in his covenant of grace:

He has shown his people the power of his works,
    in giving them the inheritance of the nations.

Indeed, the land of Canaan was a gift. In the same way, our entire salvation is a gift, from beginning to end, for which you and I have done nothing ourselves. Our salvation costs us nothing. Two thousand years before we were born, the Lord Jesus paid the entire cost of our salvation. And how much have we been privileged to hear about him from our youth onward, at home and at school? What a gift of God, such knowledge of him! For that is thoroughly reliable.

Verses 7–8:
The works of his hands are faithful and just;
    all his precepts are trustworthy;
they are established forever and ever,
    to be performed with faithfulness and uprightness.

In Scripture, the word truth refers especially to stability and faithfulness. So then, everything that God has done, said, and commanded is equally reliable.

Take his commandments. Have you ever found one of them about which you've had to say, "This commandment I have kept, but oh, how I was tricked! This commandment is so out of touch with the way I ordinarily live that keeping it makes me so unhappy!" On the contrary! With all of God's commandments your well-being is always guaranteed. God's commandments are the path of life, the path of happiness, beneficial for anyone who keeps them, good for your heart and your nerves, good for your marriage and your family, good for the church, state, and society.

Verse 9:
He sent redemption to his people;
    he has commanded his covenant forever.
Holy and awesome is his name!

For Israel, that referred especially to their salvation from Egypt. But we naturally view our salvation as referring to what God has done for us by sending his Son. What don't we owe to that great gift? We have forgiveness of sins through Christ's blood, and the sanctification of life through Christ's Spirit. But we also have perfect knowledge about heaven and earth, insight into our situation, and perspicuity enabling us to peer through the night of history to the light of heaven on earth.

As believers, whenever we sing this psalm we think of the new covenant. "He sent redemption to his people," it says. To paraphrase the Heidelberg Catechism, we know "that in life and in death I am not my own, but I am the dearly bought possession of him who saved and preserves me from head to toe."

God has ordained his covenant for eternity. All of world history is governed by that, in terms of both blessing and curse. That is the golden thread running through everything. And this is what makes his name and fame so holy and awesome. Everything we know about him from his Word, all his efforts on behalf of the church world, can be characterized with those two words: *holy* and *awesome*. That is why the psalmist ends with verse 10 by saying:

Verse 10a–b:
The fear of the Lord is the beginning of wisdom;
  all those who practice it have a good understanding.

To ignore God our Creator is the height of folly. Unfortunately, millions live as though he is nothing. Astonishing blindness! But having loving respect for him and for what he has revealed is the foundation of all perfect knowledge and life wisdom.

Glamorous diplomas and titles play a subordinate role in this connection. In Psalm 14 the Bible refers to a doctored professor who argues, "There is no God," and has this to say about him: "The fool says in his heart, 'There is no God.'" But someone who has barely graduated from elementary school and has difficulty spelling correctly, yet has respect for God and his Word, possesses "good understanding" in the biblical sense: refined understanding and praiseworthy insight.

For all true wisdom—including all forms of science—begins and ends with the "fear of Yahweh." That means deep and loving respect for God the Lord, the Creator and law giver, whose covenant governs everything in heaven and on earth. The fear of Yahweh is the key to knowledge. Only by that means do you know the meaning of your existence and the purpose of living, namely, for the honor of God and for our eternal happiness in the kingdom of God.

Now all we have remaining is the last little sentence.

What we have read and done up to this point is nothing other than praise: praising God, our Father in heaven, in the highest; telling of God's honor; boasting of his great deeds. Now the psalmist ends his brief and concise praise poem with the following brief but poignant sentence:

Verse 10c:
His praise endures forever!

That's how it is! People's names can be on others' lips for a long time. That's how people often talk about an athlete—his name is on the front page in a huge headline. And then such people are quickly forgotten, and few of those names end up in the history books. But God's praise is exalted as high as the heaven above. "His praise endures forever!" Throughout all the ages, believers have proclaimed that praise in hundreds of languages. How about us? Do we join in? Sundays in church, but also during the week? Do we talk about and exalt him in a conversation, and surely in our prayers?

Indeed, his praise endures forever! When, soon, the heavens will be split open and Jesus Christ, God's Son, will appear in undiminished divine glory on the clouds, then at that very same moment there will be only One who is great! Then all people, angels, and devils will have to boast, willingly or unwillingly, about the power and glory of the triune God, Father, Son, and Holy Spirit.

Indeed, everything will redound to the honor of God. *Soli Deo Gloria*! In the Revelation that he was privileged to receive, John heard this in advance and wrote it down in his book:

> Hallelujah!
> For the Lord our God
>   the Almighty reigns.
> Let us rejoice and exult
>   and give him the glory. (Rev. 19:6–7)

CHAPTER 12

Psalm 119: The Prayer of a Solitary Persecuted Person in a Church World Full of Contempt for God and His Word

On May 31, 1567, two Reformed ministers were hanged publicly in the town of Valenciennes. They were Guido de Bres, who authored the Belgic Confession, and his friend, Peregrin de la Grange.

Books about martyrs tell about their imprisonment, about how they were mocked and harassed. By whom? By brothers and sisters who were fellow Christians, people who also prayed the Lord's Prayer and occasionally were so religious that they wore a crucifix of the Lord Jesus on a cord around their waist. More than once the bishop of Atrecht, a genuinely prominent church leader, came in search of both prisoners so he could debate them. But they remained faithful to the end. Standing on the stairs of the scaffold with the noose around his neck, De Bres testified to his love for God and his commandment by warning the gathered crowd: "Do you wish to respect the government? I have never taught anything other than the pure truth of God." At that point, the hangman threw him from the stairs, and De Bres died a martyr's death at only forty-five years old.

This execution occurred at the command of Roman Catholic officials who themselves were being obedient to the Roman Catholic governess Margaretha. She in turn was obeying the Christian king, Philip II, who maintained close ties with the church leaders in Rome, the bishops, the cardinals, and the pope. The execution of De Bres was but one of many examples of the church persecuting the church.

Psalm 119 was written by someone resembling the persecuted righteous De Bres, and in a similarly distressing situation. This poet lived through intense need, distress, and tension. He was not hanged for his faithfulness to God's Word, but he was persecuted and oppressed for that reason, and in a way similar to what De Bres would experience: persecution by godless church leaders, in a godless world.

The Poet and His Opponents

At first glance, or if one knows only a few verses of the psalm, this distressing context is not immediately apparent. For the structure of this psalm is very artistic. It consists of twenty-two stanzas, each of which has eight verses beginning with one of the letters of the Hebrew alphabet. Since this alphabet has twenty-two letters, the psalm consists of 22 stanzas × 8 verses per stanza = 176 verses. Some Bible versions indicate at the top of each stanza which Hebrew letter forms the beginning of each verse (*aleph*, *beth*, *gimel*, *daleth*, etc.). According to the standards of beauty that existed in the world around Israel, this was an especially beautiful poem. But could it really have been the work of someone being persecuted?

Were we to focus only on this clever poetic technique, we

would easily be able to characterize the psalm as merely a product of the poet's desk, a curious song praising the glory of the Law in general, as the superscription in some Bible versions leads us to assume. But when we read Psalm 119 several times, paying special attention to what the poet says about himself and his opponents, we see clearly that throughout this longest of the psalms, a sharp line of demarcation runs between the one who was being persecuted and those who were persecuting him.

The poet

We get the impression that the writer of this psalm was a relatively young man. In verse 141 we read, "I am small and despised." The Hebrew word translated "small" (*tsa'ir*) can also mean "young." Perhaps he was thinking primarily of himself when he asks in verse 9, "How can a young man keep his way pure?" We ought to remember, though, that Scripture uses the word *young man* to refer to someone who was forty-one years old (1 Kgs. 14:21; 2 Chr. 13:7). In addition, verses 99–100 point to a youthful writer: "I have more understanding than all my teachers.... I understand more than the aged." Someone who is elderly would not write this.

In any case, this young man was experiencing distress. In verse 50 he speaks about "my affliction," about which he gives us quite a few details throughout the rest of the psalm. He is bowed low under derision and contempt (v. 22) and occasionally weeps from deep sorrow (v. 28). He is oppressed (vv. 67, 78, 84, 143) so severely that he cries out, "I am severely afflicted" (v. 107). He is persecuted (vv. 84, 161). Indeed, he may not have been executed as De Bres was, but he was certainly familiar with mortal danger: "They have almost made an end of me on earth" (v. 87; cf. v. 95). "I hold my life in my hand continually" (v. 109). People smear him with lies (v. 69), and he is treated unjustly (v. 133). As a result of all this distress, he feels like a sojourner and stranger in the land (v. 19). Some have explained the special alphabetical structure of the psalm as a poem written by a prisoner who supposedly spent time in his cell artistically arranging laments and reasons for consolation.

His opponents

What did he call his persecutors? He calls them "evildoers" (v. 115), "insolent" (vv. 51, 69, 78, 85), "accursed ones" (v. 21), and "the wicked" (vv. 53, 61, 95, 110, 119, 155). Among them were some powerful people: "Princes persecute me without cause" (v. 161). "I will also speak of your testimonies before kings and shall not be put to shame" (v. 46). In this connection, just as with Psalm 2:2, we could perhaps understand this to refer to various local and regional authorities.

With all of these descriptions, the psalmist is portraying a battlefront within Israel, for, as we saw in the first volume of the Psalms commentary, the psalms use terms like *wicked* and *insolent* and the like to refer not to pagans but to church people who do not fear God, disobedient members of God's people, Israelites who had turned their back on Yahweh and his Word. That becomes clear from other details in this psalm. In verse 53 the writer complains, "Hot indignation seizes me because of the wicked, who forsake your law." The term *law* here refers to the Word of God available at that point. He expressed such complaints somewhat often: In verse 21 we read of "insolent, accursed ones, who wander from your commandments." Verse 85 talks about "the insolent . . . [who] do not live according to your law." "For your law has been broken" (v. 126). "My foes forget your words" (v. 139). "They draw near who persecute me with evil purpose; they are far from your law" (v. 150). The wicked "do not seek your statutes" (v. 155). "I look at the faithless with disgust, because they do not keep your commands" (v. 158).

Included among these people were "princes" (vv. 23, 161) and "kings" (v. 46). The writer was being persecuted and oppressed by prominent leaders in Israel, the church of that day. Leaders in God's church of that day were out to get the psalmist. Just as they were with De Bres and, before him, David, Elijah, Elisha, Amos, Jeremiah, and our Savior together with his apostles. Every one of them was persecuted by his brothers, and by kings and princes in Israel, like Saul; Ahab; the church leader Amaziah, who banished Amos from Bethel as a troublemaker (Amos 7:10); and later official representatives within the Jewish church, like the high priests Annas and Caiaphas and the members of the Sanhedrin, with their powerful arm that reached all the way to Damascus (Acts 9:1–2).

We don't know the name of the person who composed Psalm 119, but many who suffered the kinds of oppression mentioned above could be suggested. He could have been someone like Jeremiah, whose preaching work was cut up into shreds and thrown into the furnace by a wicked prince in Israel (Jer. 36). These prophets and apostles, but especially our Savior, could have seen this psalm being fulfilled afresh in their own experience, and all the more as they focused on what the poet says about the methods that his oppressors used. In those methods, many righteous people after him who suffered recognized the methods of their own opponents. Our poet was not opposed with transparent weapons but with dirty, sneaky means, like mockery, contempt, reproach, lies, and snares. "The insolent smear me with lies," he complains (Ps. 119:69). He prays, "Put false ways far from me" (v. 29). We might speak of a campaign of lies. The poor psalmist was being opposed by underhanded enemies: "The insolent have dug pitfalls for me" (v. 85). They were harsh oppressors, lacking an ounce of sympathy: "Their heart is unfeeling like fat" (v. 70). And they constituted a large majority as well: "Many are my persecutors and my adversaries" (v. 157). All of this was happening for no legitimate reason!

Psalm 119 is replete with the poet's declarations of innocence. It would not be difficult to point to more than sixty instances of this. We will cite a few: "Even though princes sit plotting against me, your servant will meditate on your statutes" (v. 23). "The insolent utterly deride me, but I do not turn away from your law" (v. 51). "Though the cords of the wicked ensnare me, I do not forget your law" (v. 61). "The insolent smear me with lies, but with my whole heart I keep your precepts" (v. 69). "I hold my life in my hand continually, but I do not forget your law" (v. 109). "I am small and despised, yet I do not forget your precepts" (v. 141).

As we saw when we discussed Psalm 26, we absolutely may not identify this manner of speaking as pharisaical, for you can hear many righteous people using this tone in Scripture with God's approval. This is exactly how De Bres talked as he stood on the steps of the scaffold: "I have proclaimed sound doctrine to you!"

Not a work of timeless poetry

Psalm 119 is hardly a timeless poetic production about the glory of the Law; rather, it is a psalm in which a poor sufferer like Jeremiah could have recognized himself, someone who for his entire life had to remonstrate against political and ecclesiastical leaders in Judah who took counsel against him and spread lies about him (see, e.g., Jer. 36).

But the greatest fulfillment of Psalm 119 occurred with our chief Prophet and Teacher, who was smeared by prominent leaders in the Jewish ecclesiastical life of his day (he was called "Beelzebul, the prince of demons" by the Pharisees, Matt. 12:24). He also encountered "princes" like those members of the Sanhedrin who laid snares for him (trick questions) and were just as harsh as the opponents of our psalmist. And the servants of Jesus Christ were no greater than their Master. Church history often displays the pattern of Psalm 119: "princes" who "take counsel together" against innocent righteous ones who desire nothing more than to respect God and his Word.

It lies beyond the purpose of this book to discuss this psalm verse by verse. We would encourage Bible readers, however, to read each verse of this psalm from the point of view of the historical situation of the writer. Then you will see the

12. Psalm 119: The Prayer of a Solitary Persecuted Person

haze of "generality" and "timelessness" that covers this psalm for some people automatically disappear, and you will hear this psalm in terms of its flaming, polemical, confessional language—in the church world of our day, as well, which is just as full of contempt for the Word. We want to show this with the help of several verses.

Verse 136: "My eyes shed streams of tears, because people do not keep your law"

Our psalmist has at his disposal an entire group of terms for referring to the Scriptures of his day: the law of Yahweh, your testimonies, your commands, your ordinances, your commandments, your word, your counsels, the word of truth, your promise, your words. Weighed properly, these expressions naturally differ in nuances and meaning, but in fact they are all synonyms for God's Word. Moreover, each of them is defined covenantally. A term like *command* refers often in Scripture not to a single command of God but actually to the entire Horeb covenant that includes all of God's instruction (cf. *mitswah*). The term *testimony* refers to the covenant documents in the ark. The phrase *your promise* indicates the promises of life, happiness, and protection under the great king, promises Yahweh had given his vassal Israel if she would keep Yahweh's covenant (see the commentary on Lev. 18:5). In short, all of these expressions refer to the Teaching that Yahweh had given through Moses and the prophets, regarding his covenants, his kingship over all of Israelite life, and the lawsuit that he had to initiate against his apostate vassal Israel at several points in history.

During the time when this, the longest psalm, was being written, this good, divine teaching was being arrogantly neglected by many Israelites, including prominent leaders. The psalmist complains about this repeatedly: "Your law has been broken" (Ps. 119:126). "They are far from your law" (v. 150;

cf. vv. 21, 53, 85). This means nothing less than that the foundations undergirding Israelite society were eroding (cf. 11:3).

Earlier we saw something of the bitter sorrow that entered many an Israelite home when the Torah—the shield of the poor!—was broken. The breaking of the law mentioned by the psalmist occurred so often in biblical history that the term *poor* is often used, especially in the psalms, to refer to the righteous! Recall the covetous Ahab, another one of those Israelite princes, who broke the Torah and brought disaster upon Naboth and his family.

Certainly the psalmist was angry and deeply incensed about this: "I look at the faithless with disgust, because they do not keep your commands" (Ps. 119:158). "Hot indignation seizes me because of the wicked, who forsake your law" (v. 53). In this outrage and disgust, stabs of cold orthodoxism pierced through, but the psalmist also shed bitter tears because of the apostasy of his brethren: "My eyes shed streams of tears, because people do not keep your law" (v. 136).

Crying on behalf of the church is something we heard the writer of Psalm 74 do as well. By virtue of such laments, Psalm 119 joins the list of lamentations on behalf of Zion, and the writer demonstrates that his is a kindred spirit along with the writers of the book of Lamentations. Our Savior was also "moved with compassion" when he saw the hounded multitudes like sheep without a shepherd (Matt. 9:36 KJV; cf. 23:37). And for those suffering genuine sorrow on behalf of the desolate situation within modern Christianity, Psalm 119 is highly relevant.

Verse 172: "My tongue will sing of your word"

The sadness of the psalmist because of the contempt for God's Word must have been so bitter because he loved the Scripture so fervently. "My tongue will sing of your word"—well, that is exactly what he did! From verse 4 on, he addresses Yahweh

12. Psalm 119: The Prayer of a Solitary Persecuted Person

directly, so that his psalm constitutes a prayer of 173 verses or 347 lines, only seven of which omit mention of God's Word. His psalm is indeed a praise song about God's Word. To mention but a few of his expression of praise:

> *Blessed* are those who do what the Torah teaches (vv. 1–2).
> God's rules are so *righteous* (vv. 7, 62, 106, 164).
> God's rules are *good* (v. 39).
> Your entire Word is *truth* (vv. 43, 142, 151, 160).
> All of God's judgments are *righteousness* (vv. 75, 123, 138, 144).
> All your commandments are *faithful* (v. 86).
> God's Word *abides forever* (vv. 89, 152, 160).
> *Heaven and earth rest* upon God's Word (vv. 90–91).
> God's commandment is *without limit* (v. 96).
> Your commandment *makes wise* (v. 98).
> Your commands *give insight* (vv. 100, 104, 130).
> Your Word is a *lamp* for my feet (v. 105).
> Your testimonies are *wonderful* (v. 129).
> The unfolding of your words *spreads light* (v. 130).
> Your rules are *right* (v. 137).
> Your Word is well *tried* (v. 140).
> Behold, those who love your law have *great peace* (v. 165).

It was this good Word of God that the psalmist saw many people around him rejecting! Just as today in modern Christianity, "the man of lawlessness" appears more and more, "the son of destruction, who opposes and exalts himself against every so-called god or object of worship, so that he takes his seat in the temple of God, proclaiming himself to be God" (2 Thess. 2:3–4). The words of praise that we read above, which the psalmist devoted to God's Word, many within Christianity today dedicate to the sciences: "Science is wonderful: it spreads light." So we stand with the psalmist in opposition to the same battlefront even today: the choice between divine wisdom or human wisdom. Once again we have an example of the fact that Psalm 119 does not provide universal pious verses but rather sounds forth polemical praise to the wisdom of God in opposition to the fantasy wisdom of the world, including that of modern autonomous man.

Verse 82: "My eyes long for your promise"

Often, forsaking God's Word goes hand in hand with the scarcity of God's Word. In Samuel's youth, "the word of the LORD was rare in those days" (1 Sam. 3:1). It was the same during the time of Elijah, when Hosea lived, when the Lord Jesus was on earth, and also in the medieval church. And this despite the presence of impressive "piety." Such a scarcity can itself be a punishment of Yahweh. Through Amos, Yahweh said that he would send a hunger throughout the land, not for bread but for God's Word, and people would find it nowhere (Amos 8:11–12). Was the psalmist living in such a time? In Psalm 119:99–100 he says, "I have more understanding than all my teachers, for your testimonies are my meditation. I understand more than the aged, for I keep your precepts." Had the priests and Levites, the appointed teachers of God's Word, "lost their way" and been the same sort of people as the Pharisees in Jesus's day, who had taken away the key of knowledge, and like the teachers of the law in Paul's day, who had fallen into idle chatter, teachers of the law who had no understanding of God's Word (1 Tim. 1:6–7)?

How intensely the psalmist longed for the opening of God's Word: "My soul is consumed with longing for your rules at all times" (Ps. 119:20). "Behold, I long for your precepts" (v. 40). "Take not the word of truth utterly out of my mouth" (v. 43). "My soul longs for your salvation" (v. 81). "I open my mouth and pant, because I long for your commandments" (v. 131). For him, the sound of God's Word is music

(v. 54). It is more valuable to him than a thousand pieces of gold or silver (v. 72). It tastes sweeter than honey in his mouth (v. 103).

These lines of the psalm have been fulfilled in many periods of the history of Christianity, such as in 1538, when Bullinger preached every day in Zurich, from 6:00 to 7:00 in the morning, and a large multitude always came to listen.

Verse 18: "Open my eyes, that I may behold wondrous things out of your law"

In times when the Word of God is scarce, it can nonetheless be quite available in book form. God's people can still possess it and read it themselves, but they no longer understand what they are reading.

There is a cover that lies over the Scripture.

A Cover over God's Word

That cover can be anything.

In the days of Jesus's sojourn on earth, the Pharisees and Sadducees encrusted Scripture with their explanations of the Law, so that those poor folk attending synagogue got to hear the Torah read like a religious labor contract instead of as God's gospel that invites people: "Believe and you will live." This leaven of the Pharisees corrupted Scripture interpretation in the apostolic and medieval church in many places. God's Word was covered by legalism and Judaism, by the dust of medieval Roman Catholicism and even Reformed theologians with their scholastic or mystical system, full of fantasy ideas about God and his truth. Tradition can constitute just such a covering and make Scripture unreadable: "I have always heard . . ." is its prelude. Or consider the teaching about our lovely Lord in heaven who never gets angry, and about a nice Jesus who wants to be everybody's friend. All of these are coverings over God's Word.

Open my eyes

Our psalmist does not talk, however, about coverings over God's Word, but about a covering over his eyes. That means practically the same thing. Paul wrote about the unbelieving Jews: "Yes, to this day whenever Moses is read a veil lies over their hearts. But when one turns to the Lord, the veil is removed" (2 Cor. 3:15–16). We speak of reading through colored glasses. But our psalmist prayed, "Open my eyes." Here the word used for *open* (*galah*) is the same word used in Numbers 22:31: "Then Yahweh *opened* the eyes of Balaam," who initially had not seen the Angel of Yahweh standing with drawn sword, but when Yahweh had "opened" or "uncovered" his eyes, he saw the Angel. At that point the covering fell from his eyes. That is what the psalmist asked: "Yahweh, uncover my eyes, so that I may behold wondrous things from your law (which now I perhaps do not yet see)."

A humble and spirited prayer

In periods of church history like that in which the composer of Psalm 119 lived, times when the knowledge of God is despised and scarce, the righteous run the risk of being overwhelmed by the streaming anti-Word sentiment in the church of their time. For example, recall the messianic expectation of the apostles: thanks to the teaching of their misguided scribes, they knew nothing more than that the Messiah would be a powerful national leader. Despite impressive "piety" and Pharisaic law keeping, people could hear the opened Word of God only from John the Baptist and the Lord Jesus.

Did the composer of Psalm 119 experience similar circumstances? In view of his long prayer, he considered that he could have become deficient in his understanding of Holy Scripture, with a covering over his eyes. How earnestly he prayed, therefore, for the deepening of his insight into the Word of Yahweh. Six times we read, "Teach me your statutes" (vv. 12, 26, 64, 68, 124, 135). "Hide not your commandments from me!" (v. 19). "Make me understand the way of your precepts, and I will meditate on your wondrous works" (v. 27). "Graciously teach me your law!" (v. 29). "Teach me, O LORD, the way of your statutes; and I will keep it to the end" (v. 33). "Give me understanding, that I may keep your law and observe it with my whole heart" (v. 34). "Give me understanding that I may learn your commandments" (v. 73). "Teach me your rules" (v. 108). "I am your servant; give me understanding, that I may know your testimonies!" (v. 125). "My lips will pour forth praise, for you teach me your statutes" (v. 171).

At the same time, we see here why the psalmist prayed for the uncovering of his eyes: "that I may behold wondrous things out of your law" (v. 18). "Give me understanding, that I may keep your law and observe it with my whole heart" (v. 34). He wanted to become a better doer of the Word. That is a petition of a humble and sturdy believer!

For such a person does not know ahead of time what he will get to see when Yahweh answers this prayer. Our poet obtained a sharpened perspective of the situation of God's people in his time. He saw the causes of various forms of distress in Israel: "Your law has been broken" (v. 126). The more one understands God's Word, the more deeply one is able to discern various forms of church decay: cold-hearted principles, systems of thought that destroy church and society, the corrupting power of "church princes" among God's people, religion exercised apart from the Word and the covenant. The poet of Psalm 119 sensed his loneliness in the Israelite church even though he had people around him (vv. 74, 79), and he learned to see the redemptive dimension of his oppression in the Israelite church world.

Verse 71: "It is good for me that I was afflicted"

We should not pry this verse loose from the larger context of the psalm. This is not a general declaration of someone who is meditating about the benefit of affliction, but the acknowledgment of a God-fearing man who was being persecuted by his brothers for the sake of the Word.

His many prominent and insensitive opponents had caused him so much sorrow, and yet he had learned this lesson: "It is good for me that I was afflicted, that I might learn your statutes" (v. 71). For "before I was afflicted I went astray" (v. 67). Earlier he perhaps had not encountered a king as his opponent, but then, "I have gone astray like a lost sheep" (v. 176). And now prominent leaders among God's people may well gather and conspire against him, and afflict him with "snares" and "pits," but now he keeps God's Word! "Even though princes sit plotting against me, your servant will meditate on your statutes. Your testimonies are my delight; they are my counselors" (vv. 23–24). He feels more bound to Yahweh more closely than ever: "I am yours" (v. 94). "Your statutes have been my songs in the house of my sojourning" (v. 54). His being oppressed on behalf of the Word had increased his joy in God's Word!

The same has been the experience of many righteous people who have suffered. As simple Galilean fishermen, the apostles had enjoyed a far quieter life than when they came to stand as witnesses of Jesus Christ before unbelieving Judaism with its "princes" among the Sanhedrin. But with Psalm 119 they could confess, "Before I was afflicted [formerly as a fisherman] I strayed [what did I know at that point about the coming of God's kingdom? What kinds of coverings lay over my eyes as I read the Law and the Prophets back then?], but now I keep your Word." The teaching of the Lord Jesus had opened their eyes, so to speak (Matt. 13:16). Similarly, as a pupil of Gamaliel, Paul had strayed, but as the suffering apostle of Jesus Christ, he understood the Law and the Prophets for the first time.

In the sixteenth century, church history displayed the

pattern of Psalm 119 once again. Before his affliction, Luther had become a respected Augustinian monk and professor. But princes like Charles V, Philip II, the duke of Alva, and cardinals like Granvelle set out traps and dug pits in order to bring down this godly reformer. Yet precisely at that time, many Christians received joy in God's Word like they had never experienced before. The gospel sounded forth like music in the house of their pilgrimage (cf. Ps. 119:54), in Emden, London, and Geneva, where many of those persecuted at that time fled. There Psalm 119 was fulfilled: "I rejoice at your word like one who finds great spoil" (v. 162). "It is good for me that I was afflicted, that I might learn your statutes" (v. 71). "Even though princes sit plotting against me, your servant will meditate on your statutes" (v. 23).

Verse 66: "Teach me good judgment and knowledge"

We could also translate this as "Teach me to taste well," for in 2 Samuel 19:35 the same Hebrew verb is used for tasting food. We want to avoid generalizing this petition as well, but want to read it in the context of the entire psalm. Then we could paraphrase it this way: "Teach me to test well what is going on in the church world, and teach me from your Word to know you as you really are for your people, for I am placing my trust in your covenant promises."

This capacity for discernment was altogether lacking in the Pharisees and Sadducees (Matt. 16:1–4). They failed to recognize the messianic age (Matt. 13:14–15). And despite their fanatic religious zeal, the Savior spoke to his Father about the Jewish ecclesiastical world this way: "The world does not know you" (John 17:25).

It is understandable that the psalmist would pray for the capacity of discernment, for especially in times when forsaking

God's covenant is camouflaged with impressive "religiosity," it is not always easy for the godly to "taste" such situations. Amos was chased from Bethel by the "respectable" high priest, Amaziah (Amos 7:10–17). The Lord Jesus was despised by Pharisees, the same ones who stood praying on street corners. In the sixteenth century, Christians were persecuted by monks and church leaders who had denied themselves marriage for the Lord's sake. All those supposedly pious people did not make it easy for the godly in those times to distinguish between good and evil! For that, one needs the gift of discernment, listed by Paul in 1 Corinthians 12:10 among the gifts of the Spirit. The poet of Psalm 119 prayed for that gift, but he confessed at the same time, "For I put my trust in your commandments." It seems that he expected this gift of the Spirit to come from his relationship with the Book of the Spirit, namely, Holy Scripture. Along those lines, God's Spirit desires to grant people the gift of "testing the spirits" (1 John 4:1–6). For then one will be able to peer through various false fronts to identify those leaders demanding respect—the Amaziahs and the Pharisees, the bishops and church leaders—as "evildoers" and "insolent" (to use language from Psalm 119), and to identify the animal farmer Amos and the carpenter Jesus of Nazareth and the imprisoned Guido de Bres as those who, just like our psalmist, were persecuted for the sake of the truth.

All of Psalm 119 is a demonstration of how God has heard this prayer for the gift of discernment. This faithful brother was able to discern clearly the battlefront in the church of his time, so much so that he prayed with clear-headed discernment! When he prayed for his persecutors, he did not say, "O Yahweh, please remove the battle lines between those who keep your Word and those who forsake your Word." In the same way, our Savior did not pray for "the world" (which referred to the Jewish world, together with their leaders, who rejected him) but for those whom the Father had given him:

his disciples and all those who believed him (John 17:9). This is how our psalmist prayed as well; he didn't pray indiscriminately, for every Tom, Dick, and Harry, but because he discerned the real battle line, he prayed in terms of those who were forsaking the Word: "Plead my cause and redeem me" (Ps. 119:154). "When will you judge those who persecute me?" (v. 84; cf. vv. 78, 126). And as for those who loved God's Word, he declared, "I am a companion of all who fear you, of those who keep your precepts" (v. 63). He did not pray for unity with those who forsook Yahweh, but stated, "I am a companion of all who fear you, of those who keep your precepts" (v. 79). Our Savior also had in mind that unity which comes from unanimity in the Word when he prayed "that they may all be one, just as you, Father, are in me, and I in you, that they also may be in us" (John 17:21).

"Blessed are the persecuted"

"The prayer of a solitary persecuted person in a church world full of contempt for God and his Word." That is how we've entitled this chapter on Psalm 119. Taken strictly, this does not do justice to the entire psalm, for although the poet addresses Yahweh in verses 4–176, he precedes this with a confession of his faith in verses 1–3. This is the same faith as that with which Psalm 1 opened.

Are the genuinely godly in the Israelite and Christian church worlds often afflicted by reproach and persecution? Can they occasionally sob on account of the contempt for God's good Word? Do they yearn for deeper insight into Scripture and pray for the opening of their eyes? Let them dry their tears, for even though the "leaders" have driven them into a corner, nevertheless the godly have it good! For Yahweh stands on their side and he defends them, though that happens after a brief time of suffering (1 Pet. 5:10).

In that faith the poet of Psalm 119 addresses God, which is why he could introduce his long prayer with the confession that actually constitutes not only the beginning but also the conclusion of the psalm (cf. vv. 174–176):

> Blessed are those whose way is blameless,
> > who walk in the law of the Lord!
> Blessed are those who keep his testimonies,
> > who seek him with their whole heart,
> who also do no wrong,
> > but walk in his ways! (Ps. 119:1–3)

CHAPTER 13

Psalm 139: O Yahweh, You Have Searched Me and Known Me![1]

"Yahweh, you have searched me and known me!" There in one sentence you have all of Psalm 139, which is why we must study that sentence very closely. First we have the Hebrew name for God, Yahweh, a wonderful name that recalls Israel's deliverance from Egypt. Practically speaking, "Yahweh" means "He will surely be with you": It means Deliverer, Helper, Healer, Savior, Life-rescuer—except that now we have learned from the Lord Jesus a still more wonderful name, for he said "Call God your Father, just as I do." So then, you cannot address God any more intimately than with the warm and tender word *Father*. So we are going to read Psalm 139:1 this way: "Father, you have searched me and known me!"

God's eyes look right through us, down to the bottom of our heart: "No creature is hidden from his sight, but all are naked and exposed to the eyes of him to whom we must give

---

1. [Translator's note: This chapter, authored by F. van Deursen, did not appear in the Dutch original, and has been added to this translated volume.]

account" (Heb. 4:13). Nevertheless, that is not something that should make us tremble, for then we forget two things. First, we forget the thoroughly heartwarming name Yahweh or Father. Secondly, we forget that David says not only "You have searched me" but also "You have known me."

There you have once again that warm biblical word: God *knows* us so thoroughly, something that means far more than that he is "up-to-date" in a cool and dispassionate manner about the personal details of our lives. In the Bible, *know* is in fact another word for "love" and "show faithfulness." Scripture uses this term, for example, for the intimate relations between a husband and wife.

So when David confesses, "You have searched me and known me," he is referring to the exact opposite of some cold, dispassionate impersonal observation and the bare registering of facts. He is addressing his heavenly Father who, with paternal love and interest, sympathized with him more intensely and stood closer to him than anyone else.

We distinguish five sections in his psalm. "Yahweh, you have searched me and known me" (1) in the small details of my daily living (vv. 2–6); (2) as part of the immeasurable universe (vv. 7–12); (3) from my conception to my rising from the dead (vv. 13–18); (4) in my abhorrence of the wicked (vv. 19–22); and (5) in my sinful weakness (vv. 23–24).

You Know Me in Terms of the Small Details of My Daily Living (vv. 2–6)

> Verses 2–3:
> You know when I sit down and when I rise up;
>   you discern my thoughts from afar.
> You search out my path and my lying down
>   and are acquainted with all my ways.

That is how you could summarize our daily living. It consists in sitting down and rising up, coming and going. Every morning you get up. You eat breakfast standing or sitting. You go to work. There you sit or stand. You return home, and there you sit again until you lie down. What else do we do day in and day out?

In all of that, Yahweh knows us, in the warmest sense of that word. He is intimately involved in all that sitting and standing, with fatherly love and interest, in the same way that fathers and mothers of small children observe all the movements of their toddler with intense interest and deep love. That is how he sees our sick ones lying in bed and our children going to school.

Our thought world also belongs to those "ways" familiar to Yahweh. Often they are filled with matters that are anything but pretty, with cares and sadness that can keep us awake for hours during the night. Naturally, we take these in our prayers before his throne, but in so doing, we're not telling him any news, for

Verse 4:
Even before a word is on my tongue,
  behold, O Lord, you know it altogether.

That is how well he knows us! Even before we speak, he already knows what we want to say. What a rich comfort this is during those times when we don't know what to pray or when we're too tired or sick to pray. Even if we should slip into a coma and evidence not a twitch of life, our heavenly Father knows what we would say if we were conscious. He knows that we love him, and he remembers his covenant with us, even in our unconsciousness.

Verse 5:
You hem me in, behind and before,
  and lay your hand upon me.

As a father takes his toddler's hand when they cross the street together, and as a mother puts her arm around a sobbing child, that's how our heavenly Father "embraces" us from behind and in front. He does that for each of his millions of children! What a great divine work: knowing each of them, searching each of their hearts, following their getting up and lying down and their life's activities. David found this to be something incomprehensible:

> Verse 6:
> Such knowledge is too wonderful for me;
> it is high; I cannot attain it.

You Know Me as Part of the Immeasurable Universe (vv. 7–12)

Nowadays we know better than the poet did that the cosmos is so immensely huge that you could more easily find a needle in a haystack than locate our earth from deep space. Does God's benevolent love extend so far that he pays attention, despite that incomprehensible space between billions of heavenly bodies, to one particular man or woman living on that great planet called Earth? Yes, that is precisely what David confesses in verses 7–12.

> Verses 7–8:
> Where shall I go from your Spirit?
>   Or where shall I flee from your presence?
> If I ascend to heaven, you are there!
>   If I make my bed in Sheol, you are there!

God's "face" is his most intimate presence. Wherever I go, I am in your immediate presence. I can never escape your care and love. Even if I climbed up to heaven, you would be there with your care and love. Indeed, imagine that I could descend into the realm of the dead; even there I would not be apart from you. For if I could be there, I would find you there, and you would know me there as well.

In verses 9–10 David is fantasizing: Imagine that I could fly!

> Verses 9–10:
> If I take the wings of the morning
>   and dwell in the uttermost parts of the sea,
> even there your hand shall lead me,
>   and your right hand shall hold me.

Yes, even if early in the morning I flew on the wings of the first sunlight rising in the east, to the farthest west, farther than the farthest sea, even that great distance would not separate me from Yahweh. For there as well, his faithful fatherly hand would continue to hold me fast and guide me.

> Verses 11–12:
> If I say, "Surely the darkness shall cover me,
>   and the light about me be night,"
> even the darkness is not dark to you;
>   the night is bright as the day,
>   for darkness is as light with you.

Imagine that I could invite the darkest darkness to surround me, so that the midday became night: even that blackest darkness could not hide me from Yahweh. For his loving eyes, there is no difference between light and darkness, and he would continue to follow me in that deep darkness. This is something all believers may echo from David, for their encouragement.

You Know Me from My Conception to My Rising from the Dead (vv. 13–18)

How is it that God knows us so thoroughly? Because he himself formed us inside our mothers.

> Verses 13–16:
> For you formed my inward parts;
>   you knitted me together in my mother's womb.
> I praise you, for I am fearfully and wonderfully made.
> Wonderful are your works;
>   my soul knows it very well.
> My frame was not hidden from you,
> when I was being made in secret,
>   intricately woven in the depths of the earth.
> Your eyes saw my unformed substance;
> in your book were written, every one of them,
>   the days that were formed for me,
>   when as yet there was none of them.

David realizes that Yahweh has known him from the time of his embryonic existence in the womb of his mother. That was not hidden from Yahweh. His eyes watched over David's earliest formless beginning—the fertilized egg of his mother, whom in the span of nine months God caused to grow into a complete human baby.

At that point Yahweh already knew David, and everything about him was already written in God's book: whether he would be born as a boy or a girl, everything about his bones, his brains, his psychological disposition, his poetic ability, his handsome looks. Nothing was left to chance, but everything was included in God's plan for his life. He knew what he was doing and did it all in love. This should be an encouragement to pregnant mothers: your baby is already now surrounded by God's care and love.

13. Psalm 139: O Yahweh, You Have Searched Me and Known Me!

Verses 17–18:
How precious to me are your thoughts, O God!
    How vast is the sum of them!
If I would count them, they are more than the sand.
    I awake, and I am still with you.

When David contemplated God's government of the world, he encountered billions of divine thoughts, each of them far too exalted and far too profound for our understanding. But one thing he understood well: The covenant of grace that God established with his people is unbreakable. It cannot be broken even by death. He knew this for certain: When I awake from the sleep of death, then I will still be with you.

You Know Me Also in Terms of How I Abhor the Wicked (vv. 19–22)

We read how full David was with God's love for his children. But to his amazement he also saw Israelites who spurned God's love and often exchanged Yahweh for the idols of the pagans. Because he himself loved Yahweh so intensely, he laid before him this petition:

Verses 19–22:
Oh that you would slay the wicked, O God!
    O men of blood, depart from me!
They speak against you with malicious intent;
    your enemies take your name in vain.
Do I not hate those who hate you, O Lord?
    And do I not loathe those who rise up against you?
I hate them with complete hatred;
    I count them my enemies.

Here David is suddenly praying for the defeat of the wicked. Is David allowed to pray for that? Wasn't he supposed to love his enemies? According to many, these verses are completely foreign to the tone of this lovely psalm, and they certainly do not convey a New Testament spirit. We discussed this sentiment extensively in the chapter on Psalm 59. And in the opening chapter of the previous volume on the Psalms we devoted a large section to identifying the characteristics of the wicked. We will suffice with directing the reader to those places, and limit ourselves here to the following remarks.

You know that Saul almost pinned David against the wall with his spear twice, but when David twice had Saul lying powerless at his feet, he spared his life. Only one thrust of the spear was needed, and he didn't even have to do it himself (1 Sam. 24:2–6). In those circumstances he acted in the Spirit of Christ, who taught, "Love your enemies and pray for those who persecute you" (Matt. 5:44).

Moreover, for us the term *hate* makes us think most often of feelings of hatred. But in Scripture, the term *hate* can also mean to show abhorrence, to ignore something or someone and push it aside. Jesus once said, "If anyone comes to me and does not hate his own father and mother and wife and children and brothers and sisters, yes, and even his own life, he cannot be my disciple" (Luke 14:26). In saying this, Jesus was not requiring specific feelings toward one's father or mother. But if ever you would need to choose between Jesus and your parents or your wife or your children, then you must put him in first place and push the others aside.

When we understand the term *hate* in this way, then we are able to see David not as someone walking around with constant and intense feelings of hatred, but as someone who wants nothing to do with the principles and practices of those who rejected God and his Word. And so he avoided such people as much as possible (cf. Ps. 1). This abhorrence proceeded from his intimate love for the One who had loved David so wonderfully from the time of his most primitive beginning in the womb.

You Know Me in My Sinful Weakness (vv. 23–24)

No, David did not express his abhorrence of the wickedness in the church and world from a position of self-sufficiency sitting in an ivory tower. On the contrary, he knew his own weakness far too well for that (cf. Ps. 51). Woe to him if Yahweh were to abandon him to himself! Thus he turns once more to Yahweh, who by means of his covenant of grace has placed him together with Israel on the path leading to eternal life.

But how often do we walk that path with uncertain steps! What a seductive power proceeds from wickedness, affecting even believers. We experience daily the same thing the apostle Paul experienced when he confessed, "So I find it to be a law that when I want to do right, evil lies close at hand" (Rom. 7:21). David was deeply conscious of the fact that if God did not intervene, he would be able to slip from the eternal path to the dead-end path of the wicked (cf. Ps. 1:6). His heart and his thoughts often contained much that was not pretty, and so he concluded with a prayer:

> Verses 23–24:
> **Search me, O God, and know my heart!**
>   **Try me and know my thoughts!**
> **And see if there be any grievous way in me,**
>   **and lead me in the way everlasting!**

After all, it was possible that, without realizing it, he may have landed on a wrong path. In Psalm 19:12 he prayed, "Who can discern his errors? Declare me innocent from hidden faults." Open my eyes to that, and forgive me those sins. Lead me with your Word and Spirit along the path that endures and leads to eternal life.

Psalm 139 teaches us to know the One who in Christ Jesus has become our God and Father. No one stands closer to us than he. No one knows us better and is more involved with us than he. No one can promise us what he has promised us, and make good on what he has promised. He never loses sight of us and never lets go of our hand. In the darkest valleys he surrounds us from behind and in front.

The apostle Paul put it this way: "If God is for us, who can be against us? He who did not spare his own Son but gave him up for us all, how will he not also with him graciously give us all things? . . . For I am sure that neither death nor life, nor angels nor rulers, nor things present nor things to come, nor powers, nor height nor depth, nor anything else in all creation, will be able to separate us from the love of God in Christ Jesus our Lord" (Rom. 8:31–32, 38–39).

Chapter 14

Psalms 145–150: The Book of Psalms Ends with Pure Praise

Has it ever impressed you how the Psalter ends? Throughout this book of the Bible there is so much crying out and beseeching, so much groaning and weeping. But under the leading of God's Spirit, how did those who arranged the Psalter arrange the conclusion? With six psalms of pure praise! To be sure, some view Psalms 145–150 as a self-contained entity because all of these psalms begin and end with "Hallelujah" and because, from Psalm 145 onward, we hear no more laments and no more requests to God. Such features have disappeared. That is why we believe that Psalm 145 marks the beginning of the finale of the Psalter, which consists of a closing choral arrangement of six psalms, each and all of them filled with praise and worship. All of it leads to the close of Psalm 150: "Let everything that has breath praise Yahweh. Hallelujah!"

The Bible's own book of prayer closes with pure praise.

What Does It Actually Mean to Praise God?

To praise is something other than to give thanks. We teach our children to say thank you in various situations. Little children sometimes forget to do that. When you give a young boy a toy car or put a doll in the arms of a little girl they may perhaps forget to say thank you, but with their face they are praising and complimenting you for your present. Even their hands might be raised, and from their lips comes the cry, "O how nice!" This is how they have praised your action. Thanking is often a rule of etiquette, but praising is part of a child's spontaneity. In short, in terms of our conduct, asking and receiving should be followed by thanking; in terms of the psalmists' conduct, asking and receiving from Yahweh is followed by praising, magnifying God. In fact, Hebrew does not have a distinct word for "to thank"! So praising is more than thanking!

In his book *The Praise of God in the Psalms*, Claus Westermann has helpfully described the differences between praising and thanking, which we summarize in this way:

1. Thanking is often an act of acquired etiquette, more or less a question of one's training and sense of duty. But praising happens spontaneously. A person does that voluntarily and experiences joy in doing it.
2. Thanking is something we do with only one or two words: "Thanks" or "Thank you." Even so, the one doing the thanking remains central. He is the subject of the sentence: "*I* thank you." Praising, by, contrast is not something we do with one or two words; we use entire sentences for it. And not the one who is praising, but the one who receives the praise is central: "*You* are so kind! *You* did such a wonderful thing!"
3. Thanking does not make the one who is thanked any greater than he is. He remains what he was. Praising, by contrast, inherently magnifies (cf. the Latin, *magnificare*). With praising, the giver together with the gift

14. Psalms 145–150: The Book of Psalms Ends with Pure Praise

is "magnified," "exalted." The words of praise "lift him up" and "elevate him on high."

4. Thanking happens mostly without notice. It is a matter between two people and can even be done by letter. Praising is more than thanking, even in this respect. Praising inherently seeks publicity. One who wants to praise seeks a forum in which to praise someone. Moreover, praising prefers to work contagiously: it prefers to incite others on behalf of the one who is worthy of praise.

As we have already observed, Hebrew has no distinct word for "to thank," but Hebrew has an assortment of expressions for praising. It is especially the psalmists who summon people numerous times to "praise" God, to "exalt" God, to "magnify" God. In addition, we have all those Scripture passages where God is praised even though the word *praise* is never used.

What, then, does praise look like? You can praise someone in one of two ways. You can simply say, "I must praise you for that." But you can also praise someone without using that word *praise*, namely, when we tell about someone's deeds. This is how a teacher talks to a student: "What a great essay you've produced, and written so well!" In this instance the teacher proudly summarizes the deeds of his student. And that is just like praising: publicly, in the hearing of others (a class, other colleagues), telling about someone's deeds.

In Holy Scripture we encounter both ways of praising, especially in the Psalms. Numerous times the psalms summon us, "Praise Yahweh," but they especially summarize God's mighty deeds. They do so publicly, as the opening of Psalm 78 shows: "Give ear, O my people. . . . We will not hide them from their children, but tell to the coming generation the glorious deeds of the Lord, and his might, and the wonders that he has done" (Ps. 78:1, 4; cf. Ps. 66). Next the poet summarizes God's deeds performed from the time of Egypt to the time of David. In praising God, one can confess his involvement with God's historic redemptive deeds. The author of Psalm 105 does the same thing: apparently he offers a history lesson in poetic form, about the great events narrated in the Torah and the book of Joshua. But these stories stand in an altogether different context in the psalm. In the Torah and the book of Joshua, they are framed as prophetic instruction, but in Psalm 105 they are given in the context of the praise of God. This is similar to the way Psalm 104 puts into poetic language facts drawn from the world of creation.

These concluding psalms of the Psalter operate the same way. The writer of Psalm 145 introduces his praise song thus: "I will extol you, my God and King. . . . One generation shall commend your works to another, and shall declare your mighty acts. On the glorious splendor of your majesty, and on your wondrous works, I will meditate. They shall speak of the might of your awesome deeds, and I will declare your greatness. . . . All your works shall give thanks to you, O Lord. . . . [They will] make known to the children of man your mighty deeds" (vv. 1, 4–6, 10, 12). Then comes a summary of those famous deeds.

This affects our daily living as Christians. In this conclusion of the Psalter, the Holy Spirit supplies us with important instructions for our prayers! We need not always be asking something from God. The Bible's songbook and prayer book ends with six psalms that in reality ask nothing from God. Shouldn't we learn from this that we can seek God's face with nothing other than praise? In fact, in the Lord's Prayer, doesn't our Savior teach us to regularly begin and end our prayers with praise to God? Are there times when you don't know what to pray? Then simply summarize a few of those mighty redemptive deeds that God has done for us through his Son, Jesus Christ. Don't you find it remarkable that despite containing all sorts of petitions that beseech God for something, the Psalter does not have the Hebrew title *tefillim* (prayers), but *tehillim* (praise songs)?

So then, let our praying be especially praising God!

14. Psalms 145–150: The Book of Psalms Ends with Pure Praise

For what great deed is Yahweh being praised at the conclusion of the Psalter?

"Great is Yahweh, and greatly to be praised" (Ps. 145:3). In fact, he is so worthy of praise that no one can ever praise him according to his full worth. "Who can utter the mighty deeds of the Lord, or declare all his praise?" the psalmist asks (Ps. 106:2; cf. Neh. 9:5). The thread uniting Psalms 145–150 appears to be this: the glorious splendor of his kingdom (Ps. 145:12). Psalms 146–150 embroider on this pattern of Psalm 145. "I will extol you, my God and King" (Ps. 145:1). This is the melody of the finale in the Psalter: the praise of Yahweh, Israel's mighty great king who at Horeb ascended his throne in the midst of Israel and who has since that time behaved with such thorough loyalty toward his vassal and covenant partner Israel.

Yahweh's greatness

Psalm 145 begins the praise of Israel's great king by telling of his greatness (Ps. 145:3). What vassal nation in that time had a covenant with such a mighty great king as Israel did? "His greatness is unsearchable" (Ps. 145:3). This is a great verse for hanging on the wall in one's study or laboratory! The scholars will never exhaust the study of God's works. Praising is also "tell[ing] of your power" (Ps. 145:11). "Great is our Lord, and abundant in power; his understanding is beyond measure" (Ps. 147:5). God's insight is unmeasured. He is the Creator of heaven and earth, the sea, and everything in them (Ps. 146:6). He is the one who "covers the heavens with clouds; he prepares rain for the earth; he makes grass grow on the hills. He gives to the beasts their food, and to the young ravens that cry" (Ps. 147:8–9). Snow and frost, ice and balmy weather, thawing winds—all of these stand under the authority of Yahweh the great king, together with the Israelites, whom he gathered from the Persian Empire and led back to Jerusalem (Ps. 147:2, 15–18).

In our discussion of Psalm 104, we saw that the faithful remnant's talk about Yahweh's kingship over the heavenly bodies and the rain clouds was polemical praise in opposition to the worship of sun, moon, and stars that was occurring in the pagan world and in the paganized church of that time. The faithful remnant that is being given a voice in the psalms held firmly to the good confession: "Yahweh, our King, has created heaven and earth through his commanding words." As far as sun, moon, and stars are concerned, "He established them forever and ever; he gave a decree, and it shall not pass away" (Ps. 148:6). This explains the summons "Praise him in his mighty heavens!" (Ps. 150:1).

Yahweh's kingdom rules over all (Ps. 103:19).

Israel's election unto God's covenant

This almighty Creator of heaven and earth chose Israel to be his own people, and as her great king he established his vassal covenant with her. Praise is sung to God about this fundamental redemptive event in the finale of the Psalter as well (Ps. 148:14; 149:2, 4). Amazement about this grace of God is expressed most loudly, however, in the conclusion of Psalm 147, when with this note it reaches its climax:

> He declares his word to Jacob,
>   his statutes and rules to Israel.
> He has not dealt thus with any other nation;
>   they do not know his rules.
> Praise the LORD!   (vv. 19–20)

Included in "his word" are the covenant stipulations that Yahweh placed upon Israel and summarized in "the Ten Words" or "the words of the covenant" (Exod. 34:28; Deut. 4:13; cf. Exod. 20:1; Deut. 10:1–5). The *statutes* (Heb. *khoqqim*) and *rules* (Heb. *mishpatim*) are the additional stipulations belonging to that covenant.

In that covenant Israel possesses everything. In that

covenant, as their great king, the God of heaven and earth promised his vassal nation Israel his eternal loyalty, declared her to be holy, and promised forgiveness of sins and eternal life. Is it any wonder that people in Israel praised God for this election to covenant partnership with him?

For centuries Israel possessed this privilege as the only nation in the world. But that changed after the great day of Pentecost. For then God established his covenant with the kind of pagan peoples from whom we are descended: Frisians, Franks, Saxons, and Batavians. We do not get the overwhelming impression that God is praised daily among Christians for this undeniable historical fact.

The great goodness of Israel's King

We should read the conclusion of the Psalter especially against the background of the often harsh rulers in the world around Israel. The pharaoh of Egypt, a genuine great king with vassal nations, had all the newborn Israelite boys thrown into the Nile. Nebuchadnezzar threatened to hack all his seers into pieces if they did not quickly interpret his dream for him. Darius had his prime minister, Daniel, thrown into a lion's den. With a mere flip of his thumb, Nero decided the life or death of his subjects. And in the Germany of our "civilized" twentieth century, Hitler exterminated six million Jews. That is how millions have been governed throughout world history: in a manner that was heartless, lawless, pitiless, and faithless.

But this is Yahweh the great king of Israel, the God and Father of our Lord Jesus Christ! He is the God who gives life to all flesh. In him we live and move and have our being (Acts 17:28). He could cause the billions of people living on earth today to drop dead in a second. Compared to him, nations are like a drop in a bucket and dust on a scale (Isa. 40:15). "His greatness is unsearchable" (Ps. 145:3). "Great is our Lord, and abundant in power" (Ps. 147:5). But these same psalms praise him for his goodness. For the King of kings is so good! "The LORD is gracious and merciful, slow to anger and abounding in steadfast love" (Ps. 145:8). About what great king can people say that? But "the LORD is good to all, and his mercy is over all that he has made" (Ps. 145:9). The poor nations of this world are often ruled by harsh masters who lack sympathy for their subjects, but Israel's great king does not consider it beneath his divine dignity, despite his unfathomable greatness, to look with inner compassion on a widow or a blind person. Those among his people who are bowed low, oppressed, fallen, hungry, imprisoned, and suffering other distress enjoy the most attention from this King. Psalms 145 and 146 rejoice at God's royal goodness and compassion toward the helpless. Isn't that what the Israelites who were in captivity really were? Many of them were "brokenhearted" (Ps. 147:3). But with his divine power Yahweh had gathered together his own scattered Israel from all the corners and crevasses of the Persian Empire, had healed their wounds, had rebuilt his ancient residence in Jerusalem, and had satisfied her "children" (inhabitants) with the finest wheat. That is what Psalm 147 is singing about.

So then, praising means to draw attention to God's mighty deeds, especially his miracles of compassion, sympathy, and help for all those among his people who are weak.

Yahweh's faithfulness as Israel's great king

In addition to praising his great power and goodness, Psalms 145–150 praise God for his faithfulness! We should read this especially against the background of the faithlessness of many earthly potentates! Isn't politics often simply another word for subterfuge? In fact, only God is trustworthy. Therefore Psalm 146 sings, "Blessed is he whose help is the God of Jacob, whose hope is in the LORD his God, who made heaven and earth, the sea, and all that is in them, who keeps faith forever" (vv. 5–6).

One cannot possibly direct such commendation toward people who have placed their trust in an earthly potentate. One finds no genuine salvation with such a ruler: "When his breath departs, he returns to the earth; on that very day his plans perish" (Ps. 146:4). Princes before whom nations have trembled are reduced to dust or lay as motionless bones in a tomb. But in Israel people sang, "The LORD will reign forever, your God, O Zion, to all generations" (Ps. 146:10). "Your kingdom is an everlasting kingdom, and your dominion endures throughout all generations" (Ps. 145:13).

Moses and David lived under the dominion of the same king, Yahweh, as the Israelites who centuries later returned from Babylon and sang Psalm 147. And when their time comes to "go the way of all the earth," the godly may still be comforted with the knowledge that after their departure their children and grandchildren will continue to live under the protection of our King, "who keeps faith forever" (Ps. 146:6).

Those earlier themes of Psalms 1 and 2

Yahweh is faithful not only to his promises, however, but also to his threats. To those who are faithful he will show himself faithful, but to those who do evil he will show himself an opponent. On that condition he accepted his royal rule over Israel, and Yahweh remained faithful to that relationship. Psalms 145–150 praise "the glorious splendor of his kingdom." And so the finale of the Psalter echoes once more the earlier themes introduced in Psalms 1 and 2.

These introductory psalms introduced Israel's songbook and prayer book with a double confession and a double commendation. Yahweh defends the righteous ones and their life bears fruit (Ps. 1). The kingdom of Yahweh and his Messiah-King will nonetheless achieve the final victory (Ps. 2). For these reasons, those righteous who are often impoverished and oppressed will, despite all appearances to the contrary, be blessed because they keep God's Word and await his kingdom. But the often prosperous wicked will appear as unfruitful as chaff because they followed their own principles, and they will be smashed like pottery because they rejected Yahweh's royal rule.

These fundamental motifs echo throughout the finale of

the Psalter. Psalm 145 praises Yahweh with the words "The Lord preserves all who love him, but all the wicked he will destroy" (v. 20). Psalm 146 sings, "The Lord loves the righteous . . . but the way of the wicked he brings to ruin" (vv. 8–9). Can you hear the echo of Psalm 1:6, "For the Lord knows the way of the righteous, but the way of the wicked will perish"?

Those righteous ones suffered terribly under God's judgment upon the Israelite church known as the Babylonian captivity. The crisis of God's people tore their heart. But Yahweh brought those deported back home, and then they sang from Psalm 147: "The Lord lifts up the humble; he casts the wicked to the ground" (v. 6). Once again we hear the earlier theme of Psalms 1 and 2.

We hear this very clearly in Psalm 149.

Psalm 149: Praise for God's execution of wrath

The Psalter doesn't just discuss this quarrel between the righteous and their opponents in its opening pages; this remains a continual subject of discussion until the closing pages as well, as we see in Psalm 149. There we read in verses 4–9:

> For the Lord takes pleasure in his people;
>   he adorns the humble with salvation.
> Let the godly exult in glory;
>   let them sing for joy on their beds.
> Let the high praises of God be in their throats
>   and two-edged swords in their hands,
> to execute vengeance on the nations
>   and punishments on the peoples,
> to bind their kings with chains
>   and their nobles with fetters of iron,
> to execute on them the judgment written!
>   This is honor for all his godly ones.
> Praise the Lord!

When the psalmist has in view an execution of vengeance

against pagan nations, we recognize that in Psalm 149 we are reading a very ancient psalm that is singing about Israel's execution of judgment upon the Canaanite nations. These nations were under "the judgment written," prescribed already in the Torah (Deut. 7:1–2). As Yahweh's platoon of sacred executioners, Israel had to execute God's punishment on the perverse Canaanite nations. One sees this "judgment written" being carried out against Amalek (Exod. 17:14–16; Deut. 25:17–19; 1 Sam. 15:1–3). But we know of no command that God gave to Israel to slay other pagan nations with the complete ban. Certainly this is no "judgment written" that Christians should use to exterminate each other, as has occurred more than once. During the Peasants' War, Thomas Müntzer used Psalm 149 to arouse the desire for vengeance on the part of the peasants against the princes: "Do not let your sword become cold!" Appealing to the same psalm, Roman Catholic princes were incited to undertake the Thirty Years' War (1618–1648).

On the other hand, should we apply the terms *peoples*, *nations*, and *kings* in Psalm 149, just as we did in Psalm 2, to Israelite entities, to wicked Israelite kings? As we said in our discussion of Psalm 2, this explanation of the terms is certainly possible. Often *kings* referred to nothing more than something like mayors or regional rulers. Should we also be thinking here in Psalm 149 of the ancient line of demarcation between the righteous and the wicked in Israel? If so, then we should understand "the judgment written" that is mentioned in Psalm 149:9 to refer to the judgment repeated innumerable times in the Prophets and the Psalms upon the wicked among God's people. One day the roles will be reversed, and the wicked oppressors of the righteous will have to repent. If we understand it in this way, the Psalter begins and ends with the same proclamation: "The righteous are nevertheless to be congratulated, for Yahweh and his Messiah, in whom they take refuge, will achieve the final victory!" (Pss. 1, 2).

Whatever the case may be, the Psalms not only mention

the quarrel between the righteous and the wicked even in the conclusion of the Psalter; they also praise God for the outcome of that quarrel: "Hallelujah! Our King will soon vindicate the righteous and enlist them with the execution of the judgment upon their tormentors!" The church under the old covenant not only dared to ask Yahweh for this judgment in their so-called imprecatory psalms; they even praised him in advance for this judgment in Psalm 149!

Nevertheless, this psalm has not become obsolete in the new covenant. Granted, the church in the present dispensation fights not with a sword of steel but with "the sword of the Spirit, which is the word of God" (Eph. 6:17; cf. Matt. 26:52; 2 Cor. 10:4). But our Savior and the apostle Paul have taught us that the church will be involved in the final judgment. "Or do you not know that the saints will judge the world?" (1 Cor. 6:2; cf. Matt. 19:28; Dan. 7:22, 27). This judgment will not consist merely of words; it will involve a lake of fire and sulfur. That is how little the New Testament differs "spiritually" from the Old Testament. Moreover, we hear the theme of Psalm 149 throughout Scripture, even to the last page of the Bible, where we find a description of the fall of great Babylon, which is compared to a woman drunk with the blood of the saints and of those who bore witness to Jesus (Rev. 17:6). John heard a heavenly song of praise and then a summons given to the church at her fall: "Praise our God, all you his servants, you who fear him, small and great" (Rev. 19:1–5).

The finale of the Psalter supplies the prelude to this praise song!

Whom Do the Psalmists Summon to Praise God, and How Must They Do That?

According to Psalms 145–150, each and every thing in heaven and on earth must praise God: "All your works," "all flesh," "everything that has breath"—let them praise Yahweh (Ps.

14. Psalms 145–150: The Book of Psalms Ends with Pure Praise

145:10, 21; 150:6). Even the sun, moon, and stars, mountains, hills, snow, and hail are summoned to give such praise (Ps. 148). But at the head of the line, naturally, are "your gracious ones," "Jerusalem," "Zion" or "the children [citizens] of Zion." In short, "the congregation of the godly," as Psalms 145–150 entitle them.

Do these congregations adequately take into account how often the Holy Spirit—for Scripture is his book, after all—summons them at the end of the Psalter to give praise to God? In Psalms 145–150 you can easily discover thirty such appeals. And we hear the same in the other psalms: "Come, praise Yahweh," "Praise Yahweh," "Sing praise to his name," "Sing a new song to Yahweh," "Rejoice before Yahweh, all the earth," "Come before him with gladness," "Enter his gates with praise," "Give unto Yahweh the glory due his name," "Make his praise glorious," "Give God the sacrifice of praise," "Praise be to Yahweh, the God of Israel, from eternity to eternity." The word *Hallelujah*, which appears twenty-two times in the psalms, is in fact a command, for it appears literally in the imperative mood: "Praise Yahweh!" In short, Psalm 147 is saying, "Praise Yahweh, for it is good to sing praises to our God; for it is pleasant, and a song of praise is fitting" (v. 1; cf. Ps. 92:2). This too belongs to preserving the pure doctrine of salvation: putting into practice the numerous mandates to sing forth God's great deeds. In his commentary on Psalm 135:1–3, Calvin warned against "the exercise of misguided zeal, to spend our labor upon trifles, and in this respect imitate the example of too many who have wearied themselves with ridiculous attempts to invent additions to the service of God, while they have neglected what is of all other things most important. This is the reason why the Holy Spirit so repeatedly inculcates the duty of praise. It is that we may not undervalue, or grow careless in this devotional exercise" (*Commentary on the Psalms*).

One generation of God's people needs to take over the giving of this praise to God from the preceding. "One generation shall commend your works to another" (Ps. 145:4). "Praise Yahweh . . . old men and children!" (Ps. 148:7, 12). It is so lovely when this happens in families and in the gatherings of the church: the older voices of grandfathers and grandmothers mixed with the mature voices of their children and among them the clear voices of the grandchildren. From all those mouths "your mighty acts" are sounding forth, "the glorious splendor of your majesty," "the fame of your abundant goodness" (Ps. 145:4, 5, 7). Only we must remember that, for the sake of the praise of Yahweh from generation to generation, we should not remove children from the church's worship services.

As she praises, the church will naturally distinguish among time, place, and manner of praising. Psalm 147 does that when it praises Yahweh for Israel's return from the Babylonian captivity and conversion from worshiping the stars. But there is also the praise of God that is suited for daily expression, such as praise for our salvation from paganism and receiving the gift of God's covenant. The poet said on one such occasion, "Every day I will bless you and praise your name forever and ever" (Ps. 145:2). Psalm 146 seeks to arouse others to praise with these words: "I will praise Yahweh as long as I live; I will sing praises to my God while I have my being" (v. 2). These brothers saw it as their calling to let no day of their lives pass by without having said or sung something good about our heavenly Father. Do we as Christian families sing God's praise daily?

Psalm 148: Praising God with and without a voice

How should the church praise God? That is easy: in the first place, she must do so with her mouth. In Psalms 145–150, praising God is synonymous with rejoicing before God, singing songs to God, even though you can exalt God's deeds also by merely speaking.

The psalmists were also familiar with singing God's praise with the accompaniment of musical instruments: "make

14. Psalms 145–150: The Book of Psalms Ends with Pure Praise

melody to our God on the lyre" (Ps. 147:7), "mak[e] melody to him with tambourine and lyre" (Ps. 149:3). Psalm 150 calls people to praise God with a full-blown orchestra: trumpet sound, harp, lute, tambourine, stringed instrument, flute, and cymbals. The tambourine and cymbal served in this context not so much for accompaniment as for keeping the beat properly and supporting the rhythmic hand clapping (Ps. 47:1).

In the psalms it was not only the Israelite church that was summoned to praise God, however, not even simply "all flesh" or "everything that has breath" (Ps. 145:21; 150:6), but they exclaim: "all your works will praise you!" This comes out forcefully in Psalm 148.

The most massive choral music is made with the instruments mentioned in Psalm 148: a choir and orchestra consisting of sun, moon, stars, angels, waters, sea creatures, land animals, snowstorms, fruit trees, mountains, hills, kings, old people, young people, princes, and peoples. The stage for this performance is the entire universe, and the performers are all of God's creatures. Actually there are two choirs. For in verse 1 we are told, "Praise Yahweh from the heavens; praise him in the heights!" Then in verses 2–6 the psalmist summons the angels, together with the sun, moon, and stars and the waters above the heavens (the rain clouds). That is the heavenly choir. But then in verse 7 we read the summons: "Praise Yahweh from the earth," and then come the sea creatures, the water deeps, storms, animals, trees, mountains, and people to play their part in this great oratorio.

Two choirs: one in heaven and one on earth.

And who is the director? Who points to both the angels and the heavenly bodies to join the earth with all its inhabitants? That is the composer of Psalm 148, as well as the church who joins in singing his song.

We know that the angels are continually praising God. Isaiah can understand what they say during the vision in which he was called (Isa. 6:3). But sun, moon, and stars have no mouth, right? The composer of Psalm 19 knew that too, but nonetheless, when he looked to the sky, he heard the heavenly bodies singing: "There is no speech," he said, "nor are there words, whose voice is not heard. Their voice goes out through all the earth, and their words to the end of the world" (vv. 3–4). Do we also not hear with the ears of faith that mighty heavenly choir of billions of suns, moons, and stars, praising our heavenly Father? Without tongue and without language, but praising, always praising! Although many people ignore God, for centuries now the moon has stood like a heavenly chorister in the night sky, always singing impressive nocturnal recitatives. Why must angels and heavenly bodies praise God? Because he created them out of divine delight: "For he commanded and they were created!" (Ps. 148:5; cf. 33:6). In this way, the praise of God in the psalms remains anti-Canaanite to the very end, shaming all worldly wisdom.

With that same ear of faith we can hear the second choir mentioned in Psalm 148, as the sea creatures and water deeps praise God voicelessly. Recall along these lines when you have seen movies about the exotic plant and aquatic world in the depths of the oceans. This is how we can hear God's praise in the thundering of a severe storm and in the blossoming meadows and fruitlands.

When Psalm 148 has sung so majestically of the majesty of the Creator, it sounds like a climax when we then read, "His majesty is above earth and heaven. He has raised up a horn for his people, praise for all his saints" (vv. 13–14). To raise up someone's horn means to grant him power and prosperity. Had Israel just achieved a victory, or is Psalm 148, like Psalm 147, referring to the return from Babylonian captivity? In this context we cannot help but think of our Lord Jesus Christ, whom God exalted as the "horn of salvation" (the spear of liberation) in the house of David (Luke 1:68–69). God has exalted him for the good of his church, or, as the psalmist expresses it, "for the people of Israel who are near to him" (Ps. 148:14). The King of heaven and earth is very near to us!

14. Psalms 145–150: The Book of Psalms Ends with Pure Praise

Nothing Is More Exalted and Glorious Than Praising God

When else does our human living reach its best, if not in those moments when we are praising God, the Father of our Lord Jesus Christ?

A. Janse has observed that the most glorious and exalted thing a person can do isn't to eat, drink, and take pleasure in those moments—although Scripture does indeed appreciate such enjoyment of God's gifts (Eccl. 9:7). Nor is it to be clothed elegantly and enjoy the luxuries of life with all our modern comforts and affluence—although Scripture praises this for the one to whom God grants it (Eccl. 9:8).

Nor is it the wonderful intimacy between husband and wife—although Scripture repeatedly presents that as a gift of God (Eccl. 9:9).

Nor is it doing one's work in full strength, whether manual labor or scientific research or art or business or whatever else—although Scripture says that we must do everything with all our strength and that enjoying such endeavors is God's gift (Eccl. 9:10 and 5:18).

Nor is it being rich and amassing wealth, for Scripture often calls that foolish—and dangerous (Prov. 30:8–9).

Nor is it music and song and stringed instruments, although Solomon loved those and was allowed to enjoy them very much.

Nor is it speaking words of wisdom, although Scripture values that highly.

Nor is it rendering justice in fair measure and in court, something again that Scripture values highly.

Nor is it living a good, moral life, although God's commands warn his people sharply that they must do that, threatening God's wrath if they bring shame to him through their living.

Nor is it even believing in Christ, although the entire Scripture calls for accepting God's Word and believing in the Son.

Nor is it rendering great service in God's kingdom,

although the Lord has promised great reward for that.

Nor is it becoming a martyr for believing in Jesus, although the Lord says that such persons will receive the crown of victory.

But the highest is that love which so grips the church as bride that she continually praises her Bridegroom for his beauty.

Praising God, exalting our Maker in the highest, sounding forth the joys of our King (Num. 23:21; Ps. 150:5), proclaiming God's redemptive deeds done through Jesus Christ—that is the highest thing a person can do.

The Psalter ends with pure praise for that Great King who established a covenant with his people, who revealed himself in Christ as the incomprehensibly great God, but nonetheless is very patient, very gracious, and very good, toward all his creatures.

"Let all the mighty kingdom of Yahweh worship his great name and honor his great deeds. Let all join in praising Yahweh!" That has not yet happened universally on the earth. But the praise that we offer to God now is the prelude to the royal joy of the church, which will one day be raised from the dead and, once united on the new earth, will praise God and his Christ. Then it will no longer be a mere wish but a glorious reality: "Everything that has breath, praise God, the Father of our Lord Jesus Christ!"[1]

---

1. [*Translator's note:* Omitted from this translation is §28 (pp. 347–91 in the original), entitled "Singing about God and Flourishing Life in his Covenant, or about Ourselves and Our Devoutness? A Comparison of the Psalms with the 'Evangelical' Hymns." In this chapter the author provides a historical overview of singing hymns and concludes with a plea for the priority of psalm-singing, while identifying requisite qualities of New Testament hymns. Sufficient literature on this question already exists in the English language, and this chapter serves mostly as an appendix in the original.]

Name and Subject Index

A
Aaron, 233, 240, 242
Abel, 21, 113
Abiathar, 118–19, 128
Abigail, 25, 55, 69, 85, 127
Abijam, 208
Abimelech, king of Gath, 82
    See also Achish
Abimelech, king of Gerar, 188
Abishai, 4
Abner, 188–89, 192
Abraham, 144–45, 178, 281
    covenant, xii–xiii, 155–56, 164, 183, 195, 231
    Pharaoh and, 187–88, 191–92
    promises to, 274–75, 287
accumulated wrath of God, 197–202, 204–5, 230–33, 240
    Christians and, 208–10, 251
    Israel and, 239–40
    See also wrath of God
Achan, 192, 193–94, 208
Achish, 44, 46–47, 52, 61, 82–83, 88–89
acrostic psalms, 83
activism, 18, 60, 210
Adam, 196, 237, 292
    eternal life and, 227, 287
    sin of, 195–96, 220

Adullam, cave of, 66–67, 73, 75, 82, 109
afflictions, 110–11, 315–16
    redemptive dimensions of, 325–27
    See also troubles
Africans, 209
Ahab, 169, 187, 317, 320
Ahaz, 291
Ahimelech, 116–18
ahistorical orientation, 176, 178, 208–9
Akhenaten, 290
'al tashkhet (do not destroy), 4–5, 6, 104
Amalek, 118, 351
Amaziah, 317
Amon, 291
Amos, 317, 322, 328
Amran, 183, 242
Anabaptists, 9, 31
Ananias and Sapphira, 189, 192
Anathoth, 10
'anawim (meek), 24, 56, 84–86, 88–90, 95–96
ancestors, 175–76, 185–86, 235–36
    solidarity with, 186–89, 191–94, 200–202
Angel of Yahweh, 92–95, 324

angels, 92–93, 144, 196, 276, 355–56
animals/beasts, 158, 270–71
Annas, 317
answers to prayers, 36, 56, 88–89, 166
anthropomorphism/anthropopathism, 143
Antiochus IV Epiphanes, 167–68
apostasy, 140, 166, 170–71, 284, 320–21
apostles, 30–31, 317, 324–25, 326
   Gnosticism and, 298
   See also John; Paul; Peter
Apostles' Creed, 288
argument with God, 18–19, 147, 150–51, 223
ark of the covenant, 27–28, 136, 203, 319
arrogance, 24–25, 106–7, 195
Asa, 219
Asaph, 133, 135–37, 156, 166, 213, 223
   deliverance, 160
   focus on God, 171
   humility of, 163–64, 171
   Lamentations and, 152–53
   Maccabees and, 173
   psalm composing, 142–44, 151–52
   sons of, 131, 135
   wrath of God, 148–49
Ashurbanipal, 291
Assyrians, 106, 158, 207, 254, 291
Astarte, 266, 298
Athaliah, 128
atheistic technocracy, 255, 286
atheism, 273–74

B
Baal, 254, 262, 266, 282, 298
Baasha, 6, 16, 142, 187

Babylon / Babylonian Empire, 17, 254
   captivity, 107–8, 109, 141, 147, 201–2, 293, 350
   destruction of Judah/temple, 133–35, 142, 146–47
   fall of, 31, 352
   judgement of, 37–38, 156
   as Leviathan, 158–60
   religion, 279–80, 289
   reproach of God's name, 150, 162, 165–66
Balaam, 324
baptism, 98, 139–40
St. Bartholomew's Day massacre, 8–9
Baruch, 142, 156
Belgic Confession, 7, 33–34, 313
Benjamites, 116
Bethel, 186, 317, 328
Bethlehem, 67–68, 72, 90, 103, 194
betrayal, 53, 73, 233
Bible/Scriptures, xii–xiii, 319, 328
   criticism of, 16, 147, 278
   deeds of God, 305–6
   Holy Spirit and, xii–xiii, 16, 81, 213, 353
   insight into, xi, 324–25
   Law of Moses, 283, 299–300, 323
   love for, 59, 75, 320–23
   understanding, 149, 245–46, 323–25
   See also New Testament; Old Testament; Torah; Word of God
bitterness, 69, 320
blessing, 182–84, 185–86, 194
blindness, 31, 123, 141, 309, 324
   of Christians, 123, 197, 210

blindness (*cont.*)
  of Maccabees, 170–71
  of Saul, 116, 124
bloodthirsty, 7–9
Boaz, 71
body, 196, 219
bones, 112–13
Bosch, Hieronymous, 165
de Bres, Guido, 7, 33, 313–14, 317–18, 328
brokenhearted, 105–9, 107–8, 348
brothers, 7–9, 67–68, 73
Bullinger, Heinrich, 323

C

Caiaphas, 317
Cain, 21, 113
Caleb, 20, 100, 232, 240
Calvin, John, 8–9, 140, 292, 353
Canaan, 158–59, 351
  as Israel's inheritance, 21–22, 230–32, 307–8
Canaanite religion, 27, 254–55, 279–79, 285–86, 289
  Astarte, 266, 298
  Baal, 254, 262, 266, 282, 298
  Leviathan, 271, 282
  sea as god, 282, 295
Canaanized Israel, 19–21. 22, 254–55, 285–86
chaos, 157, 264, 286, 295
children, 37–38, 97–99, 197–98, 354
  instructing, 97–99, 111–12
  parent's sin and, 186–87, 191, 198–99, 201
  prayer for, 248, 251
Christians/Christianity, 7–9, 10, 57, 208, 218, 222, 264
  accumulated wrath, 208–10, 251

Christians/Christianity (*cont.*)
  activism, 18, 210
  ahistorical orientation, 176, 178, 208–9
  apostasy, 57–58, 140, 166, 284, 321
  blindness, 123, 197, 210
  confession of ancestral sin, 208–10
  connection with former generations, 176, 196–97, 238
  covenant relationship with God, 139–40
  domination of human power, 122–23
  enemies of, 147–48
  foolish, 162–63
  hero worship, 50–51, 57–58
  humanism in, 15–16, 40–41, 50–51
  imprecatory psalms and, 15–16, 31, 32–34, 39–41
  individualism, 176–78, 208
  intercession for, 145, 164–65, 167
  judgment of, modern, 140, 197, 210
  persecution of, 32–34, 53, 313–18
  prayer, 31–32, 160–61
  religiosity, 221–22, 224–25
  rights, 17–18, 28, 85–86
  science and, 321–22
  self-focus, sufficiency, 87–88, 140
Chronicles, books of, 133, 171
church, 196–97, 303–4, 354–55
  leaders, 120–21, 313, 326–27, 328
  persecution inside, 53, 313–18

church (*cont.*)
  Satan and, 122–23, 160–61
  See also Christians/Christianity; Roman Catholic Church, medieval
church history, 297, 318, 324
  false members, 53, 73, 120, 128
  sixteenth century, 7–8, 20, 326–27
circumcision, 98, 168, 183
Cocceius, Johannes, 4
commandments, 308, 314, 319
community, 178–82, 191–92
  confession for, 194–95, 206
complaining, 219, 224, 230–33
confession of sin, 153–54, 164, 279, 307
  of ancestral/parents, 176, 208–10
  for community/nation, 194–95, 203, 205–8
Corinth, 189–90, 222, 239
covenant partners, 139–40, 164
  God as, 110, 282, 287, 296, 345
  Israel as, 27, 102, 113, 139, 183, 347
covenants, 91, 309, 319, 337, 346–47
  Abrahamic, xii–xiii, 155–56, 164, 183, 195, 231
  breaking, 138–39, 149, 153–54, 163–64, 198–99, 319–20
  curses, 27–28, 91, 133, 140, 240
  God's faithfulness to, 72, 119, 163–64, 305, 348–49
  Horeb/Sinai 139–40, 155–56, 164, 186, 230–33

covenants (*cont.*)
  new, xiii, 139–40, 160, 164, 307–9, 347
  prayer for renewal, 166–67
creation, 255, 258–63, 267–68, 270, 292, 304
  as evil, 274–75, 281, 285–86, 300
  ongoing, 272–73
  myths, 255, 282, 284–86, 295
  psalms, 253–56, 269, 284–86, 297–99
  water and, 284–86
crocodile, 158
curses, 16, 125, 186
  communal punishment, 194–95, 207
  covenant, 27–28, 91, 133, 140, 240
  solidarity with ancestors and, 186–89, 191–94, 200–202

D

Dahood, Mitchell, 121, 128
Damacus, 317
Dan, 186
Danites, 188
Daniel, 128, 150, 173, 277–78, 347
  prayer of, 150, 164, 166, 205
  as remnant, 91, 108, 142, 156
  world powers as beasts, 158
Danites, 188
Darius, 347
darkness, 221, 224–26, 280–81, 299–300, 335
David, 27–28, 55, 59, 77, 113–14, 189, 203
  answers to prayers, 36, 56, 88–89
  argument with God, 18–19
  in the cave, 65–66

Name and Subject Index

David (*cont.*)
- faith of, 17, 57, 61–62, 75–76, 128–30
- family of, 67–68, 90
- fear, 44, 47, 49–51, 88–89
- followers, 68–70, 84–86, 88–89, 96–97, 109
- friends of, 46, 48–49, 86, 90–91, 104
- future deliverance, 35, 62, 128
- in Gath, 44–47, 49–50, 52, 63, 67
- innocence, 10–11
- insanity / nerves crisis in Gath, 44–47, 59, 67, 82–83
- Joab and, 188–89, 192
- Jonathan and, 3, 25, 185
- lament, 49, 63
- on liberation, 283–84, 292
- love for enemies, 18
- love for God, 18–19, 74–75, 173, 337–38
- loyalty to Saul, 6, 10
- meekness/humility, 9, 56, 95
- as messiah/deliverer, 20–21, 23
- persecution of, 1–5, 13, 24, 46, 54, 73, 317, 338
- as poor man, 90–92
- praise of God, 80, 84
- prayer for deliverance, 5–6, 104
- prayer against enemies, 2, 7–8, 11–12, 14–16, 122, 337–38
- psalm composition, 3–4, 35, 43, 66, 82, 91–92, 99
- reform of Israel and, 19–24, 97–98

David (*cont.*)
- relationship with God, 331–32, 334–35, 336–37
- Samuel and, 6, 19, 27–28, 59
- as shepherd of Israel, 60, 69–70, 74
- as teacher of wisdom, 81–82, 89, 96–101, 111–14
- troubles of, 90–92, 111
- trust in God, 35, 60, 61–62, 71–72, 76–77
- vows, 61–62
- waiting on God, 4–5, 6–7, 13–14, 17, 53–54, 71
- weakness of, 58–59, 70, 92, 339
- in wilderness of Judah, 48, 53

days of old / prehistory, 144–45, 153–54, 156, 160, 164
dead, the, 222–23
death, 113, 216–18, 219–20, 222–23, 236–37, 337
- didactic poetry on, 211–12
- of Israelites in wilderness, 238–42
- joy and, 225–26
- of Saul, 75, 105, 128
Deborah, 69, 94
deliverance, 92–95, 110–11, 160, 215
- David and, 20–21, 23
- future, 35, 62, 128
- prayer for, 5–6, 104
delusion, 243–44
demons/spirits, 279–81, 283–84
- demonic teaching, 298, 300
didactic poetry, 126, 173
- on death, 211–12
- insight, 141, 145
- intercession, 160–61, 164
- *maskil*, 120, 133, 138, 212

didactic poetry (*cont.*)
  superscript, 131–33, 137–38
  wisdom teachers and, 96, 99
discernment, 327–28, 339–40
Doeg the Edomite, 104, 116–19, 122–24, 125–26, 128
dogs, 12, 34
do not destroy (*'al tashkhet*), 4–5, 6, 104
doubt, 165, 214–15, 231–32
doves, 163
dragon/dragons, 157–59, 161
dust, 236–37
Dutch Psalter (1773), 87

E

earth, 75, 79, 262–64, 277–78
  See also creation
Eastern mysticism, 209
Ecclesiastes (*see* Preacher, the)
ecumenism, 165
Edom, 37, 38, 179
ego, 87, 122–23
  religion of, 177–78, 197, 209–10
Egypt, 144, 151, 158–59, 187–88, 233, 277
  captivity in, 230, 347
  exodus from, 156–59, 184
  religion, 201, 254, 255, 289–90
  as Tannin/Leviathan/Rahab, 158–59
  See also Pharaoh
electricity, metaphor for holiness, 125–26
Eli, 26, 28, 32
Eliab, 67–68
Elijah, 20, 51, 53, 111, 317, 322
Elisah, 276
Emden, 327
enemies, 18, 36, 147–48

enemies (*cont.*)
  love for, 15, 18, 338
  prayer against, 2, 7–8, 11–12, 14–16, 122, 337–38
  prayer for conversion, 31–32
Ephraim, 180
Eratosthenes, 277
Esau, 113, 118
eternal life, 76, 130, 220, 222–23, 226–27, 307
  path to, 339–40
eternity, 22, 220–21, 236
Ethan, 135, 213, 223
Eudoxus, 277
evangelical, 68–69, 212, 282
Eve, 196, 227, 292
evil, 15, 113, 148, 200
  creation as, 274–75, 281, 285, 300
  turning from, 101, 104–5
evolutionism, 16, 147, 181, 190–91, 264
  science, 275–78
  worldview, 299, 300–301
exaggeration, 96–97, 110–12
exceptions, 96–97, 110–11, 192
exodus, the, 144, 156–59, 184, 230, 243, 347
experience, 88–89, 95–96, 177, 209, 276–77
Ezekiel, 111, 162, 201–2
  individual punishment, 190–91
  on judgment, 148–49, 153
  on name of God, 150–51
  as remnant, 91, 108, 142, 156
Ezra, 108, 164, 206–7

F

faith, 38, 96–97, 111, 143, 212
  binoculars of, 35, 75, 129–30

faith (*cont.*)
    of David, 17, 57, 61–62,
        75–76 , 128–30
    miracle of, 75–76
faithful, the, 85, 92
faithfulness, 124, 348–49
    God's covenant, 72, 119,
        163–64, 305, 348–49
fathers, 97, 111, 183
    accumulated wrath and,
        197–98
    connection to, 177–78,
        184–85, 196–97, 208–9
    God as, 78, 97, 110, 114, 163,
        198, 331–34
    religion of, 171–73, 184
    sins of, 176, 181, 186–87,
        190–91, 198–204, 209–10
    spiritual, 98–99, 111
fear, 52, 300
    ancient Near Eastern, 279–
        81, 295–96, 299–300
    of God, 97–101, 207, 244–45,
        309–10
    of David, 44, 47, 49–51,
        88–89
    liberation from, 282–84,
        299–301
fertility, 129, 254, 274, 287
flood, the, 264, 279
focus on God, 87–90, 150, 171
food, God's provision of, 257,
    266–67, 273, 306–7
fools, 13, 162–63, 309
forgiveness, 307–8
French Revolution, 98–99
friends
    of David, 46, 48–49, 86,
        90–91, 104
    God as, 110
    loss of, 216, 219, 221, 223,
        225
future promises/hope, 79, 277,
    310
    deliverance, 35, 62, 128

G

Gamaliel, 326
garment, fold of, 151
Gath, 44–47, 49–50, 52, 63, 67
Gedaliah, 156
generations, connection with,
    176, 196–97, 238
Genesis, creation story, 255,
    258–63, 267–68, 270
    six days of, 258–59
Geneva, 327
geologists, Christian, 264
Germany, 347
Gideon, 20, 94
Gilboa, 36, 56, 100, 105, 114
    death of Saul, 75, 105, 128
Gilgal, 185
glory, of God, 74–75, 250, 254
Gnostic/Gnosticism, 226, 298,
    300–301
    Marcionite-Gnostic spirit,
        226
    neo-Gnosticism, 147, 209
    Old Testament and, 245–46
    soul religion, 209, 226, 250
God, 87, 125, 214, 236, 260
    against his people, 169–70
    anger, 147–48, 244
    answers to prayers, 36, 56,
        166
    argument with God, 18–19,
        147, 150–51, 223
    as Creator, 157, 253–56,
        258–63, 265–68, 282,
        292–97, 304–5
    compassion, 166, 250, 348
    Covenant Partner, 110, 282,
        287, 296, 345

God (*cont.*)
  deeds of, 137–38, 145, 160–61, 287–88, 305–6, 343–44
  deliverance of, 92–95, 110–11
  discipline, 141–43, 168–69, 190
  displeasure, 244–45
  dwelling/presence with his people, 144–45, 147, 149, 231, 334–35
  exaltation, 74–75, 87
  faithfulness, 72, 119, 163–64, 305, 348–49
  Father, 78, 97, 110, 114, 163, 198, 331–34
  fear of, 97–101, 207, 244–45, 309–10
  focus on, 87–90, 150, 171
  forsaking his people, 168–71, 224–25, 245–46
  foundational deeds, 145, 160–61
  glory, 74–75, 250, 254
  goodness, 95–96, 260, 347–48
  grace, 306–7, 346
  greatness, 256–57, 283–84, 304–5, 345–46
  hand, 151, 218–19
  holiness, 125–26
  honor, 18, 74, 89, 95, 255
  housekeeping, 256–57
  inheritance, 144–45
  judgment, 25–28, 55–56, 85, 123, 240–42, 350–52
  justice of, 37, 104–5, 305
  King, 154–55, 160, 337, 345, 347–48, 358
  kingdom, 345, 349–50
  knowledge of, 16, 55–56, 331–33, 336

God (*cont.*)
  Lord (*'adōn*), 29–30, 235, 251
  Lord of history, 286–88, 293–94
  LORD of hosts, 11
  love, xiii, 250, 281
  mercy, 306–7
  name of, 120, 147, 149–51, 162, 166, 167
  nature and, 268–69
  nose, 142–43
  order, 99, 102, 257, 272–73
  order, reversing, 27, 38, 247
  patience, 198, 230–32
  promises of, 35, 76, 230–32
  protection, 155, 168–71, 333–34, 349
  provision, 96–97, 257, 266–67, 273, 306–7
  redemptive work, 40, 145, 156–57, 246–48, 286–88
  as refuge, 71, 95–96, 235
  reproach of, 150, 162, 165–66
  return, 155–56, 245–46, 247–48
  righteous, 102–4
  rights of, 86, 130, 230
  as Shield, 23–24
  as Suzerain of Israel, 154–56, 161, 163–64, 173
  thanks, 303–4, 342–43
  time, 237–38, 272–73
  vengeance of, 37–39, 113–14, 350–51
  way back, 155–56, 202–3
  wicked and, 103–4
  wisdom, 260, 272–73, 345
  wrath of, 20, 25–28, 54, 142–43, 197–202, 219–21, 239–40

God (*cont.*)
  See also Angel of Yahweh; Holy Spirit; Jesus Christ; praise of God
God's people, 8–9, 19–24, 197, 181, 329
  dwelling/presence with, 144–45, 147, 149, 231, 334–35
  See also Christians/Christianity; Israel, nation of; Judah, nation of
God's Word. *See* Bible/Scriptures; Word of God
gods, pagan, 157, 162, 168, 170, 279–82, 287
  Baal, 254, 262, 266, 282, 298
  Babylonian, 162, 279–82, 284–86
  creatures as, 254, 268
  divination, 280–81
  psalms against, 262, 266, 291, 346
  queen of heaven, 153–54, 255, 292
  Ra/Aten, 289–90
  sea, 282, 295
  Shamash/Shemesh, 289
  Sin, 291
  sorcery/necromancy, 148, 279, 281
Goliath, 2–3, 18, 20, 25, 29, 74
  sword of, 44, 117
Gonzalez, Juan, 40
good/goodness, 99–101, 113
  of God, 95–96, 260, 347–48
gospel, the, 214, 232–33
  of Jesus, 33, 140, 145, 160, 305–6
  in Law of Moses, 283, 299–300, 323
  government, 120–21
  persecution by, 33–34, 316–17, 347
grace, 57, 58, 220, 306–7, 346
de la Grange, Peregrin, 313–14
grapes, as metaphor, 195
Greek thought, 157, 168, 170, 277–78
  religion, 157, 168
  truth, 123–24
guilt, 186–90, 202, 219–21

H
Hallelujah, 353
Hananiah, 169
Hannah, 20, 23, 85, 111
  prophecy of, 26–28, 38, 54, 59, 72
hate/hatred, 21, 113, 338
heart, 106–8, 220, 244
  brokenhearted, 105–9, 107–8, 348
heathens, 11–12
heavenly bodies, 254–55, 272, 281, 355–56
  worshiping, 289–92, 297–98
heavens, 79, 256, 261–62, 267–68
Heidelberg Catechism, 32–33, 309
Heman, 135, 136–37, 211–13
  argument, 222–26
  prayer of, 214–19
  wrath of God, 219–21
Herod, 128
hero worship, 50–51, 57–58, 171–73
Hezekiah, 173, 185, 203–4, 226
historical psalms, 288–89
historical unity, 178–82
history, 178, 181–82, 237–38
  church, 297, 318, 324

history (*cont.*)
   God as Lord of, 286–88,
      293–94
   God's work in, 40, 145,
      156–57, 246–48, 286–88
   prehistory (days of old),
      144–45, 153–54, 156, 160,
      164
Hitler, Adolph, 347
holiness, 125–26
Holy Spirit, 26, 189, 220, 227,
      309, 328, 353
   Bible composition and, xii–
      xiii, 16, 81, 213, 353
   new covenant, 140, 160
   prayer and, 11, 344
   Saul and, 19–20, 24
honor, 63, 283–84
   of God, 18, 74, 89, 95, 255
Hophni, 27–28, 32, 169
Horeb/Sinai covenant, 139–40,
      155–56, 164, 186, 230–33
   as foundation, 72, 100, 127,
      183, 214, 230, 284
Horeb/Sinai, Mount, 136,
      144–45, 231, 234–35
   foundational events, 242–43
   wrath of God and, 239–40
Hosea, 111, 322
Hoshea, 6
humanism, 15–16, 40–41, 50–51,
      147, 283–84
human race, 178, 195, 209–10
humans, 22, 195–96, 283–84
   mortal, 236–37, 239
   power, idolatry of, 19–21, 23,
      50–51, 164–65
   praise of God, 357–58
humility/humble, 5, 16, 108–9,
      199, 325
   of Asaph, 163–64, 171
   of David, 9, 56, 95

humility/humble (*cont.*)
   return of God and, 155–56
Hunger Winter (1945), 97
Hymenaeus, 222
hymns, 40, 177, 226
   ancient Near Eastern,
      290–91
   imprecatory, 39–41
   self-focused, 87, 177

I
idolatry, 243, 254–55, 286, 298
   calf worship, 186, 233
   Canaanite, 27, 254–55
   Egyptian, 201, 254, 255,
      289–90
   of human power, 19–21, 23,
      50–51, 164–65
   in Judah, 200–201, 291–92,
      297
   punishment for, 186–87
illness, 217–18, 221
Immanuel, 23
imprecatory psalms/prayers, 2,
      7–8, 11–12, 14–16, 21–22,
      352
   of apostles, 30–31
   Christians and, 15–16, 31,
      32–34, 39–41
   hymns, 39–41
   in New Testament, 30–31
   prophecy and, 36–39
individual, 177, 190–91
   representing group, 192–93,
      203–8
individualism, 176–78, 181, 194,
      197, 208
individualizing, 87, 132
inequality, 98–99
injustice, 6, 68–69, 86, 142, 173
   social, 209

innocence, confessions of, 10–11, 317–18
Inquisition, the, 9, 39–40
insight, 114, 122, 145
    lament and, 138–40
    maskil, 120, 130, 137–40, 141
    into Scripture, xi, 120, 130, 141, 324–25
intercession, 23, 55, 145, 160–61, 164–65, 167
    of Jeremiah, 32, 166
    of Moses, 152, 231, 234–35, 239–40, 245–46
Irenaeus, 298
Isaiah, 37–39, 152, 195, 297, 355–56
    on hearts, 106, 107–8
    on judgment, 141–42
    on remnant, 51–52
Israel, nation of, xiii, 281
    accumulated wrath of God, 239–40
    apostasy, 170–71, 320
    Assyrians and, 106, 141
    Babylonian captivity, 107–8, 109, 141, 147, 201–2, 293, 350
    Canaanized, 19–21, 22, 254–55, 285–86
    covenant breaking, 163–64, 319–20
    covenant partner, 27, 102, 113, 183, 347
    created by God, 144–45
    Egyptian captivity, 206, 230, 347
    exodus, 144, 156–59, 184, 230, 243, 347
    historical unity of, 178–82
    inheritance, 21–22, 230–32, 307–8
    Jesus and, 8

Israel, nation of (*cont.*)
    Moses and, 230–31
    nature and, 253–54
    pride, 242–44
    punishment of, 231–33, 237–39, 243–44
    reform of, 19–24, 97–98
    remnant in, 27–28, 69
    twelve spies/princes, 231–33
    in wilderness, 159, 206, 230–33, , 238–42, 243–44
    See also Judah, nation of

J

Jabesh Gilead, 19, 24
Jacob, 113, 118, 178–79, 226
Jeduthun, 136–37
Jahaziel, 137
Jehoiakim, 199
James, 73
Janse, A., 22, 233, 357
Jeremiah, 56, 111, 156, 158, 162, 189, 255
    on accumulated wrath, 199–201, 204–5, 240
    confession of national sin, 204–5
    fulfilled prophecies of, 128
    intercession, 32, 166
    on judgment, 138, 142, 148–49, 153
    persecution of, 9, 10, 51, 317, 318
Jericho, 93–94, 156
Jeroboam, 186–87
Jerusalem, 139
    accumulated wrath, 200–201, 205–6
    church in, 128
    destruction of, 107, 133–35, 142

Jerusalem (cont.)
　return to, 109, 135–36, 206, 295, 345, 348–49
Jesse, 68–69
Jesus Christ, xii–xiii, 8, 63–64, 339–40, 349–50
　as Angel of Yahweh, 93–94
　body of, 196
　fear, 52
　justice and, 305–6
　modern views of, 39, 94
　new covenant, 160
　persecution of, 9, 317, 328
　Pharisees and, 108–9, 181, 318, 328
　prayer, 15, 328–29
　return, 310
　salvation through, 196, 318
　Sanhedrin and, 113, 318
　as Shepherd, 69–70
　teaching, 61, 324, 338
　temptation of, 215
　waiting on God, 6–7
　unity of God's people, 181, 329
Jezebel, 159
Joab, 188–89, 192
Job, 84, 221
John, apostle, 311, 352
　imprecatory prayers, 30–31
John the Baptist, 324
John of Leiden, 31
Jonathan, 3, 18, 46, 48–49, 55
　blessing of descendants, 185
　defense of David, 3, 25, 185
　as remnant, 69, 127
　Saul and, 20, 116–17
Jordan River, 159, 184–85
Joshua, 20, 93–94, 100, 160, 185, 193, 242
　book of, 344
　spies and, 232–33, 240

Josiah, 173, 198–99, 204
joy, 224–26
Judah, nation of, 162
　accumulated wrath, 200–201
　Babylonian captivity, 141, 155
　covenant breaking / rebellion, 138, 149, 153–54, 162, 198–99
　destruction of, 133–35
　judgment of, 138, 142–43, 148–49, 153
　idolatry of, 200–201, 291–92, 297
　prayer for, 158–59
　reformation of, 198–99
　return of, 109, 135–36, 166–67, 206, 295, 345, 348–49
Judaism, 225, 323, 326
Judaizers, 225
Judas Maccabeus, 168, 169, 172
judges, period of, 19–20, 21, 26–28, 51, 85, 188
judgment, 145, 148–49, 153
　of Babylon, 37–38, 156
　final, 55–56, 275, 352
　of God, 25–28, 55–56, 85, 123, 240–42, 350–52
　of Israel, 231–33, 237–39, 243–44
　of Judah, 142, 148–49, 153
　modern time of, 140, 197, 210
　Philistines as, 20, 23, 91
　repentant remnant and, 192
　of Saul, 20, 23, 24–25
　universal, 220
　written, 351
justice, 6, 37, 104–5, 305–6

K

Kadesh, 237, 239, 241–42, 245, 250
kings, 154, 200, 316–17, 351
    God as, 154–55, 160, 337, 345, 347–48, 358
Kings, books of, 133, 171
knowledge/knowing, 16, 244, 277–78, 309
    of God, 16, 55–56, 331–33, 336

L

Lamentations, book of, 133–35, 143, 152–53, 320
    confession of national sin, 205–6
laments, 49, 63, 152, 212, 233, 240–41
    insight and, 138–40
    prayer and, 215
    of Zion, 131, 132, 139–40, 320
Lamparter, H., 84
Law of Moses, 9, 198–99, 283 *See also* Torah
legalism, 225, 323
leprosy, 217
Leviathan, 157–60, 161, 271, 282
Levites, 126–26, 194
    singers, 136–37, 213, 223
Leviticus, 68, 91, 125–26, 202
liberation, 281–82, 283–84, 292, 299–301
lies/lying, 124
    persecution and, 13, 24, 53, 73, 315, 317
life, 216–18, 241–42, 270–71, 282
    daily, 332–33, 344, 354
    eternal, 76, 130, 220, 222–23, 226–27, 307
    good, 99–101

life (*cont.*)
    of grace, 57, 58
light, 62, 256, 258, 260–61
    in heavens, 267–68
London, 327
loneliness, 143, 225, 325
Lord (*'adōn*), 235, 251
Lord's Prayer, 313, 344
Lot, 182, 193
Luther, Martin, 56, 84, 327
love, 22
    for enemies, 15, 18, 338
    for God, 18–19, 74–75, 173, 337–38
    of God, xiii, 250, 281
    for Scriptures, 59, 75, 320–23
loyalty, 6, 10, 117–18, 120, 183, 185
    to covenant, 102, 113, 134, 345, 347

M

Maccabees, 18, 131, 135, 210
    blindness, 170–71
    "God is with us," 168–70
    hero worship, 171–73
    modern, 165
    spirit of resistance, 167–68, 208
Maccabees, books of, 168–72
Manasseh, 148, 198–99, 291–92, 297, 299
manna, 246–47, 307
Marcionite-Gnostic spirit, 226
Margaretha, 314
Mark, 98
martyrs, 32–33, 297, 313–14
Mattathias, father of Judas Maccabeus, 168
meditation, 138, 256, 260, 274–75, 293, 322

Mediterranean Sea, 265, 294–95
meek, the (*'anawim*), 24, 56,
    84–86, 88–90, 95–96
meekness, 9, 56, 95, 240–41
Menahem, 6
Mephibosheth, 185
Meribah, 249–50
Michael, 93
Michal, 1, 2–3
Midian/Midianites, 94, 234, 250
mighty men, 93–94, 104, 119–20
miktam, 4
military language, 5, 10, 13–14
    shield, 23–24
military power, 13–14, 19–20,
    37–38, 72
    Maccabees, 171–72
    protection, 23–24
    rule by, 119
military tactics, 37–38, 44
miracles, 75–76, 149, 305–7
Miriam, 231, 242
monsters, legendary, 157–59
moon, 257, 268
    worship of, 255, 282, 291–92
Mordecai, 128
Moses, 20, 22, 110, 124, 143,
    277–78
    age of, 233, 235, 242
    ancestors and, 235–36
    circumcision and, 183
    covenant curses, 133, 240
    Edom and, 179
    God's way back, 202–3
    intercession, 152, 231, 234–
        35, 239–40, 245–46
    Israelites and, 230–31
    laments of, 241–41
    Law of, 9, 198–99, 283
    meekness, 240–41
    prayer of, 229–30, 234
    prophets and, 148, 234

Moses (*cont.*)
    psalms composer, 234
    on sins, 240–45
    Torah of, xii, xiii
    work of, 247–50
mothers, 71, 90, 103, 133, 208,
    333–34, 336
    accumulated wrath and,
        197–98
    connection to, 177–78, 184,
        196
mountains, 234–35
Müntzer, Thomas, 31, 351
murmuring, 219, 224, 230–33
mysticism, 209, 323
    Eastern, 209
myths, 157–59, 282
    Bible and, 264
    creation, 255, 282, 284–86,
        295
    psalms against, 255, 285–86,
        295

N

Naioth, 25, 55, 59, 127
Name of God, 120, 147, 149–51,
    162, 166, 167
    reproach of, 150, 162, 165–66
    Y{\sc hwh}/Yahweh, name of
        God, 214, 331–32
nations, 12, 77–78, 351
natural law, 218, 254, 269
natural science, 117, 269, 273–74,
    278, 298–99
nature, 253–55, 268–69, 287,
    295–97
Nebuchadnezzar, 133–34, 347
    divination, 280–81
    as God's servant of judg-
        ment, 139, 200
Nebuzaradan, 183
Nehemiah, 108, 164, 207–8

neo-Gnosticism, 147, 209
Nero, 347
Netherlands, 166, 264–65
new covenant, xiii, 139–40, 164, 160, 347
    Holy Spirit and, 140, 160
    salvation and, 307–9
New Testament, xii–xiii, 93, 189–90, 220, 299–300
    imprecatory prayers, 30–31, 54, 338
    Old Testament and, 54, 226–27, 352
New Year's Eve, 229–30, 242, 249, 279
nihilism, 147
Nile River, 158
Nimrod, 50
Noah, 182, 193, 194, 281
Nob, 43, 46, 117
    priests of, 69, 104, 116–18
nose of God, 142–43

O

obedience, disobedience and, 7–8
oceans 265, 271, 295, 297
offerings, 61
Old Testament, 8, 15, 93, 189
    attitude toward, 125, 139
    belief, 54, 79, 215, 223, 275
    Gnosticism and, 245–46
    New Testament and, 54, 226–27, 352
olive trees, 129–30
Omri, 6
oppressed, the, 68–70, 79, 348
oppression, 56, 315–16
    social/economic, 68–69
order of God, 99, 102, 257, 272–73
    reversing, 27, 38, 247

P

paganism, modern, 288
Paris, 8–9
Pashur son of Immer, 169
Passover, 184, 243
paternalism, 98–99
Paul, apostle, 98, 219, 304, 324, 340, 328
    communal guilt, 189–90
    on death, 220, 239
    Gamaliel and, 326
    imprecatory prayers, 30
    on joy, 225
    liberation of Torah, 300
    on peace, 90
    on persecution, 63
    Philippian jailor and, 185–86
    on prayer, 161
    sea and, 294–95
    on sin, 339
    teachers of the law and, 322
    tears of, 56
peace, 90
    offering, 61, 79, 275
    seeking, 101–2
Peasants' War, 351
Pekah, 6
Pentecost, 347
persecution, 32–34, 62–64, 316–18, 329–30
    of Christians, 32–34, 53, 313–18
    of David, 1–5, 13, 24, 46, 54, 73, 317, 338
    by government, 33–34, 316–17, 347
    inside the church, 53, 313–18
    of Jeremiah, 9, 10, 51, 317, 318
    of Jesus, 9, 317, 328
    lies and, 13, 24, 53, 73, 315, 317

persecution (*cont.*)
   psalms and, 40–41
   sixteenth century, 32–34, 40
Peshitta, 4
Peter, apostle, 98, 209
piety, false, 13, 322
Pharaoh
   Abraham and, 187–88, 191–92
   exodus, 144, 159, 230, 243, 347
Pharisees, 322–23, 324, 327
   Jesus and, 108–9, 181, 318, 328
Philetus, 222
Philip II, 314, 327
Philippian jailor, 185–86, 193
Philippians, 225
Philistines, 82, 100
   Achish, 44, 46–47, 52, 61, 82–83
   Gath, David in, 44–47, 52, 67, 82–83
   as God's judgment, 20, 23, 91
   Saul and, 19–21
Phinehas, son of Eli, 27–28, 32, 169
   wife of, 110
Phoenicians, 294
pleading, 70, 145
poetic language, 157–58, 256–58
polemic, psalms as, 298, 319
   creation myths and, 255, 285–86, 295
   gods and, 262, 266, 291, 346
   modern ideas and, 262, 268
   spirit of resistance and, 173
   wisdom and, 322, 356
Ponce de León, Don Juan, 39–40
Pontius Pilate, 220, 288

poor, the, 27, 68–69, 85, 90–92, 163, 320, 348
   oppression of, 100
   prophet's widow, 68
   rebellion of, 142
power, 157–59
   government by might, 120–21
   human, 119, 129, 122–23
   idolatry of, 19–21, 23, 50–51, 164–65
   military, 13–14, 19–20, 37–38, 72
   relationships, 60–61
praise, of God, 260, 263, 304–9, 310, 357–58
   all creation, 354–56
   children and, 354
   as Creator, 253–55, 292–97
   for covenant, 346–47
   of David, 80, 84
   for deeds, 343–44
   for faithfulness, 348–49
   focus on, 87–89, 171
   for goodness, 347–48
   greatness, 345–46
   Holy Spirit and, 353
   for judging the wicked, 350–52
   Levitical singers, 136–37, 213, 223
   musical instruments, 355
   nations and, 77–78
   offering, 61
   singing, 354–55
   thanks and, 342–43
prayer, 31–32, 66, 160–61, 164, 333–34
   answers to, 36, 56, 88–89, 166
   for children, 248, 251
   for covenant renewal, 166–67

prayer (*cont.*)
    in crisis, 155–56
    of Daniel, 150, 164, 166, 205
    for deliverance, 5–6, 104
    against enemies, 2, 7–8,
        11–12, 14–16, 122, 337–38
    of Heman, 214–19
    Holy Spirit and, 11, 344
    of Jesus, 15, 313, 328–29, 344
    of Moses, 229–30, 234
    prophecy and, 32, 36–39
    psalms as prayer book,
        40–41, 86
    See also imprecatory psalms/
        prayers
Preacher, in Ecclesiastes, 223,
    238
prehistory (days of old), 144–45,
    153–54, 156, 160, 164
priests, 125–26, 322
    of Nob, 69, 104, 116–18,
        125–26
primitive
    biblical worldview as, 218,
        275–78
    progress from, 183–84, 190
princes, 316–17, 318
    twelve spies/princes, 231–33
Pritchard, James B., 291
promises, of God, 76, 130, 319,
    230–32
    to Abraham, 274–75, 287
    believing response to, 35
    for future, 79, 277, 310
    of promised land, 230–32
Prophets, books of, xiii, 137, 192
prophets/prophesying, 106–7,
    128, 148–19
    faith and, 38
    Hannah, 26–28, 38, 54, 59,
        72

prophets/prophesying (*cont.*)
    imprecatory prayers and,
        36–39
    Levitical singers, 136–37
    miraculous signs, 149
    Moses and, 148, 234
    psalms and, 38, 126, 128
prosperity/fertility, 129, 254, 274,
    287
proverbs (*mashal*), 89, 112
    composing, 98, 112, 314–16
Proverbs, book of, 113
providence, 260, 272
Psalms, book of, xiii–xvi, 132
    acrostic psalms, 83
    creation/nature psalms,
        253–56, 269, 284–86,
        297–99
    deathbed poem, 212
    historical, 288–89
    introductory, 349–50
    liberation and, 281–84, 299
    as prayer book, 40–41, 86
    singing, 64, 87–88, 132, 139
    as songbook, 40–41, 344
    teaching psalms, 82, 121–22
psalms, composing, 1–4, 26, 38,
    138–39, 234
    Asaph, 142–44, 151–52
    David, 35, 43, 66, 82, 91–92,
        99
    for/in historical situations,
        21, 48, 62–63, 70, 132
    as memorials, 18
    motivations, 18, 23
    prophecy and, 38, 126, 128
    teaching psalms, 122
psychologizing, 86
punishment, 127–28, 186–87, 190
    communal, 194–95, 207
    individual, 190–91

punishment (*cont.*)
    of Israel, 231–33, 237–39, 243–44
Pythagoras, 277

Q

queen of heaven, 153–54, 255, 292

R

Ra/Aten, 289–90
Rachel, 110
rage, 46–47, 171–73, 251
Rahab of Jericho, 3, 156, 182, 193
Rahab the monster, 156–58
rain, 262, 266–67, 287
rationalism, 147, 209
reality, 110, 123–24, 197, 257
    invisible, 276–77
redemption, 34
    God's work in history, 40, 145, 156–57, 246–48, 286–88
    history of, 181–82
Red Sea, 157, 159, 185, 230, 296–97
reform of Israel, 19–24, 97–98, 198–99
    of Samuel and, 20–21, 49, 69
Reformation, 20
Reformed confessions, 32–33
Reformed ministers, 313–14
Reformed theology, 323
refuge, in God, 71, 95–96, 235
relationships, 60–61
    blessings and, 186, 194
    covenant, 139–40
    curses and, 186, 194–95
    with God, 331–32, 334–35, 336–37
    punishment and, 190

relationships (*cont.*)
    See also covenant partnerships
religion/religious, 171–73, 184
    Babylonian, 279–80, 289
    Canaanite, 254–55, 278–79, 285–86, 289
    cyclical, 286–88
    of the ego, 177–78, 197, 209–10
    Egyptian, 201, 255, 254, 289–90
    fanaticism, 31
    fertility, 274–75, 287
    Greek, 157, 168
    hatred, 21, 113
    personality, 209–10
    progression, 190
    self-directed, 87–88, 188
    sentiment, 132, 338
    solemn, 279–80
religiosity, 221–22, 224–25, 328
reminding God, 72, 144–45, 155, 161–63, 167
remnant, 51–52, 64, 91, 108, 127–28, 292, 329
    Babylonian captivity, 91, 108, 142–43, 156
    brokenhearted, 107–8
    Christian, 41
    in Israel, 27–28, 55, 69, 127, 154
    judgment and, 192
    mouthpieces for, 154
    promises to, 130
    return of God and, 155–56
repent/repentance, 155–56, 199
reproach of God's name, 150, 162, 165–66
resurrection, 215, 222–23, 337
Réveil, 166

Name and Subject Index

righteous, the, 102–3, 128, 320, 324
    confession of ancestor's sins, 202–8
    death of, 113
    responses of, 121–23, 127
    suffering of, 62–64, 69–70, 91–92, 110–11, 350
    wicked and, 349–52
rights, 17–18, 28, 85–86, 173
    of God, 86, 130, 230
Roman Catholic Church, medieval, 314, 323, 351
Romans, 173, 264
Ruth, 71

S

Sadducees, 323, 327
salvation, 170, 214–15, 248, 299–300, 353
    answers and, 89
    horn of, 356
    new covenant and, 307–9
    through Jesus, 196, 318
Samuel, 23, 27, 124, 322
    David and, 6, 19, 27–28, 59
    reform work, 20–21, 49, 69
    as remnant, 55, 127
    Saul and, 24–25, 32
Sanhedrin, 113, 317, 318, 326
Sarah, 144, 187–88
Satan (devil), 275
    church strategy, 122–23, 160–61
    temptation, 215
Saul, 49, 113, 129
    blindness, 116, 124
    death of, 36, 56, 105, 128
    descendants, 185
    as fool, heathen, 11–13
    God's judgment of, 20, 23, 24–25, 127–28

Saul (*cont.*)
    Holy Spirit and, 19–20, 24
    injustice of, 6, 68–69, 86
    Jonathan and, 20, 116–17
    murder of priests, 116–18, 125–26
    persecution of David, 1–4, 24, 46, 54, 73, 317, 338
    Philistines and, 19–21
    rule of, 19–20, 49, 120–21
    worldliness, 49, 58
sea, 294–95
    as a god, 282, 295
self-centeredness, 74, 87–88
Semitic monster myths, 157–59
Seville, 39–40
science, 164, 217–18, 277–78, 321–22
    evolutionistic, 276–77
    natural, 117, 269, 273–74, 278, 298–99
    wisdom and, 310, 321–22
Shallum, 6
Shamash/Shemesh, 289
shamelessness, 141–42
Shear-jashub (repentant), 192
Sheol, 216
shield, 23–24
Sikkel, J. C., 57–59, 120–21, 122–23
Silas, 185–86
Simon Maccabeus, 172
Sin, moon god, 291. *See also* moon
singing, 64, 87–88, 132, 139, 354–55
sinners, 8–9
sins, 190, 240–45, 339
    of Adam, 195–96, 220
    of ancestors, 176, 181, 186–87, 190–91, 198–204, 209–10
    guilt for, 219–21

sins *(cont.)*
   See also confession of sin; guilt
Sisera, 94
slander, 13, 24, 53, 73
Sodom, 182, 208
solidarity, with ancestors, 186–89, 191–94, 200–202
   blessings of, 182–86, 194
Solomon, 79, 135, 212–13, 278
   temple of, 145
   prayer of, 164
son, 181
songbook, psalms as, 40–41, 344
sorcery/necromancy, 148, 279, 281
souls, murdering of, 164–65
spies/princes, twelve, 231–33
spirit, arrogance in, 106–7
   crushed in, 105–9
   of resistance, 167–68, 208
spirits/demons, 279–81, 283–84,
   demonic teaching, 298, 300
spiritualizing, 132, 164–65
Spurgeon, Charles, 2, 130
stars, 94, 254–55, 268, 282, 298–99
   horoscopes, 284
Stephen, 15
Stoics, 170
suffering, 24, 219, 227
   general, 62–63, 91
   for righteousness, 62–64, 69–70, 91–92, 110–11, 350
sun, 257, 268, 298–99
   worship of, 254–55, 282, 289–91
superscriptions, 47, 53–54
   of Asaph, 135–36
   didactic psalms, 131–33, 137–38

superscriptions *(cont.)*
   geographical, 66–67
   historical, 2, 11, 43–44, 47, 66–67, 82–83, 115
   maskil, 120, 133, 138, 212
   prayer of Moses, 229–30, 234
suzerain, 23–24, 29
   God as, 154–56, 161, 163–64, 173
symphony orchestra, as metaphor, 193

T

tabernacle/tent, xiii, 231, 243, 256, 261, 275
Tannin, 157–58, 161
teaching psalms, 82, 121–22
teaching wisdom, 27–28, 81–82, 212–13, 224
   David, 81–82, 89, 96–101, 111–14
   didactic poetry, 96, 99
   exaggeration, 96–97, 110–12
   from experience, 88–89
tears, 51, 55–56, 75
temple, in Jerusalem, 136–37, 145
   destruction of, 132, 134–35, 142, 145–47
   laments for, 138–40
temptation, 214–15
thanks to God, 303–4, 342–43
Thirty Years' War, 351
time, 237–38, 268, 272–73, 282
Timothy, 98, 300
Titus, 98
toil, 243
Torah, xii–xiii, 68–69, 249, 287, 292–93, 344
   on creation, 285–86
   as foundation, 69, 145, 249, 284

Torah (*cont.*)
  future promises, 274–75
  gospel, 323
  liberation and, 281–82, 300
tree, as metaphor, 177–78, 191
tribe, 178–80
troubles, 90–92, 110–11, 214–15, 225
  underlying causes, 170–71
trust in God, 20, 35, 60, 61–62, 71–72, 76–77
truth, 123–24, 255, 308

U
Ugarit, 295

V
vengeance, 4–6, 16–17, 33–34
  desire for, 101–2
  of God, 37–39, 113–14, 350–51
violence, 103, 119, 122
  anti-Christian, 161
  bloodthirsty, 7–9
votive offering, 61
vows, 61–62

W
waiting on God, 86, 130
  David, 4–5, 6–7, 13–14, 17, 53–54, 71
  of Jesus, 6–7
water, 261–64
  creation and, 284–86
  oceans 265, 271, 295, 297
  rain, 262, 266–67, 287
  sea, 294–96
way back, 155–56, 202–3
weakness, 60, 163, 220, 227
  of David, 58–59, 70, 92, 339
  sin and, 190
weather, 262, 266

wicked, the, 13, 27, 103–4, 128, 316, 337–38
  evil and, 113
  righteous and, 349–52
  suffering of, 91
wilderness
  David in, 48, 53, 65–66
  Israel in, 159, 206, 230–33, 240, 243–44
  manna, 246–47, 307
wisdom, 81–82, 212–13, 321–22
  ancient Near Eastern, 277–78, 279–80
  fear of the Lord and, 244–45, 247, 309–10
  of God, 260, 272–73, 345
  praying for, 244–45
  psalms and, 322, 356
  science and, 310, 321–22
  See also teaching wisdom
Word of God, 16, 64, 85, 87, 147, 239, 271
  cover over, 323–25
  cultural traditions and, 229, 323
  famine / scarcity of, 148–49, 322–23
  forsaking / rebelling against, 90–91, 102, 104–5
  as history, 287–88
  insight and, 120, 130, 141
  as law, 316–17
  liberation of, 300–301
  living according to, 169–70
  love of, 59, 75
  praise of, 320–21
  psalms and, 38, 137
  return to, 20, 49
  teaching, 19, 97
  See also Bible/Scriptures
world powers, as beasts, 157–59
worldview, 263

worldview (*cont.*)
    ancient Near Eastern, 278–81
    biblical, 218, 275–78
    evolutionistic, 299, 300–301
World Wars I and II, 251
worship, 354
    See also praise of God
wrath of God, 20, 25–28, 54, 142–43, 197–202
    Asaph on, 148–49
    Heman on, 219–21
    Horeb/Sinai covenant, 239–40
    See also accumulated wrath of God; judgment

Y

Y<small>HWH</small>/Yahweh, name of God, 214, 331–32

Z

Zaccheus, 185
Zealots, 170–73, 210
    See also Maccabees
Zechariah, 40, 106
Zedekiah, 134, 169, 171, 193
    Jeremiah and, 182–83
Zedekiah son of Chenaanah, 169
Zerubbabel, 135
Zimri, 6
Zion, 145
    laments of, 131, 132, 139–40, 320
Ziph, men of, 73
Zurich, 323

Scripture Index

OLD TESTAMENT

Genesis
1 . . . . 258–60, 263
1:3–5. 258
1:6–8. . . . . .258, 261
1:9–13 258
1:11. 266
1:14–15. 268
1:14–19. 258
1:20–21 270
1:24 270
1:26 270
1:29 258
1:31. 273
2:2 273
2:5 266
3:15 274
3:17–19. 275
3:19 237
4:26 237
6:7. 143
6:9 194
7:13 182
8:21 265
11:31–32 291
12:3 274
12:4 291
12:14–15 192

Genesis (*cont.*)
12:17 188
15:18 232
17 193
17:9–14. 183
17:10 183
17:12 183
17:23 183
18 208
19:12 194
19:12–16 182
20:2 188
20:7 188
20:9 188
20:17 188
20:18 188
28:4 232
28:11 253
35:12 232
49:18 226
49:26 236

Exodus
1 124
2:23–24 230
2:24 208
4:24–26 183
5:1 144
5:22 152

Exodus (*cont.*)
6:5–6. 144
6:20 242
12:12–13 243
12:24–27 184
12:29 243
13:8 184
13:14 184
14:11 230
15:1–21 234
15:8 143
15:16 144
15:24 230
16:3 231
16:14 246
17:3 180
17:4. 231
17:5–6 159
17:7. 231
17:14–16 351
19:5–6 155
19–24 155
20 281
20:1 346
20:4–6. 186
20:12. 232
23:4–5 15
23:13 286
34:6 230
34:28 346
36:8–38 249

Leviticus
1–7 223
3 61
4 240
11:4 168
11:7 168
13–14 217
16 20
18:5 . . . . 100, 230, 243, 319

Leviticus (*cont.*)
19:18 15
25 68
25:43 68
26 . . . . 22, 91, 202
26:3 170
26:14 170
26:31–39 171
26:40–42 . . . . . 155, 156, 164

Numbers
3:12 194
8:16 194
11:1–3 231
11:4–35 231
12 231
12:3 240
13:2 231
13:27–28 232
13:33 232
13–14 233
14:3 233
14:5–10 240
14:11 . . . . 231, 233
14:23 231
14:27 233
14:32 244
14:33 233
14:34 . . . . 244, 245
14:37 233
14:39–45 169
16:30 231
20:1 242
20:2–13 250
20:11 159
20:14–21 . . . . 118, 179
20:19 249
20:29 242
22:31 324
23:8 250
23:21 358
30:3 61

Numbers (*cont.*)
32:9 232
33:39 . . . . 233, 242
33:53 232

Deuteronomy
4:5 292
4:13 346
4:19 292
5:16 232
6:20–22 184
7:1–2 351
7:14 26
8:3 . . . . 269, 271
9:23 232
10:1–5 346
12:1 232
14:8 168
15 68
17:3 292
18:15 234
18:16–18 148
23:21–23 61
24:16–26:16 124
25:17–19 351
28 . . . . 20, 22
28:7 155
28:18 26
28:49–68 171
28:53 68
28:54–57 133
28:55 68
28:57 68
28:63 133
28–30 91
29:16 184
31:19–20 234
32 234
32:6 . . . . 144, 162
32:8–9 144
32:28 244
32:29 138

Deuteronomy (*cont.*)
32:35 17
33:2 155
33:10 143
33:23 247
33:27 236
34:7 . . . . 233, 242

Joshua
2 . . . . 3, 124, 193
2:9 232
2:10–11 156
2:12–20 . . . . 182, 194
2:14 232
3 160
4:21–24 185
5:14–15 93
6:2 93
6:16 232
6:25 . . . . 182, 194
7:1 . . . . 193, 208
7:11–12 . . . . 193, 194
7:21 192
10 . . . . 11, 160
18:3 232
24:15 193
24:29 . . . . 233, 242
24:31 242

Judges
1:25 . . . . 182, 194
2:1–3 94
2:6–3:4 266
5:4–5 155
5:20 94
5:23 . . . . 28, 94
6–7 94
13:6 234
13:8 234
17:10 98
18:25 188

Ruth

2:12	71
4:9	194
4:11	194

1 Samuel

1	85
2	54, 59
2:1–10	27, 71
2:9	23
2:10	27, 72
2:22	27
2:25	32
2:27	234
2:27–36	26
3:1	148, 322
4	28, 169
4:1	19
5	28
6:12	289
8:7	20
8:20	19, 20, 95, 120
9:6–10	234
9:16	19, 24
9:26	253
10:6–7	19
10:10–11	19
10–11	24
13:11	20
14:29	20
15:1–3	351
15:26	25
15:35	32
16	32, 124
16:1	25
16:14	25
17:26	20, 29
17:28	67
17:36	20
17:36–37	74
17:45	20
17:45–47	29

1 Samuel (*cont.*)

17:47	20
18:7	3
18:8–9	3
18:11	18
18:16	6
18:20–21	11
18:23	9
18–19	2
19	11
19:1	11, 73
19:1–3	185
19:10	18
19:11	3
19:11–17	3
19:18	6, 19, 25
19:19–24	25
20:3	48
20:15	185
20:17	185
21	45, 46, 47, 49, 83
21:7	116
21:10	44
21:10–15	43
21:10–22:2	82
21:11	44
21:12	46
21:12–13	45
21:13	44, 45, 46, 47
22	68, 69
22:1	67, 82, 90
22:1–2	23, 97
22:2	68
22:6–19	104
22:6–23	116
22:7–8	116
22:9–10	117
22:11	117
22:12–13	117
22:14–15	118
22:16	118
22:17	126

1 Samuel (cont.)

22:17–19	118
22:22	119
22:23	69, 128
23	73
23:14	67
23:19–24	73
23:26–29	36
24	5, 18
24:2–6	338
24:3	67
24:11	10
24:18	18
25	85
26	5, 18, 73
26:1	73
26:8–9	5
26:19	90
27:3	97
29:6–7	44
30:1–3	97
31	36, 114

2 Samuel

1:17–27	18
1:18	97
3:20	192
3:28–29	189
4:4	185
5:2	25
9:7	185
12:14	163
19:35	327
22:9	143
22:16	143
22:21–24	203
22:25	203
23:13–17	67
24:13	189

1 Kings

4:25	230

1 Kings (cont.)

4:31	212
5	78
8:29	147
8:46–51	164
10:24	277
11:14	118
12:22	234
13:1–31	234
13:34	187
14:10	187
14:13	187
14:21	315
15:4	208
15:29–30	187
15:33–16:7	187
16:3	187
17:18	234
17:19	256
17:23	256
17:24	234
19:4	51
22:22	187
22:24	169

2 Kings

1:9–14	234
3:2–3	187
4:1–7	68
4:10	256
6:15–18	276
8:19	185
8:26	187
9	187
9:35	159
10:11	187
11	128
11:1	187
17:16	254, 291
17:19	291
19:3	91
19:34	185

2 Kings (*cont.*)
21:3 291
21:5 291
21:3–9 254
21:10–15 297
21:16 297
23:4–5 254
23:11 291
23:12 291
25 134
25:1 133
25:18–21 134

1 Chronicles
2:6 212
6:33–38 213
8:29–38 185
13:3 203
15:17 213
15:19 213
16:5 135
16:7–36 136
16:30 . . . . 136, 145
16:41 213
16:41–42 . . . . 213, 223
21:3 189
23:14 234
25:1 . . . . 136, 213
25:2 136
25:3 137
25:4 213
25:5 . . . . 137, 213
25:6 213

2 Chronicles
5:12 213
8:14 234
13:7 315
16:12 219
20 136
20:14–17 137
24:22 126

2 Chronicles (*cont.*)
28:17 204
28:21 204
29:2 203
29:6 203–4
29:9 203–4
29:14 213
29:30 137
33:6 148
34:1–8 198
34:2 204
34:19 . . . . 198, 204
34:21 . . . . 198, 204
34:25 198
34:27–28 199
35:15 . . . . 137, 213
36:5–8 199
36:13 134
36:17 134
36:21 149

Ezra
2:41 135
3:10–11 136
9 . . . . 164, 176, 177
9:6–7 207
9:10 207

Nehemiah
1:6 . . . . 195, 207
1:9 202
7:44 135
8:13 138
9 . . . . 164, 176, 177, 207
9:5 345
9:33–34 207
9:37 . . . . 91, 207
12 136

Esther
7 128

Scripture Index

Job
1:21	84
2:9	214
3:8	157
3:23	221
9:13	157
14:21	223
17:13	216
19:8	221
21:21	223
26:12	157
31:29–30	15
33:4	271
34:14–15	271
38:10–11	265
40:15–20	157
41	158

Psalms
1	267, 329, 338, 349–50, 351
1:6	339, 350
2	349–50, 351
2:2	316
5	2, 15
8	253, 258, 283–84, 292, 292
8:1	283
8:1–3	284
8:3	255, 292, 299
8:4	236
8:4–8	284
8:5	283
8:6–8	283
8:9	283, 284
9:15	11
10:1	152
11	69, 127
11:2	55
11:3	72
13:1	152
14	309

Psalms (cont.)
16	4, 16, 66, 223, 275
16:4	286
18	143, 288
18:8	143
18:11–12	256
18:15	143
18:20–23	203
19	292, 293, 355
19:1	293
19:12	339
20:6	151
24	288
24:6	179
24:1–2	275
25:22	91
26	10, 11, 318
28:5	128
29	253
29:11	287
30	215, 216, 219, 223
33	253, 293
33:6	255, 285, 293, 356
33:9	285
34	4, 45, 47, 81–114
34:18	109
35	2, 15
35:20	85
42	87
44	131, 139, 155, 180
44:1	144
44:3	151
44:5–7	180
44:12	152
44:23–24	152
46	140, 169
46:1	112
47:1	355
50	137, 304

Psalms (*cont.*)
50:14 61
51 . . . . 107, 339
51:4 107
51:10 272
52 . . . . 4, 104, 115–130
56 . . . . 4, 43–64, 66, 67,
70, 82, 83, 88
56:4 75
56:8 49
57 . . . . 4, 5, 65–80, 82,
85
58 . . . . 2, 5, 15, 29
58:11 30
59 . . . . . . 1–41, 54–55, 66,
104, 125, 126,
338
59:2 55
59:4 8
59:5 52
59:8 36
59:9 36
59:11–13 21
59:12 25
60:5 151
64:9 137
65 253
65:3 180
66 . . . . 288, 343
67 253
68 288
68:5 256
68:7–8 155
69 . . . . 2, 15
69:22–23 30
69:25 30
73 . . . . 112, 132
74 . . . . 131, 131–73, 175,
202, 212, 288,
320
74:1 245
74:11 202

Psalms (*cont.*)
74:12–17 289
74:14 157
74–83 137
75 5
76:9 73
77 . . . . 91, 131, 139
77:15 144
77:16 296
77:19–20 296
77:20 143
78 28
78:1 343
78:4 343
78:13 296
78:15–16 159
78:35 144
78:54 151
78:65–66 26
78:67 28
79 . . . . 131, 135, 139, 156,
164, 175–76, 195,
196, 202, 205
79:7 179
79:8 . . . . 154, 175–210,
233, 235, 238
79:13 143
80 . . . . 131, 139
80:1 143
80:11–13 148
80:15 151
82:1 73
83 152
87:4 . . . . 157, 158
88 211–27
89 . . . . 131, 139
89:10 157
90 . . . . 131, 229–51
91 276
92:2 353
93:4 297
95:3 295

Scripture Index

Psalms (*cont.*)

95:5	295
96	293
96:5	293
100:3	144
101	121
101:5	106
102	131, 139, 156, 292, 293
102:14	140
102:25	293
103	84, 240, 241, 256, 306
103:10	240
103:19	346
104	253–301, 344, 346
104:6–8	236
104:26	157
105	136, 256, 288, 342, 344
105:6	178
105:41	159
106	164, 176, 177, 205, 208
106:2	345
106:6	206
106:7	138, 206
106:9	296
106:13–33	206
106:34–36	206
106:36–39	206
107	288
109	2, 15, 40
109:8	30
111	303–11
113	26
114:3	296
114:5	296
115:17–18	223
116:13–14	61
116:15	113

Psalms (*cont.*)

118:16	151
119	313–30
119:143	68
126	206
126:2	166
128	129
130	211
132	203
135	288
135:1–3	353
135:6	297
136	288
136:1	296
136:3	293
136:4	296
136:5	293, 299
136:7	293
136:13–15	296
137	2, 15, 17, 37, 38, 165
137:7	118
139	331–40
139:8	216
145	344, 348, 350
145:2	354
145:3	347
145:4	354
145:5	354
145:7	354
145:8	346
145:9	348
145:10	353
145:13	349
145:20	350
145:21	353, 355
145–150	341–58
146	348
146:2	354
146:4	349
146:5–6	295
146:6	345, 348, 349

Psalms (cont.)
146:8–9 350
146:10 349
147 . . . . .107, 253, 292,
348, 349, 354,
356
147:1 353
147:2 . . . . .109, 345
147:3 . . . . .107, 348
147:4–5. 294
147:5 . . . . .345, 347
147:6 350
147:7 355
147:8–9. 345
147:15–18. 345
147:19–20 346
148 . . . . 253, 353,
354–56
148:3 285
148:3–6 294
148:5 . . . . 255, 285, 356
148:6 . . . . 299, 346
148:7 354
148:12 354
148:13 . . . . .294, 299
148:14 346
149 350–52
149:2 346
149:3 355
149:4 346
149:4–9 350
149:6–7. 286
149:9 351
150 355
150:1 346
150:5 358
150:6 . . . . 353, 355

Ecclesiastes
1:13 276
5:4–5. 61
5:18 357

Ecclesiastes (cont.)
7:17 . . . . 238, 242
9:2 62
9:5 223
9:7 357
9:8 357
9:9 357
9:10 357
9:11 112
11:7 62
12:11 112

Isaiah
1:5–7 179
2:1–5 275
3:18 292
5 108
5:12 141
6:3 . . . . 75, 355
6:10 149
7 192
8:17 143
8:19 148
9:10 106
9:13 141
11:1–10 275
12 180
13:16 38
13–14. 38
22:11–3. 142
25:6–12 275
26:11 142
27:1 . . . . 157, 158
28:23–29. 250
30:7 . . . . 157, 158
32:1–8 275
34:1–17. 37
38:10 . . . . 226, 242
40:12–31 160
40:15. 347
40:22. 256
40:27. 179

Scripture Index

Isaiah (*cont.*)
41:14	163
41:20	137–38
41:29	243
42	108
42:3	108, 109
44:2	144
44:18	138
45:7	261, 272
46:12	106
47	38
48:21	159
51:9	157, 158
51:9–10	144
53:1	244
53:2b–3	52
53:5	195
54	179
54:5	144
57:15	109, 110
57:15–16a	108
57:18	108
61	90, 108
61:1	108, 109
61:3	109
63	152
63:10	170
63:15	152
63:17	152
65:5	143
65:6–7	199
65:17–18	272
65:20	242
66:2	108, 109, 167
66:3	243

Jeremiah
2:2	204
2:19	142
2:30	142
2:35	142
3:3	142

Jeremiah (*cont.*)
3:13	142
4:22	162
5:3	142
5:21	162
5:22	265
5:23	106
6:15	142
7:18	255, 292
7:29	240, 251
8:2	291
8:12	142
8:21	194
9:1	56
9:24	138
10:12	261
11:16	129
11:19	9
14:11–12	32
14:20	204
15:1	32
15:4	204
15:6	32
15:10	51
15:11–12	149
16:10–12	200, 204
16:11–12	205
19:9	68
19:13	291
20	169
20:7–8	51
25:16	46
26:4–5	180
26:14–15	189
26:19	194
27:6	139
27:7	149
28	169
28:1	128
28:17	128
29	169
29:10	149

Jeremiah (*cont.*)
31:18–19 180
31:22 272
32 200
32:18 200
32:30–33 200
32:33 142
36 . . . . . . 142, 149, 317, 318
37 133
38:17 . . . . 183, 193
39:2 134
40:3 183
40:7–43:7 153
40–44 153
41:16–43:13 154
44 . . . . 153, 154
44:1–8 200
44:9–11 200
44:10 . . . . 142, 153
44:15–19 153
44:17 201
44:26–30 154
49:7–22 37
50–51 38
51:7 46
51:34 158
52:6 134
52:12 134
52:23 146
52:24–27 134

Lamentations
1 . . . . 154, 179
1:4 135
1:6–7 135
1:12–22 154
1:19 133
2:5 134
2:9 148
2:10 133
2:11 153
2:11–12 37

Lamentations (*cont.*)
2:12 133
2:17 . . . . 144, 201
2:19 37
2:20 . . . . 134, 153
3 206
3:7 221
3:31–33 143
3:42 206
4:4 . . . . 37, 133
4:5 133
4:10 133
4:13 206
4:16 134
4:20 134
5:7 . . . . 201, 206
5:11 134
5:12 134
5:15 135
5:18 . . . . 135, 165

Ezekiel
1 256
2:4 106
3:7 . . . . 106, 142
7:26 148
10:18–19 147
11:9 106
16 179
17:13–24 134
18 191
18:2 197
18:20 . . . . 186, 190–91
18:20–21 191
20 201–2
20:4 201
20:8 201
20:11 230
20:13 230
20:14 201
20:21 . . . . 201, 230
20:27 201

Scripture Index

Ezekiel (*cont.*)
20:30 201
20:33–38. 201
21:21 280
25:12–14 37
29:3–5 158
32:2 158
36:22 166
36:22–23 151

Daniel
1:4 227
2:48 227
6 128
7 158
7:10 93
7:22 352
7:27 352
8:27 51
9 . . . . 164, 176, 177
9:2 149
9:4–8 205
9:17–18 150
9:22 138
12:10 138

Hosea
2:15 275
8:14 144

Joel
2:13 246

Amos
1:11 . . . . 37, 118
3:1–2 184
4:13 . . . . 261, 272
5:13 138
7:10 317
7:10–17 328
8:11–12 322
9:11 275

Obadiah
1:1–21 37
1:10 118

Micah
4:4 230
6:9 142
7:20 144

Habakkuk
3:3 155
3:6 236

Zephaniah
1:5 291

Haggai
2:17 142

Zechariah
7 106
7:11–12 106
12:1 256

NEW TESTAMENT

Matthew
5:44 . . . . 54, 338
5:44–45 15
5:45 267
7:24–25 238
9:36 320
10:5 8
10:16 . . . . 8, 73
11:25 109
11:28 109
11:28–30 70
12:14 9
12:20 108
12:24 318
13:14–15 327

Matthew (*cont.*)
13:15 106
13:16 326
16:1 9
16:1–4 327
16:24 63
19:28 352
22:15 9
23:35 181
23:37 320
24:30–31 93
26:3–5 9
26:14–16 9
26:38 52
26:47–48 9
26:52 352
27:51 132
28:19 8

Mark
3:5 106
3:21 52
5:39 124

Luke
1:46–55 26
1:68–69 356
1:71 40
4 90
6:27–28 15
12:4–5 61
14:26 338
16:15 23
18:8 105
19:8–9 185
19:43–44 132
22:44 52
23:30 284
23:34 . . . . 15, 126
24:44 . . . . xii, 9

John
3:36 76
5:22 79
8:33 178
16:20 12
16:33 12
17:9 329
17:21 329
17:25 327
18:20 12
19:32–36 113

Acts
1:20 30
2:31 113
3:17 126
5:1–11 189
5:2 192
5:41 63
7:22 277
7:42 291–92
7:60 15
9:1–2 317
9:4 196
12:7–10 276
12:23 128
16:30–31 186
16:31–34 193
17:26 196
17:28 347
27:12 295
27:14–15 294

Romans
1:20 . . . . 297, 304
2:5 198
5:12 195
5:12–21 . . . . 196, 220
7:18 221
7:21 339
7:24 219
8 227

Scripture Index

Romans (cont.)
8:11 219
8:18 227
8:21 275
8:21–22 275
8:31–32 . . . . 227, 340
8:38–39 340
9:14 192
11:9 30
12:5 196
12:14 15
12:19 . . . . 15, 16
14:17 225

1 Corinthians
1:28–29 51
2:8 126
6:2 352
6:15 196
10:17 196
11:30 190
11:30–32 239
12:10 328
12:12–31 196
13:7 124
15:12 222
15:20 196
15:22 196
15:23 196
15:32 284
15:50 221
15:50–57 220
16:22 30

2 Corinthians
3:15–16 324
4:17–18 276
5:4 220
10:4 352
11:25 294

Galatians
1:9 30

Ephesians
1:23 196
4:5–6 140
4:12 196
5:8 . . . . 145, 160, 280
5:19 39
6:11–12 161
6:12 161
6:17 352
6:18 161

Philippians
1:25 225
2:6–7 94
2:17–18 225
3:18 56
4:4 . . . . 84, 225
4:7 90

Colossians
1:15–16 276
1:15–20 93
1:18 196
1:24 . . . . 64, 196
3:16 39

1 Thessalonians
5:15 15

2 Thessalonians
1 33
2:3–4 321

1 Timothy
1:1–2 98
1:6–7 322
4 . . . . 298, 300
4:7 300

2 Timothy
1:2 98
2:1 98
2:17–18 222
3:12 63
3:15 300
3:16 . . . . 81, 262
4:14 30

Titus
1:4 98

Hebrews
4:13 332
7–8 140
8:13 132
10:29 140
11:11–12 144
11:37 297
12:25 140
12:29 140

James
3:6 73
3:8 73

1 Peter
1:3 301
2:9–10 . . . . 145, 160
2:23 . . . . 6, 17
4:11 197
4:15 31
4:19 15
5:6 143
5:10 329
5:13 98

2 Peter
1:21 . . . . 81, 213
3:8 209

1 John
2:25 76
4 298
4:1–6 328

Revelation
3:9 12
6:9–10 31
6:16 284
7:17 56
12 . . . . 93, 161
12:3 161
12:4 161
12:10 215
13 . . . . 158, 161
17:6 352
18 31
19 31
19:1–5 352
19:5 31
19:6–7 311
21:4 56
21:23 75

APOCRYPHA

1 Maccabees
2:12 171
2:22 172
2:44 171
2:64 172
3:2 172
3:26 172
3:43 . . . . 171, 172
3:58 171
4:30 169
5:63 172
6:44 172
9:21 172
10:74 172
12:1 173

1 Maccabees (*cont.*)
13:3 172
13:27–30 172
14:4–5 172
16:23 172

2 Maccabees
5:17 170
6:12 . . . . 169, 170
6:16 168
6:18–7:42 172
7:18 170
14:37–46 172
15 169
15:7–8 169
15:7–10 169

Contributors

Cornelis Vonk (1904–1993) was a Reformed preacher and pastor in the Netherlands during the middle third of the twentieth century. His sermons and studies are widely known and appreciated today as a warmly devotional and pastoral treatment of the Bible text.

Frans van Deursen (b. 1931) was ordained to the ministry of the Reformed Churches in the Netherlands (Liberated) in Barendrecht in 1957 and served congregations in Haarlem, Apeldoorn, and Wezep. He was a minister in the Nederlands Gereformeerde Kerken (NGK) from the late 1960s until his retirement in 1986. He currently resides in Barneveld with his wife, and has four children and fourteen grandchildren.

Nelson D. Kloosterman serves as executive director of Worldview Resources International and labors as the translator of the volumes in this series. He is an ordained minister (PCA) and lives in Indiana.

Jordan J. Ballor is a research fellow at the Acton Institute for the Study of Religion & Liberty and serves as executive editor of the *Journal of Markets & Morality*.

Stephen J. Grabill serves as senior research scholar in theology and director of programs at the Acton Institute for the Study of Religion & Liberty.

Made in the USA
San Bernardino, CA
22 June 2016